Benedikt Schmid
Making Transformative Geographies

Social and Cultural Geography | Volume 37

Für Rosi

Benedikt Schmid holds a doctorate in geography from the University of Luxembourg and is a post-doctoral researcher at the chair of Geography of Global Change at the University of Freiburg. His research focuses on the role of community initiatives and social enterprises for the transition towards a post-growth economy.

Benedikt Schmid
Making Transformative Geographies
Lessons from Stuttgart's Community Economy

[transcript]

This book is based on a PhD dissertation in human geography at the University of Luxembourg, supervised by Christian Schulz and co-supervised by Tim Freytag and Gerald Taylor Aiken. This publication is funded by the Department of Geography and Spatial Planning at the University of Luxembourg.

uni.lu | UNIVERSITY OF LUXEMBOURG
Department of Geography
and Spatial Planning

Bibliographic information published by the Deutsche Nationalbibliothek
The Deutsche Nationalbibliothek lists this publication in the Deutsche Nationalbibliografie; detailed bibliographic data are available in the Internet at http://dnb.d-nb.de

© 2020 transcript Verlag, Bielefeld

All rights reserved. No part of this book may be reprinted or reproduced or utilized in any form or by any electronic, mechanical, or other means, now known or hereafter invented, including photocopying and recording, or in any information storage or retrieval system, without permission in writing from the publisher.

Cover layout: Kordula Röckenhaus, Bielefeld
Cover illustration: Birgitt Gaida
Printed by Majuskel Medienproduktion GmbH, Wetzlar
Print-ISBN 978-3-8376-5140-9
PDF-ISBN 978-3-8394-5140-3
https://doi.org/10.14361/9783839451403

Printed on permanent acid-free text paper.

Contents

Introduction 9
Focus and research question 11
Contributions 14
Limitations 16
Structure 17

Part I: From a growing economy to a-growth economies

Chapter 1: Growth in the Capitalocene 25
Why are we growth addicted? 27
Escalation 29
Limits 31
Green growth – an oxymoron? 34
Why grow in the first place? 35
Interim conclusion 37

Chapter 2: Alternative economies 39
Alterity and diversity 39
Degrowth 43
Postcapitalism 45
Towards a radical theory and praxis 47

Chapter 3: Transformation, transition, and agency 51
Sustainability transition research 52
Grassroots innovations and the social economy 55
Agents and allies of transformation 58
Transition, transformation, and politics 65

Interlude I: Geographies of change 69

Part II: Transformative geographies: space, politics and change

Chapter 4: Reimagining togetherness 79
Community 80
Community economy 83
Economic diversity 85
Poststructuralist transformative geographies 87
Epistemic fallacy? 89

Chapter 5: Materialization 93
From regimes of signification to practice 95
Practice theories 96
Working with the concept of practice 99
Institutions and organizations in practice 103

Chapter 6: Scale and power in transformative geographies 107
Scale 108
Power 111

Chapter 7: From transformative geographies to a degrowth transition 115
Interventions in practice 115
Towards a degrowth transition 117
Degrowth practices and politics 119
Operationalization: the diverse logics perspective 120

Interlude II: Strategies for transformation 125

Part III: Researching transformative geographies

Chapter 8: A practice theory methodology 133

Chapter 9: Planning and conducting research on a degrowth case study 137
The case of Stuttgart 137
Research design 144

Chapter 10: Research as practice 155
Participatory action research 156
Positionality and self-reflection 158

Chapter 11: Data analysis 161
Coding and coding frames: an overview 161
From conceptual framework to coding frames 163
Triangulation and final coding 170

Part IV: Stuttgart's community economy
Of infidels and agnostics 178

Chapter 12: Alternatives 181
Slow technology – supporting sufficiency and subsistence 181
Unlocking a sustainable local economy 184
A politics of pragmatism 187
Trust-based economies 189
Cultivating subjects for other worlds 191

Chapter 13: Constraints 195
Consuming to save the planet? 195
Money makes the world go 'round 196
For-profit policy 199
The tragedy of (artificial) scarcity 202
Me, myself, and I 203

Chapter 14: Enablement 207
Supportive infrastructures 207
Sustainability-related business models 209
Institutional support 210
In community we trust 212
Trusted subjectivities and devotion 213

Chapter 15: Compromise 215
Trade-off 215
Alternative income sources, charity projects, and social tariffs 216
Diversified business and Trojan Horse? 218
Self-restriction 219
Grey zones 220
Self-management 221
Non-confrontative confrontation 221

Interlude III: Of transition 223

Part V: A degrowth transition in practice

Chapter 16: Sketching a degrowth transition 235
Stuttgart's politics of place beyond place 237
Economy.. 238
Governance 241
Communality 243
Subjectivity... 246
Technology... 248
A multifaceted transition 251

Chapter 17: Degrowth practices 253
Repair... 255
Sharing 257

Chapter 18: Degrowth organizations 261
Symbiotic organizations 262
Interstitial organizations... 264
Pragmatic organizations 266

Chapter 19: Degrowth strategies... 269
Transformative Infrastructures 270
Politics of hybridity 273
Hybrid infrastructures 276

Chapter 20: Transformative geographies and socio-spatial strategies 279
Networked interstitial strategies for economic transformation........................... 280
Territorial ruptural strategies for transformations in governance 282
Place-based symbiotic strategies for transformations in communality 284
Putting socio-spatial strategies into perspective 285

Concluding thoughts on making transformative geographies............................ 289
Advancing research on transformative geographies 291
Autocritique and potentials for future research 295
A false sense of realism... 299
Skeptical hope 301

Acknowledgements 303

References 309

Introduction

> Capital against the earth – one or the other may survive but not both.
> *Hardt and Negri, 2017, p. 167*

"Something largely unnoticed is happening in cities across the world," Paul Chatterton (2019, p. 1f.) notes in his recent book *Unlocking sustainable cities – A manifesto for real change*. "There are countless projects where people from all walks of life and city sectors are creating, resisting and intervening in their unfolding urban story. In spite of the overbearing weight of corporate power, loss of public space, bureaucratic hierarchies, ingrained inequalities and even the presence of war and violence, people and projects are emerging to lay down markers for very different urban futures." A few years before, Paul Mason (2016, p. xv) popularized the term "postcapitalism" to describe this development: "almost unnoticed, in the niches and hollows of the market system, whole swathes of economic life are beginning to move to a different rhythm. Parallel currencies, time banks, cooperatives and self-managed spaces have proliferated." Chatterton and Mason are in good company as there are numerous scholars that draw attention to old and new forms of community economies (Gibson-Graham, 2006; Gibson-Graham, Cameron, et al., 2013), alternative economic spaces (Leyshon et al., 2003), social and solidarity economies (North and Cato, 2017), commoning (Bollier and Helfrich, 2012), and reconsiderations around well-being and the good life (Gudynas, 2011; I.L.A. Kollektiv, 2019; Rosa and Henning, 2018).

These hopeful gestures, however, contrast with an incessant flow of bad tidings. Global climate continues to destabilize; species become extinct; rainforests and other ecosystems turn into wastelands; soils erode; pesticides, plastic, nuclear waste, and toxic chemicals contaminate oceans, freshwater, lands, animals, and people "all feeding into a multi-dimensional sustainability crisis that leaves politicians (as well as the market) utterly helpless" (Blühdorn, 2017, p. 42). Lately, four of nine planetary boundaries have been crossed, threatening to change the earth's ecosystems uncontrollably and irreversibly (Steffen et al., 2015). Economic growth and progress in the name of which parts of humanity exploit nature and lives (Patel and Moore, 2018), thereby, fail the mass of population. Billions lack clean drinking water, sanitation, nutrition, shelter, safety, access to education, and political participation. Others work "bullshit jobs" (Graeber, 2018) to keep alive an extractive economy that deepens inequality (OECD, 2011; Piketty, 2017) and entangles existences in ways that pitch interests against each other so one person's well-being becomes another person's exploitation (Brand and Wissen, 2017).

While all this is going on, daily routines in the Global North persist seemingly unperturbed by the possibilities and threats of planetary futures. Judging by the continuation of business-as-usual, ecological and social crises appear to be little more than small nuisances that require the shift of some habits, market expansion to hitherto non-marketized areas, and the technological innovation of not-yet-so-smart cities. The green economy – like its predecessors ecological modernization and sustainable development – sets out to reconcile capital accumulation with social justice and the earth's ecosystems. Virtually no government in the Global North seriously questions an economy based on self-interest and dependent on continuous growth, ignoring the evidence that makes an absolute decoupling of growth and resource consumption highly implausible and employing economic metrics that have limited significance for general social well-being (Jackson, 2017).

Taking a sincere look at things raises a number of profound questions. What is the real scope of the global social and ecological crises? Can progressive politics reconcile markets and states with the requirements of a truly sustainable future? Or does humanity need a revolutionary break with growth economics and interest-driven politics? Will community-based initiatives and peer-to-peer economies creepingly replace a rampant global capitalism? Can autonomous, democratic, and decentralized associations oust corrupt governments? Should we be hopeful to realize the possibilities of other forms of economic organization and togetherness? Or does optimism veil the difficulties and contradictions of community activism? Should we be devastated, horrified, and furious in view of the sweeping contempt for human and non-human lives? Or does pessimism turn into paralyzing nihilism and cynicism? Are we responsible to change our lives dramatically to avoid emissions and exploitation? Or is it the responsibility of politicians and managers to enable a sustainable lifestyle for everyone? Who should we vote for, address, judge, and organize with?

Geography and other disciplines cannot provide clear answers to these questions (and if they attempt to, one should be rather careful). They do, however, provide a number of conceptual and methodological tools to approach the complexities of transformation. Situated between natural sciences and the humanities, geography links social practices and ecological processes to capture the complex spatialities of more-than-human interaction. It sheds light on both sides of transformation. Transformation as the fundamental change of ecological, technological, cultural, and institutional relations that unfolds seemingly removed from anyone's sphere of influence. And transformation as the engagement, struggles, and promises of activists, communities, eco-social organizations, and progressive politicians for a more just and sustainable future. Transformative geographies, consequently, unfold through and between global change and local agency, collective engagement and individual resubjectivation, grant narratives and small actions. In this sense, the notion of 'transformative geographies' captures the *spatial struggles and negotiations over just and sustainable forms of (more-than-) human co-existence*.

This work explores the forces and possibilities of transformation in a polarized world of elating community economies and an ostensibly overwhelming global capitalism. It looks at 24 eco-social organizations, projects, and groupings – at some of them closer than others – in the city of Stuttgart (Germany) and its vicinity. By means of qualitative exploratory research methods, the study develops an understanding of the complex interplay of possibilities and constraints, individual efforts and community organizing, politico-economic coercion and windows of opportunity, place-based practices and politics beyond place that all feed into processes of transformation. Drawing on the processual ontologies of community economy and practice theory scholarship, the work develops a perspective that acknowledges agential and structural moments of transformation and articulates inspirations for hope as well as reasons for concern. The remainder of this introduction elaborates on the study's focus and research question as well as its contributions and limitations. It concludes by giving an overview of the structure of this work.

Focus and research question

Thematically, this work situates itself within the debates on degrowth and postcapitalism in critical geography and cognate disciplines (Chatterton and Pusey, 2019; Gibson-Graham, 2006; Kallis, 2018; Latouche, 2009). Degrowth convenes a number of theoretical and practical approaches that seek to abandon economic growth and related narratives of development, innovation, and progress as guiding principles of human co-existence and instead propose a reflective recalibration of economic, political, and social institutions to support a temporally and spatially equitable, sustainable, and dignified survival of human and non-human species (Schmid, 2019a). Opposing economic growth inevitably challenges the institution of capital and thus involves perspectives on a postcapitalist future that abandons the societal project of "accumulation of surplus value, individualization, commodification and enclosure" (Chatterton and Pusey, 2019, p. 15). Both degrowth and postcapitalism entail critiques of incumbent social institutions and foster dialogues about new values that guide potential futures.

Despite a sophisticated case made by social and natural scientists on the perils and glaring injustice of current patterns of overconsumption and exploitation, there is a lack of adequate policy and planning responses. Much critical research, therefore, shows discontent with top-down responses to climate change; biodiversity loss; soil erosion; contamination of water, lands, animals, and people; exploitative economic relations; social inequality; and human suffering due to a lack of access to fresh water, nutrition, shelter, and sanitation. Instead, many scholars turn to community activism and civic engagement. Although the present work does not dismiss the necessity and possibility of transformative impulses from incumbent political and economic institutions entirely – and indeed provides a sophisticated framework to include such a perspective – it places its primary focus on community-type initiatives and organizations.

This work centers around the question, *how can community activism and civic engagement channel transformative geographies towards a degrowth trajectory?* It is interested in the diverse and often ambiguous practices of community-led initiatives, activists, and eco-social enterprises that devote energy and reflection to social and ecological issues and devise strategies to have a positive effect. Notions of sustainability, thereby, vary as much as the approaches to remedy grievances. The study's interest translates into three connected research questions:

a. What practices follow from and accompany (radical) critiques of unsustainable and unjust social relations?
b. How do facilitating and constraining moments become relevant in sustainability-related practice?
c. How can a deeper understanding of transformative geographies contribute to the development of knowledge and strategies for a degrowth transition?

Research question a. focuses on different notions of sustainability and "narratives of change" (Avelino et al., 2017, p. 3) as well as the ways in which individuals and organizations translate these ideals into practice. The main focus at that is on organizations that advocate a shift away from a narrow perspective on economic growth and are skeptical of current neoliberal attempts on market-based sustainability transitions. Research question b. builds on that by carving out various internal and external factors that facilitate and catalyze or inhibit and blight sustainability and degrowth-oriented practices in particular. In doing so, the book attempts to paint a differentiated picture that includes both, the possibilities of a postcapitalist future and the forces that militate against it. Eventually, question c. takes this work in a more hopeful direction. Instead of getting bogged down in quarrels over the probability of change in the magnitude required, the book develops a degrowth research agenda that takes both possibilities and constraints into account to devise strategies for a degrowth transition.

Geographically, the book's focus primarily pertains to the Global North. I use this established but partially misleading term to refer to spaces of a relative (material) wealth that is generally related to the exploitation of social and environmental conditions elsewhere (the Global South) (Brand and Wissen, 2017; Patel and Moore, 2018). The Global North does not necessarily map onto national territories (Trefzer et al., 2014) but rather encompasses the places, bodies, and networks which profit materially from currently instituted global economic relations. Consequently, while global relations continue to be important for the book's argument and, in fact, constitute a major aspect of the crises it addresses, the book revolves around the role of the Global North.

Empirically, this orientation translates into the focus on 24 eco-social organizations, projects, and groupings in the city of Stuttgart. Stuttgart is located in the South of Germany, in a prosperous region with a strong manufacturing sector. It is home to a number of global players but has also a long-standing tradition of small and medium sized enterprises. In this context, Stuttgart's landscape of alternative organizations and actors provides a compelling window into the possibilities of alternative economizing. It is a highly dynamic case which shows a number of substantial social and technological innovations in conjunction with degrowth-oriented practices and strategies. Above all, a strong interconnectedness between several sustainability-related organizations opens a perspective beyond individual projects. A prominent role of supra-organizational connections, furthermore, feeds into the book's interest on the possibilities of broader (institutional) change.

Conceptually, this book turns to processual and relational perspectives that reject the ontological privileging of spatial hierarchies. Practice theory and community economy thinking, each in their own way, renounce and counter determinative conceptions of structures, systems, and globalism (Schmid and Smith, 2020). Instead they turn to performances and practices in and through which the social world is (re)enacted, bringing diverse routines and possibilities of social co-existence into focus. Despite being bonded over a processual ontology, both perspectives conceptualize the world in quite different ways. Community economy scholarship (Gibson-Graham, 1996, 2006; Gibson-Graham and Community Economies Collective, 2017; Roelvink et al., 2015) cuts capitalism's ground by exposing economic relations as a site of radical difference. Drawing on a wide variety of inspirations from feminism, poststructuralism, queer theory, and antiessentialist Marxism, community economy thinking deconstructs capitalocentric narratives and subjectivities and seeks to resocialize and repoliticize economic practice. In doing so, the focus is on becoming and difference of postcapitalist subjectivities. Critics, however, see community economy's research agenda around the disidentification with capitalism as attempt to think away its institutions, materialities, and power relations (Castree, 1999; Glassman, 2003). A gap which practice-theoretical perspectives can help to fill.

Practice theory is grounded in a long genealogy of thought around the writings of Marx, Heidegger, Wittgenstein, Dewey, Bourdieu, Giddens, and others (Geiselhart et al., 2019; Nicolini, 2013; Reckwitz, 2002). While community economy scholarship localizes the social primarily in discursive orders and epistemes, practice theory turns away from representationalism towards routinized performances that assemble bodies, artefacts, meanings, and discourses into relative stable patterns of activity that establish, order, and uphold social co-existence (Reckwitz, 2002; Schatzki, 1996; Shove et al., 2012). Practice theory advances a perspective on the materialization of social performances that productively speaks to community economy's focus on contingency and diversity. The book sees merit in combining both approaches to acknowledge the possibilities that dwell in economic difference – liberated by community economy's ontological politics and put into perspective through practice theory's appreciation of routinized activities that institute, condition, and channel possibly transformative activity.

Methodologically, the work turns to ethnographic research methods and interviewing. Participant observation, in a way, is the methodological counterpart of practice theory (Reckwitz, 2016). It allows the researcher to capture the 'silent' part of human activity – the supposedly irrelevant, the taken-for-granted, the clandestine, the ineffable, the routinized, and the unconscious. Participant observation, however, faces a number of limitations around accessibility, temporality, and expenditure. Interviews partly make up for these shortcomings, in particular by easing access and providing orientation. Furthermore, the work follows action research methodologies in their rethinking of data collection, knowledge production, and research objectives along notions of empowerment and social justice. While truly collaborative co-production of knowledge faces a number of issues in the present study, such as the limited availability of co-researchers, action research informs the study's active participation in Stuttgart's community economy.

Contributions

This book contributes both conceptually and empirically to the research and activism of transformative geographies. In joining a community economy perspective with practice theorizing, it combines two strands of scholarship that explore possibilities of a societal shift towards more sustainable trajectories but hitherto lack productive interaction (Schmid and Smith, 2020). Community economy's ontological politics and practice theory's grounding of change in the repetitive enactment of conventionalized patterns of activity inspire a research agenda around the materialization of postcapitalist possibility. Such a research agenda reacts to critiques of community economy's emphasis that to change our understanding of the world is to change the world (Gibson-Graham, 2006). The book makes an elaborate argument that emancipatory research requires the consideration of both possibilities and restrictions to formulate strategies for societal change. In doing so, it speaks to pertinent debates in the literature on social change. In particular to the tension between antagonism and imagination – that means opposition against 'undesirable' practices on the one side and the emphasis of plurality, possibility, and openness on the other side – as different modalities of resistance (Zanoni et al., 2017; see also R. Lee, 2016; North and Cato, 2017).

Based on a practice-theoretical reading of community economy scholarship, this book develops an analytical framework that operationalizes a degrowth research agenda through a perspective on the diverse patterns of practices' relatedness ('logics'). As such it reacts to spatially naive approaches that focus on locally bound community activism on the one hand and an abstract globalization, which is frequently conceived of in aspatial terms, on the other hand. Following relational notions of space, such as Massey's (2005, 2008) demand for a politics of place beyond place, the 'diverse logics perspective' embeds empirical findings in a conceptually grounded notion of practices' broader alignments. In doing so, the book develops notions around degrowth practices and degrowth politics that describe *conventionalized patterns of activity that reflectively relate to practices' broader alignments in ways that found the assumption that these activities have an effect in line with degrowth's principles*. Transformation, or more precisely a degrowth transition, then, is the *change of practice-alignments towards a degrowth trajectory following breaks, substitutions, and shifts of dominant patterns in practices' relatedness*. The work, thus, makes an important contribution to bridge the conceptual and methodological chasm between context-specific enactments of alternatives and more general notions of social change.

Space is not only at the root of the book's conceptual argument but also informs a differentiated view on the geographies of transformation, acknowledging different forms of socio-spatial relatedness. Drawing on the spatial concepts of place, scale, network, and territory, the book explores the different spatialities through which transformative processes unfold. It attunes different social dimensions with transformative strategies through common spatialities, carving out particularly viable socio-spatial degrowth strategies.

Empirically, the study investigates a highly dynamic case in a prosperous context in the Global North. In contrast to places with a longer trajectory in alternative organizing, the case of Stuttgart is relatively inconspicuous at first. Lacking a significant "alternative milieu" (Longhurst, 2015) until recently, a contemporary generation of activists and organizations create a rather undogmatic and pragmatic landscape of alternatives, addressing a broad range of issues around social inequality and environmental unsustainability. In terms of its empirical focus, the study stands out in at least two ways. First, it covers the dynamic unfolding of alternative forms of economic organization in a place without a long-standing tradition of community-led activism. By capturing both enabling and constraining moments in that development, this book sheds light on the possibility of building alternative economies outside and beyond the 'usual' places. Second, the work pays close attention to the links between organizations, which is crucial for the development of an alternative milieu beyond disparate hubs of alternative organizing. Both aspects broaden the focus and contribute to a better understanding of transformative processes.

Limitations

Research on transformation in general, and this study in particular, faces a number of limitations that require further reflection. First, due to its orientation towards possible futures, research on transformation inevitably involves speculation – something scientific studies are inherently uncomfortable with. Simply extrapolating possibilities from the present, however, ignores the wealth of possibilities that remain hidden and underacknowledged. This book takes on this challenge by grounding future-oriented assumptions in conceptually and methodologically sound argumentation. It finds an optimistic and hopeful tone, while being aware of and transparent about the hypothetical character of its forward-looking orientation. Second, research on transformation involves a politics. While research is never simply neutral or objective, the prospective character of research on transformation renders it distinctly normative. As a consequence, any articulation needs to be transparent about its origin and intent. I do acknowledge this circumstance at different points throughout this work. Specifically in part I, which establishes the study's critical stance against growth-based economic and political institutions, and in part III, in which I reflect on the study's methodology and my own positionality. Finally, research on transformation deals with complex processes that involve dispersed moments and places. It needs to engage the limited resources at its disposal to generate useful and empowering knowledge. This last point needs further elaboration to explain the study's approach.

Broadly speaking, there are two ideal-typical (in a Weberian sense) strategies on how research can mobilize its limited resources to account for the complexity of transformative geographies. On the one hand, it can focus on a particular object or practice and its relations across different places and times. On the other hand, it can look at the complex interplay of objects, practices, and relations in a specific geographical context. The former enables the research to gain insights into the effects, tendencies, and interdependencies across dispersed sites. It can, however, only make limited assertions about the processes and interdependencies outside of the relations in focus. The latter, in turn, works to capture the complexity of relations in place. It can, however, only make limited assertions about the relations beyond that geographical and temporal context. Of course, there are also numerous combinations of both strategies.

This work primarily follows the latter strategy but seeks to include the former by creating conceptual and methodological tools to link its empirical focus to moments and places beyond. In concrete terms that means, although the work's empirics are geographically and temporarily bound to the context of Stuttgart between 2016–2019, it considers the relations beyond place which remain outside of its direct focus. This 'outside' is a simplified and homogenized space that emerges through literature and experience – sometimes on/of specific sites, sometimes on social relations more generally – such as analyses of value chains, research on social and environmental injustice, and involvement in translocal networks. My discussion of transformation, consequently, is grounded in rich empirical data from a specific site squared with the many-sided (and sited) but less direct insights beyond place. This work spends much time on providing a thematic overview and developing conceptual tools to enable a perspective on a politics of place beyond place (Massey, 2005, 2008), as reflected in its structure.

Structure

This book structures into five parts that follow the classical trajectory of literature review, conceptual framework, methodology, findings, and discussion. Each part divides into a number of chapters that are consecutively numbered for simpler orientation and cross-referencing and build towards the question how community activism and civic engagement can shift transformative geographies towards a degrowth trajectory. Part I contours the field of tension between (economic) growth, capitalist cheapening, sustainable consumption, and community economies that activism and civic engagement challenge, co-create, and navigate. Part II, then, advances a conceptual argument how different sites interlink in practice and works towards the development of a research agenda to trace the complex processes of transformation and transition. Part III translates the foregoing considerations into methodological tools that guide data collection and analysis of transformative practice. Part IV presents empirical evidence on alternatives, as well as enabling and constraining moments thereof. Part V, finally, returns to the initial question and examines the (im)possibilities of a degrowth transition in practice. The individual parts are interspersed by interludes that explicate transformations' spatialities and draw out its decidedly geographical character. While the book exhibits a spatial sensitivity throughout, these sections highlight the merit of developing a sophisticated spatial literacy and provide a corresponding groundwork. The remainder of this introduction gives a more detailed overview that looks at the individual chapters.

Part I discusses social and ecological crises in the context of growth-based economic, political, and cultural institutions in the Global North and traces the various responses of scholars, activists, policy-makers, and entrepreneurs. Chapter 1, thereby, exposes both the unsustainability and the institutionalization of economic growth. It outlines the ensuing contradiction that modern societies depend on growth which, at the same time, runs up against social and ecological limits. Approaches around sustainable development and green growth that continue along present trajectories, the chapter concludes, ultimately deepen social and ecological crises and constitute an implausible orientation for a sustainability transition. Chapter 2, then, scans the landscape of political and economic alternatives for approaches that question existent relations of work, property, and decision-making, which lay at the base of modern growth-dependency. It drills down into degrowth and postcapitalism, two approaches that oppose economic growth and capital accumulation, as guidance for a radical (as in addressing the root cause) theory and praxis. Chapter 3, lastly, turns to transformation and its agents. It traces the diverse actors involved in translating more or less radical critiques into social practice, including community grassroots initiatives, eco-social enterprises, and policy-makers. Furthermore, it sets up the conceptualization of transformative geographies – deepened in part II – by proposing an etymologically grounded distinction between transformation and transition. While transformation means to 'change in shape', which, at first, does not imply a particular agent or directionality, transition emphasizes the (strategic) passage from one state of affairs to another and thus includes both the notion of an orientation and the active connotation of an agent.

Part II formulates a conceptual agenda of transformative geographies around politics and its disagreements, encounters and identities; space and its materialities; and the dynamic unfolding of the social through its routines, shifts, and ruptures. Chapter 4 propounds a political sensitivity by exploring the inherent togetherness of human co-existence. It follows the philosophical thought of Jean-Luc Nancy – brought into Geography most prominently through the writing partnership of Katherine Gibson and Julie Graham – to ground economic practice in an ontological sociality. From the vantage point of a 'community economy', the chapter explores the contingency and politics of economic being-in-common alongside the limitations of poststructuralist transformative imaginaries. Chapter 5, in response, turns towards the materiality of social life. Drawing on practice theory, it traces how human togetherness materializes in bodies, artefacts, and things, stabilizing across time and space. The notion of practice, with its processual and materially grounded ontology, adds to a perspective on social reproduction and change in the spirit of a poststructuralist materialism. Chapter 6 deepens this perspective on the materiality of social co-existence by looking at concepts of scale and power. This brisk chapter prepares the operationalization of transformative geographies, an issue the subsequent chapter turns to. Taking up the conceptual grounding of space, politics, and change, chapter 7 translates the deliberations on transformative geographies into a perspective on concrete practices. Based on notions of degrowth practices and politics, this chapter proposes to consider diverse logics – patterns in practices' relatedness – to structure the research on transition.

Part III expands the books's thematic and conceptual thrust of a poststructural-materialist perspective on degrowth transitions with methodological and empirical deliberations. Chapter 8 outlines the implications of the work's conceptual orientation for its methodological and analytical set-up. Against the background of practice theory's non-dualistic sensitivity, the chapter conceptualizes implicitness/explicitness and discourse/practice along continua of explicitness and material engagement. Chapter 9, then, translates the general methodological considerations into a research design that guides this work empirically. It schematically presents the different methods the study draws on – desktop research, semi-structured interviewing, participant observation, and focus groups – and relates them both methodologically and chronologically. Chapter 10 takes a more reflexive angle and contemplates research itself as a practice which is exposed to and imbued with cultural, political, ethical, and economic moments. After situating the present study within action research methodologies, it turns to issues around positionality and normativity. Chapter 11, finally, weaves in foregoing critical reflexivity with the book's thematic and conceptual deliberations to formulate an elaborate coding scheme. It details the procedures around data analysis to bare the study's handling of the different kinds of data collected through different methods.

Part IV presents the study's findings. In continuation of the conceptual and methodological considerations which find expression in the study's coding scheme, presented in the previous section, this part is structured into four chapters – alternatives, constraints, enablement, and compromise. Chapter 12 focuses on the ways in which individuals and organizations diverge from incumbent practice. Oriented by the diverse logics identified in parts II and III – economy, governance, communality, subjectivity, and technology – the chapter exposes a range of activities that jar with prevailing norms and rules. Chapter 13 continues by highlighting moments of constraint that impede the enactment and stabilization of heterodox practices. In contrast, the subsequent chapter 14 traces moments that enable and encourage alternative practices. Chapter 15, then, brings together alternatives, constraints, and enablement by tracing the compromises that characterize the everyday practices of sustainability- and degrowth-oriented organizations. Part IV closes with some considerations on transformation, sounding the bell for the ensuing discussion.

Part V, reviews the study's research findings and insights. Chapter 16 (re)turns to the question of a politics of place beyond place and combines the study's conceptual and contextual insights with its empirical findings to sketch the possibility of a degrowth transition. Chapters 17 and 18, then, propose more nuanced perspectives on practices and organizations respectively, elaborating on the concepts of degrowth practices and degrowth organizations. Against the background of a notion of degrowth politics, these chapters discuss how practices and organizations reflectively relate to practices' broader alignments in ways that found the assumption that they have an effect in line with degrowth's principles. Chapter 19 discusses the difficulties in identifying, let alone singling out, transformative processes of a degrowth transition. Rather than losing itself in the hybridity, contingency, diversity, and processuality of transition, it traces the development of possible strategies for a degrowth transition around 'hybrid infrastructures'. Finally, chapter 20 links the social, spatial, and strategic dimensions of transformation to identify particularly viable socio-spatial strategies for a degrowth transition.

This work wraps up with a reflection on its contributions and limitations as well as the possibilities it identifies. Transformation towards a sustainable future, it concludes, while still involving much speculation and hope, is most likely to come about through tactical compromising – informed by socio-spatial strategies – to build up potential for alternative organizing.

Part I: From a growing economy to a-growth economies

Outline

Growth is a lynchpin in current debates on economic futures. 'Realists' of one sort point towards the progress and prosperity that (only) economic growth can bring, or, if that argument feels under threat, reiterate the lack of workable alternatives. 'Realists' of another sort point out that the societal fixation on continuous and endless growth is about to irreversibly destroy humanity's own means of subsistence. Furthermore, the latter tackle other forms of progress that occur alongside economic growth – individual self-enhancement, political expansion, technological advancement, and a general inquietude that characterizes modern societies. The debates on growth, green-growth, degrowth, and a-growth, however, are more complicated than that. Advocates of the green economy promise a decoupling of economic growth from ecological destruction and social entrepreneurs work to rectify issues around exclusion and injustice. Yet others remain agnostic about the advantages and disadvantages of growth and the possibilities of its decoupling, arguing for a-growth or a 'preventive post-growth position' (Petschow et al., 2018). Beyond the theoretical discussion in academic, public, and (to a severely limited extent) political arenas, a wide variety of community-born initiatives, projects, and enterprises implement and experiment with economies that deviate from the conventional entrepreneurial focus on profits and growth. Although they alternately align with, position against, remain agnostic to, or simply ignore growth narratives, a perspective on their diverse practices strains narrow conceptions of economy, fuels questions on social and environmental justice, inspires debate on economies' objectives, and sparks hope for transformative politics.

Part I lays the foundations for a critical perspective on transformative geographies. It starts out by tracing current social and ecological crises as outcomes of the ways capital positions humans in relation to each other and the more-than-human world. Drawing on pertinent literature, the first chapter contextualizes growth in the fields of political economy, world ecology, and social theory. In doing so, it aims to disentangle the diverse accounts of growth's inevitability, flexibility, promises, and failures. It touches on the structural necessity of growth, its ecological and social limits, and on systemic responses. Chapter 2 continues by sketching the landscape of alternatives that question existent relations of work, property, and decision-making and shift practices of production, consumption, distribution, financing, and governance towards sustainability, equity, and justice. Contouring the breath of approaches, it scopes out degrowth and postcapitalism as radical (in a literal sense) alternatives that address some of the root causes of the multiple crises. Chapter 3, then, discusses transformation and transition. That means, on the one hand, the fundamental shifts in social and ecological systems that comprise multiple interacting dimensions including political, economic, demographic, cultural, juridical, technological, climatic, biological, aquatic, and pedological moments. And, on the other hand and central to this book, the purposive responses to ecological and societal issues involving changes in the configuration of policy, industry, mobility, technology, and supply towards more sustainable alignments. The chapter emphasizes the diverse actors involved in translating more or less radical critiques into social practice, including community-led initiatives, eco-social enterprises, and policy-makers. By proposing an etymologically grounded differentiation of transformation and transition, it sets up the conceptualization of geographies of change that follows in part II. To that effect, the chapter closes with a translation of transformation into spatial terms.

Chapter 1: Growth in the Capitalocene

> Clearly capitalism is all too impossible.
> Lee, 2016, p. 283

The Anthropocene marks an epoch of considerable human influence on earth systems. The term was first proposed by Crutzen and Stroemer (2000, p. 17) to "emphasize the central role of mankind in geology and ecology" and has since been discussed in various disciplines including geography (Castree, 2014). Speaking of the Anthropocene, however, is misleading in two respects. First, it suggests that the current transgression of "planetary boundaries" (Rockström et al., 2009) at alarming rates is "just humans being humans in the way that kids will be kids or snakes will be snakes" (Patel and Moore, 2018, p. 2). Second, and related therewith, referring to human influence in general hides the fact that it is by no means humankind as such that dramatically threatens its own base of existence. Environmental impacts distribute highly unevenly alongside racial and socio-economic divides. Patel and Moore (2018, p. 3) go on to argue that rather than humankind as a whole, it is the particular way of "organizing the relations between humans and the rest of nature" that is destabilizing the climate, eradicating species, and destroying ecological balances from food chains to nutrient cycles: capitalism.

"If 'the Anthropocene' is an indefensible abstraction at the point of departure as well as the end of the line," Malm (2014, p. 391) asks, "might there be a more adequate term for the new geological epoch?" Malm concludes that instead of speaking of the Anthropocene, it seems more appropriate to speak of the *Capitalocene* – the epoch of capital. Before thinking about a conception of capitalism and the peril of singling it out as name giver for a whole epoch, it seems prudent to start with a definition of capital. At its very basic, capital refers to money that is "put into circulation in order to get more money" (Harvey, 2010, p. 76), or to use Marx's familiar formula: M-C-M' (Marx, 1981 [1867], p. 251). Capital, therefore, is predicated upon a particular organization of production, exchange, and consumption that allows the extraction of surplus and its reinvestment to generate further surplus (accumulation of capital). The ways in which capitalist forms of organization are institutionalized differ across time and space. At this point, however, I am not interested in the particularities of capitalist institutions and their spatialities (see for instance

Peck and Theodore, 2007 for the notion of "variegated capitalism"). Rather, I am interested in a minimal definition of capitalism as a form of temporal and spatial organization of society. Capitalism, at its very basic, is a set of social relations that generate an "imperative to unlimited accumulation of capital by formally peaceful means" (Boltanski and Chiapello, 2018, p. 4).

Capital, thereby, neither determines social relations nor is it the only way how people relate to each other and the more-than-human world (Gibson-Graham, 2006; see part II). In capitalism, however, accumulation and circulation of capital are deeply inscribed into mental infrastructures, social institutions, and the built environment. To use Adorno's notion of real abstraction: by continuously engaging in capitalist practices, capitalist relations are 'made real' and reproduce the material basis in which social practice is grounded (Belina, 2013; Swyngedouw, 2012). In other words, capitalist relations are both the basis and the outcome of a dialectical dynamic (see part II). This has profound consequences for the individuals of capitalist societies. Although their actions are not determined by capitalism, individuals are continuously coerced to participate in capital's accumulation and thus in the reproduction of capitalist social relations. Reproduction, of course, entails a diverse range of economic and non-economic moments (Althusser and Balibar, 1977). For now, it suffices to acknowledge the demanding if not impossible challenge of foregoing products from profit-oriented enterprises and relying fully on alternative circuits of value or self-provisioning (see below).

Capital, therefore, while not determining, is nevertheless a driving force in modern societies. Capturing the essence of capital in the pointed equation M-C-M', Marx goes on to remark: "But in buying in order to sell [...] the end and the beginning are the same [...] and this very fact makes the movement and endless one" (Marx, 1981 [1867], p. 252). Capitalist accumulation does not have a target, final purpose, or endpoint – for example when an appropriate level of material wealth is reached or negative externalities threaten the bedrock of humankind. Instead, accumulation has to continue – infinitely. This is not just a (mis)perception by neoclassic economic theory. Rather, social institutions are set up in a way that they are deeply dependent on the continuation of accumulation and thus economic growth.[1] Recessions can throw millions into poverty. State budgets depend on fiscal revenue and with it pension, health, education, and other social systems (Seidl and Zahrnt, 2010). Furthermore, progress and the expectation of a continuous increase in options of consumption are firmly fixed in mental infrastructures (Welzer, 2011).

---

1   Accumulation, here, refers to the "reproduction of capital on an expanding scale through the reinvestment of surplus value" (Andreucci and McDonough, 2015, p. 60). It is therefore distinct from economic growth, generally considered to refer to the increase in the aggregate of all goods and services produced in a set time period as expressed by GDP. But the latter reflects the former, which is implied when speaking of (de)growth in the following.

Along these lines, Rosa et al. (2017, p. 54) speak of dynamic stabilization – the notion that modern societies require continuous "(material) growth, (technological) augmentation and high rates of (cultural) innovation" in order to maintain and reproduce their present configuration. What's at issue beyond economic growth – the continuous accumulation of capital – then, is also acceleration in general in its various shapes and forms: as progress, augmentation, self-optimization, expansion, development, and inquietude.

The positioning of individuals, groups, and societies within global capitalist relations, however, is highly uneven. The societies that scholars variously refer to as 'modern' or 'capitalist' are primarily located in the Global North. The term Global North, here, is a coarse descriptor for the places, bodies, and networks which profit materially from currently instituted global economic relations. Consequently, while capital is grounded in global relations, the subsequent focus revolves around the institutions and the role of the Global North. Before turning to the consequences of capitalism's "escalatory tendencies" (Rosa et al., 2017) that continuously push its "frontiers" (Patel and Moore, 2018), therefore, the next section reviews different dimensions of growth-dependency.

Why are we growth addicted?

A basic but tautological answer to the question of why capitalist societies need growth is: capitalist societies have to grow because they are capitalist. As outlined above, capital is predicated on growth. That means "an economic system in which capital no longer accumulates is no longer capitalism, whatever one might want to call it" (Skidelsky and Skidelsky, 2012, cited in D'Alisa et. al., 2015, p. 11).

To move beyond this tautology, however, one needs to look at how capital materializes in socio-economic relations. Richters and Siemoneit (2017) group arguments that identify growth drivers into six categories: (1) individual aspirations, (2) credit and interest, (3) property, (4) competition and capital, (5) technological progress, and (6) state institutions. The arguments differ widely as to which of these factors are causal drivers of a growth imperative, in how far they can be substituted, and to what extent this substitution is desirable. Reviewing the debate in its entirety is beyond the scope of this book. In the following, however, I will review growth imperatives on three levels that are relevant for the further argument: First, formal economic structures; second, state institutions; and third, subjectivities and mental infrastructures.

Formal economic structures

Money mediates the practices of the formal economy. This ranges from individuals' and households' consumption of basic goods and services such as food, housing, or mobility to large-scale production of cars and the trade of financial derivatives. Economic agents who do not have enough money at their disposal to finance their endeavor – be it buying a car or setting up an automobile factory – enter a credit relation (or abandon their endeavor). Credit relations enable the acquisition of goods or the investment in economic activities. Whereas the former – the consumer – enters the credit relation to purchase a good or service, the latter – the capitalist – enters it to invest the money as *capital*. The former, in turn, generally depends on an income source through labor and thus on the profitability of the activities of the latter. An economy that is shot through with credit relations does not only allow for growth but imposes it (van Griethuysen, 2010).

> Debtors who fail to meet those constraints [solvency, profitability, time pressure] will be eliminated from the property-based economy (through the seizure, foreclosure or acquisition of their property). This also means that any economic behavior motivated by alternative criteria will be discouraged, even eliminated by the capitalist requirements (van Griethuysen, 2010, p. 591).

A fundamental driver of growth, thereby, lies in the structuring of the monetary system itself. Through fractional reserve banking, banks create money "out of thin air" (R. A. Werner, 2014, p. 1) when issuing credits that eventually have to be repaid with interest (H. C. Binswanger, 2013). As a consequence, debt and money supply are continuously misbalanced, which can only be compensated through further loans starting the circle anew. In the aggregate, then, there is a flow of money from firms to credit institutions, requiring a sustained increase in money supply to compensate for this loss. "But only a growing economy can sustain a continuous inflow of new money by credit expansion, which compensates for the increase in bank owner's capital" (M. Binswanger, 2009, p. 725). A credit-based economy, therefore, needs continuous growth to remain stable.

State institutions

For the most part, there is consent across political parties for economic growth. Seidl and Zahrnt (2010) identify three major relationships between state finances and economic growth. First, economic growth is meant to increase fiscal revenue. Second, it ought to decrease the expenses for social welfare. Third, and redundant from a degrowth perspective, it is supposed to increase investor confidence to stimulate further growth. State institutions, therefore, have an intimate interest in growth because in the absence of growth "companies close down, jobs are lost, and, by consequence, public revenues decrease and expenditures increase, and the ensuing monetary and fiscal crisis can put political legitimation at risk, too." (Rosa et al., 2017, p. 54).

Furthermore, on a more basic level, states are debtors themselves and face the threats of bankruptcy and concomitant dispossession. This can be seen in recent developments in Greece and many countries of the Global South. Programs of 'structural adjustment', thereby, create relations in which states are even more dependent on growth to continue functioning (Brand and Wissen, 2017).

Subjectivities

Growth and progress are also inscribed in Western cultures and identities. The history of the idea of progress and its role in capitalist relations can be traced from cultural (Konersmann, 2015), state-centered (Scott, 2017), economic (Wood, 2017), and ecological (Patel and Moore, 2018) perspectives. Welzer (2014) speaks of mental infrastructures – solidified patterns of thinking and being – to acknowledge the deeply embodied cultural-ideological norms that drive economic growth. Concretely, this translates into expectations of continuously increasing consumption options (Rosa, 2016), a feeling of entitlement to, and defense of, resource-intensive high standards of living (Brand and Wissen, 2017), forms of self-optimization (W. Brown, 2015), and naive techno-optimism (Kerschner et al., 2018).

Rosa (2018, p. 42) captures the subjectivities of modern societies through the triple-A approach: "the modern way of acting and being-in-the world is geared towards making more and more of its qualities and quantities available, accessible, and attainable". Individuals are driven by a fundamental desire to expand their reach and scope and to maximize the part of the world available to them. Money, as a universal means of exchange, represents the potentiality of goods and services. An increase of money, then, equals an increase in the share of the world that is available, accessible, and attainable. Since expansion itself is the imperative, there is no target or endpoint in the desire for accumulation. The endless pursuit of more in order to reach the "good life" ironically renders the latter an impossibility by definition. Rather, "we end up turning the business of increasing our scope and horizon of the available, attainable, and accessible […] into an end in itself, into an endless, escalatory cycle which permanently erodes its own basis and thus leads nowhere" (Rosa, 2018, p. 45).

Escalation

In its current form, formal socio-economic institutions depend on growth. Stagnation or recession destabilizes formal political, economic, social, and mental structures. Due to the close relation between capital, state, and social subsistence, economic downturns are not just a problem for capital but for society as a whole. On the surface, this tight linkage has forged a false coalition of capital and public welfare, which is, however, trapped in a "spiral of escalation" (Rosa et al., 2017, p. 60). For growth to continue, capital has to penetrate non-capitalized spaces ever further. Capital has to find new strategies of cheapening natures, including humans, and thus continuously transgressing its frontiers (Patel and Moore, 2018). Cheapening, "a strategy, a practice, a violence that mobilizes all kinds of work – human and animal, botanical and geological – with as little compensation as possible [...] makes possible capitalism's expansive markets" (ibid., p. 19ff.).

Precarity, as a result, is not an exceptional state – that which "'drops out' from the system" (Tsing, 2015, p. 20) – but it is the very condition of capital at work. Global value chains incorporate different forms of "salvage accumulation" in strategies of cheapening. Tsing (2015, p. 63) defines salvage accumulation as "the process through which lead firms amass capital without controlling the conditions under which commodities are produced". Examples abound, not least the sourcing of lithium and tantalum in the recent boom of electro-mobility where slave and child labor are ever-present. In general, it is close to impossible to purchase high-tech products requiring the use of materials such as tantalum, tin, and gold without contributing to the salvage accumulation of capital. Even *Fairphone*, a company whose focus is explicitly on sustainably sourced materials and which goes to great lengths to trace its supply chain, is only able to set up transparent supply chains for a fraction of the 40 materials it uses.

> While many of the materials evaluated deserve more attention, the findings of our materials scoping study helped us to create a shortlist of 10 materials to examine more closely: tin, tantalum, tungsten, gold, cobalt, copper, gallium, indium, nickel, rare earth metals. These materials are all frequently used in the electronics industry, have a range of mining-related issues, and are not likely to be substituted in the near future. While we certainly won't be able to improve all these supply chains, these minerals currently represent the most compelling potential to make a lasting impact. We have already set up transparent supply chains for some of these minerals. For the rest, we'll continue to evaluate options for improvement one material at a time (fairphone.com).

Economic relations in place are tightly interwoven with global capital, making it highly challenging to establish production, transfer, and consumption practices that withdraw from salvage accumulation. While it is important to say that capitalist social relations are neither the only (Gibson-Graham, 1996; Roelvink et al., 2015), nor the preferred form (White and Williams, 2016) how people relate to each other and the more-than-human world, it is also true that for most of humanity, everyday life depends on global capital one way or another. From the perspective of the

Global North, this is expressed in the fact that it is almost impossible to avoid participating in the exploitation of close and distant "earth others" (Plumwood, 2002) without simultaneously ceasing to participate in everyday social interactions (for instance through telecommunication). Brand and Wissen (2017, p. 43) describe the fact that everyday life in capitalist centers is based fundamentally on the appropriation of human and ecological relations elsewhere as "imperial way of life". Like Patel and Moore's notion of cheapening, it exposes the social and environmental injustices that accumulation on an expanding scale – growth – implies.

Capital not only shapes significant fractions of economic conduct but is also "undoing basic elements of democracy, [including] vocabularies, principles of justice, political cultures, habits of citizenship, practices of rule, and above all, democratic imaginaries" (W. Brown, 2015, p.17). Its interference with the democratic processes of collectively negotiating the parameters and principles of social togetherness goes beyond the corruption of subjects and institutions through money, power, and vested interests. Rather, "neoliberal reason, ubiquitous today in statecraft and the workplace, in jurisprudence, education, culture, and a vast range of quotidian activity, is converting the distinctly political character, meaning, and operation of democracy's constituent elements into economic ones" (ibid.). Growth and commodification penetrate deeply into the fabric of democracy, absorbing collective forms of decision-making for the purposes of endless accumulation and growth (Foucault, 2008).

Limits

Accumulation and economic growth face social and ecological limits. Socially, capital accumulation is bounded by the interlinked moments of discursive-ethical limits on the one hand and counter-movements and social unrest on the other hand. The cheapening of nature, work, care, and lives in capitalism begs questions about their intrinsic worth. Quite diverse schools of thought reiterate democracy, justice, equality, and responsibility as central values of modern societies. Capital's transgression of moral boundaries and the erosion of democracy (W. Brown, 2015; Rancière, 1998), freedom (Shannon et al., 2012), and rights – including the right not to partake in the imperial way of life (I.L.A. Kollektiv, 2019) – undermine these values and thus the central moral and political institutions of modern societies. Justice and rights are a slippery ground, in particular from a post-foundational perspective that navigates the ridge between essentialism and relativism. Barnett (2017, p. 248), against this background, emphasizes the "priority" of the sense of injustice which is "independent from a prior formulation of a universal principle of justice". The conceptual prioritization of injustice shifts the focus to the multiple emergent sites of "felt experiences of injustice" (Barnett, 2017, p. 237) that arise in social struggles. These are the places and moments when capital encounters, contests, or defers to its social limits.

Social limits to accumulation, then, materialize in social movements, disobedience, resistance, unrest, or simply withdrawal from capitalist production and exchange that slow down, hinder, or outright challenge capital circulation. While social struggles can ensue from a sense of injustice, they can be quite different in their focus, scope, strategy, and tactics. Particularistic struggles address, for instance, animal rights, environmental protection, or wages, opposing and limiting capital's exploitation of nature, work, and lives. Broader movements might follow when the cost of capital surviving its own contradictions becomes "unacceptable to the mass of the population" (Harvey, 2014, p. 264). Yet, capital is not idle pushing back and dismantling resistance through counterrevolution (Marcuse, 1972), appropriation (Rosa et al., 2017), conventionalization (Kjeldsen and Ingemann, 2016), cooptation (Zanoni et al., 2017), integration (Hardt and Negri, 2017), and commodification of progressive ideas, practices, and projects. This double movement – here in a slightly different sense than Polanyi's (2001 [1944]) two opposing movements of disembedding economy from and reembedding it in society – is crucial for understanding both capital's persistence and the possibilities of postcapitalist politics.

While moral and social frontiers are negotiable – in the sense that they are subject to ethical and political debate – capital also encounters ecological limits. Pushing capital's frontiers deep into global ecologies sets off mechanisms that are beyond human control (Malm, 2018). Rockström et al. (2009) identify nine planetary boundaries – climate change, ocean acidification, stratospheric ozone depletion, atmospheric aerosol loading, biochemical flows, interference with phosphorus and nitrogen cycles, global freshwater use, land-system change, rate of biodiversity loss, and chemical pollution – which human activity has to respect if it does not want to risk abrupt and possibly catastrophic global environmental change. Three boundaries – rate of biodiversity loss, biochemical flow boundary of nitrogen, and climate change (in order of severity of transgression) – had already been overstepped at the time of Rockström et al.'s publication. Since then, the trend has continued. Adding land-system change, an updated version from 2015 considers four out of nine planetary boundaries as crossed (Steffen et al., 2015).

Numerous metrics, furthermore, show the scope of current resource consumption and its unsustainability. Most straightforwardly, the 'earth overshoot day' – the day of each year when all the amount of resource use exceeds earth systems' ability of renewal. Since the 70s, the earth overshoot day has moved from December to early August, signaling a global resource use of 170% of earth's carrying capacity. Similarly, the ecological footprint and the material footprint are abstractions which describe the amount of resources necessary to sustain a particular lifestyle. The concept of ecological footprint was developed by Wackernagel and Rees (1997) to calculate the surface area required while the material footprint reflects the amount of resources and materials in weight measures. All metrics can be scaled differently – globally, nationally, regionally, locally, individually – showing fundamentally different results alongside north/south, racial and class divides.

Attempts to abstract nature and human impact face a number of issues. Apart from the inherent problem in converting "heterogeneous forms of data into the single metric of carbon or physical land units, thus often replacing rigor for simplified headline figures" (T. Smith, 2019a, p. 26), rendering nature and society calculable shades a number of other issues. Numbers easily veil power relations and injustices such as the export of dirty industries and the greatly unequal distribution of causation of, and suffering from, environmental destruction. Like the "indefensible abstraction" (Malm, 2014, p. 391) of the Anthropocene – veiling the stark social and spatial differences in human-nature relations and ecological destruction – the abovementioned calculations can be (mis)used to evoke the sense of an inherently human rather than a socio-economic causation. Furthermore, they easily pave over the fact that the effects of environmental change are both spatially and socially uneven, creating a reality of vastly differentiated vulnerabilities in which there are "lifeboats for the rich and privileged [and] class divisions will become matters of life and death" (Malm, 2014, p. 391). On a deeper level, furthermore, the abstraction through numbers does violence to the concrete and everyday of human and more-than-human togetherness. Taylor Aiken (2015a, p. 88), for instance, criticizes the instrumentalization of community through a focus on numbers noting that "once accountancy and numbers became a core means, the end of a community of belonging, togetherness and living justly with environmental others was sidelined".

Despite the need to tread these metrics with caution, they clearly point towards the fundamental unsustainability of human activity in earth's ecosystems. Beyond moral and social limits to growth that are deferred through institutionalized injustice, ideology, and violence, capitalist expansion runs up against ecological frontiers, the transgression of which increasingly destabilizes earth's support systems. The present, near, and far future impacts of this transgression are difficult to ignore and pressure to act comes from both scientific and non-scientific communities. Global politics of late pushes a range of agendas to face ecological and social challenges, in particular climate change. Yet, growth itself remains sacrosanct and is not up to debate. Instead it is further enshrined into institutional frameworks such as UN's sustainable development goals. With goal number 8 – decent work and economic growth – the international community commits itself to "sustained economic growth, higher levels of productivity and technological innovation" (undp.org). Capital, then, remains at the core of global politics disguised as green, smart or sustainable growth.

Green growth – an oxymoron?

The green economy comprises a range of strategies and policy measures that aim to reduce negative environmental impacts and resource consumption while maintaining economic growth (Bina, 2013; Schulz and Bailey, 2014). By and large, green growth strategies are based on technological innovation for efficiency and productivity gains as well as marketization of ecosystem services. Green growth is thereby premised on two assumptions that are not subject to further debate rendering the green economy a largely technocratic and postpolitical project (Kenis and Lievens, 2015). First, capitalist economies based on private property, deregulated markets, and competition are the most efficient way to meet social and ecological challenges and are without considerable alternatives. Second, economic growth is needed to counteract social inequality and can be reconciled with planetary boundaries through technological innovation and dematerialization. To understand and finally challenge these assumptions, it is necessary to reflect briefly on different notions of sustainability.

The concept of sustainability can have quite different meanings. A main distinction can be drawn between conceptions based on an overlapping and those based on a nested model of sustainability. The former places economy, society, and environment on equal footing as dimensions of comparable significance. Sustainability, then, means targeting a triple bottom line by balancing society, environment, and (a capitalist) economy. This endeavor, however, often "turns out to be a 'good old-fashioned single bottom line plus vague commitments to social and environmental concerns'" (Norman and Macdonald, 2004, p. 256).

An overlapping model of sustainability creates skewed priorities due to its conception as such. Placing economy, society, and environment on equal footing ignores the fundamental asymmetries between these dimensions. Nested conceptions of sustainability, instead, acknowledge that society is embedded and ultimately dependent on more-than-human ecologies while economic relations are socially produced and should be conceived of as a subset of social relations.

Nevertheless, green economy approaches continue the project of sustainable development that proposes more of the same to solve the current crises. Market mechanisms, privatization, competition, and growth are the ingredients for sustainability's recipe. Or as Nyberg et al. (2013, p. 450) put it: "the only solution to the problems of capitalism is more capitalism". The tenacious adherence to growth is premised on an overlapping conception of sustainability. The Global Green Growth Institute, for instance, is "founded on the belief that economic growth and environmental sustainability are not merely compatible objectives; their integration is essential for the future of humankind" (cited in Kenis and Lievens, 2015, p. 4). In this sense, the green economy is heralded as an opportunity to create further growth and jobs. In other words, to continue the transgression of capitalism's frontiers for instance through carbon trading and ecosystem services as business opportunities. This also deepens the abstraction of ecologies whose life-sustaining balances are torn into a set of priced commodities. It is, then, not nature or community as such that has (intrinsic) value. For capital, their worth is determined by and imposed through markets, fragmenting human and more-than-human relations and ultimately rendering them replaceable (Kenis and Lievens, 2015; T. Smith, 2019a).

Green growth advocates claim to be able to reconcile economic growth and planetary boundaries, basing their argument on increasing gains in efficiency. This presumably allows for a decoupling of growth from resource consumption. There is, however, a crucial distinction between absolute and relative decoupling. Relative decoupling refers to the decrease in use of materials or greenhouse gas emissions *relative* to GDP (growth). Absolute decoupling, instead, refers to the total decline of resource consumption and greenhouse gas emission independent of GDP growth (Jackson, 2017). While examples for relative decoupling abound, absolute decoupling is not only out of sight but also highly unlikely (Hickel and Kallis, 2019). Only focusing on climate change – leaving aside the multiple other ecological challenges – an absolute decoupling would require rates of reduction of GHG emissions per unit of GDP that are 50 times higher than they have been within the last 10 years (Jackson, 2017). Green growth's basic premise, consequently, is highly problematic. Nevertheless, proponents cling firmly to this "decoupling myth" (Paech, 2010). But even if growth were to be reconciled with planetary boundaries, there remains the question whether continuous growth is actually desirable and for whom.

Why grow in the first place?

Capitalist societies cannot simply stop growing and, if they do, they face a number of dire consequences. Stagnation and its negative economic and social consequences are certainly a major reason for the perseverance of the growth paradigm in political and public discourses. The fact that current economies need to grow, however, does not explain why growth should be desirable in the first place. Neither does it answer the question why – in the face of ecological destruction with the highly unlikely chance of absolute decoupling – global society should not embark on the endeavor to reshape economic, political, and social institutions to become independent of growth. In this section, I will deconstruct some pro-growth arguments that green economy approaches are based on.

Political and public debates generally associate economic growth, as measured by GDP, closely with prosperity (Rosa and Henning, 2018). A growing economy, the assumption goes, leads to an increase in prosperity and quality of life. GDP, however, is a very partial and poor measure for several reasons of which I will only detail the most important ones. First, GDP aggregates *all* traded goods and services irrespective of their social and environmental desirability. A fairly sourced and produced climate-neutral product is registered exactly like a same-priced product produced through child labor. For GDP, exporting weapons is equal to exporting solar panels. Storms, floods, accidents, and other disasters might contribute positively to GDP if the ensuing follow-up costs exceed the economic outages.

Second, GDP *only* aggregates commodified goods and services and does not reflect the quality of social and ecological relations. Intact ecosystems and communities, trust, friendships, unconditional help, and altruism are indifferent to GDP. In contrast, GDP might actually grow when social relations are destroyed. For instance, when neighbors don't help each other out but hire professionals, or a unique forest ecosystem is destroyed and commodified.

Third, GDP is an aggregate that ignores inequality. Although it is often accounted per-capita, it is an average measure that does not reveal the actual distribution of material wealth. Actually, in many countries, income inequality is currently higher than anytime during the 20th century (Jackson, 2017). The wealthiest profit disproportionally from economic growth while marginalized populations are often worse off due to stagnating incomes and rising prices. Piketty (2017) propounds a detailed account of the increasing concentration of wealth and the concomitant inequality in the second half of the 20th century in parallel to economic growth – a tendency that can be observed throughout many countries of the Global North and South (OECD, 2011). Rather than a trickle-down effect, economic growth causes a trickle-up effect (Jackson, 2017). Economic growth currently intensifies social inequality and (relative) poverty rather than (dis)solving it.

GDP, therefore, is a poor measure of well-being in advanced capitalist societies (Rosa and Henning, 2018; Wilkinson and Pickett, 2010). A frequently cited example is the Easterlin paradox (Easterlin, 1974). According to Easterlin's work, GDP per capita "does not correlate with happiness above certain levels of satisfaction of basic needs" (Schneider et al., 2010, p. 512). Although some criticize Easterlin's findings for difficulties associated with the measurement of subjective well-being (J. O'Neill, 2018), others take their cue from these and similar findings to explore alternative measures of well-being (Hayden and Wilson, 2017).

Proponents of alternatives to GDP often turn to Bhutan's measure of 'gross national happiness', a metric that quantifies the collective happiness of its citizens. The metric is calculated on the basis of general indicators and subjective well-being, the latter being survey-based. While alternative metrics such as Bhutan's gross-national happiness have potential to radically challenge the role of GDP in current politics, they remain subject to the limits and perils of quantification. Thomas Smith (2019a, p. 49) states that "the realization of research explicitly referring to concepts of 'wellbeing' and 'happiness' in recent decades has been noted to have been one-sided, tending towards what has been called a 'science of happiness' perspective which prioritizes the quantitative measurement of happiness." GDP-critical perspectives, in this sense, need to remain wary of the reduction inherent in the abstraction of numbers.

Interim conclusion

Thus far, chapter 1 has problematized the growth paradigm – "a worldview institutionalized in social systems proclaiming that economic growth is necessary, good, and imperative" (Kallis et al., 2018, p. 45) – both on ecological and social grounds. At the same time, it has acknowledged that modern societies depend on growth and can only stabilize through the perpetual transgression of capital's frontiers – cheapening nature, work, and lives. Continuing pushing capital's social and ecological limits, however, (further) dismantles societal values such as democracy, justice, and (more-than-) human rights and ultimately threatens the natural basis of human activity itself. Taking into account the failed promises of growth as well as the unlikeliness of reconciling an increasing GDP with social and ecological sustainability, then, raises the question why political and public discourses tenaciously adhere to growth. Institutional inertia and mental infrastructures explain part of the story. Another part are power relations that adapt and stabilize capital's accumulation regimes – an issue that will accompany us throughout this book.

Power is best approached by taking a look at the forces that challenge the incumbent social make-up. Growth and current modes of economic organization, indeed, are not unanimously accepted. Different approaches challenge business-as-usual and propose, practice, and institute "alternative economic spaces" (Krueger et al., 2017). The subsequent chapters explore the diverse individuals, organizations, and institutions that alter, challenge, resist, and withdraw from capital accumulation. Within the wide variety of approaches, chapter 2 foregrounds projects and practices that aim to transition towards "an era in which the societal project is redefined beyond the pursuit of economic growth" (Cassiers and Maréchal, 2018, p. 2). To that effect, it explores two (partly interweaving) schools of thought: degrowth and postcapitalism (Schmid, 2019a). After tracing alternative forms of production, transfer, and governance in degrowth and postcapitalist economies, chapter 3 works towards the question of how societal trajectories might shift from growth-dependence towards sustainability and justice.

Chapter 2: Alternative economies

> We invite our readers to reconsider and rebalance our individual and collective engagement between theorizing and denouncing the multiple ways capitalism denies economic, social, and epistemic justice on one hand, and non-capitalist experiences redress economic, social, and epistemic justice on the other. And then to act in service of these latter.
> *Zanoni et al., 2017, p. 584*

Alterity and diversity

Alternative economies – more specifically alternative economic and political spaces and practices – here, refers to the "performance and enactment of economies and polities through socio-spatial relations and networks that are to a greater or lesser degree distant or disengaged from global capitalism and the system of territorial states" (Fuller, Jonas, and Lee, 2016, p. xxiii). While I am particularly interested in alternative *economies*, they cannot be severed from alternative politics and, in fact, move closer in and through the theories and practices presented in the following. Alternative economies, therefore, is an umbrella term for a range of approaches including: degrowth, post-growth, steady-state economy, post-capitalism, diverse economies, solidarity economy, and commons (Bollier and Helfrich, 2012; Cassiers and Maréchal, 2018; Gibson-Graham, 2006; Gritzas and Kavoulakos, 2016; Johnsen et al., 2017; Kerschner, 2010; North and Cato, 2017; Schneider et al., 2010; Zademach and Hillebrand, 2013). Green economy approaches and the related notions of green growth, smart growth, ecological modernization, and sustainable development, in contrast, do not fall within the notion of alternative economies as it is used here – although their proponents, at times, portray them as such – since these approaches remain firmly rooted in capitalist institutions. Furthermore, the roles of sharing economy, collaborative economy, collaborative consumption, circular economy, and social economy are ambiguous in that they all comprise a broad range of practices that relate differently to mainstream economies (Cohen and Muñoz, 2016; Hobson, 2016; Martin, 2016a; Richardson, 2015).

Alternative economy approaches reconceptualize and restructure capitalist forms of socio-economic organization and, in various ways, (aim to) shift practices of production, consumption, distribution, financing, and governance towards sustainability, equity, and justice. In doing so, they question, in different ways, the existent relations of work, property, and decision-making. Although Marxist, anarchist, feminist, postcolonial, and queer theory(ies) are pivotal references, there is no common alternative economies framework (Notz, 2011). As a consequence, tensions and contradictions ensue and there is no sharp dividing line separating alternative from non-alternative approaches. The distinction between green economy and alternative economy approaches, as suggested above, rarely fits onto actually existing alternatives. Rather, it is a normative and often tactical question of drawing the line between business-as-usual and progressive pathways.

A number of authors have suggested typologies to capture the width and breath of alternative economies or to put them into relation to more conservative concepts. Schulz and Affolderbach (2015), for instance, differentiate between weak ecological modernization, strong ecological modernization, and alternative economies, presenting a continuum that increasingly moves from an efficiency orientation to politics of sufficiency. In a similar vein but with a stronger institutional focus, Bina (2013) distinguishes between almost business-as-usual, greening, and 'all change' policy responses to the double crisis of economy and ecology.

Fuller and Jonas (2003) are interested in different degrees of alterity and distinguish between alternative-additional, alternative-substitute, and alternative-oppositional forms (see also Jonas, 2016; R. Lee, 2016). Alternative-additional refers to alternatives that exist in addition to – respectively in symbiosis with – a capitalist economy and do not question its underlying relations of property, work, and governance. Examples are fair trade markets, corporate social responsibility, and similar measures. Alternative-substitute forms are a fill-in where formal economies fail and thus constitute a surrogate for capitalist sustenance. This is particularly visible in the context of austerity politics (Amanatidou et al., 2015). Alternatives that are a substitute can also become an opposition to existing economic relations. Alternative-oppositional, then, describes alternative circuits of value that are deliberately set up to oppose capitalist relations (R. Lee, 2016).

Scholars have proposed concepts such as variegated capitalism (Peck and Theodore, 2007), the ordinary economy (R. Lee, 2006), and diverse economies (Gibson-Graham, 2008) to challenge both the uniformity of the formal economy and the narrowing of economic practice to the former. The present work takes up the notion of diverse economies, in particular, to acknowledge that economies are "intrinsically heterogeneous spaces composed of multiple class processes, mechanisms of exchange, forms of labor and remuneration, finance, and ownership" (Healy, 2009, p. 338). Gibson-Graham's heuristic of capitalist, alternative-capitalist, and non-capitalist forms of labor, transactions, and enterprises has been used widely to explore the diversity of economic practices beyond wage labor, commodity exchange, and for-profit enterprises (see also Gibson-Graham, Cameron, et al., 2013). Gibson-Graham (2006, p. 60) introduce a language of economic diversity to widen "the identity of the economy to include all of those practices excluded or marginalized by a strong theory of capitalism". In doing so, Gibson-Graham explicitly avoid presenting a "'ready-made' alternative economy" (ibid.) in order to "resist the closures that come with every positive economic articulation" (Miller, 2013, p. 521). Gibson-Graham's concept of a diverse economy will play a pivotal role in chapter 4. Here, I am mainly interested in their thrust to problematize the notion of alternative.

The concept of a diverse economy raises an important issue about the notion of alternative. The word alternative "underscores a fundamental insight from modern linguistic theory – that no term derives its meaning self-referentially" (Healy, 2009, p. 338). Economies that are described as alternative, then, appear to derive their identity primarily from what they are an alternative to – a seemingly homogenous and omnipresent 'norm(al)' (capitalist) economy. Yet, although alternatives do emerge as substitution in cases where capitalist relations fail (see Fuller and Jonas' notion of alternative-substitute), they are much more than a fill-in for capitalist relations. On the contrary, the practices and institutions discussed as alternatives are frequently the "preferred and desired way to get tasks undertaken" (White and Williams, 2016, p. 6). Alternative economic practices, therefore, are not marginal phenomena but different expressions of 'economic being-in-common' (see chapter 4) in their own right. In contrast to the connotation of alternatives as an inferior choice to the mainstream economy, alternative economies, here, refer to "[p]rocesses of production, exchange, labor/compensation, finance, and consumption that are intentionally different from mainstream (capitalist) economic activity" (Healy, 2009, p. 338). This implies also that, counter to common perception, alternative economies are neither less structured (stabilized), less important for human (re)production, nor less spatially or temporally extensive than capitalist economies (Schmid and Smith, 2020).

Emphasizing diversity over alterity, however, eclipses the evaluation of and opposition to undesirable economic practices and relations. Andrew Jonas (2016, p. 22) argues that critical scholarship should approach alternatives with a "healthy skepticism". He points out that alternatives are not desirable *per se*. Michael Samers (2005) makes a similar point, problematizing that non-capitalist practices are not necessarily less exploitative than capitalist practices. Roger Lee (2016), furthermore, underlines the political significance of alterity (see also Glassman, 2003).

> As an alternative is defined in terms of something else, it is its 'other' – or, at least, an 'other' – and thereby legitimates and maintains the centrality of something else. By contrast, the notion of diversity simply implies that there are many possibilities. However, the political significance of alternative versus diversity is also crucially important (R. Lee, 2016, p. 276).

Acknowledging the economy as diverse, therefore, does not suffice in the identification of alternative economies. Instead, transformative geographies require a discussion on what alternatives are desirable and how they can shift societal trajectories away from current patterns of unsustainability. The notions of alterity and diversity both have political implications. Diversity "opens up ways of thinking about the circumstances under which such decisions are made" (Jonas, 2016, p. 14), unlocking potentials and possibilities for other economies. Alterity, in turn, dissociates particular economic activities from an 'other' and thus distances, for instance, from exploitative and ecologically destructive forms of economizing. The notion of alternative economies, then, includes both a broadening and a narrowing moment. Alternatives are more than capitalism's 'other' and include a wide variety of imaginaries and practices that exist(ed) before, aside, with and despite of capitalist relations. On the other hand, alternative economies do not refer to an arbitrary collection of diverse imaginaries and practices, but to those that are positioned against exploitation, dominion, injustice, and ecological destruction. This narrowing excludes, for instance, the technological and market-based green economy approaches that continue along the trajectories of commodification and economic growth as well as undesirable non-capitalist alternatives like authoritarian socialism. Alterity and diversity, hence, lead to two different "modalities of resistance – through antagonism and social imagination, respectively" (Zanoni et al., 2017, p. 578). These are frequently seen as contradictory but, as I argue below, can be productive when put into a co-constitutive relation.

Still, the question of what constitutes (desirable) alternative economies remains subject to political and ethical negotiation, leading to blurred boundaries and ambiguous allies. Greening, modernization, and to some extent also alternative-additional approaches might provide short-term remedies to ecological and social issues but perpetuate the escalatory tendencies of dynamic stabilization in the long run. Sharing economies, social enterprises, cooperatives, and non-profit organizations, furthermore, might challenge some aspects of capitalist relations of work, property, and appropriation of surplus while endorsing others. Following the call for diversity, a preemptive exclusion of potentially emancipatory alternatives is counterproductive and deeply problematic. At the same time, scholars on the antagonistic side of things rightly caution against unruly allies that uphold a (disguised) exploitation of natures and lives. To drill deeper into the politics of complementary-, additional-, substitute-, and oppositional alternative economic practices, I will now turn to two increasingly influential strands of scholarship, namely degrowth and postcapitalism. Both concepts are grounded in radical critiques of capitalist social relations and propose a range of linked ideas and practices to challenge social and environmental issues.

Degrowth

Degrowth is both an activist slogan and an academic debate challenging the hegemony of growth as economic, political and social imperative. In recent years, degrowth has emerged as quilting point for a wide range of approaches from disciplines and fields as diverse as environmental sciences (Kallis, 2018), economics (Jackson, 2017; Paech, 2012), geography (Krueger et al., 2017), and sociology (Rosa and Henning, 2018) questioning economic growth and related notions such as development and progress (Bendix, 2017; Demaria and Kothari, 2017; Latouche, 2009). Rather than simply opposing growth, development, and progress, degrowth scholars combine a variety of approaches that are concerned with alternative imaginaries, principles, practices, and institutions of socio-economic organizing centering around well-being, justice, and sustainability. Along these lines, degrowth aims for an "equitable downscaling of production and consumption that increases human well-being and enhances ecological conditions at the local and global level in the short and long term" (Schneider et al., 2010, p. 512).

Degrowth's roots go back to the 1970s, which witnessed a number of events and interventions – partly related and partly independent – that shape the emergence of today's degrowth debate. In 1971, Nicholas Georgescu-Roegen has published a thermodynamic rethinking of economics entitled *Entropy and the Economic process* (Georgescu-Roegen, 1971) that links economic activity to the physical conditions which pose (energetic) limitations to the former. One year later, Donella Meadows and colleagues presented their work on the *Limits of Growth* to the Club of Rome, demonstrating the material boundaries of compound growth (Meadows and Club of Rome, 1972; see also Meadows, Randers, and Meadows, 2004). The integration of ecological conditions and economic theory led some ecological economists and scholars from other disciplines to question "growthmanship" (Kallis et al., 2018) and propose alternatives. Quite influential for today's degrowth debate is also the work of Herman Daly on a "steady-state economy" (Daly, 1973; see also Kunkel and Daly, 2018).

The French intellectual André Gorz was the first to use the term *décroissance* in posing the question: "is the earth's balance, for which no-growth – or even degrowth [*décroissance*] – of material production a necessary condition, compatible with the survival of the capitalist system?" (Gorz, 1972, cited in Kallis et al., 2015, p. 1). However, apart from some notable exceptions – such as the title of the French translation of a collection of Georgescu-Roegen's work *demain la décroissance* – the term gained little traction beyond a small circle of activists and academics until the early 2000s. In 2002, then, Bruno Clémentin and Vincent Cheynet edited a special issue of *Silence* in tribute to Georgescu-Roegen, which "was probably the starting point for today's degrowth movement" (Kallis et al., 2015, p. 2). Both activists and academics – arguably the most influential being Serge Latouche with his post-developmental critique of Western economism – mobilized with *décroissance* as a slogan in the years to follow. The English translation of *décroissance* – degrowth – officially emerged in 2008 with the first international degrowth conference in Paris signaling the consolidation of an international exchange (Kallis et al., 2015).

Décroissance originates in the spirit of a radical critique of consumerism, development, and capitalism (Demaria et al., 2013; Martínez-Alier et al., 2010). With the recent development and spread of the debate, however, a range of understandings has emerged that do not retain this critical stance. The term degrowth is often narrowed to GDP degrowth, consumption degrowth, work-time degrowth, or physical degrowth (van den Bergh, 2011). It is problematic, though, to reduce degrowth to a particular area or metric. Degrowth "should not be understood in its literal meaning (i.e. negative growth of GDP) or just as shrinking of material throughput" (Asara et al., 2015, p. 377). Currently, most economic and social institutions are based on continuous growth and destabilize or break in times of recession (Rosa et al., 2017; Kallis et al., 2012; see above). Degrowth, therefore, loses its critical purchase if decontextualized from a broader critique that seeks to transform growth-dependent institutions.

The strategies, priorities, and scope of transformative ambitions vary between different degrowth approaches. Moderate degrowth advocates propose reforms of growth-based economic, political, and social institutions, for instance through eco-taxes, basic-income schemes, internalization of costs, and alternative indicators for prosperity (Seidl and Zahrnt, 2010a). By and large, moderate degrowth perspectives hold on to market and state institutions as central pillars of societal organization while aiming for a restructuring of health care, pension, education, tax systems, financial markets, and others to become growth-independent. Existent political institutions are central actors in this vision. On the other end of the "degrowth spectrum" (Eversberg and Schmelzer, 2018) are advocates of a radical shift beyond capitalist forms of work, transfer, and property relations as well as the state. Proponents of a radical degrowth question the ability of state and market institutions to work in the name of social and environmental justice. While institutional reforms are part of the repertoire, radical degrowth focuses on social movements and community initiatives that prefigure alternatives beyond market and state institutions as central agents of transformation (see below).

Irrespective of specific orientations within the degrowth debate, opposing growth as economic and political objective entails the abandonment of the institution of capital. Degrowth questions (infinite) capital accumulation as basis of economic organization, instead privileging economic practices that address social and ecological needs. Consequently, it moves beyond social institutions that enforce and secure the "unlimited accumulation of capital by formally peaceful means" (Boltanski and Chiapello, 2018, p. 4; see above). It's vision, foundation, and ambition, thus, are essentially postcapitalist. Nevertheless, some degrowth scholars eschew an explicit stance *against* capitalism. Andreucci and Mc Donough (2015) identify three principal reasons for this reluctance. First, degrowers want to avoid the reification of capitalism as unified, ubiquitous, and powerful object. Second, many degrowth scholars and activists propose decentralized, autonomous, and horizontal projects that evade the imaginary of a centralized revolutionary struggle against a uniform opponent. And third, to facilitate the spread of degrowth across academic and political spheres, degrowth advocates avoid adopting an explicitly anticapitalist language. All three reflect aforementioned unease with alterity and opposition (see above) and beg further investigation of the relation between degrowth and anti- or postcapitalism.

Postcapitalism

The foregoing analysis identifies antagonism and social imagination as different modalities of resistance. Arguing for the integration of both, Zanoni et al. (2017, p. 578) assert that critical scholars should "keep developing sophisticated critique that fosters antagonism and become more proactively performative of alternatives". In a similar vein, Miller (2015, p. 364) caricatures the apparent juxtaposition between postcapitalism and anticapitalism before arguing for the necessity to blend both dynamics.

> We are asked, it seems, to choose: be an anticapitalist revolutionary, building organized political power by marching arm in arm with the unified force of the new Communist party; or be a postcapitalist ethical subject, eschewing critique, disavowing capitalism, and strengthening emerging communal practices through engaged research.

Postcapitalism, anticapitalism, and degrowth share significant common ground, yet there is only limited reference across these different debates (Schmid, 2019a). Anticapitalism comprises theories, movements, and groupings that stand in opposition to capitalism (Tormey, 2012). Anticapitalists, consequently, are primarily defined by what they are against: capitalism, neoliberalism, globalization, and transnational corporations (Morland, 2018). Despite this shared opposition, anticapitalism is not a coherent movement or fixed ideology. Anticapitalist thought builds on a rich tradition around thinkers like Rousseau, Godwin and Marx (Tormey, 2012) of which the latter in particular sticks out for his systematic critique of capitalism. Harvey asserts that "the contributions of Marxism in general and Marxist political economy in particular are foundational to anti-capitalist struggle. They define more clearly what the struggle has to be about and against and why" (Harvey, 2015, p. 2). Marxism, of course, has diversified into a plethora of approaches that exceed the label anticapitalist.

Here, it is illuminating to track the post-Marxist critique of figures like Laclau and Mouffe and Gibson-Graham (see also part II) to understand the sensitivities of postcapitalism and its relation to anticapitalism. Gibson-Graham criticize the Marxist representation of capitalism as unified singular totality and – inspired by poststructural feminist thought – seek to establish a *post*capitalist, rather than an anticapitalist, politics around performativity, plurality, and hope. In line with aforementioned turn from alterity to diversity, the emphasis shifts from opposition to difference.

Postcapitalism is also used by other schools of thought. Chatterton and Pusey (2019) identify post-work and autonomous perspectives as further strands of the postcapitalist debate. Post-work imagines technological progress as a way out of capitalism. Mechanization and automation in conjunction with the provision of universal basic services are proposed to lead to a "fully automated luxury communism" (Bastani, 2018; see also Srnicek and Williams, 2016). In this sense, post-work scholars seek to accelerate technological innovation. Along similar lines, but less 'accelerationalist', Mason (2016) argues that the rise of information technology and collaborative production surmount capitalism's ability to adapt and thus open the possibility (or rather necessity) of postcapitalism.

Autonomous perspectives, as third strand of postcapitalism, focus on "autonomous social forms and practices and their potential to build methodologies of organization and social (re)production that challenge capitalism" (Chatterton and Pusey, 2019, p. 11). Autonomous perspectives emphasize self-managed projects that exist and thrive within capitalism's temporal, spatial, and institutional interstices. Theory and practice of autonomous postcapitalist literature stresses prefiguration – the pursuit of micro-political tactics and the creation of alternative spaces in the here and now – as opposed to a "politics of waiting" (Springer, 2014b, p. 262; see also Pickerill and Chatterton, 2006) that is often associated with Marxist and anticapitalist positions.

The (false) antagonism between anticapitalism and postcapitalism that Miller (2015) and others observe links to the debate between Marxism and anarchism that characterizes large parts of the history of the socialist left (Kellermann, 2011, 2012, 2014) and is reiterated recently in human geography (Harvey, 2015; Springer, 2014b, 2017). This debate is largely between the more utilitarian, institutional, oppositional, and ruptural imaginaries of Marxism and the prefigurative, spontaneous, pluralistic, and interstitial imaginaries of anarchism. Arbitrating voices such as

Pickerill (2017, p. 255) redirect the conversation towards the real issues at stake: "the central question remains: how can we stop the hegemony of capital and capitalism?" The diverse approaches of anticapitalism, postcapitalism, and degrowth might provide different answers. But in the end their commonalities (should) prevail. Any emancipatory project needs to reflectively negotiate between orientation (a directionality that includes a horizon and knowledge of what it aims to get away from), strategy (a method and plan for how to affect change including the anticipation of opposition and constraints), and possibility (the hopes, dreams, desires, and creativity needed to imagine a different future). Different approaches have different focal points. But none has the ability to predict the future and decide on a master plan. In their extreme – and that is what critics jump at – degrowth, anticapitalism, postcapitalism, and other approaches overemphasize one dimension at the expense of others. Most thinking and practice, however, transcends the narrow confines of labels.

Following Chatterton (2016, p. 404f.), postcapitalism "points to a desire to reinvent and reinvigorate the revolutionary process away from older top-down, elite-led models of change" while it remains "deliberately open and provocative [since] as soon as we begin to deal with what comes next, we enter the terrain of speculation, conditionality and advocacy, as well as hope and imagination" (ibid., p. 405). And yet postcapitalism's agenda is not arbitrary.

> If the capitalist system generates deep social and spatial unevenness, then postcapitalism has to work towards the opposite. Postcapitalist social and spatial formations should inhibit the accumulation of surplus value, individualization, commodification and enclosure, as well as build commons, socially useful production and doing (Chatterton and Pusey, 2019, p. 15).

In this vein, postcapitalism refers to both a critique of and opposition to capitalist hegemony as well as a vision of a future beyond capitalism and the prefiguration of hopes and imaginations in the here and now. Together, degrowth and postcapitalism inform a radical theory and praxis beyond accumulation and growth to which I turn next.

Towards a radical theory and praxis

Postcapitalism speaks to the aforementioned reluctance of degrowth scholars to explicitly position themselves against capitalism. First, in the same vein of Gibson-Graham's post-Marxist critique, postcapitalism seeks to make visible the diversity of provisioning and (re)productive practices in order to disidentify with capitalism as only form of economic relatedness. Second, postcapitalism is an open and plural process that provides a horizon rather than a universalistic counter project to capitalism. And third, postcapitalism joins different strategies and paths towards an alternative future that range from the "ruptural desire to break the system [to] symbiotic moves to work within existing institutions, and interstitial activities that break free and lay down prefigurative future markers" (Chatterton and Pusey, 2019, p. 15).

Degrowth and postcapitalism also speak to each other through the practices they manifest in and draw on. Associations, collectives, enterprises, and individuals experiment with different forms of ownership, collective processes of decision-making, voluntary simplicity, and non-monetary forms of exchange (Alexander, 2013; Burkhart et al., 2017; Chatterton and Pusey, 2019; Demaria et al., 2013; Johanisova and Wolf, 2012; Sekulova et al., 2013). In doing so, they oppose capitalist hegemony, prefigure alternative economies, and sketch the possibilities of other forms of economic interaction. Experimentation spans a wide diversity of economic activities – such as production, work, property, transactions, decision-making, finance, and surplus allocation – and sectors – food, housing, energy, mobility, and consumer goods.

Both in theory and in practice, degrowth and postcapitalism overlap with a range of other perspectives. Approaches such as the steady-state economy (Buch-Hansen, 2014; Kerschner, 2010), participatory economics (Hahnel and Wright, 2016), the solidarity economy (Miller, 2010; North and Cato, 2017), buen vivir (Acosta and Brand, 2018; Gudynas, 2011), and commons (Bollier, 2015; Bollier and Helfrich, 2012; Caffentzis and Federici, 2014); and concepts such as social and spatial justice (Peet and Watts, 1996; Soja, 2010), sufficiency (Schneidewind and Zahrnt, 2014), and conviviality (Illich, 1973; Vetter, 2018) are used by, alongside, or in lieu of degrowth and postcapitalist perspectives.[1] Depending on theoretical take, research agenda, and empirical focus, many scholars impose their viewpoint onto alternative projects and practices. In this vein, empirical examples are studied from and sometimes claimed by a number of approaches simultaneously. Co-housing, for example, is investigated from degrowth (Lietaert, 2010), postcapitalist (Chatterton, 2016), and commons (Noterman, 2015) perspectives, with considerable overlaps. Some practitioners and activist themselves use labels such as degrowth, postcapitalism, sharing economy, circular economy, or social entrepreneurship (see below), sometimes in quite diverse ways, sometimes several labels at once. Others engage in alternative practice but do not subscribe to particular traditions, discourses, or movements.

---

1 Approach, here, refers to a broad take on alternative economies (such as solidarity economy), while concepts are more selectively applied within alternative economy literature alongside other concepts (such as sufficiency). The distinction between approaches and concepts is not clear cut. Commons, for example, is both an approach in itself (e.g. Bollier and Helfrich, 2012) and used as concept alongside others (e.g. in the degrowth debate).

Digression: Commons

The notion of commons is central to both degrowth and postcapitalist perspectives but constitutes also an approach in its own right (Bollier, 2015; Bollier and Helfrich, 2012; Caffentzis and Federici, 2014; Helfrich and Bollier, 2019; Noterman, 2015). Enclosure of common resources, in particular land, is at the heart of capitalist development (Wood, 2017). Dispossession and social dislocation accompany the push of capitalism's frontier both in the capitalist heartlands and in the Global South. Enclosure and primitive accumulation (Glassmann, 2006) are not historical phenomena but occur to this day through land-grabbing, the privatization of city space, and the commodification of animal and plant species, amongst other things (Linebaugh, 2014). (Re-)asserting collective ownership beyond market and state institutions, then, becomes a crucial means of resistance that withdraws capital's foundation of private property.

Commons are collectively owned and administered goods, ideas, and resources. Commoning – the process of collectively managing, negotiating, using, and maintaining commons – incorporates property relations that are beyond the binary of private and public. Due to the intimate relation between a community, its rules, patterns, and institutions (Helfrich, 2015; Ostrom, 2010), "commons cannot be conceived as a pre-existing object or good" but are instead "fundamentally rooted in praxis" (Enright and Rossi, 2017, p. 7). Commons, therefore, premise a community that regulates access, use, conditions, and participation. As commonly administered resources, commons dissolve the division between owners and users or producers and consumers, along with the concomitant forms of alienation and heteronomy. The common regulation of basic goods and services opens up possibilities beyond market and state relations. Hardt and Negri (2009, p. 273) write "what the private is to capitalism and what the public is to socialism, the common is to communism" – referring to a third way besides socialism centered on state-property and capitalism based on private property.

The complex and diverse landscape of alternatives renders any rigid categorization a futile endeavor. Yet, there are tendencies within and between the various approaches that help both practitioners and scholars to navigate and communicate. Different approaches highlight different aspects and add various qualities and subtleties to both theories and practices of alternative economizing. Sharing economy, social economy, circular economy, and collaborative economy all propose a particular form of praxis – for instance the *sharing* of resources, use, access, and ownership; or the *circulation* of resources and materials through production, consumption, and recycling – to address social and ecological issues. Degrowth, postcapitalism, and commons, instead, target fundamental capitalist institutions – such as property, accumulation, and economic growth – that engender social and spatial inequalities. Alongside other perspectives such as buen vivir, they remain rather general in their ideas and propositions. This does not preclude links to yet other approaches such as the economy for the common good, participatory economics, and some strands of degrowth and the social and solidarity economy that propose quite concrete blueprints for building alternative economic institutions (Felber, 2018; Hahnel and Wright, 2016; Paech, 2009).

Differences in the approaches and concepts vivify the landscape of alternative economizing. The rather particular focus of sharing economy and circular economy, for instance, does not mean that these approaches are irrelevant for a radical theory and praxis. In fact, they constitute empirically highly relevant contributions for that very reason. Compromises, hybridities, and particularisms are important features of actually existing alternative economies (see below). Approaches that do not challenge the fundamentals of capitalist institutions, therefore, are still important allies for degrowth and postcapitalist perspectives. However, mainstream economies frequently rope in innovative concepts for the purposes of capital. Circular economy, for instance, echoes the promises of efficiency narratives (Hobson and Lynch, 2016), and highly flexible on-demand platform economies adorn themselves with the progressive ring of 'sharing' (Frenken and Schor, 2017). Approaches that lack a radical orientation, then, merge easily into mainstream economic practice without asserting an opposition to, and distance from, capitalist profit seeking and exploitation.

The remainder of this work draws on a range of the aforementioned approaches and concepts. Degrowth and postcapitalism, however, remain the primary perspectives and guiding frameworks of this book. Since degrowth and postcapitalism have considerable overlaps they feature interchangeably at times. Yet, both perspectives carry different sensitivities that thread their way through the following chapters. I use degrowth primarily to refer to the contours of an agenda or proposal of change that addresses different issues by way of how they relate to growth (causing growth, affected by growth etcetera). Degrowth, on that note, is close to the notion of transition that the next section establishes as the (strategic) passage from one state of affairs to another. On the other hand, I use postcapitalism to refer to the ontologies and politics of change. This is more closely related to the notion of 'transformative geographies' as changing spatialities that emerge from the power-laden struggles of human co-existence (see part III). Chapter 3, now, turns to the question of how change unfolds and looks at the politics, agents, and strategies of change to further clarify the notions of transformation and transition.

Chapter 3: Transformation, transition, and agency

> People in fact are conscious initiators of actions, even if they are also creatures of unconscious habit and often act in highly scripted ways. This is critical, because unless people are agents in this sense, there really would be no point in writing books to clarify the harms generated by capitalism, the desirability of an alternative and the dilemmas of realizing those alternatives. The very possibility of strategy depends on people being conscious initiators of acts.
> Wright, 2019, p. 123

Chapter 3 tackles two questions that remain implicit in the preceding chapter. First, that of transformation and transition and second, that of their agents. Transformation is a widely used term in recent debates on sustainability, global change, and alternative economies. For the most part, however, the notion remains rather vague. Generally, transformation refers to fundamental shifts in social and ecological systems comprising multiple interacting dimensions that include politics, economy, technology, and ecology. Perspectives on transformation commonly take one of two angles. On the one hand, a passive approach, in which transformation in ecological, economic, and social systems challenges individuals, communities, companies, nations, and the international community to adapt. On the other hand, an active approach, in which individuals, communities, entrepreneurs, and organizations steer economic, political, cultural, and technological change towards sustainability and justice or away from it. Both dimensions, of course, intersect, raising questions of governance, politics, and power. From an emancipatory point of view, then, transformation is the process of channeling social and ecological dynamics into a desirable direction (Schneidewind, 2018).

Transition, meanwhile, emerges as twin concept to transformation, most notable in sustainability transition research (Hansen and Coenen, 2015; Loorbach et al., 2017; Markard et al., 2012). Reviewing recent debates in transition and transformation research, this chapter drills deeper into different conceptualizations and pathways of change as well as the agents thereof. Albeit critical of the apolitical tendencies in some socio-technical and policy-focused approaches, this chapter sees merit in a deeper engagement. In this sense, chapter three moves from sketching different conceptual angles towards a discussion of the politics of transformation and transition.

Sustainability transition research

Sustainability transition research encompasses a wide range of conceptual and empirical perspectives that inquire into the inertia of unsustainable socio-technical alignments and trace – often actively advocate – transformations, de- and re-alignments, substitutions, and reconfigurations of technology, policy, markets, industry, science, and culture towards more sustainable arrangements (Geels and Schot, 2007; Loorbach et al., 2017). Transition, consequently, involves "far-reaching changes along different dimensions: technological, material, organizational, institutional, political, economic, and socio-cultural" in the course of which "new products, services, business models, and organizations emerge, partly complementing, partly substituting for existing ones" (Markard et al., 2012, p. 956). Despite a number of different conceptual takes, focal points, and topics, transition literature shares a number of basic assumptions about socio-technological change.

Transition literature, by and large, follows a processual and emergent notion of change that plays out through the dialectic of agents and the configurations that structure their activities. Apart from some notable exceptions developing around practice-theoretical thinking (see chapter 5), large parts of transition research see change as unfolding through the dynamic interaction of different levels of structuration – commonly referred to as niche, regime, and landscape – in the course of which less institutionalized, formalized, and experimental technologies, practices, or organizational modes replace, modify, or infuse with incumbent configurations. Furthermore, different elements, sectors, and regimes interact in processes of stabilization and destabilization rendering transition a highly complex, non-linear, and co-evolutionary dynamic (Loorbach et al., 2017).

In conceptual terms, a number of frameworks and theoretical lenses constitute the field of transition research including the multi-level perspective [hereafter: MLP] (Geels, 2011; Geels and Schot, 2007; A. Smith et al., 2010), transition management [TM] (Loorbach, 2010), strategic niche management [SNM] (Seyfang and Haxeltine, 2012; Seyfang and Smith, 2007), technological innovation systems [TIS] (Bergek et al., 2008; Jacobsson and Bergek, 2011), and social practice theory [SPT] (Hargreaves, 2011; Shove and Walker, 2010; Spaargaren, 2011; Strengers and Maller,

2015). Pertinent reviews often do not include the latter in the field of sustainability transition research (Hansen and Coenen, 2015; Markard et al., 2012). I will do so for two reasons. First, many contributions from SPT follow the thrust of sustainability transition research in proposing a perspective on the non-linear, complex, and co-constitutively structured dynamic of change (Gram-Hanssen, 2011; Hoffman and Loeber, 2016; Shove et al., 2015; Warde, 2005). Second, there is a vivid debate on the synergies and differences of SPT and the MLP in particular (Hargreaves et al., 2013) and transition literature more broadly (Shove and Walker, 2007, 2010). For reasons of scope, I will focus on the two approaches most relevant for the argument of this book in the following – MLP and SPT – only touching upon other approaches – such as SNM – where appropriate.

The multi-level perspective

The multi-level perspective conceptualizes (sustainability) transitions as interplay between different levels of structuration: niches, regimes, and landscape (Geels, 2011; Geels and Schot, 2007). Regimes are dynamically stable configurations of practices and rules that are relatively coherent while interpenetrating and co-evolving with other regimes. The trajectories of socio-cultural, market, science, policy, and technological regimes are thus characterized by lock-ins and path dependencies. Niche and landscape are defined in relation to regimes. Niches are protected spaces of experimentation such as small market niches, laboratories, subsidized projects, or spaces of community activism. Through different processes – for instance articulation (and adjustment of visions), building of social networks, and learning processes (Kemp et al., 1998) – niches can develop to challenge incumbent regimes. In conjunction with pressure from the landscape-level – external long-term trends and ideologies, values, and economic patterns – niche innovations might change the configuration of regimes.

Geels and Schot (2007) propose four transition pathways which they derive from the possible combinations of timing of landscape pressure and niche development on the one hand and the relation between niche-innovation and regime on the other. 'Transformation', according to Geels and Schot's typology, results from "moderate landscape pressure at a moment when niche-innovations have not yet been sufficiently developed" (ibid., p. 406). This leads to the modification of development paths but does not cause major changes. 'De- and re-alignment', as second transition pathway, follows from major landscape changes at a time of insufficiently developed innovations. As a result, multiple niche-innovations compete, with one eventually asserting dominance. 'Technological substitution' occurs if niche innovations have developed at the time of strong landscape pressure. A technology, then, substitutes another during the "window of opportunity" (ibid., p. 410) opened through the external shock. Lastly, 'reconfiguration' ensues from developed symbiotic innovations at times of moderate landscape pressure, resulting in adjustments of the regime.

The multi-level perspective and the transition pathways it envisions are primarily focused on technological innovations. Geels and Schot's examples of transitions from cesspools to sewage systems, from horse-drawn carriages to automobiles, from sailing ships to steamships, and from traditional factories to mass production – which they use to illustrate aforementioned transition pathways – evidence this narrow focus. Accordingly, much application of MLP is in line with eco-modernization and green economy approaches. Particularly problematic here, however, is the notion of landscape as an external or residual category. Landscape dynamics – macro-economic trends, societal values, and political patterns – are removed from the range and scope of agency and conceived of as largely outside of the influences of innovations. MLP only allows for secondary effects of new regimes on landscape, which, however, it hardly thematizes. This external force of landscape is highly misleading and risks determinative and essentialist notions of social reproduction and change.

Social practice theory

Social practice theorists take issue with both MLP's narrow focus on technological innovations and its hierarchical ontology of niche, regime, and landscape (Shove and Walker, 2010). The focus on practices – patterns of social activity that exist through the interconnectedness of materials, meanings, and competences (Shove et al., 2012) – introduces a different angle to transition research (here, I am primarily interested in the relation between MLP and SPT, a deeper conceptualization and contextualization of the latter follows in chapter 5). In contrast to the verticality of the multi-level perspective, SPT foregrounds the horizontality of practices, their elements, and their links with other practices (Hargreaves et al., 2013). "In emphasizing the horizontal circulation of elements and in arguing for a flatter model characterized by multiple relations (rather than hierarchical levels) of reproduction across different scales" social practice theory counters MLP's tendency to "overemphasize processes of (market) competition and selection resulting in stabilizing levels or moments of provisional closure" (Shove and Walker, 2010, p. 474).

Theories of practice, therefore, seek change in practices' circuits of reproduction – the "processes of enactment which simultaneously limit or facilitate the transformation of the practice in question, its integration with other practices and the reproduction of elements" (Pantzar and Shove, 2010, p. 450). A first circuit of reproduction can be found in the ways practices' materials, meanings, and skills hang together and cohere. Like the elements of practice, practices themselves interconnect and form systems of practice, which is the second circuit of reproduction. Finally, a third circuit ensues from practices' temporality and the evolvement from past practices through the ways they shape future practice.

A perspective on practices, rather than on niches, regimes, and landscape, opens different avenues for policy intervention. Spurling and McMeekin (2015, p. 79ff.) suggest three "intervention framings", that is ways in which policy can intervene to shift towards more sustainable trajectories. First, recrafting practices: changing the elements that make up resource intensive (or more generally undesirable) practices. Second, substituting practices: replacing unsustainable practices with other practices. Third, changing how practices interlock: intervention in the patterns that practices form. Spurling and McMeekin's typology largely parallels an earlier proposal by Shove et al. (2012) who identify four ways how change in practice occurs.

Social practice theorists depart from MLP's conception of different levels in conceptualizing transition. While some scholars try to replace MLP's verticality with SPT's horizontality (Shove et al., 2012; Shove and Walker, 2010), others argue for the merits of an integration of both perspectives (Hargreaves et al., 2013). The former, however, maintain that the 'levels' of MLP jar with the flat conceptual plane on which elements, practices, and practice formations form and interact. Niche, regime, and landscape divide practices, technologies, institutions, and actors at the outset into more densely and more loosely structured realms and thus fail to "capture the complexity and contingency of sustainable and unsustainable developments" (A. Smith et al., 2010, p. 443). Furthermore, although MLP's levels are not 'spatial levels' as such, their temporal and structural scaling is frequently recast as spatial argument (for a critique see Raven et al., 2012). Some authors even conflate MLP's levels with territorial boundaries such as nation states. Spatially sensitive conceptualizations of transition, therefore, are crucial to refine the multi-level perspective and incorporate important criticisms by SPT and other theories (Coenen et al., 2012; Hansen and Coenen, 2015; Raven et al., 2012; A. Smith et al., 2010). I will return to these conceptual issues in part II. Next, I turn to a central notion throughout different strands of sustainability transition research – that of innovation.

Grassroots innovations and the social economy

Innovation research is a major intellectual root of the sustainability transition literature (Loorbach et al., 2017). The MLP, in particular, was significantly developed around technological innovations in niches that act as "incubation rooms" from which "radical novelties emerge" (Geels and Schot, 2007, p. 400). Innovation, thereby, is not limited to technology. Concepts such as social innovation (Marques et al., 2017; Moulaert et al., 2013; Moulaert et al., 2005; Westley et al., 2013), transformative social innovation (Avelino et al., 2017), system innovation (Rauschmayer et al., 2015), grassroots innovation (Longhurst, 2015; Seyfang and Smith, 2007), and conceptual innovation (Longhurst, 2015) show a broad interest in the role of novel configurations for societal change. Innovation, for Avelino et al. (2017, p. 2), encompasses "any initiative product, process, program, project, or platform that challenges and over time contributes to changing the defining routines, resources and authority flows of beliefs of the broader social system in which it is introduced; successful social innovations have durability, scale and transformative impact". *Transformative* social innovation, then, is "the process through which social innovation challenges, alters and/or replaces dominant institutions" (ibid., p. 2).

Looking not just at innovation but also at the innovators brings transformative agents and dynamics into view that other transition perspectives miss. The notions of grassroots innovations (Seyfang and Haxeltine, 2012; Seyfang and Smith, 2007) and alternative milieus (Longhurst, 2015) foreground the role of community and civil society in sustainability transitions. Community actors differ significantly from the policy-makers and market actors that stand in the center of much transition literature. Since community actors are situated outside of market economics and state bureaucracy – in the sense that they do not represent market or state institutions – they exhibit a more contingent orientation towards the rules and dynamics of incumbent institutions. For Seyfang and Smith (2007), grassroots innovations develop in the context of the social economy rather than the market economy. This is important insofar as the "social economy differs from the market economy; appropriation of profits by capital under the latter is suspended in favor of reinvesting any surplus into the grassroots under the former" (Seyfang and Smith, 2007, p. 591). Instead of reproducing the principles and values of markets, grassroots innovations "emphasize different social, ethical, and cultural rules" (ibid.). A perspective on grassroots innovations, then, both broadens the scope of transition research to include non-market and non-state agents and challenges the apolitical assumption of markets, states, and other institutions as given (landscape).

Social economy and a range of other terms such as third sector, solidarity economy, voluntary sector, and non-profit sector refer to economic activities that divert from the market-state duopoly of public provision and private (profit-oriented) enterprises. Using these terms interchangeably, however, neglects their diverse genealogies and differences in focus (see Moulaert and Ailenei, 2005 for an overview). The term 'third sector', arguably, reflects the idea of a space outside public and private provision most straightforwardly. It describes a sector that is "different from the traditional public 'general interest serving' and the private market sectors" (Moulaert and Ailenei, 2005, p. 2042). This 'third sector' combines "formal and informal elements at the level of organization (market, state, volunteering, self-help, and the domestic economy), market and non-market-oriented production and valorization of goods and services, monetary and non-monetary resources at the level of funding" (ibid.). Consequently, the third sector might be portrayed as the middle ground of a tri-polar economy with three types of agents – public agencies, households, and private firms – that represent three major forms of transfer – redistribution, reciprocity, and markets. Combining these different logics, the third sector transcends the boundaries of public/private, formal/informal and profit/non-profit.

Social economy follows this thrust in hybridizing market, alternative-market, non-market, and non-monetized economic practices. On a basic level, the prefacing of economy with the qualifier 'social' emphasizes that "the relationship of embeddedness between society, economy, and nature is an inevitable feature of the socioecological metabolism, and that any attempts to make the real-world economy autonomous of social and political control will produce [...] destructive outcomes" (Coraggio, 2017, p. 19). More profoundly, social economy reiterates the intention of 'oikonomia' – the management of resources and enabling of subsistence – that capitalism replaced with 'chrematistics' – a term Aristotle used to critique the 'unnatural' practices of accumulation and enrichment (Felber, 2018). Social economic activity, therefore, is directed at providing "services to its members or to a wider community, and not serve as a tool in the service of capital investment" (Defourny et. al., 2000, cited in Huybrechts and Nicholls, 2012). The social economy, consequently, comprises the "voluntary, non-profit, and co-operative sectors that are formally independent of the state" (Moulaert and Ailenei, 2005, p. 2042).

Although the co-operative sector is not necessarily non-profit, there is a tendency to define the social economy through legal forms or even alongside the for-profit/non-profit divide (Huybrechts and Nicholls, 2012; Johanisova et al., 2013). This is problematic due to difficulties in finding adequate legal forms, issues in common public interest law, and organizations' legal status not reflecting their orientation towards the common good (see chapter 13). By fitting into legal categorizations, the concept, furthermore, feeds capitalist imaginaries of a 'real economy' on the one hand and subsidized, donation-, and voluntary-based alternatives on the other. Some see the social economy therefore as a complement to market economies rather than a transformative force and propose concepts such as the solidarity economy instead (Miller, 2010). North and Cato, for instance, discuss the notion of social and solidarity economies side by side maintaining that while the former mainly addresses the inclusion of those ignored by the market, the latter raises more fundamental questions such as "how can we live in inclusive ways, with dignity, safeguarding the needs of the environment and future generations, given that millions currently cannot do so" (North and Cato, 2017, p. 8)?

Agents and allies of transformation

Against the backdrop of the discussion around innovation and the social economy, sustainability transitions can be said to involve at least three groups of actors: (social) enterprises, public institutions, and civil society. Social and solidarity economy perspectives, furthermore, show the former can be driven by a range of motivations and goals beyond pure profit-maximization (North, 2016). Hybrid organizations (Doherty et al., 2014; Dufays and Huybrechts, 2016) that combine different institutional logics weaken the boundaries between enterprises, public institutions, and civil society, marking the contingency of this distinction. Institutional logics, thereby, refer to "socially constructed, historical patterns of cultural symbols and material practices, including assumptions, values, and beliefs, by which individuals and organizations provide meaning to their daily activity, organize time and space, and reproduce their lives and experiences" (Thornton et al., 2012, p. 2). Of course, each actor group also includes counter forces. In the following, however, I will focus on possible carriers and allies of sustainability transitions. First, I turn to community-led initiatives and social movements primarily engaging in protest and non-commodified alternative economies. They overlap significantly and blur with, second, social entrepreneurs, ecopreneurs, and others who engage in market activities as a means to further ecological and social ends. Last but not least, I turn to politicians and planners who are committed to pushing back capital to privilege non-economic objectives as important allies for transformation.

Community-led initiatives and social movements

Communities-led initiatives comprise actors, organizations, and networks that create spaces for sustainability-related activities and in doing so practice and prefigure alternative economies. The labels community activism, community-based initiatives, or grassroots initiatives are often used interchangeably. Seyfang (2009, p. 64) defines grassroots initiatives as "networks of activists and organizations generating novel bottom-up solutions for sustainable development and sustainable consumption; solutions that respond to the local situation and the interest and values of the communities involved". This definition, however, exposes two common difficulties with respect to defining community initiatives. First, community is often equated with the local (Taylor Aiken, 2017). While most networks commonly referred to as community initiatives are indeed place-based and their activities are mainly bound-up with local processes, they are often simultaneously part of broader translocal movements (such as for example the Transition Town Movement). Reducing their activities to the local misses the translocal significance of their practices (Brickell and Datta, 2011). In addition, many are concerned with narratives and practices that are beyond place (Schmid, 2018). Second, when acknowledging the different thrust of green economy approaches on the one hand and degrowth or postcapitalist ones on the other hand, framing community initiatives one-sidedly under rubrics such as 'sustainable development' – a descriptor advocates of the latter would reject – is problematic. Many authors insufficiently consider "divergences, contestation and struggle within initiatives" (Fischer et al., 2017, p. 1988). Furthermore, the practical implementation of (radical) alternatives generally comes with a range of internal and external compromises. This makes it particularly difficult to lump community initiatives into any one category (see chapter 2).

Community-led initiatives cover a wide variety of different areas and include community-supported agriculture (Bloemmen et al., 2015), open source projects (Mason, 2016), time banking (Amanatidou et al., 2015; Seyfang, 2016), Transition Towns (Aiken, 2012; Hopkins, 2014), repair cafés (Schmid, 2019b), collective energy projects (Kunze and Becker, 2015), open workshops and hackerspaces (Lange and Bürkner, 2018; T. Smith, 2019b), alternative currencies (North, 2014), ecohousing (Pickerill, 2016), community-led cohousing (Chatterton, 2016), alternative food networks (Rosol, 2018), food sharing (Morrow, 2019), and eco villages (Lockyer, 2017). Across these examples, communities experiment with alternative forms of organizing, production, consumption, transfer, property, and financing.

Community-supported agriculture [CSA], for example, is premised on the cooperation between consumers and producers. The consumers guarantee the financial resources for fair production and thereby share the risks as well as the fruits, literally and figuratively, of a good or bad harvest. Being based on needs and possibilities, CSA schemes often also incorporate solidarity amongst the participants themselves. Individual contributions are proposed in bidding rounds until the required amount is reached to be able to operate. Collective and politically motivated renewable energy projects, again, link sustainable energy production with "participation [,] collective legal ownership, a collective benefit allocation mechanism, or collective decision-making processes." (Kunze and Becker, 2015, p. 426). On the basis of inclusive organizational set-ups, communities push both ecological and social alternatives through decentralized and collectively owned means of energy production. Other organizations are less branch specific and work more broadly on issues such as climate change or social exclusion. The Transition Town Network [TTN], for instance, connects Transition initiatives worldwide that identify with the network's general principles around resource limits, social justice, subsidiarity, learning, and collaboration (Hopkins, 2014). TTN describes itself as "community-led response to the pressures of climate change [and] fossil fuel depletion" (cited in Aiken, 2012, p. 92).

A community-based response to environmental and societal issues that has recently gained attention from geographers and other scholars working on transformation is the maker movement (Lange and Bürkner, 2018; Schmid, 2019b; T. Smith,

2017; 2019b). The term 'maker movement' refers to a broad range of communities that form around practices of 'making' and engage in decentralized forms of value creation and organization (C. Anderson, 2012; Davies, 2017a). The spaces in which these communities operate are variously referred to as hackerspaces, Fab Labs, makerspaces, and open workshops – depending on the author's emphasis and the communities' orientation. Although there is no common value system that unifies the heterogeneous movement, a range of topics reoccur in different patterns and intensities, such as do-it-yourself and do-it-together approaches, open-source, use of high-technology, haptic interaction with materials and reskilling, local (sustainable) production, and (technological) democratization (Baier et al., 2016; Hielscher and Smith, 2014; Lange, 2017; Simons et al., 2016; Walter-Herrmann and Büching, 2013).

The maker movement's proximity to locality, community, and "geographies of making" (Carr and Gibson, 2016) has sparked a scholarly discussion relating its practices to sustainability transitions (e.g. Baier et al., 2016; Lange and Bürkner, 2018; Davies, 2017b; Hansing, 2017; Lange, 2017; T. Smith, 2017; 2019b). Local production, construction, repair, and hacking are discussed in relation to sustainability, degrowth, and postcapitalism. Various authors argue for or against the potential of 'commons-based peer production' for sustainability transitions (M. Bauwens et al., 2019; Lange, 2017; Petschow and Peuckert, 2016). In particular the use of high technology such as 3D printing attracts much attention in recent debates. While some herald 3D printing's potential to disrupt global value chains and re-localize production (Baier et al., 2016), others note its limitations in actual practice (Hielscher and Smith, 2014).

Civic engagement also takes explicitly oppositional forms in protest and social movements. While aforementioned alternative practices tend to be constructive in orientation, collective action can also be explicitly contentious (Tarrow, 2011). Both lines of action, of course, are not mutually exclusive. Terms like 'maker movement' or 'Transition Town Movement' hint at the combination of practical and oppositional activities. Tarrow (2011, p. 9) defines social movements around four properties: collective challenge, common purpose, social solidarity, and sustained interaction. Social movements, consequently, are expressions of "collective challenges, based on common purposes and social solidarities, in sustained interaction with elites, opponents and authorities" (ibid., p. 9).

Della Porta and Diani (2006, p. 145ff.) distinguish between three types of social movement organizations. Professional movement organizations, such as Greenpeace or Amnesty International, command the resources to finance a management structure. These organizations often include a complex (and often costly) bureaucracy. Members are largely donors rather than active participants. Della Porta and Diani contrast this with participatory movement organizations, which they further divide into two subcategories. Mass protest organizations combine "attention to participatory democracy with certain levels of formalization of the organizational structure" (2006, p. 147). Grassroots organizations, as third type, are even more strongly orientated towards participation while exhibiting low levels of formal structuration. In contrast to the former two, the existence and functioning of grassroots organizations hinges entirely upon the active contribution and engagement of their members. Whereas social movement research as such is beyond the focus of this book, the organizational forms that contentious politics take, in particular that of grassroots organizations, are of relevance (a point I return to in part V and the conclusion).

(Eco-)Social enterprises

A second group of potentially transformative actors and organizations is that of (eco-)social entrepreneurs and enterprises. Social entrepreneurs and (just) ecopreneurs (Affolderbach and Krueger, 2017; Huybrechts and Nicholls, 2012; K. O'Neill and Gibbs, 2016) managing and working for (eco-)social enterprises (Defourny and Nyssens, 2012; Johanisova and Fraňková, 2017) comprise a heterogeneous group of actors and organization that plays a difficult-to-define role in sustainability transitions. On the one hand, green and social entrepreneurship is the epitome of the market-based approach of the green economy to social and environmental issues. Introducing business models to yet non-commodified areas perpetuates capital's encroachment into social and ecological relations. On the other hand, (eco-)social enterprises de-emphasize profit maximization and thus benefit communities and ecologies (Johanisova et al., 2013). They are a means to divert financial resources towards social and ecological ends while implementing more just economic relations. In addition, social entrepreneurs can be "effective change agents" (North and Nurse, 2014) by showcasing alternative economies. Research on (eco-)social enterprises and entrepreneurship reflects these diverse expectations and framings, discussing social enterprises alternatively as a means to "deliver sustainable new social value" and bring about "systemic change" (Nicholls, 2006, p. 3), as providers of failed state welfare (Nyssens et al., 2006), and a means of creating new markets (Karamchandani et al., 2009).

Huybrechts and Nicholls (2012, p. 33) link the different terms by stating that "'social entrepreneurship' is the dynamic process through which specific types of individuals deserving the name of 'social entrepreneurs' create and develop organizations that may be defined as 'social enterprises'". This apparently simple coupling, however, cannot be extended to the 'social economy'. In contrast to the social economy, which is often defined in a static way alongside largely non-profit legal frameworks (see above), social entrepreneurship generally includes a distinct orientation towards markets. Social enterprises "have a continuous production of goods and/or services and take economic risks – bankruptcy is always a possible outcome" (Huybrechts and Nicholls, 2012, p. 35). At the same time, social enterprises mark themselves off from traditional businesses by putting social and environmental outcomes over the maximization of profits. The combination of market orientation on the one side and social and ecological purposes on the other side requires technological and social innovations such as "new organizational models and processes [,] new products and services, [or] new thinking about, and framing of, societal challenges" (Huybrechts and Nicholls, 2012, p. 34).

Defining (eco-)social entrepreneurs through their ecological and social orientation, innovation, and market orientation alone, however, restricts considerations of their transformative agency to green economy imaginaries. Markets, in this frame, are a given – located on the landscape level, to use MLP terminology (see above) – and are merely a means of transformation but never its objective. In other words, by defining social entrepreneurship through its market orientation without considering the ways in which social entrepreneurs challenge and shift economic frameworks themselves, fails to address more fundamental issues as exposed by scholarship on degrowth and postcapitalism (see chapter 2). Literature on social enterprises largely accepts the "capitalist growth paradigm and its theoretical underpinnings and sees social enterprises merely as a vehicle for generating employment and providing services to socially excluded groups" (Johanisova and Fraňková, 2017, p. 509). This does not mean that market orientation *per se* thwarts any ambitions for radical transformation – parts IV and V of this work consider the role of hybrid market and non-market constellations in more detail. It highlights, however, that social entrepreneurship needs a framing that accommodates more radical orientations beyond markets and beyond the imaginaries of a green (growth) economy, the shortcomings of which are summarized by Hardt and Negri (2017, p. 145):

> Social entrepreneurship, true to its social democratic roots, does not question the rule of property and the sources of social inequality but instead seeks to alleviate the worst suffering and make capitalist society more humane. This is certainly a noble task in itself, but it makes social entrepreneurs blind to the potentially autonomous circuits of cooperation that emerge in the relationships of social production and reproduction.

Three notions that propose a more radical framing are that of "eco-social enterprises" (Johanisova and Fraňková, 2013, 2017), "post-growth organizations" (Rätzer et al., 2018; Schmid, 2018), and of "postcapitalist entrepreneurship" (Cohen, 2018). Johanisova and Fraňková (2017, p. 511) define eco-social enterprises through five characteristics: other-than-profit goals; the use of profits for social and ecological purposes; democratic and local ownership and governance; rootedness in place and time; and non-market production, exchange or provisioning patterns. In emphasizing democratic control and embeddedness as criteria, Johanisova and Fraňková decenter the role of markets as allocative (and governing) mechanisms and turn towards community (see also chapter 4). Eco-social enterprises' engagement in non-market practices, furthermore, challenges the market logic and thus the deeper economic ontology that social enterprise literature fails to address.

Building on Johanisova and Fraňková's definition of eco-social enterprises, elsewhere, I propose the notion of post-growth organizations as "organizational associations that (1) address social and environmental concerns and (2) simultaneously engage in post-growth politics – the initiation and support of parallel and mutually enforcing processes of cultural and institutional change within the diverse meanings of post-growth" (Schmid, 2018, p. 283). Post-growth organizations include social enterprises that go beyond market-based solutions for ecological and social problems and innovate new organizational structures, technologies, and modes of operation, through which they reflectively relate to and challenge capitalist economies. With this in mind, I do not reject the notion of social entrepreneurship and instead follow Arthur et al. (2016, p. 219) who explore social enterprise as potential agents for radical transformation: "social enterprises can be seen to be alternative social spaces and, as such, can contend transgressively". Chapter 18, below, further develops this notion and, for reasons of terminological continuity, speaks of 'degrowth organizations'.

Postcapitalist entrepreneurship, in a similar vein, addresses and challenges the rule of property and the sources of social inequality. Reclaiming the notion of entrepreneurship – as the creation of "new combinations among already existing workers, ideas, technologies, resources, and machines" (Hardt and Negri, 2017, p. 140) – for emancipatory politics opens new and creative paths towards resistance and alternative futures. Hardt and Negri (2017, p. 145ff.) go as far as to call for an entrepreneurship of the multitude:

> Once these neoliberal notions of entrepreneurship are cleared away, we can begin to glimpse some characteristic of a potential (or even already existing) entrepreneurial multitude, that is, a multitude that is author of 'new combinations' that foster autonomous social production and reproduction.

Carving out the transformative potential of strategic bottom-up organizing to reclaim the creative power of entrepreneurship and innovation are a central task for a postcapitalist project. I will return to and elaborate on this issue below, particularly in part V.

Politics and planning

A third group of transition agents comprises policy-makers and planners. I touch on this group only briefly since the key focus of this work lies with community initiatives and eco-social enterprises.

A number of contributions to transition literature explore and evaluate policy interventions and their role in sustainability transitions (Hendriks and Grin, 2007; Macrorie et al., 2015; Spurling and McMeekin, 2015), often under the labels of 'transition governance' or 'transition management' (Avelino and Grin, 2017; Loorbach, 2010; Loorbach and Rotmans, 2010). In line with MLP's focus on regimes, perspectives on policy are generally sectoral, for instance on housing (Macrorie et al., 2015), mobility (Spurling and McMeekin, 2015), or energy (van der Laak et al., 2007). By and large, the sectoral focus excludes more fundamental questions that transgress the market- and state-centered imaginaries of green economy perspectives.

Radical research on transformative politics, in turn, is often abstract and speculative or ignores state institutions as potential allies altogether (Gibson-Graham, 2006; see also Fickey, 2011; Jonas, 2016). Important impulses, however, come from the proposition of 'non-reformist reforms' – political work in which "each reform demanded [is] articulated into a general project aiming at producing a global change" (Gorz 1968, 124). In other words, the challenge is to change state institutions in ways to prepare and facilitate more radical transformations. Adler (2017, p. 27f.) notes three criteria for a 'degrowth politics'. First, degrowth politics are structurally compatible with degrowth approaches but (legally) enforceable under the present socio-economic conditions of capitalist relations. Second, degrowth politics limit the causes and conditions of the (re)production of alienated desires and concomitantly the corresponding imaginaries of prosperity and progress to facilitate the transition towards a degrowth culture. Third, degrowth politics ought to address not only progressives and avant-garde milieus but should appeal to a broader audience and their political representatives. Concrete proposals for radical transformative policies include universal basic income schemes (van Parijs and Vanderborght, 2017, 2018), working time reduction (Schor, 2010), ecological and green taxes (Daly, 1996), egalitarian taxes (Piketty, 2017), and taxes on financial transactions (Latouche, 2009). For an overview and additional degrowth policy proposals, see Kallis (2018, p. 128).

Although the mentioned proposals for radical transformative policies have thus far failed to materialize, formal politics remains an important potential ally in sustainability transitions. Policy unfolds on multiple intersecting levels – local, regional, national, international, and global. While much state and federal policy does not promote but rather stifle radical transformation, it is not the only avenue for policy intervention. Place-sensitive approaches to sustainability stress the role of local (policy) contexts in facilitating transformative practice (Hansen and Coenen, 2015; Späth and Rohracher, 2012). The crucial question, then, is twofold: "what institutions [...] must be established in order to create and support the necessary collective actions?" (T. Bauwens and Mertens, 2018, p. 45) and how can they be established? Polycentric notions of governance entail two key ideas. First, (the rehabilitation of) localism as a meaningful source of governance. And second, the appreciation of self-organization and actors' capacity thereof (T. Bauwens and Mertens, 2018). Transition governance, therefore, exceeds the narrow realm of formal politics and plays out through interactions of all actor groups – civil, entrepreneurial, and political – that increasingly blur, merge, and hybridize the deeper we dig into the complex processes of transformative geographies.

Transition, transformation, and politics

Agency and governance accentuate the question of who actually shapes socio-technical transitions. Politics and power, however, remain largely underexplored in transition literature (Avelino et al., 2016; Lawhon and Murphy, 2012; Patterson et al., 2017). Frequently, uncritical and naive positions prevail, so that "elites such as corporate and state leaders, innovators, and scientists appear to have only progressive, environmentally responsible interests or values." (Lawhon and Murphy, 2012, p. 363). Scoones et al. (2015, p. 11) infer that "a deeper understanding of processes of knowledge politics, political conflict and accommodation, bargaining and disciplining, as niche experiments challenge existing regimes, is clearly highly pertinent". On that note, a number of recent contributions carve out the micro-politics of transformation (Avelino and Wittmayer, 2016; Hoffman and Loeber, 2016). In line with critiques around the neglect of community as a site of innovative activity (Seyfang and Smith, 2007), they shift the focus from markets, policy, and technology towards grassroots activism and bottom-up organizing.

Political ecology (Lawhon and Murphy, 2012), community economy scholarship (Gibson-Graham, 2006), and earth system governance (Patterson et al., 2017) provide crucial impulses for the politicization of transition studies. They address questions around governance, politics, and power such as, "who is (or is not) represented and included in transition decisions; where and at what scale decisions are made; whose knowledge counts and why; how power relations influence regime dynamics, landscape features, and the prospects for niche innovations; what checks are in place to qualitatively evaluate the representativeness and fairness of transition processes; what are the expected social consequences of the adoption of particular technologies; and how these can be better predicted, shaped, and/or mitigated" (Lawhon and Murphy, 2012, p. 371).

To sharpen a perspective on the politics of social change, it is expedient to take a closer look at the respective etymologies and uses of transition and transformation. Transformation and transition both "express the ambition to shift from analyzing and understanding problems towards identifying pathways and solutions for desirable environmental and social change" (Hölscher et al., 2018, p. 1). For the most part, both terms are used interchangeably. Yet, different research communities tend to privilege either transformation or transition to describe processes of change, with some putting both terms in relation to each other – such as Geels and Schot (2007), for whom transformation is one among several pathways for transition (see above). Hölscher et al. (2018) consider transition's and transformation's etymological differences that hint at the diverging emphases they express. Transformation, etymologically, means to 'change in shape' which, at first, does not imply a particular agent or directionality. Transition, in contrast, is best described as 'going across' and hence carries both the notion of an orientation and the active connotation of an agent. As detailed below, this book takes these etymological cues to hone both notions and propose, although not sharply delimited, still nuanced conceptual differences that tie in with the broader sensitivities of the respective literatures on transition and transformation.

Transformation, as a change in shape, has a two-sided character. First as a fundamental shift through multiple interacting dimensions that include political, economic, demographic, cultural, juridical, technological, climatic, biological, aquatic, and pedological moments. And second as the individuals, communities, entrepreneurs, organizations, planners, and policy-makers that are enlisted in and differently shape unfolding changes. Transformation, in this sense, does not presuppose an orientation towards sustainability. Yet it can – and often does – include the aspiration to channel social and ecological dynamics towards sustainability and justice and break with undesirable infrastructures, institutions, and routines. In the following, I disentangle three different 'meanings' of transformation that closely interrelate, overlap, and implicate each other: transformation as adaptation, transformation as analytical framework, and transformation as emancipatory project.

A large body of literature around global change, climate change, adaptation, and resilience discusses transformation as reaction to the profound destabilization and stress in ecological and social systems (Bouzarovski and Haarstad, 2018; K. Brown, 2014; Cretney, 2014). Katrina Brown (2014, p. 112) notes that "it is argued [...] that global environmental change will enforce radical, unplanned and detrimental transformation, especially through impacts of climate change." Environmental changes, in this perspective, cause and force social institutions to fundamentally transform and adapt resulting in "different controls over system properties, new ways of making a living and often changes in scales of crucial feedbacks" (ibid.). Transformation, in this sense, is a reaction or adaptation to environmental change.

Framing transformation solely in terms of social adaptation to environmental change, however, conveys a lopsided notion of human-environment relationships in which social institutions are primarily reactionary. A second meaning of transformation, consequently, acknowledges the diverse ways in which transformations can be shaped. It revolves around transformation as analytical framework to explore the interactions between social and environmental dynamics and the proposition of measures which lead towards more sustainable pathways. The notion of 'great transformation' as used by the academic advisory council for the German Federal Government, for example, describes the profound ecological, technological, and social transformative dynamics and the possibilities of shaping and steering these dynamics into a desirable direction (WBGU, 2011; Schneidewind, 2018). By using the term 'great transformation' the academic advisory council draws on the economic historian Karl Polanyi (2001 [1944]) who traces the transformation to industrial capitalism in the 19th century. Polanyi's analysis of the metamorphosis of capitalist social relations exposes capital's encroachment on nature and work, compromising its own foundation. Despite this radical reference, large parts of public and political discourse on transformation remain superficial. Brand and Wissen (2017, p. 37, author's translation) criticize that a "new critical orthodoxy considers itself critical towards the dominant developments, however, remains fixated on the existing institutional system and confides in the realization [Einsicht] of the elites".

Brand and Wissen point towards a third meaning of transformation, as emancipatory project. Critical scholars acknowledge that "transformation means different things to different people or groups, and it is not always clear what exactly needs to be transformed and why, whose interest these transformations serve, and what will be the consequences" (O'Brien, 2012, p. 670; see also Lawhon and Murphy, 2012, quoted above). Transformation as emancipatory project, consequently, involves a fundamental shift in power relations. Dussel, for example, understands transformation as "a change in the form of the innovation of an institution or the radical transmutation of the political system in response to new interventions by the oppressed or excluded" (cited in Barnett, 2017, p. 29). Much scholarship on community-based activism and alternative economies follows such an emancipatory notion of transformation (see above).

As emancipatory project, transformation entails an orientation towards autonomy, social justice, and empowerment. Developing a sense of direction, the meaning of transformation converges with that of transition – 'going across' from one state of affairs towards another. In contrast to transformation's detour through politics, however, transition generally already knows where it is headed. Sustainability transitions, according to one definition that captures well its overall use in transition research, are "goal-oriented or 'purposive'[...] systemic changes [that] involve alterations in the overall configuration of transport, energy, and agri-food systems, which entail technology, policy, markets, consumer practices, infrastructure, cultural meaning and scientific knowledge" (Geels, 2011, p. 24f.). Herein lies a central issue of transition as carved out above. Transition is concerned with getting from status quo to a defined 'other' rather than with the politics that shape its directionality.

From a critical perspective, transformation and transition both require an orientation, but they put very different emphases on the development thereof. While transition is premature in determining its directionality – often showing manage-rial and technocratic tendencies – transformation, at least when taking cue from its etymology and emancipatory use, leaves much room for politics and possibility. Given the issues associated with either term, a theory of transformation and transition needs to articulate clearly the orientation, visions, and strategies of societal change, as well as the politics that allow for an inclusive negotiation, adjustment, and correction of the former. Transition without transformation runs the risk of being apolitical or ontologically naive. Transformation without transition, on the other hand, might lack practicability and clarity. Using either term in the following, therefore, implies an awareness of the respectively other. These tendencies reflect aforementioned discussion of and distinction between degrowth and postcapitalism. Degrowth, as used here, carries the sensitivities of transition in that it contours an agenda or proposal of change which addresses different issues by way of how they relate to growth – inferring possibilities and constraints for a (strategic) passage from the present state of affairs to a degrowth society. Postcapitalism, in contrast, highlights the politics of change and premises a sophisticated conceptual foundation that establishes an ontology of social dynamics.

For Wright (2010), the elaboration of a theory of social transformation is a key task of an emancipatory social science, next to a critique of society and a theory of alternatives. Thus far, the book reflects Wright's proposal with chapter 1 issuing an elaborate critique on capitalist growth-based economies and chapter 2 engaging with economic and political alternatives. This chapter, subsequently, has started to develop the notions of transformation and transition by looking at different conceptions thereof and the trajectories and agents they bring into view. Part II, in the following, fleshes out a spatial theory of transformation in greater detail, taking its cue from community economy and practice theory scholarships. Community economy's work opens political and ethical spaces in which new 'becomings' can be imagined, negotiated, experimented, and practiced, thus highlighting the politics of transformation. Practice theory provides a perspective on the materialities of social dynamics and their grounding in relations of power. Part II, to that effect, develops a perspective on transformative geographies as *spatial struggles and negotiations over just and sustainable forms of (more-than-) human co-existence materializing in the antagonistic, divergent, adjusting, and synergistic practices of its everyday (re)production.*

Interlude I: Geographies of change

Transformation and transition are fundamentally spatial processes. Change unfolds and is rooted in places, connects close and distant sites, shifts horizontal and vertical relations, and involves the negotiation of territories and boundaries. A number of recent contributions explore the spatialities of transition and transformation (Bouzarovski and Haarstad, 2018; Chatterton, 2016; Chatterton and Pickerill, 2010; Coenen et al., 2012; Hansen and Coenen, 2015; Longhurst, 2015; Raven et al., 2012; A. Smith et al., 2010; Vandeventer et al., 2019). Yet, most argue that research on transition and transformation still lacks genuinely geographical theorizing. Hansen and Coenen (2015, p. 105), for instance, maintain that "most studies on the geography of transitions have primarily layered on top of existing theory in the transitions literature, relying largely on concepts and frameworks such as MLP, TIS and SNM yet adding spatial sensitivity". As a consequence, "few studies in the geography of transitions field suggest alternative frameworks to study sustainability transitions and thus challenge current theorizations of transitions and its geographies" (ibid.).

This book develops a decidedly spatial perspective on transformation and distills socio-spatial strategies to give more practical leverage to community activism and civic engagement working towards degrowth and postcapitalism. It takes its cue from Jessop et al. (2008) whose seminal paper, *Theorizing Sociospatial Relations*, emphasizes four spatial concepts – territory, network, place, and scale – each referring to a distinct form of social spatiality (see figure 1). While Jessop et al. (2008, p. 392) acknowledge other spatial concepts that are not part of their framework (such as environment and positionality), they identify the aforementioned as "most salient in work on contemporary political-economic restructuring". Applying what Jessop et al. call a TPSN (for territory, place, scale, and network) research agenda, allows both to conceptually isolate and sharpen particular spatial dynamics and to integrate said spatial concepts, making visible the complexity of socio-spatial relations. This book engages in a systematic TPSN analysis to further the development of socio-spatial strategies (see chapter 20).

Places constitute ensembles of bodies, artefacts, things, meanings, and practices that meet in time and space. They are meaningful locations where historical

Figure 1 Spatial dimensions of transformation

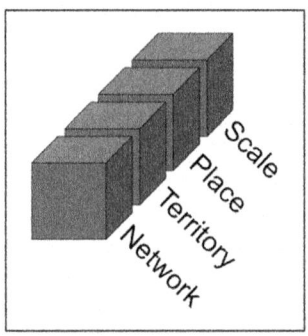

trajectories arise, interact, stabilize, and change. That means both the forces sustaining current social relations and impulses for change do not reside in an abstract placeless global sphere but in concrete locales. Transformation, consequently, is always bound up with concrete temporal and spatial contexts. Understanding these contexts is important for understanding transformation and its processes, possibilities, and obstacles.

Doreen Massey (2008) makes a strong case using the example of the City of London to show how the 'global' is produced in a specific place. In the same way that far reaching economic and political dynamics emanate from place, the potentials of emancipatory transformations are woven into localized contexts. Longhurst (2015, p. 184), for instance, emphasizes the importance of a "localized density of countercultural institutions, networks, groups, and practices" that he calls "alternative milieu". Alternative milieus are protected contexts which allow new ideas to emerge, invite experimentation, support alternative practices, and spawn imaginaries about the place itself as locality for radical innovation. Authors who stress the importance of proximity also speak of informal local institutions as catalyzers for transformative practice (Coenen et al., 2012; Hansen and Coenen, 2015; Späth and Rohracher, 2012). With this they refer to the norms, values, trust, social networks, and cooperation cultures that impel (or constrain) social and technological innovation.

Transformation, then, includes a "politics of place" (Gibson-Graham, 2006, p. xxiv). Such a politics is situated in the "here and now" of everyday practice (Beveridge and Koch, 2018; Gibson-Graham, 2006; Pickerill and Chatterton, 2006). Place, here, has both spatial and temporal significance. Akin to anarchist imaginaries, transformation is not deferred to an elsewhere (for instance the abstraction of a national or global 'level') or an else-when (an indefinite future) but is part of concrete human activity that seeks to prefigure alternatives. Politics of place, then, materialize in local economies (Parker, 2017), place-based activism (Gibson-Graham, 2006), and communities (Taylor Aiken, 2015b).

Places, as a matter of course, do not exist on their own terms and independently. A focus on place, therefore, has to be wary not to equate place, community and the 'local' (Taylor Aiken, 2015b) neglecting other spatialities and succumbing to place-centrism (Jessop et al., 2008). Still, the notion of place contextualizes (global) power relations that are always produced in concrete sites. A critical appreciation of the local, then, extends a politics of place to a politics of place *beyond place* (Massey, 2008).

A politics of place beyond place considers the diverse translocal connections between individuals, organizations, and locales. While a lens on place-specific contexts is important to understand the constellations of values, communities, and technologies from which transformative practices develop and radiate, it is equally important to consider the people, ideas, and goods that travel through places, connecting them to other close and distant sites. Networks, as the horizontal connectedness of different entities and the spatialities that emanate from their interactions and interdependencies, describe and capture decentral and multi-sited socio-spatial textures.

Networked perspectives highlight the distributed agency of individuals, groups, and communities that shape social relations in close and distant places, as well as the politics and ethics these agencies involve. In this way, the horizontal spatiality of network metaphors is a recurrent figure of thought in recent theorizing of transformative geographies (Chatterton, 2016; Springer, 2014a). Transformation is imagined as shifting discourses or assemblages connected through "webs of signification" (Gibson-Graham, 2006, p. xxiv) and diverse performances (Roelvink et al., 2015). These imaginaries "shift strategy away from merely scaling-up niches towards a multiplicity of ways to corrode the overall regime and landscape through more networked forms and distributed social relations" (Chatterton, 2016, p. 405). The relationality of social phenomena, here, extends to supposedly large and stable structures such as states and markets. Some geographers criticize representations of monolithic and coherent macro-spatial systems that abstract from the practices, processes, and bodies which produce these phenomena while being differently positioned within existing relations of power. As consequence, scholars and activists "cultivate a politics of horizontal extent, reach, and association, rather than a 'politics of scale'" (Roelvink et al., 2015, p. 16).

Aside from networked transformative imaginaries that center around representational and discursive shifts (as in community economy scholarship explored in chapter 4), organizational networks which connect places, people, institutions, and communities play a crucial role also. Umbrella organizations, city networks, and other translocal institutions coordinate and support the exchange and diffusion of alternative ideas, values, and technologies. The *Verbund offener Werkstätten* [German network of open workshops], for instance, supports organizations that revolve around local production and associated practices (see discussion on maker movement above). It does so both by connecting similar projects that pursue related strategies and encounter the same difficulties, and by centralizing services such as insurance and counselling. The networks that emerge from translocal activities can consist of both denser and looser connections, creating proximity across distances in (Euclidian) space. Coenen et al. (2012, p. 969) similarly note that "regular interactions between actors can build up into more solid connections, institutions, and networks which in turn can support further 'remote' relationships".

While there is an emancipatory moment in horizontal perspectives that think space primarily through network metaphors, some geographers redirect attention to the vertical differentiation that emanates from different practical or institutional densities and relational forms of power that "constrain and structure space" (M. Jones, 2009, p. 493). The debate around the horizontal and vertical dimensions of space and politics is central for a spatial research agenda on transformation (Barnett, 2017; Hardt and Negri, 2017; see also Schmid, 2019a). Shaped by many misunderstandings – in particular the confusion of ontological perspectives with arguments pertaining to relations of power – the 'scale debate' shows a need for a differentiated consideration of two issues. First, a spatial ontology that does not presuppose different structural levels separating micro from macro processes. And second, a conceptual perspective that captures the structuring moments of (large) social phenomena and the unevenness of power relations. Vertical differentiations, then, are not pre-structured conditions but become visible as products of social practice (see chapters 5 and 6).

Nonetheless, depending on which of the two issues takes center stage, different positionings towards the possibilities and constraints of transformative practice follow. A 'politics of hope' emphasizes the potentialities that become visible through a flat ontology (Marston et al., 2005; Gibson-Graham, 2006). Rejecting local and global as static conceptual categories opens "intensive capacities for change and newness" (Marston et al., 2005, p. 425). Others, in turn, emphasize present institutional orders which, although socially produced, follow path-dependencies and exert strong influence on social practice (Joutsenvirta, 2016). Scale, for them, remains an important spatial category. Andrew Jonas (2006, p. 399) warns that "to reject 'scale' altogether would be to miss out on an important dimension of thinking about and acting upon contemporary economic, political, social, and environmental change". Martin Jones (2009, p. 498), in this context, provides a reconciling perspective, arguing that socio-spatial relations are produced through "a mutually transformative evolution of inherited spatial structures and emergent spatial strategies within an actively differentiated continually evolving grid of institutions, territories, and regulatory activities".

Irrespective of the nuances of the broader debate this section only touched upon (and chapter 6 returns to in more detail), there is a fundamentally scalar moment in different imaginaries of transformation as 'upscaling', diffusion, institutionalization, or polycentric shifts in meanings and practices. Whether the term scale is used, or rejected for its conceptual baggage, notions of spread, dissemination, and expansion of alternative (economic) practices remain central for perspectives on transformative geographies.

Territory, lastly, is another important spatial category for research on transformation. Territories are generally understood as bounded portions of space. Boundaries as well as territories themselves are – analogues to the foregoing discussions of other spatial categories – both a product of social practice and a materialization of socio-spatial dynamics directing human activity. Critical scholars, consequently, emphasize the processuality of territory as territorialization (Belina, 2013; Elden, 2010; Painter, 2010). Territory "is not the timeless and solid geographical foundation of state power it sometimes seems, but a porous, provisional, labor-intensive und ultimately perishable and non-material product of networked socio-technical practices" (Painter, 2010, p. 1116).

Territories are relevant for transformative processes, both in their effects as well as in their production. Territorially organized and enforced local, regional, national, and international policy can facilitate or constrain sustainability-related practice. Administrative territories constitute a significant restraint for practices that jar with incumbent institutions – in particular legal frameworks that are (potentially violently) enforced by police and military. At the same time, actors tactically draw on different administrative territories and levels to navigate policy, obtain funding, and spread alternative practices to other places. Territories themselves can and must be renegotiated through transformative practice.

Place, network, scale, and territory, to be sure, do not constitute independent spatial dimensions. The separated presentation above is a conceptual move to further systematic analyses of different socio-spatial relations and their transformative dynamics. The interdependencies between places and their embeddedness in translocal networks or the interaction between nested territories expressing different administrative scales are only the most conspicuous examples, demonstrating that actually existing socio-spatial relations are polymorphic and complex. Scalar, networked, place-based, and territorial spatialities intersect and co-constitute each other in the variegated politics of transformative geographies part II turns to.

This book provides a detailed argument for the importance of acknowledging transformation's spatialities. Conceptually, notions of scale are of particular importance. While it is clear that transformation requires some sort of spread, diffusion, expansion, dissemination, or 'growth' of sustainability-related practices, simplified concepts of 'upscaling' have proved problematic. A challenge I take on in part II, then, is to further deconstruct the problem of assuming different (temporal, structural, or spatial) levels a priori and the development of alternative concepts thereto. Relational perspectives that emphasize horizontal networks in lieu of hierarchical spatialities (M. Jones, 2009; Marston et al., 2005) support this endeavor. Relational thinking is also crucial to complement place with the concept of site (Schatzki, 2003). Territory, for reasons of scope, will remain underexplored. I return to this issue in chapter 20, which, in a concluding manner, pulls together different forms of socio-spatial relations once again.

Part II: Transformative geographies: space, politics and change

Outline

Transformative geographies describe the spatial struggles and negotiations over just and sustainable forms of (more-than-) human co-existence materializing in the antagonistic, divergent, adjusting, and synergistic practices of its everyday (re)production. Space, politics, and transformation, thereby, are intimately bound up with each other. Laying a conceptual foundation for the exploration of transformation requires the consideration of each: space and its materialities; politics and its disagreements, encounters, and identities; and the dynamic unfolding of the social through its routines, shifts, and ruptures.

Starting from the claim that human existence is inherently plural – in the sense that being is always a being with an 'other' – chapter 4 traces the political implications of 'togetherness'. This vantage point exposes the contingency of the ways in which humans coexist with each other and the more-than-human world, opening a space of possibility for different arrangements of common survival and wellbeing, as emphasized by community and diverse economy perspectives. Against the background of critical voices that challenge the primarily discursive thrust of community economy scholarship – the book's primary source of inspiration for thinking through a politics of (economic) possibility – chapter 5 turns towards the materiality of social life. Human togetherness, it demonstrates, materializes in practices constituting the spaces in which political subjectivities co-exist and act. Transformative geographies, then, are shown to emerge through a complex dynamic of resistance and cooptation, politics and submission, endeavor and coercion, conditioned and conditioning moments, and constituent and constituted power. Understanding transformation, consequently, premises a concept of social dynamics itself. The notion of practice with its processual and materially grounded ontology provides such a perspective on social reproduction and change. Chapter 6 continues to develop the emergent synthesis of community economy and practice theory scholarship around the concepts of scale and power. This brisk chapter prepares the operationalization of transformative geographies, an issue chapter 7 turns to. Taking up the conceptual grounding of space, politics, and change, this final chapter of part II translates transformative geographies into a perspective on concrete practices. Based on the criticism of capitalism's escalatory tendencies in part I, it explores practices that resist the capitalization of nature, lives, and social relations. In developing the notions of degrowth politics and practices, chapter 7 formulates a research agenda to trace the possibilities of a degrowth transition.

Chapter 4: Reimagining togetherness

> If we wish to emphasize the becoming of new and as yet unthought ways of economic being, we might focus on the multiple possibilities that emerge from the inessential commonality of negotiating our own implication in the existence of others.
> Gibson-Graham, 2006, p. 88

Capitalism is a mode of social existence in which human and more-than-human relations are substantially organized around the continuous movement of capital. Capitalist social relations are sedimented across mental, social, and material infrastructures and institutions, leaving little leeway to individual withdrawal from participation and reproduction. Nevertheless, capital is neither omnipresent nor inevitable. That means, first, waged labor, the commodity market, and capitalist enterprises are not the only way of organizing provision, transfer, compensation, surplus allocation, and governance (Gibson-Graham, 2006, p. 53ff.). A range of theoretical lenses and a vast number of empirical examples make perspectives that describe the world solely in terms of capitalist relations untenable (Fuller et al., 2016; Gibson-Graham, 2006; Krueger et al., 2017; R. Lee, 2013; North and Cato, 2017; Roelvink et al., 2015; White and Williams, 2016). Second, other-than-capitalist modes of social and economic organization do not constitute inferior, less relevant, or secondary choices *per se* but comprise practices that exist(ed) before, aside, with, despite, and instead of capitalist relations.

Although capitalist relations challenge and sideline alternative forms of economic relatedness, capital and state are no totalizing forces but are themselves products of and abstractions from human practice and organization. A conceptual grounding of transformative geographies, then, cannot start with individual actions or the structuredness of economic and political institutions. While the former easily conceal the broader relations which condition, curtail, force, and prohibit human activities, the latter closes off the agency, autonomy, and plurality of subjectivities and groups that question, subvert, and confront hegemonic structures. Transformative geographies, rather, are grounded in dynamic unfolding of human togetherness itself: community.

Community

Community is the "never-ending process of being together, of struggling over the boundaries and substance of togetherness, and of coproducing this togetherness in complex relations of power" (Gibson-Graham and Community Economies Collective, 2017, p. 5). Community, much like transformation, is not emancipatory in and off itself (Taylor Aiken, 2017). But it can be mobilized as an emancipatory concept that denaturalizes capitalist organization and opens spaces for alternative visions and practices of togetherness. Drawing on the philosophy of Jean-Luc Nancy (1991, 2000, 2016) – brought into geographies by figures like Gibson-Graham (2006, 2008) and Dikeç (2015) – this section explores what it means to be 'in-common' and the political consequences of togetherness for processes of transformation.

Inverting the Western metaphysics which subordinates plurality within an abstract singularity, Nancy (1991, 2000) argues that any singularity is always spaced by something surrounding it and singling it out. "A single being", he notes, "is a contradiction in terms. Such a being, which would be its own foundation, origin, and intimacy, would be incapable of *Being*, in every sense that this expression can have here" (Nancy, 2000, p. 12). Consequently, there cannot be "a singular being without another singular being" which leads Nancy to assume an "ontological 'sociality'" (Nancy, 1991, p. 28). Togetherness, consequently, is a basic condition of human existence. To be means to be together with an 'other'.

Existence, then, always entails an exposure to others (Dikeç, 2015). The "mode of existence and appropriation of a 'self'", in Nancy's words, "is the mode of an exposition in common and to the in-common" (Nancy, 1991, p. xxxvii). This ontology of being-in-common as mutual exposure suggests that human existence is fundamentally political. Nancy, however, separates the domains of politics and common, so that for him "the common is not immediately political (Nancy, 2000, cited in Dikeç, 2015, p. 62). Nevertheless, he grants that "the political is the *place* where community as such is brought into play" (Nancy, 1991, p. xxxvii). It is, then, qua the spatiality of community that the common and the political are imbricated (Schmid and Taylor Aiken, 2020).

Individualistic ontologies, by contrast, foreclose politics. A community that is built on pre-constituted subjects brings individuals together in a "constructed oneness" (Gibson-Graham, 2006, p. 85). That means, community is reduced to a common substance or identity around which commonness is set-up. Nancy (1991, p. 38) speaks of a "common being" in contrast to being-in-common. Conceiving of the common as essence precludes conflict over the common itself and thus disagreement (Rancière, 1998, 2004, 2011). Common being, consequently, produces closures that limit the possibilities of different becomings. As such it is also a closure of the political.

Still, essentialist notions of community – of a "communitarian being" (Nancy 1991, p. 15) – are widespread in economic and political thought, for instance in neoclassic theory, liberalism, or individualist anarchism. Individualistic ontologies suppress and conceal the commonality of being and thereby the "togetherness implied in any singularity, any identity or concept of being" (Gibson-Graham, 2006, p. 82). Pertaining to economic discourse, the closure of the political manifests in the hegemony of an "asocial economic atomism" which seeks to represent economic interaction as devoid of "the sticky ties of culture and social allegiance" (ibid., p. 83). By obscuring the sociality and interdependence of economic relations, their political character is hidden – economic relations are de-socialized and de-politicized.

This is particularly visible in the reduction of the notion of freedom (in economic and political discourse) to negative freedom, meaning freedom from society or community (Dierksmeier and Küng, 2016; Loick, 2017). Negative freedom abstracts from the social relations that allow for (individual) participation in social practice and thus assumes an individualistic ontology (generally referred to as methodological individualism).

Digression: Homo oeconomicus and neoliberal post-politics

Neoclassic theory – the foundation of mainstream economics – is the paragon of an individualistic ontology. A broad range of writings challenge the problematic assumptions, reductionisms, and gaps in neoclassical economics (Kallis, 2018; F. Lee, 2009; Raworth, 2017; van Treeck and Urban, 2017). A recently influential critique is Kate Raworth's (2017) *Doughnut Economics* which systemically juxtaposes misconceptions in mainstream economics with alternative proposals. In her introduction, Raworth quotes an open letter from the *International Student Initiative for Pluralism in Economics*, which summarizes the consequences of uncritical reductionism:

> The teaching of economics is in crisis ... and this crisis has consequences far beyond the university walls. What is taught shapes the minds of the next generation of policy-makers, and therefore shapes the societies we live in ...We are dissatisfied with the dramatic narrowing of the curriculum that has taken place over the last couple of decades ... It limits our ability to contend with the multidimensional challenges of the 21st century – from financial stability, to food security and climate change (Isipe, 2014, cited in Raworth, 2017, p. 2f.).

> A particular problematic tenet of neoclassic theory is the conception of humans as *Homines oeconomici* – "solitary, calculating, competing, and insatiable" (Raworth, 2017, p. 95) individuals. The world of neoclassical economics is populated by self-centered and instrumental beings who, ideally, act as "responsible self-investor[s] and self-provider[s]" (W. Brown, 2015, p. 84). Because, as we know from Margaret Thatcher: there is no such thing as society. Instead, through the "bizarre mechanism" of the invisible hand, homo oeconomicus functions "as an individual subject of interest within a totality which eludes him and which nevertheless founds the rationality of his egoistic choices" (Foucault, 2008, p. 278). Instead of building and engaging in relations of co-dependence, the rational economic man (and woman) "accepts reality" (Foucault, 2008, p. 269) – the "truth" of the market (W. Brown, 2015, p. 67). Rationality, here, is an economic rationality that negates any other system of reference as legitimate.
>
> By implication, it is irrational to refuse the truth of the market. While liberalism saw the economic sphere next to politics and other dimensions of society, neoliberalism generalizes economic principles. That means, "neoliberal rationality disseminates the model of the market to all domains and activities – even where money is not at issue – and configures human beings exhaustively as market actors, always, only and everywhere as homo oeconomicus" (W. Brown, 2015, p. 31). Homo oeconomicus thus eliminates homo politicus. To rehabilitate the latter, the intimate co-dependency of humans on each other and their environments has to be reinvigorated. Rendering visible the multiplicity of relations at the foundation of human and more-than-human existence makes individualistic ontologies untenable.

Essentialist notions of individuality, identity, and community, however, are not solely a function of liberalism or neoclassic economics. Counterhegemonic projects frequently mobilize an 'other' – the evil banks, governments, or wrong-headed initiatives – in constituting a common being. Similarly, "equating community economic development only with growing the local capitalist economy, *or* with attempts to establish 'small-is-beautiful' green self-sufficiency, *or* with achieving community self-determination through promoting homegrown, locally oriented community business" (Gibson-Graham, 2006, p. 86, emphasis in original) forecloses alternative becomings. Against this background, some scholars advance critiques on static and reified notions of community in social and environmental activism (for a discussion pertaining to the Transition Town Movement see Taylor Aiken, 2017).

Community economy

Community economy scholarship understands the economy as inherently plural, recognizing the interdependencies of being-in-common and the contingencies that emerge from economic diversity. In doing so, community economy scholars avoid specifying the substance of an alternative economy. Taking their cue from Nancy's philosophy of community, Gibson-Graham (2006, p. 86) – whose work is at the base of the broader community economies research agenda – resist the urge to conceive of the properties of an "ideal economic organization", instead acknowledging the communitarian dimension of economy. Taking economic being-in-common as the starting point has (at least) two major consequences for rethinking 'the economy'. First, in affirming co-dependence, the notion of economic being-in-common opens a discursive space to negotiate the key coordinates of a *community* economy. Community economy scholars thus, "resocialize" and "repoliticize" (Gibson-Graham 2006, p. 88) economic practice. Second, by not assuming a prediscursive commonness, community economists avoid excluding 'other' forms of economic practice – that is forms of survival and provisioning that any given specification of an alternative would ignore. Community economy, therefore, is a heterogeneous field which is radically open to new possibilities, identities, and becomings.

Through their notion of community economy, Gibson-Graham deconstruct the discursive dominance of economic imaginaries that revolve around capitalist forms of transfer, work, and organization. Capitalocentrism, the reduction of 'the economy' to the capitalist practicalities of commodity exchange, wage labor, and for-profit enterprises, manifests in the pervasive claim of political and public debates that the current (neoliberal, growth-based, capitalist) economy is without alternative, also known as TINA (there is no alternative). TINA expresses the 'truth of the market' in neoliberal ideology that further solidified with the demise of the planned economy of the Soviet Union – for some even marking the end of history itself (Fukuyama, 2006). While there are and always have been criticisms and counter projects to capitalist economies, Gibson-Graham (1996, p. 41) problematize the representation of capitalism as the "central or dominant identity" in relation to which non-capitalist spaces are defined (see chapter 2). Gibson-Graham's post-capitalist critique, therefore, is fundamentally also a critique of Marxist political economy that tends to "theorize capitalism as totality and all-encompassing entity" (Fickey, 2011, p. 238). Capitalocentrism places capitalist relations at the center of any economic narrative – whether affirmative or dismissive – tending to marginalize the pluriform possibilities that exist outside, in addition to, and despite of capitalism. Defining alternatives in relation to capitalism denies them an own and independent identity, which, in a roundabout way, reproduces the hegemony of capitalocentric discourse.

In deconstructing this discourse, Gibson-Graham see a way to destabilize economic identity and disidentify with capitalism as a natural form of economic being-in-common. By "widening the identity of the economy to include all of those practices excluded or marginalized by a strong theory of capitalism" (Gibson-Graham, 2006, p. 60), other subject positions can emerge. Following Nancy's postfoundationalist take on community, Gibson-Graham rid the economy of "all essential content" (Miller, 2013, p. 522) and in doing so propose an economic ontology that is perhaps the closest it can come to non-essentiality "without rejecting the term 'economic' itself" (Miller, 2013, p. 522). Gibson-Graham (2014) speak of a "weak theory", that means a theory that intentionally stays open to new becomings by not foreclosing other forms of (economic) being-in-common. Methodologically, a 'thick description' (Geertz, 2003) accompanies this weak theory, capturing the diversity of practices and articulations without imposing a particular interpretative frame or (capitalist) identity onto them (Gibson-Graham, 2014). The community economy, thus, provides an "emptiness" that "awaits filling up by collective actions in place" (Gibson-Graham, 2006, p. 166) and therefore allows the negotiation of how to shape and design economic being-in-common. Community economy, consequently, "refers to a praxis of co-existence around which economic decisions are negotiated and made" (Roelvink et al., 2015, p. 9).

Radical deconstruction and the opening of the discursive space to allow for new becomings and un-fixed imaginaries has its limits. To be relevant as "a politics of collective action" (Gibson-Graham, 2006, p. xxxvi), community economy has to involve a closure. That means a standpoint or horizon that guides collective struggle and excludes unjust alternatives. Excluding slave labor, for instance, as legitimate economic practice seems self-evident but constitutes a closure of possibilities. In his reading of community economy, Miller (2013) traces three constitutive moments: the ontological moment (CE1), the ethical moment (CE2), and the moment of politics (CE3) to elaborate the movement between deconstruction and reconstruction of economic being-in-common.

CE1, the "ontological moment", emphasizes the openness of the concept. That is, the anti-essentialist ontologies of economy and community. CE2 and CE3, by contrast, are "movement[s] towards a positivity" (Miller, 2013, p. 525) – the emergence of desire and the articulation of possibilities. CE2, the "moment of ethical exposure", revolves around a "preliminary affirmation" (ibid.). Rather than stipulating any concrete values and norms for such a process, it demands the space for ethical negotiation itself. Hence, it is the site of multiplicity, diversity, and possibility, coming close what others have called the political (Rancière, 1998). The "moment of politics" (CE3), finally, is the moment in which a political construction occurs and is thus the collective enactment of positivity (Miller, 2013, p. 525). The moment of politics, here, expresses the necessity to make decisions and develop concrete practices. Besides creativity, connection and transformation this moment also entails struggle and exclusion. While it is essential to fix certain values, ideas, relations, and identities in order to perform economies at all, it is also crucial to move back to CE1 and CE2 in order to avoid universal closures. In other words, to keep the moments "in constant play, affirming positive practice yet always returning to an explicit recognition of its dangers" (ibid., p. 529). As such, community economy attends to particular desires while excluding others. However, never doing so against the backdrop of universal principles but the temporary and open affirmation of inclusive ethical decision-making.

Economic diversity

Developing a language of economic diversity is the principal strategy to cultivate community economies. The so called 'iceberg model' and the 'diverse economy framework' – probably the most widely known pieces of work from community economy scholarship – provide heuristics to represent economic practice as a variegated and heterogeneous field involving a "wide range of people, processes, sites, and relationships" (Gibson-Graham and Community Economies Collective, 2017, p. 10). Below the surface of paid wage labor, production for markets, and capitalist businesses – the capitalocentric representation of the economy – there are alternative and non-capitalist activities and sites that fundamentally contribute to well-being, survival, and sustenance, thus constituting forms of economic practice in their own right. While these remain invisible for capitalocentric perspectives and are widely ignored in economic discourse, they "possibly keep ... us afloat as a society" (Gibson-Graham, Cameron, et al., 2013, p. 11).

Inspired by the iceberg, a more systematic framework breaks down the diverse economy into capitalist, alternative-capitalist, and non-capitalist forms of labor, enterprise, transactions, property, and finance (older versions are without the latter two). This results in a three by five – or respectively three by three – matrix that can be used to guide the examination of a field, a community, or an organization, portraying its activities beyond a narrow formal economy. A range of studies have applied the diverse economies framework in different cases such as social enterprises (Houtbeckers, 2018), rural municipalities (Gibson et al., 2015), and local initiatives (K. Werner, 2015). Representing the economy as inherently diverse has two quite practical consequences for the repoliticization of economic being-in-common. First, it shows that individuals and communities already employ a broad range of non-capitalist forms in everyday practice. Second, it sketches the breadth of possibilities and helps to identify "building blocks" (Gibson-Graham and Community Economies Collective, 2017, p. 11) of postcapitalist economies.

The concept of diverse economy is situated within a broader genealogy of approaches that struggle over (re)defining economy. Quite profound and influential was the debate between formalism and substantivism, the initiation of which is generally attributed to Karl Polanyi (Peck, 2013). Substantivists describe actually existing or real economies, in doing so prioritizing the empirical content over abstract – formal – models. In contrast to the formal economy that "operates in a time and space vacuum ... the substantive economy is situated in both time and place" (Halperin, 1994, cited in Peck, 2013, p. 1554). Identifying different patterns of economic organization – reciprocity, redistribution, exchange, and house holding – Polanyi prepared a perspective on economies as "combinatory sites of multiple rationalities, interests, and values, rather than as spaces governed by singular and invariant economic laws" (Peck, 2013, p. 1555).

Economic geography itself reflects the turn from formalism to substantivism. Polanyi's critique on the formalism and methodological individualism of neoclassic theory resonates with important turns in (primarily anglophone) economic geography away from spatial science to more political and theory-based approaches. The figure of David Harvey, who withdrew his support for the "mathematically abstract and narrow conception of economic geography" (Sheppard and Barnes, 2017, p. 5) in favor of the import of Marxist theory into the discipline, reflects this shift quite vividly. In the late 1980s and 1990s, then, the cultural turn increasingly led economic geographers to include further, hitherto neglected dimensions such as meanings, identities, trust, and knowledge (Faulconbridge and Hall, 2009). While drifting further apart from economics, dominated by neoclassic theory, new points of contact with anthropology, sociology, and other social sciences opened up. Along these lines, a notion of economy emerges that is "culturally inflected, institutionally mediated, politically governed, socially embedded, and heterogeneous" (Peck, 2013, p. 1546).

These developments supported new understandings of economy beyond capitalist relations (Leyshon et al., 2003). In sum, two tendencies interweave to disentangle capitalism and economy. First, capitalism is relegated to a contingent, spatiotemporally limited form of social organization which is embedded in political and cultural institutions. Rather than equating capitalism with the economy, capitalism is a particular form of economic activity that exists besides, adds onto, appropriates, and corrodes other modes of subsistence. We might call this first tendency a narrowing of capitalism. Second, economy is liberated from its reduction to capitalism. Inspired by thinkers like Polanyi, economy, then, is grounded in the diversity of human relations. "Economy is the instituted process of interactions between humans and their environments, involving the use of material means for the satisfaction of human values" (Kallis, 2018, p. 17). We might call this second tendency a broadening of the economy. Yet, while attempts to disentangle capitalism and economy open new and potentially emancipatory perspectives, there is a need to 're'-entangle capitalism with the 'web of life' (Moore, 2015) – a point that I return to below.

Representing economy as a diverse field illustrates the importance of more-than-capitalist practice for human co-existence. Apart from Gibson-Graham's iceberg model, scholars have proposed other conceptions of a varied economy. Roger Lee (2006, p. 414), for instance, speaks of the "ordinary economy" which is "an integral part of everyday life, full of the contradictions, ethical dilemmas and multiple values that inform the quotidian business of making a living". Kate Raworth (2017, p. 44) represents the economy as doughnut which symbolizes the area of a "save and just space for humanity". Economy, then, is the navigation between the "social foundation of well-being and [the] ecological ceiling of planetary boundaries". And Hazel Henderson (1999) depicts the economy as a three-layer cake with icing. Here, the private sector (the icing) is only the visible topping that rests on the public sector, the "social cooperative caring economy", and on "nature's layer" (cited in Johanisova et al., 2013, p. 9). While all these approaches have different emphases, they demonstrate that economy comprises diverse and historically changing patterns of co-dependent human organization around the satisfaction of needs and wants that are embedded in more-than-human ecologies.

Poststructuralist transformative geographies

By suggesting 'community economy' as a discursive nodal point around which alternative meanings and practices can convene, Gibson-Graham follow a "feminist political imaginary" (Miller, 2013, p. 531). Inspired by second-wave feminism, they envision transformation not around (centralized) organizational structures but through ubiquitous shifts in discourses and practices that involve processes of dis-identification (with capitalocentric discourse) and re-identification around new nodes of signification. Transformation, then, does not come about through 'upscaling' of local initiatives or new global institutions but through dispersed shifts in many places that are "related analogically rather than organizationally and connected through webs of signification" (Gibson-Graham, 1996, p. xxvii). To better understand Gibson-Graham's strategy to "take back the economy" (2013) by "dislodge[ing] the discursive dominance of capitalist economic activity" (2006, p. 54), this section tracks Gibson-Graham's reception of Laclau and Mouffe's post-Marxist project and the formulation of a 'politics of hope'.

In *Hegemony and Socialist Strategy*, Laclau and Mouffe (2001) develop a notion of politics as a discursive field in which structures and subjects are not pre-given "but constituted and reconstituted through debate in the public sphere" (p. xvii). Discourse, here at the center of politics, shapes subjectivities and social relations through temporary fixations in meaning. Hegemony, against this background, "is best understood as the organization of consent – the processes through which subordinated forms of consciousness are constructed without recourse to violence or coercion" (Barnett, 1991, cited in Jorgensen and Phillips, 2002, p. 32). Discursively sedimented relations appear as quasi-natural, masking their contingency and foreclosing alternatives. "A poststructural theory of politics that situates discourse (and therefore language) at the center of any political project" (Gibson-Graham, 2006, p. 55), consequently, has to unfix economic identity and liberate difference from its subsumption under a capitalocentric logic.

Transformation, then, centers around a shift in meaning. Knowledge is performative, or as Gibson-Graham (2012, p. 33) expound the post-structural twist of Marx's 11th thesis on Feuerbach: "to change our understanding [of the world] *is* to change the world in small and sometimes major ways". Cultivating subjectivities that disidentify with capitalism as dominant way of organizing social relations, from this perspective, opens new economic possibilities.

> How we construct stories or narratives of transformation is important. These narratives have what some social theorists call 'performative effects'. In other words, our narratives help to bring into being the worlds they describe [...] It is therefore crucial that we cultivate representations of the world that inspire, mobilize, and support change efforts even while recognizing real challenges (Gibson-Graham and Community Economies Collective, 2017, p. 4).

Speaking about the world – including the articulations of scholarship – then, is not purely descriptive but also performative. Foregrounding possibility creates "other images of the present" (B. Anderson, 2017, p. 595) that render the diverse economy visible and encourage subjectivities to build community economies. A hopeful representation of the world in general and the economy in particular, thus, is a central tenet of Gibson-Graham's transformative imaginary of ubiquitous shifts that are linked through webs of signification.

Such a 'politics of hope' (Gibson-Graham, 2008; Roelvink et al., 2015) has consequences for community economy's notion of space. It decenters verticality and privileges a non-hierarchical spatial ontology (see interlude I). From a scalar perspective, capitalocentrism is a form of "macro-mystification" (Marston et al., 2005, p. 427). Capitalocentric discourse draws on an abstract globality and creates the image of an objective structure that is removed from the access through everyday practice. A vertically structured or scalar representation of social relations might serve as a "distraction" (Springer, 2014a, p. 7) that obscures the "sites of ordering practices, as well as the possibilities for undoing them" (Marston et al., 2005, p. 427). Community economy scholarship, consequently, turns away from the apparent verities and constraints of vertical structures and towards the possibilities of a relational and flat spatiality.

In lieu of different scalar 'levels', community economy thinking focuses on place as the site of politics, new becomings, and transformation. Place, thereby, is not reducible to the local but convenes activities of potential "global reach" (Gibson-

Graham, 2006, p. xxvi). Inspired by Massey's (2005, 2008) 'ethics of place beyond place', Gibson-Graham (2008) emphasize the relationality of place.

> This place [here the urban] has to be conceptualized [as] a meeting-place, of jostling, potentially conflicting, trajectories. It is set within, and internally constituted through, complex geometries of differential power. This implies an identity that is, internally, fractured and multiple. Such an understanding of place requires that conflicts are recognized, that positions are taken and that (political) choices are made (Massey, 2007, cited in Gibson-Graham, 2008, p. 622).

Emergence and relationality are key parameters in the ontological reframing of capitalism. Both the deconstruction of hierarchical scale and the appreciation of place with its multiple relations work towards abandoning the "ontological privileging of systemic or structural determination" (Gibson-Graham, 2008, p. 623). Poststructuralist transformative geographies, then, emerge from the cultivation of political subjectivities in diverse localities that embrace a plurality of values and engage in encouraging and nurturing forms of economic being-in-common, foregrounding openness and justice.

Epistemic fallacy?

In conceptualizing transformation as an emergent discursive project, Gibson-Graham shift the focus from the substantive to the performative. Some (often sympathetic) critiques of the community economy project problematize that a hopeful focus on resubjectivation runs the risk of ignoring the engine, mechanisms, and machinations of capital (Sharpe, 2014; Fickey, 2011). Community economy's focus on possibilities, in this view, neglects the institutions, materialities, and power relations which transformative practices are situated in and constrained by. Noel Castree (1999, p. 145) problematizes Gibson-Graham's (2008, p. 615) premise that to "change our understanding is to change the world" as "epistemic fallacy" (drawing on Roy Bhaskar). In doing so, he claims, community economy scholarship conflates epistemology with ontology and thus mistakes thinking about the world for the world itself.

By attempting to 'think away capitalism', community economy also tends to overlook the powerful entanglement of capital and state (Jonas, 2016). State power is crucial for the understanding of capitalist economies. For instance, its role in stabilizing and steering institutions such as private property and markets through regulation, intervention, and subsidies. At the same time, opposition to the state, pragmatic use of state institutions, and their subversion are part of postcapitalist resistance and struggle. Jonas (2016, p. 18) argues that "geographies of the state can play an important role in framing the tactics and strategies of alternative social and political movements". Lacking a theory of the state, community economy scholarship misses an important aspect of postcapitalist struggle.

Aside from missing a clear positioning against capitalist exploitation, community economy's emphasis of diversity, so another important point of critique, also fails to exclude undesirable non-capitalist alternatives (see also discussion on diversity and alterity in chapter 2). Samers (2005), for instance, observes a lack of critical examination into the economic relations that constitute alternative economies. Some critics, therefore, call for a more selective appreciation of non-capitalist forms of production, labor, transfer, and surplus allocation. The same goes for community economy's appreciation of projects which appear to be non-capitalist on the surface but turn out to be deeply involved with capital's reproduction upon closer examination. Kiribati – a small Micronesian island and former British colony – for instance, inspires Gibson-Graham (2006, p. 187) to think about (postcapitalist) options for consumption. The island is fairly self-sufficient and defies export-oriented resource extraction. This is mainly due to the comfortable position of having some 508 million US$ in an overseas account gained from mining its phosphate deposits. Currently, "all fund assets are invested offshore by two London-based fund managers in an equal balance of equity and fixed-income investments" (Gibson-Graham, 2006, p. 186). It seems highly questionable, however, to pass off an arrangement heavily based on the M to M' circuit of financial capital as an example to promote different economic imaginaries. By neglecting capital and state – not as reified powerful antagonists but as sets of relations that possibly undermine, divert, and coopt postcapitalist ambitions – community economy scholars run the risk of losing sight of capitalist and statist power relations and their everyday reproduction.

In another way, overemphasizing the role of language and processes of resubjectivation tends to sideline the material relevance of alternative economies for human co-existence and survival. Gibson-Graham's (2006, p. 160ff.) example of a workshop for Christmas decoration in Latrobe Valley, for instance, which they use to track processes of encounter, certainly contributes to the cultivation of new forms of community and subjectivity. Yet, it possibly diverts attention and capacities away from more substantial practices of postcapitalist transformative geographies. Inflating strongly localized and self-referential projects is liable to neglect the more fundamental inequalities these and other communities face.

Community economy thinking, indeed, acknowledges the materiality of relations of power.

> Lest ontological reframing be mistaken for a simplistic assertion that we can think ourselves out of the materiality of capitalism or repressive state practices, we should affirm that our orientation toward possibility does not deny the forces that militate against it – forces that may work to undermine, constrain, destroy,

or sideline our attempts to reshape economic futures but we should deny these forces a fundamental, structural, or universal reality and instead identify them as contingent outcomes of ethical decisions, political projects, and sedimented localized practices, continually pushed and pulled by other determinations (Gibson-Graham, 2006, xxxi).

In addition, community economy scholarship increasingly draws on assemblage thinking and other approaches to account for the material and more-than-human (Roelvink et al., 2015). Nevertheless, the prioritization of possibilities over constraints has fundamental consequences that need further exploration. While community economy scholarship focusses on a politics of hope, there is insufficient consideration about the consequences of sidelining constraints. Barriers and counterforces are crucial moments in the everyday resistance of individuals, community initiatives, and eco-social enterprises in particular, and degrowth-oriented politics in general. The reasons for a need to include constraints into the analysis of transformative geographies are at least threefold.

First, although capitalist forms of work, transfer, and enterprise are not the only mode of economic organization, nor the preferred choice for many, there is little leeway for individuals and communities to (completely) withdraw from the participation in possibly violent and exploitative relations. Commodity chains of food, clothes, building materials, electronics, and other goods abound with examples of "salvage accumulation" (Tsing, 2015; see chapter 1) – together with the services people call upon such as logistics, construction, or care. Depending on material resources, skills, social networks, and financial situation, there is often little room for maneuver not to live at the expense of others (Brand and Wissen, 2017). The same is true for alternative organizations. A social enterprise, for instance, that draws on value chains incorporating hard-to-track materials and components which cannot be avoided or substituted, continuously has to weight the harm it (re)produces against the positive impacts it may have socially and environmentally. Constraints, here, means an awareness of exploitation and violence which is needed to navigate the contradictions of economic practice and to adjust transformative politics.

Second, acknowledging constraints is important in counteracting neoliberal ideologies of responsibilization and sacrifice (W. Brown, 2015). Community initiatives often include individuals that take on a disproportionate burden of duties and functions leading to stress and in extreme cases also burnout. While it is admirable that numerous activists and social entrepreneurs work long hours for (partially) altruistic purposes with (usually) little compensation, their engagement also reproduces the tendencies of individualized responsibility and withdrawal of state welfare. Strategic niche management, in this sense, sees "widely shared, specific, realistic and achievable" (Seyfang and Haxeltine, 2012, p. 190) expectations as crucial for niche development. While I have problematized the notion of niche upscaling above (see part I), it is important to contextualize individual and group efforts by considering constraints.

Third, and most central to the thrust of this work, tactical interventions and postcapitalist strategies premise knowledge about transformation's obstacles. Only if critical activists, entrepreneurs, and politicians assess and evaluate their scope of action, they can devise appropriate strategies to enlarge alternative economic and political spaces. Finding (institutional) levers and tipping points proves to be a demanding task that requires conscious trade-offs and a constant negotiation of possibilities and constraints (see chapter 19). Transformation, therefore, is a delicate interplay of possibility – a utopian moment expressed in a politics of hope and the appreciation of difference – and the acknowledgment of constraints – sedimented power relations that stabilize an exploitative, violent, and destructive capitalism, which activism needs to oppose and position against. Privileging either moment *a priori* predetermines a particular strategy for activism centered either around the opening of possibility and the appreciation of diversity or the positioning against capitalism and the focus on alterity (see chapter 2). The following section, therefore, grounds the community economy perspective in materialities and relations of power to open a field for postcapitalist strategy *in practice*.

Chapter 5: Materialization

> If humans are part of nature, historical change – including the present as history – must be understood through dialectical movements of humans making environments, and environments making humans. The two acting units – humanity/environments – are not independent but interpenetrated at every level, from the body to the biosphere.
> *Moore, 2015, p. 28*

Community economy scholarship takes its cue from poststructuralist feminist thought which is anti-essentialist in its orientation. Subjectivities, communities, and economic relations, then, are contingent outcomes of diverse performances. Poststructuralism veers away from the ideas of truth, essence, and autonomous subjects (Kuhn, 2005) and instead turns towards difference and becoming. Processuality, as poststructuralism's central tenet, "challenges structuralism's binary abstractions – such as nature/culture, emotion/reason, space/time, non-human/human" (Woodward, 2017, p. 1) which merge in the constant becoming of a dynamic world.

Processuality, of course, is not particular to poststructuralism. One important source poststructuralism both builds on and criticizes is Marxism[1] (Kuhn, 2005). Marx's well-known assertion that "men make their own history, but they do not make it as they please; they do not make it under self-selected circumstances, but under circumstances existing already, given and transmitted from the past" (Marx, 1852) highlights the continuous (re)production of social relations. In contrast to poststructuralism's focus on contingency and difference, Marxism, however, is

---

1   Marxism does not identify a uniform or even consimilar school of thought. Detailing the historical development and breadth of Marxist inspired literature is beyond the scope of this work (for overviews see Cumbers, 2009; A. Jones, 2009). In the following, I draw primarily on spatial thinkers that develop Marx's philosophy into a historical-*geographical* materialism (Swyngedouw, 2012; Wiegand, 2016).

based on a strong materialism that foregrounds the circumstances – in particular the 'economic base' – which conditions social practice. It has, consequently, a strong emphasis on institutions and heteronomy taking effect as structures. As a critique of structuralist Marxism, geographical-historical materialism – significantly developed through the work of figures like David Harvey (1982, 2011) and Henri Lefebvre (1991, 2014) – marks a revised strand of Marxism that is supposed to "retain the powerful insights emergent from Marxian analysis while absorbing and adapting to the poststructuralist and postmodern critique" (A. Jones, 2009, p. 480). Some poststructuralists, including Gibson-Graham, however, disagree that Marxism can be reconciled with its poststructuralist censure (A. Jones, 2009) – at least not a Marxist conception of the capitalist class process (Gibson-Graham, Erdem, et al., 2013).

Much of the disagreement between Marxism and poststructuralism can be cast as a positioning vis-à-vis structure and contingency, determination and possibility, lack of reconstruction and lack of deconstruction. Critics of poststructuralist thought maintain that the dissolution of all verities ultimately leaves scholars without the categories needed to critique social relations in capitalist societies (Castree, 1999; Glassman, 2003). Perspectives that assume "a world where power is putatively highly fluid and dispersed" tend to ignore or overlook the forces constraining and conditioning human activity, limiting "the ability of studies of resistance to articulate the conditions under which political and social struggles might transcend resistance and succeed in liberating groups of humans from oppressive conditions against which they struggle" (Glassman, 2003, p. 695). Although poststructuralism seeks to overcome the dichotomization of materiality and sociality, its rejection of fixity runs the risk of neglecting the historical-geographical circumstances of social co-existence – dismissing any notion of structure, system, or truth in favor of becoming, contingency, and floating signifiers. What is at stake, therefore, is materiality in a broad sense as the stabilization of social relations.

Social theory of late has (re)turned to the question of materiality and its relation to the social, developing postructuralist-materialist approaches around actor-network-theory (ANT) and practice thinking (Gherardi, 2016, 2017; Murdoch, 2006; Reckwitz, 2002, 2016). The remainder of this chapter examines practice-theoretical approaches as way to conciliate poststructuralist with materialist perspectives. At first, it takes a step back and sketches the field of social theories within which these different approaches are situated. Tracing different types of social theories and their critiques situates community economy scholarship with respect to practice theory – as the two variants of poststructuralist and materialist thought this work is interested in. Subsequently, this chapter surveys the field of practice theories, working towards a notion of practice as conventionalized patterns of activity that integrate material arrangements, competent bodies, and configurations of meaning. Finally, it turns to broader nexuses of human activity – namely organizations and institutions – conceptualizing both from a practice theory perspective. In sum, chapter 5 prepares a poststructural-materialist perspective on transformative geographies which the remainder of part II further develops and operationalizes.

From regimes of signification to practice

Reckwitz (2003) distinguishes between various types of social theories that differ with respect to how they conceptualize sociality or, in other words, where they 'localize' the social: structural theories, individualist approaches, and cultural theories. Structural theories – to which Reckwitz counts historical materialism – localize the social in supraindividual material regularities (structures). In contrast therewith, individualist approaches conceive of the social as produced by individual actors to whom they grant considerable agency. Culturalist theories, drawing on a broad range of inspirations such as structuralism, poststructuralism, phenomenology, hermeneutics, pragmatism, and radical constructivism, take a middle way and foreground the question of how social 'orders' are produced which, in turn, enable subjects to partake in their (re)production. Language, meaning, and symbolic interactions gain importance for the construction and reproduction of "meaningful orders and their symbolic organization of reality" (Reckwitz, 2002, p. 288, author's translation). Culturalist theories themselves differ with respect to the localization of the social. Reckwitz, here, distinguishes between four forms of culturalist theories: mentalism, textualism, intersubjectivism, and practice theory. "On a very basic level these schools of thought offer opposing locations of the social and conceptualize the 'smallest' unit of social theory differently: in minds, discourses, interactions, and 'practices'" (Reckwitz, 2002, p. 245).

Textualism, or more specifically discourse-theoretical approaches – which for Reckwitz are a subcategory of textualism and within which we can situate Gibson-Graham – locate the social in complex supra-individual discursive orders, in communication, and in epistemes. Discourse theories foreground "regimes of signification" (Reckwitz, 2016, p. 53; author's translation; see chapter 8) by focusing on "sets of ideas and practices that give statements, texts, rhetoric, and narratives particular kinds of meanings" (Berg, 2009, p. 215). Language, here, is the central condition "under which we know reality" (ibid.). Discourses, therefore, might be conceived as texts – understood in a very broad sense – that can be analyzed, deciphered, and read. This privileging of ideas, meanings, and knowledges through which sociality is (re)produced led critics to accuse discourse-theoretical approaches of conceptual intellectualism and a dematerialization of the social (Reckwitz, 2003).

The world of discourse theorists, however, is not devoid of artefacts, bodies, infrastructures, and things. Community economy thinking – as the perspective of interest here – is well aware of embodied capitalist relations, material and technical elements, and more-than-human assemblages (Roelvink et al., 2015). And poststructuralist feminist theory, which is crucial to Gibson-Graham's thought, draws on the (female) body as the primary "site of resistance" (Gibson-Graham, 1996, p. 96; see also Mountz, 2018). Yet, there is a strong tendency to conceptually, methodologically, and empirically privilege regimes of signification. The community economy project revolves primarily around a "politics of language", "language of economic diversity", "imaginaries of possibility", and "representations of the economy" (Gibson-Graham, 1996, 2006; Roelvink et al., 2015).

Critiques of community economy's focus on language and meanings are situated within a broader dissatisfaction with representationalism. As a consequence, human geographers turn to more-than-representational theories (Cadman, 2009; Simpson, 2017) and the material grounding of social life (Everts et al., 2011). More-than-representational, here, does not mean that the discourses, texts, ideas, identities, and signs are irrelevant for the constitution of human co-existence. Instead, what is passed censure on are perspectives that "reduce the world to, and fix and frame it within, text or discourse alone" (Simpson, 2017, p. 1).

The "practice turn" (Schatzki et al., 2001), against this background, is a response to representationalism that seeks to rectify the dematerialization and intellectualization of the social. Various authors draw on practice theory to rekindle materiality with culturalist theorizing (Hui et al., 2017; Nicolini, 2013; Reckwitz, 2002, 2016; Schäfer, 2016a; Schatzki, 2003, 2010a, 2010b; Shove et al., 2012). In the diverse lines of thinking under the labels of practice theory or praxeology, two moments stick out that express practice theory's positioning in the field of social theories. Practice thinking turns its attention to (1) the materiality of the social and (2) its implicit and informal logic (Reckwitz, 2003). Practice theories are characterized by an anti-intellectualism that seeks to explain social life through bodily and materially grounded activities instead of representational models (Geiselhart et al., 2019). Against the foregoing critique of poststructuralist transformative geographies, practice theories constitute a promising conceptual grounding for developing a poststructural-*materialist* perspective on transformative geographies. Along these lines, this and the subsequent chapters explore practice theorizing as possible response to, and complement of, the discourse-theoretical thrust of the community economy project.

Practice theories

Practice theories are grounded in a long genealogy of thought that stretches from Marx, Heidegger, Wittgenstein, Dewey, Lyotard, Taylor, Bourdieu, and Giddens – amongst many others that are not named here – to contemporary thinkers like Schatzki, Reckwitz, and Shove. Influences and directions as diverse as pragmatism, phenomenology, structuration theory, ethnomethodology, actor-network theory, and neo-Marxism shape contemporary practice theories (Geiselhart et al. 2019; Hillebrandt, 2014; Hui et al., 2017; Nicolini, 2013; Reckwitz, 2016). This variegated legacy is important to understand the genealogy and diversity of practice theorizing (Nicolini, 2013) which, in part, merges these different traditions, terminologies, and assumptions. Some scholars, therefore, stress that practice theory is not a homogenous school of thought and avoid using the singular when talking about theories of practice in general.

Despite conceptual and genealogical differences, practice theories share an identifiable family resemblance (Hillebrandt, 2014; Nicolini, 2013). Most important, here, is their fundamentally processual ontology. The world, from a practice theory perspective, is an ongoing 'habitual accomplishment'.

> The appeal of what has been variably described as practice idiom, practice standpoint, practice lens, and a practice-based approach lies in its capacity to describe important features of the world we inhabit as something that is routinely made and re-made in practice using tools, discourse and our bodies. From this perspective, the social appears as a vast array or assemblage of performances made durable by being inscribed in human bodies and minds, objects and texts, and knotted together in such a way that the results of one performance become the resource for another (Nicolini, 2013, p. 2).

Practices, then, are recurring patterns of activity that establish, order, and uphold social co-existence. They constitute a historically and spatially situated cultural repertoire of types of behavior, such as driving or bookkeeping, that can be taken up by individuals who become carriers, reproducers, and architects of these patterns (Geiselhart et al., 2019). Practices are supra-individual in character but only exist through their continuous enactment by habituated bodies who actualize practices through performance (Nicolini, 2013; Shove et al., 2012). Human co-existence, then, materializes in body-minds and their differentiated positionings in the world of artefacts, things, and other beings – all of which are enrolled in the continuous process of social production and are thus elements of practice.

A widely used definition, on that note, defines practice as a "routinized type of behavior which consists of several elements, interconnected to one another: forms of bodily activities, forms of mental activities, 'things' and their use, a background knowledge in the form of understanding, know-how, states of emotion and motivational knowledge" (Reckwitz, 2002, p. 249). This definition advances two different foci that have been key in the development of the notion of practice as well as its operationalization. The first focus zeros in on that which binds different activities together to form an intelligible and contiguous set. The second focus identifies the different elements that constitute a set of activities.

Two approaches have gained prominence in recent theories of practice, respectively based on one of the two foci. On the one hand, Schatzki's notion of practices as open-ended sets of activities that are organized by practical understandings, rules, teleoaffective structures, and general understandings (Schatzki, 2003, 2008, 2010b). On the other hand, Shove et al.'s conceptualization of practices as the active integration of materials, competences, and meanings (Shove et al., 2012). Schatzki identifies four dimensions through which activities are linked to each other and constitute intelligible nexuses. (1) Practical understandings refer to the knowledge and skills involved in performing a set of activities. Activities are linked through a practical understanding and constitute a practice when "most participants agree on what it makes sense to do" (Nicolini, 2013, p. 165). (2) Rules, furthermore, are "explicit formulations" (Schatzki, 2003, p. 191f.) that guide human activity. They constitute elements that people consider when engaging in activities. (3) Teleoaffective structures describe the motivations, affects, and emotions that are involved in activities. As "a range of normativized hierarchically ordered ends, projects, and tasks" (Schatzki, 2003, p. 192) they link activities. Last but not least, (4) general understanding – which Schatzki adds to his tripartite of practical understandings, rules, and teleoaffective structures in later publications – refers to a reflective understanding of the context in which activities are set.

Shove and colleagues (2012, 22ff.), in contrast to Schatzki, focus on the connection of different elements that constitute a practice. In a simplifying move, they collapse the various dimensions Reckwitz proposes in the abovementioned definition into three broad categories: materials, competences, and meanings. Materials comprise artefacts, things, objects, and infrastructures as well as bodies. Pending a more detailed conceptualization of these components – which Shove et al. provide only partially – materials comprise all tangible and physical parts enrolled in human activity. Second, competences refer to the skills, practical understandings, and abilities involved in human activity. In short, all the capabilities socialized bodies (need to) possess to perform a practice. Finally, meanings comprise mental activities, beliefs, emotions, moods, affects, and objectives. This is probably the most elusive of Shove et al.'s categories including both explicit and implicit moments. Practices, then, are "defined by interdependent relations between materials, competences and meanings" (Shove et al., 2012, p. 24). They come into being, shift and fall apart by linking, substituting, altering or decoupling these elements.

A crucial difference between Reckwitz and Shove et al.'s conceptualization of practice on the one hand and Schatzki's on the other is that while the former include materials as element in their notion of practice, Schatzki places "humans, artefacts, organisms and things of nature" (Schatzki, 2010a, p. 129) outside of practice (Gram-Hanssen, 2011). Schatzki speaks of practices *and* material arrangements. Although Schatzki emphasizes that practices are "inevitably and often inextricably bound up with material entities" and uses the notion of "practice-arrangement-bundle" (Schatzki, 2015, p. 1f.), his terminology introduces an analytical distinction between practices and materials. The separation of practices and arrangements allows Schatzki to conceptualize different forms of relatedness between them: causality, prefiguration, constitution, and intelligibility (Schatzki, 2010a, p. 139). In contrast, other practice theorists, in particular those close to posthumanism and actor-network thinking, maintain that human activity and materiality co-emerge, which they emphasize by speaking of "intra-action" between things and people (Gherardi, 2016, p. 5). Like Shove et al., they see materiality as internal to practice.

Digression: The role of ANT for practice-theoretical thought

Although processuality and materiality are important points of contact between ANT and practice-theoretical approaches, there are different opinions on how they relate to each other (Nicolini, 2013; Schatzki, 2002; Everts et al., 2011). Reckwitz (2003) and Nicolini (2013), for instance, draw on Latour as an important pioneer of practice thinking, while Schatzki (2002) problematizes ANT's symmetry of human and non-human entities in relation to their capacity to act. This leads Schatzki to exclude ANT as form of practice theory. For him, the networks of ANT resemble his notion of 'arrangements'. "Arrangements, however, are only one of the two principle sorts of phenomena that make up social phenomena. The second is practices, which have no pendent in actor-network theory" (Schatzki, 2010a, 134). As a consequence, Schatzki claims, ANT lacks the means to explore how materialities and social activities hang together. Nicolini (2013, 180), in contrast, notes that Schatzki's complex theoretical architecture is fairly prescriptive and thus risks hampering rather than facilitating empirical explorations. Latour's simple principle 'follow the actor', in turn, constitutes a more open methodology which is a valuable addition to the issues "left unsolved by Schatzki and many of his colleagues" (ibid.). While it is beyond the scope of this work to trace the commonalities and differences of ANT and practice theory in more detail, it is important to note that both approaches converge around notions of processuality and materiality and thus productively speak to each other. For a more detailed discussion around ANT and assemblage thinking see Müller (2015).

Working with the concept of practice

The remainder of this book uses a concept of practice that builds on Reckwitz's and Shove et al.'s notion of several interconnected elements. Adapting Shove et al.'s tripartite model, it slightly twists and regroups the elements into (1) competent bodies, (2) meanings, and (3) materials. (1) 'Competent bodies', here, refers to physiological and cognitive abilities, tacit knowledge, desires, and habits. That means bodily qualities and capabilities that are physical and/or largely unconscious. For instance, the ability to ollie a skateboard, or handle a stressful situation. (2) 'Meanings' comprise understandings, values, ideas, ideologies, identities, explicit knowledge, and reasoning. Meanings can be explicated such as a political standpoint or the information on directions to the next supermarket. (3) 'Materials' include infrastructures, documents, goods, animals, and ecosystems, which can be grouped into artefacts and things. Artefacts designate "physical objects made or shaped by human hand" (Scholar, 2017, p. 4) while things refer to the physical world that exists largely independent of human work.[2]

Competent bodies, meanings, and materials are closely intertwined and depend on each other. Meanings, for instance, do not exist outside of bodies' capacity to memorize and reproduce information, voice political ideologies and articulate creative ideas. Bodies shape artefacts and in turn use clothing, cell-phones, and prison walls to convey meanings to, share information with, and exert physical power over other bodies and things. Materials such as documents or computers allow for new abilities to develop, such as reading or using the internet, and meanings to emerge, such as the aesthetics of a well-written novel or the notion of trolling. While there is analytical merit in distinguishing between different elements (Shove et al., 2012), one needs to be well aware that social phenomena are always the result of their complex interaction.

In the same vein, further useful theoretical distinctions – such as those between practice (non-countable) and practices (countable), and between practices-as-performances and practices-as-entities – have to be understood in decidedly analytical rather than ontological terms. The non-countable noun 'practice', here, refers to the bodily effectuation of social phenomena in their entirety. Practice, therefore, describes the "whole of human action" (Reckwitz, 2002, p. 249). Practices, in turn, are individuated segments of that 'whole' which are identified by an observer, often using everyday verb forms (Hirschauer, 2016). Practice theorists, consequently, see the world as constituted through an infinite number of "doings and sayings" (Schatzki, 2012).

The analytical distinction between practices-as-performances and practices-as-entities (Shove et al., 2012), in turn, emphasizes practices' double character as pattern and activity. Reckwitz (2002, p. 250) states that "a practice is a pattern which

---

2   Things are a particularly tricky category. While there are sophisticated arguments against the separation of nature and culture (Latour, 1993) and its political consequences (Patel and Moore, 2018), others maintain that hybridity erodes radical environmentalist politics (Malm, 2018). Lacking space to engage in a deeper discussion, this work acknowledges that things exist and unfold independently of human activity but are primarily relevant in their enrolment into human practice – for example in practices of observation, abstraction, pollution, sustenance, and so forth.

can be filled out by a multitude of single and often unique actions reproducing the practice" (see also Schatzki, 1996). The notion of practice-as-entity, consequently, abstracts from the idiosyncrasy of individual enactments in favor of a general pattern or type of doing. The focus, then, is, for instance, on the practice of driving as a type of activity rather than a singular instance of movement using a vehicle. Yet, the pattern only exists by means of multiple individual and idiosyncratic enactments that fill out the pattern and thus (re)produce driving as cultural technique. Practice-as-performance, ergo, refers to the specific actualization of a practice. The distinction between practices-as-entities and practices-as-performances, furthermore, sharpens the perspective on the interaction of performance and materialization. Practices-as-performances are situated and specific enactments of practice while practices-as-entities refer to materialized sets of interconnected elements. Whereas the former focuses on the performance of a practice which is context specific and therefore subject to certain conditions, the latter focuses on the general pattern of activity that, while conditioned, is itself part of a material context and affects other activities in turn. In their performance, 'doings and sayings' are inevitably embedded within broader alignments of related practices and, therefore, to some extent, conditioned. At the same time, each performance is a materialization of social dynamics, conditioning other practices in turn.

Locating the social in practices – conventionalized patterns of activity materialized in competent bodies, artefacts, and things which are reproduced as well as transformed through their recurrent enactment – breaks with agency and structure as explanantia. Practice theory conceives social phenomena in their historical genesis as contingent yet material performances. Human activity, from this perspective, unfolds through spatially and historically dispersed nexuses of practices. Structures, then, consist in the "routinization" of practice (Reckwitz, 2002, p. 255) while individual agents are its carriers, participants, and architects. Neither agency nor structure determine practice. Rather, both emerge from the continuous movement of practice. Practice theory's central tenet – congruent with the poststructuralist insights outlined above – is that dualisms such as structure/agency, culture/materiality, stability/change, mind/body, and micro/macro merge in this recurring making of the world. Such a 'flat ontology' (DeLanda, 2006; Schatzki, 2016b) has a number of consequences that I will shortly reflect on in the following.

First, conceiving of practices as locus of the social – rather than material structures, regimes of signification, or the minds and bodies of individuals – puts the co-constitution of cultural/mental and material/bodily moments on equal footing without privileging one over the other *ex-ante*. Practice theory, then, assumes an ontological sameness of the various elements of practice which become relevant in and through interaction. Social life transpires through the imbrication of objects, texts, bodies, knowledges, and meanings that are bounded together in the unfolding of human activity. Discourse and culture are always material – inscribed into competent and habituated bodies – while artefacts and things are socially mediated.

Second, this flat ontology has profound spatial consequences. Practice theory sees practice formations – for example markets, the education system, organizations, or friendship – as constellations or aspects of practices (Schatzki, 2016b). Like the elements of practice, all constituent parts of social phenomena share an ontological sameness. Scalar differences – as suggested by the terminology of micro/macro or local/global – are not a function of distinct planes of reality but are made in practice (including discursive practices, in reference to community economy scholarship). Instead of a (hierarchically) layered reality, practice theory proposes a 'site ontology' (Schatzki, 2003; Marston et al., 2005; Everts, 2016).[3] Site refers both to a more metaphorical interconnectedness of human activity and the temporal and spatial localities in which human co-existence unfolds. Site, therefore, spatializes the processual materiality of the social (see below).

This brings us to the third aspect, that of repetition. Stability and change, for practice theorists, are two sides of the same coin. In conceptualizing the world as dynamic, social phenomena are seen as always in the making. Markets, states, and other practice-formations are premised on their recurrent enactment and thus exist as "routines of social practice" (Reckwitz, 2002, p. 255). This, however does not make them "less solid" (Nicolini, 2013, p. 3). Social phenomena gain stability through their routinized (re)enactment and (re)constitution (see subsequent section). The continuous reproduction of social phenomena, simultaneously, leaves leeway for ruptures, mutations, and shifts and thus opens possibilities for change. Schäfer (2016a), therefore, proposes to conceptualize the continuous (re)enactment of practice as repetition – implying simultaneous moments of difference and sameness.

Finally, practice theory reflects on the practice of research itself (Geiselhart et al., 2019). Research is inevitably contextual which renders universal and decontextualized claims problematic. Practice theory, therefore, takes into account the concrete spatio-temporalities in which research practices are situated and to which they pertain. This is another strong point of contact with community economy scholarship that follows a weak form of theory that refuses to "know too much" (Gibson-Graham, 2008, p. 619). Reflecting on research as a practice has particular consequences for the study's methodological considerations (see chapter 10).

---

3   Depending on preference and emphasis different authors speak of a 'flat ontology' or 'site ontology'. In the following I use both notions with a similar meaning that all social life is made of the same ingredients and does not unfold in ontologically different spheres. Occasionally, I use the term 'processual ontology', highlighting the fact that all social entities are constantly in flux.

As "poststructural materialism" (Hillebrandt, 2016, p. 72) practice theory integrates poststructuralism's anti-essentialism, anti-universalism, and orientation towards difference with materialism's accentuation of historical-geographical patterns of human relatedness. Processual and relational thinking defuses the reductionist tendencies of structural and agential perspectives. Neither structure nor agency, materiality nor meaning precede human activity and provide a privileged perspective onto the world. Instead, structure and agency transpire through the multiform processes of human and more-than-human activity,[4] and with it the possibilities and constraints of transformation. A conception of transformative geographies, therefore, cannot build on either category alone but needs to be grounded in a perspective on social dynamics. In addition to the (discursive) openings of community economy scholarship, it needs to be able to account for stability – an issue that I turn to in the subsequent section by looking at organizations and institutions as materialized sets of interconnected practices.

Institutions and organizations in practice

Practices and institutions are two sides of the same coin. While 'practice' implies the doing of something and therefore activity, 'institution' signals stability and fixity. Institution derives from the Latin 'institutum' which is the "noun use of neuter past participle of instituere" and literally means "thing set up" (etymonline.com). This nominalization already hints at the conceptual, discursive, and material fixation of a process rather than a stable entity in and of itself. In this way, practice theory's processual ontology conceives of stability as the result of repetitive or routinized enactments. Institutions, say taxation, only exist as long as they are actualized in practice, for instance, through tax collection, accounting, control, and punishment for tax evasion. Practices are anchored (materialized) in bodies, artefacts, things, and in their positioning in relation to each other. Bodies and minds, for instance, remember – in a broad sense – meanings, bodily movements, patterns of behavior, manners, and reactions. Books, documents, films, and computers store images, sounds, writings, and other forms of text, while the layout of a city expresses past ideas, technologies, and social relations. Cleared woodlands materialize mining for coal and oceanic ecosystems a rise in CO_2 levels, the use of plastic, and practices of (over)fishing. Practices' enactment always builds on the materialization of (previous) activities and is therefore not presupposition-less,

---

4   I include the more-than-human here to acknowledge that also animal behaviour, for instance, can play an important role in social processes. I distance, however, from perspectives that equate human agency with that of animals, plants or things, the discussion of which is beyond the scope of this work.

but shaped, conditioned, and enabled. Human activities, therefore form "chains of actions" (Schatzki, 2016a; Everts, 2016) and "chains of practices" (Nicolini, 2013) – linking activities across time and space.

Taxation, for example, is an institution that developed over millennia during which its practices have continuously shifted in combination with spatio-historical contexts. From the tithe on peasants' yield revolving around royal directives, travelling tax collectors, and the estimation of harvest and possessions, to a complex system of added-value tax, income tax, dividend tax, environmental taxes, and multiple operations revolving around accounting, bookkeeping, tax offices, and tax declarations. In any point in time, these practices hang together and intersect with multiple other activities such as filling out forms, walking to the post office, and hoping for return payments. The introduction of new elements can also fundamentally change these nexuses, as computers, the internet, and programs for electronic tax declaration. All these activities hang together forming chains of action, which make and remake the institution of taxation.

Chains of action, in turn, materialize in bodies – that are capable of filing a tax form, break out in sweat at the thought of it, or rage against 'the greedy state' – and artefacts – pay slips, data-bases, and statute books. Processuality and materiality are constantly at play, conditioning, causing, necessitating, and obstructing each other. Aforementioned distinction between practices-as-entities and practices-as-performances is helpful to disentangle analytically both moments. To recap: practices-as-entities are materialized sets of interconnected elements, while practices-as-performances refer to situated and specific enactments of practice. The concept of 'practice-as-entity', then, is a snapshot in time. It fixates analytically the continuous unfolding of social life and looks at the elements that compose a practice, for instance, false tax statements, motivations to evade payments, and bodies capable of committing fraud, and deduces a pattern therefrom, such as tax-evasion. The concept of 'practice-as-performance', in turn, describes the "immediacy of doing" through which "the 'pattern' provided by the practice-as-an-entity is filled out and reproduced" (Shove et al., 2012, p. 7), for instance a specific act of fiscal evasion.

In the same vein, we can conceive of institutions-as-entities and institutions-as-performances. As entities, institutions consist of heterogeneous elements including materials, meanings, and socialized bodies. As performances, institutions are actualized in a range of activities that themselves might be conceptualized as practices. Institutions, therefore, do not exist outside of practices but "as forms of ongoing and relatively stable patterns of social practice based on mutual expectations that owe their existence to either purposeful constitutions or unintentional emergence" (Bathelt and Glückler, 2014, p. 346). Taxation, therefore, indeed is a complex nexus that binds together laws, regulations, statute books, state administrators, and accountants. But it only exists through the innumerable practices of accounting, filling out forms, controlling, and punishing. Like practice, institutions are conventionalized patterns 'filled out' through concrete performances.

Organizations, on a similar note, constitute a form of instituted practice. They are "constantly in the process of becoming – dynamic, multiple, performative, and open-ended – resulting from networks of different practices of organizing and knowing" (Pallett and Chilvers, 2015, p. 151). Like institutions, organizations are practice-formations that consist of multiple interweaving practices hanging together and forming co-dependent constellations of human activity. An accountancy firm, for instance, is not a 'thing', but a complex of communicating, accounting, filing, marketing, and a host of other practices. From a practice theory perspective, then, organizations "have to be materially produced time and again through 'eventful' practices" (Hillebrandt, 2016, p. 72; author's translation). Both organizations and institutions "can only be understood as materializations of practices *in actu*, and are *per definitionem* events" (ibid.).

Organizations and institutions share a certain degree of continuity and stability which is the result of permanent work. With respect to institutions, this work is deeply embedded in social routines and habits, making institutions often appear as natural (which is particularly problematic when used to legitimize unjust and exploitative relations). Organizations, in contrast, generally can be identified as deliberately established formations serving a definable purpose. Although there is no clear-cut distinction between organizations and institutions, the latter generally lack visible agents or members. Taxation, for instance, as described above, consists of complex chains of actions that are strongly rooted in habits and routines exceeding governmental and associated bodies. Organizations, instead, describe entities such as a particular governmental panel, taxation office, or police station involved in defining and enforcing a tax. In actual practice, of course, institutions and organizations are closely imbricated. While institutions carry a more passive and inconspicuous connotation, organizations refer to functionally linked bodies that allow distinguishing between members and non-members.

Considering organizations as practice-formations, however, blurs their boundaries as well. An organization, say a capitalist enterprise, is not a self-contained entity but a porous constellation that hinges on a vast number of performances marginal to, or outside of the organization's formal core. For instance, the cooking and care practices that enable a worker to regenerate after a day's work, the sharing of information on knowledge commons like Wikipedia that allow a manager to skim an issue, or, more broadly speaking, relatively stable social relations and the political enforcement of framework conditions such as private property rights. A processual view of organizations, therefore, "has motivated a shift away from a focus on purely internal organizational trends and changes to an awareness of broader trends and influences external to any given organization" (Pallett and Chilvers, 2015, p. 149). The same applies to institutions, say markets. Conceiving of markets as practice formations that depend on a vast number of non-market performances (re)embeds market institutions into social relations (Polanyi, 2001 [1944]).

Organizations (and institutions), then – and here it is helpful to draw on ANT and assemblage terminology (Latour, 2005; Müller, 2015) – are heterogeneous assemblages of bodies, artefacts, motivations, teloi, information, and other elements that act in networks. Or, to use a practice-theoretical wording, organizations and institutions are patterns of human activity that hang together forming "complexes" (Shove et al., 2012, p. 17) or "constellations" (Schatzki, 2016a, p. 6) of practices. Activity, here, is a function of a non-bounded network of elements that escapes action theory's focus on intentionality. This is important insofar, as references such as 'organizational practices', as used in the following, by no means construe a homogenous entity, let alone an intentional actor. Rather, organizational practices refer to the diverse conventionalized activities that (re)produce a given organization. In this respect, practice theory aligns with community economy scholarship in emphasizing the multifacetedness and performativity of organizations and institutions, an aspect that the subsequent chapter turns to in more detail.

Chapter 6: Scale and power in transformative geographies

> Rather than thinking of the emphases on domination or on constitution as belonging to two incompatible ways of thinking about power, we might be better served to view them as two emphases combined in different ways by different traditions of thought.
> *Barnett, 2017, p. 26*

Practice theory resonates with community economy scholarship in several ways. Both practice theory and community economy thinking "abandon the ontological privileging of systemic or structural determination" (Gibson-Graham, 2008, p. 623). In doing so, both focus on performance and advance a fundamentally processual view of the social. The language of practices itself goes to the heart of the community economy project. Distancing from totalizing notions of economy, the market and other capitalist institutions, community economy scholars turn towards the diversity of *economic practices* – widely opening the field of what it means to be economically in-common. They do so using a weak form of theory and a thick description of economic practice (Gibson-Graham, 2014), which resonates with practice-theoretical approaches conceptually and methodologically (a more detailed elaboration of the latter follows in part III).

Despite these commonalities, there are fundamental points of divergence between both schools of thought. As outlined above, community economy scholarship focuses primarily on shifts in meaning, in particular the disidentification with and dissociation from capitalocentric discourse. Although community economy scholars acknowledge that which "pushes back" (Gibson-Graham, 2006, p. 23) at transformative political projects, they do so primarily in the realm of meaning. Gibson-Graham, for instance, look at the numbers (ibid., p. 27ff.), vocabularies (ibid., p. 33ff.), and grids of visualization (ibid., p. 41ff.) that constitute instruments of subjection. Their perspective on economic practice, consequently, lacks considerations around the institutions, infrastructures, and resources that are involved in, facilitate, and push back at transformative geographies.

Practice theory's focus on the materialization of human co-existence in bodies, artefacts, and things, then, provides a promising corrective or addition to the discursive approach of community economists. However, applications of practice theory in transition research, too, frequently lack adequate consideration of relations of power and the role of 'large-scale' institutions (see chapter 3). Having discarded structures as explanans, practice theorists are challenged to reintroduce a notion of hierarchy – in the sense of uneven power relations – not as spatial a priori, but as socially produced differences in the capacity to act. This chapter takes on the task of formulating practice-theoretical concepts of scale and power. In doing so, it takes inspiration from community economy scholarship, offering a synergistic reading of both theoretical avenues. The two sections of this chapter, one on scale and one on power, advance two related conceptual arguments. First, the imbrication of spatial and social moments of potentiality. And second, the acknowledgement of the double sidedness of power as both domination and potential.

Scale

Practice theory and community economy scholarship both proceed from a flat ontology in their conceptualization of the social. Turning to assemblage thinking, Roelvink et al. (2015, p. 16) reason that "the local and global are outcomes of particular networks and associations rather than inherent qualities or capacities". Notwithstanding the differences between practice theory and assemblage thinking (Gherardi, 2016; see also digression above), both share a processual conception of practices, organizations, institutions, and ultimately the social itself.

> This view makes untenable old ways of theorizing that postulate separate levels of reality and the existence of superstructures and similar paraphernalia. Practice theories are inherently relational and see the world as a seamless assemblage, nexus, or confederation of practices – although not all having the same relevance (Nicolini, 2013, p. 3).

Geographers long have conceptualized space relationally (M. Jones, 2009; Massey, 2005; Thrift, 1996). Relationality, here, refers to the idea that space does not exist for itself but through socio-material objects and their relations. That means, "objects are space, space is objects, and moreover objects can be understood only in relation to other objects – with all this being a perpetual becoming of heterogeneous networks and events that connect internal spatiotemporal relations" (M. Jones, 2009, p. 491). Turning towards the continuous becoming of space, theories of relational space reject the notion that space is hierarchically structured in and of itself. Space, for thinkers like Thrift (2004, p. 59), does not constitute "a nested hierarchy moving from 'global' to 'local'" the notion of which he thinks is "absurd". Instead, horizontal metaphors such as connectivity, flow, network, assemblage, and entanglement describe the geographies of relational thought. Some geographers, therefore, turn to a site ontology and propose the elimination of scale as a concept in human geography (Marston et al., 2005).

Site, as it is interpreted and adapted here, wavers between two closely related meanings. First, as a temporal and spatial moment and locality in which human co-existence unfolds. And second, as a context constituted through the interaction of different elements and activities (Schatzki, 2003; Everts, 2016). In the first instance, site refers to something akin to place, a locale where chains of activity intersect temporally and spatially through the co-presence of bodies, meanings, and materials. In addition to this, site carries a contextual sensitivity for the patterns in which human activity is set and simultaneously is constitutive of (that is practices). The two-sidedness of site reflects the analytical distinction between practices-as-performances (human activity at concrete places and moments in time) and practices-as-entities (general patterns and types of doing that constitute the context for social activity). Only when drawn together, practices-as-performances and practices-as-entities explain the constant unfolding of human co-existence through a historically and spatially situated repertoire of types of behavior (see chapter 5). Site spatializes the processual materiality of the social insofar as it links performance and context. Without hierarchizing space, a perspective on site provides a window into the performance of social hierarchies (Schmid, 2019a).

Against the background of a site ontology, drawing a dividing line between hierarchical and non-hierarchical notions of space is misleading. In fact, many geographers would agree that scale is socially produced while still disagreeing with Marston et al.'s (2005) call for abandoning scale. Jonas (2006, p. 404) identifies a false "'site-versus-scale' dualism" in the debate around spatial hierarchy. "Many so-called 'scalists'", Jones maintains, "are not writing about 'scales-as-fixed-structures'; nor are they treating scalar territories as 'vertical structures'; or 'rational abstractions' in the realist sense". What is of concern here, instead, in the social production of scale or hierarchy. While some rightly criticize a non-reflective application of scalar categories and seek to deconstruct hierarchical space, others justifiably maintain that scale continues to have effect within social practice and constitutes an important spatial category. The latter critique argues that "the advocates of thinking space relationally seriously overstate their case. Despite the multiple potentials of space flagged in relational thinking, factors can constrain and structure space. All things considered potential does not necessarily become an actual" (M. Jones, 2009, p. 493).

There is a profoundly political moment in the site-versus-scale debate (see interlude I). The opposition of hierarchical and non-hierarchical perspectives on space translates as tension between a politics of hope and possibility on the one hand, and a focus on institutions, routinization, and material constraints on the other hand into the literature on transformation (more often so implicitly than explicitly). A focus on possibility, thereby, frees itself from the identification with capitalism (Gibson-Graham, 2006) and other forms of "macro-mystification" (Marston et al., 2005, p. 427). Instead it focuses on the sites of alternative practices that prefigure 'other worlds' (Roelvink et al., 2015) and 'autonomous geographies' (Pickerill and Chatterton, 2006). Skeptical approaches, in contrast, remind us that although hierarchies are socially produced, transformation inevitably originates from within the given socio-spatial relations and is thus conditioned by present institutional orders (Buch-Hansen, 2018; Joutsenvirta, 2016; van den Bergh, 2011).

Practice theory neither privileges scale's constructedness nor its materialization and conceptualizes scale through the links, dependencies, and tensions amongst practices. Practices form "arrays that can be thinner or thicker, more compact or spread out, continuing and fleeting, and patterned or scattered" (Schatzki, 2016a, p. 6). That means, practices transpire through different densities, coherences, and solidities that exert influence on other practices. Constellations or complexes of practices, thus, create hierarchies in the sense that they order or structure the social world (an argument that the subsequent section on power outlines in more detail). These hierarchies are not ontologically given but emerge through alignments of human activity, unfolding on a single plane of reality. Schatzki (2016a, p. 6) develops a nested terminology including activities, practices, practice-arrangement bundles, constellations (which are "nothing but larger bundles"), large social phenomena ("far-flung constellation of practices"), and the plenum (which are practices and arrangements in their entirety). In doing so, Schatzki provides a vocabulary to describe social phenomena of different extent without reverting to higher or lower orders.

Schatzki provides an approach that takes seriously the existence of extensive and tightly knit constellations of mutually reinforcing, dependent, and stabilizing practices – say, lawmaking, taxation, and policing – without locating the institutions they create – say, governments, or the state – on a higher echelon. Governments, transnational corporations, and world markets, for Schatzki, are 'large social phenomena' that result from complex and interwoven chains of mutually dependent actions and practices (see also Everts, 2016; Nicolini, 2013). Large social phenomena are real in their effects but socially produced through their continuous enactment in practice. This conceptualization does not reify constellations and large phenomena as independent entities existing outside of practice. But it acknowledges the solidities and densities that emerge from chains of actions and practices.

The neat terminology of bundles, constellations, and large social phenomena, however, runs the risk of slicing the social world into convenient building blocks that abstract from its complexity and emergence. In particular the term 'large social phenomena' is problematic is several ways. Speaking of phenomena suggests the existence of bounded empirical entities independent from an observer's perspective. Chapter 7, in this sense, turns to the issue of typing practices and constellations. Furthermore, the notion of 'large' evokes a return to the spatial hierarchizing relational perspectives seek to overcome. Upon a closer look, it is not the spatial extent of a practice or practice-formation that is of relevance but the ways it summons and orders other practices. From the relational perspective of a site ontology, then, scale works through the reach, scope, and alignment of practices and their constellations. A practice-theoretical concept of scale is closely imbricated with power to which I will turn next.

Power

In a quote introduced above, Nicolini (2013, p. 2) describes the social world as "vast array or assemblage of performances made durable [materialized] by being inscribed in human bodies and minds, objects and texts, and knotted together in such a way that the results of one performance become the resource for another". Thus far, I have primarily focused on the first part of Nicolini's statement: the materialization of performances in bodies, artefacts, things, and chains of action. This section, now, specifies how previous performances condition further activity.

Practices are always conditioned by a temporal and/or spatial 'elsewhere' (Schmid and Smith, 2020). 'Elsewhere' means that the enactment of a practice is always situated in a larger context that is beyond the direct control or influence of its practitioners. Elsewhere is both temporal – the historical trajectories that have formed subjects, discourses, and institutions – and spatial – the positioning of subjects, discourses, and institutions in relation to each other. This is what the concept of site expresses (see above). Any performance, therefore, has a site of enactment that includes the interconnectedness with other practices as well as their geographies. Grasping conditioning moments of practice premises a notion of power compatible with practice theory's processual ontology.

Power is generally used in a twofold sense (Allen, 2017). 'Power over' refers to the ability of individuals or groups to force, coerce, persuade, or nudge someone to engage in or abstain from particular activities. 'Power to', in contrast, refers to the ability to "get things done" or "make things happen" (Allen, 2017, p. 1). Against the background of practice theory's flat ontology, individual agency and structural determination drop out as sources of power. That means subjects, objects, organizations, or institutions cannot possess power in and off themselves. Rather, power, from a practice theory perspective, is fundamentally relational. Practices' conditioning emerges from the historically shaped positioning of subjects, discourses, and institutions in relation to each other. Power, therefore, "must be understood as an effect of performances of practices, not as something external to them" (Watson, 2017, p. 171). That means, while practice theory acknowledges that individuals and groups can exercise 'power over' someone or something – respectively having 'power to' accomplish something – this capacity does not reside within subjects themselves. Instead, power is highly contextual and necessitates the consideration of how subjects, the activities they engage in and the capabilities, discourses, artefacts, and things they draw on are positioned in relation to each other.

Wartenberg (1990), who takes his cue from Foucauldian and feminist theories of power, provides a helpful notion to think power relationally: that of alignment. He uses alignment "to refer to the structure of social relationships that are necessary for constituting a situated power relationship" (Wartenberg, 1990, p. 149). In doing so, he emphasizes the "'relative positioning' of social others" (ibid.). Although Wartenberg does not argue from a practice theory perspective, his notion of alignment is helpful for theorizing power. Understanding social positioning as something that happens in and through practice, exposes power as both emerging from and taking effect on practice. A practice's 'elsewhere', then, translates into the positioning of other practices in relation to it. Or, more generally, power emerges from the way practices are aligned with and towards each other. To understand the power that transpires through capitalist social relations, then, requires looking at the way economic practices relate to each other, align in particular ways, and form specific contexts that privilege some forms of sustenance over others.

> The alignment, for instance, of practices of production, distribution, and regulation through price, profit-interests, and property relations produces constraints and possibilities for the material sustenance of society. The power relationship between capitalist and non-capitalist forms of material sustenance, then, can only be understood when taking into account the ways in which different alignments condition livelihood options [...] Capitalism per se does not have power over non-capitalist practices. However, within capitalist social relations, practices are aligned in ways that impede some non-capitalist forms of sustenance and thus limit the options for non-capitalist production and distribution (Schmid and Smith, 2020, p. 9).

Conceptualizing power as practices' alignments is in agreement with practice theory's tenets of processuality and materiality. While acknowledging the situated power that emerges from capitalist social relations, to stick with the example of interest here, such a perspective simultaneously de-centers power. Power does not reside in the structure of capitalism or in the subject of the capitalist but in the ways in which economic practices relate to each other.

When power emerges from the alignments of practices, then a shift in practices can affect shifts in power relations. In this sense, transformation is a possibility which is both constrained and enabled by current alignments of practices. That means, while there is certainly a form of structuration of social relations, which in the terminology established above can be referred to as institutions-as-entities, a relational conception of power retains two important openings for change: repetition and emancipatory alignments. Repetition, the continuous work needed to reproduce practices- and institutions-as-entities, leaves leeway for ruptures, mutations, and shifts (see interlude II). Institutions, furthermore, are not necessarily dominative and restraining but can also be enabling and emancipatory.

Power, as alignment of practices, then, can be both dominative and transformative. As Barnett states in the introductory quote of this chapter, a theory of power should consider both domination and constitution making visible power's 'double-sidedness' or 'double potentiality' (Saar, 2014: 10, see also Saar, 2010; Barnett, 2017; Hardt and Negri, 2004, 2017). Following community economy scholarship, economic practices are not solely aligned through profit interest and as markets but also along non-capitalist dimensions. Power, as potential, transpires likewise through the alignment of economic practices alongside trust, volunteering, gratitude, solidarity, and dignity. Emancipation and materialization, then, are not to be thought of as opposites in the context of transformative geographies. Rather, the materialization of possibility in emancipatory alignments is an essential ingredient of postcapitalist transformation. Transformation, therefore, is not solely about overcoming power but as much about harnessing power's transformative potential to further societal change. Making visible the power that emerges from practice alignments beyond wage labor, price, private property, and others opens pathways for the recognition of the materiality of postcapitalist possibility. The next chapter, now, turns to the question of how transformation in practice might unfold through changes in practices, their elements and their alignments in more detail.

Chapter 7: From transformative geographies to a degrowth transition

> While there is no general formula, there are nonetheless some guidelines we can formulate from our analysis for forming collective actors to effectively erode capitalism.
> *Wright, 2019, p. 142*

So far, part II has laid a conceptual foundation for transformative geographies. Starting with the reimagination of togetherness, chapter 5 has continued by grounding transformation materially in the bodies, artefacts, and things of everyday practice. Subsequently, chapter 6 has proposed an understanding of scale, power, and transformation against the background of a 'poststructural materialism'. Chapter 7, now, returns to the distinction between transformation and transition which was established in part I. While transformation focuses on the unfolding human and more-than-human dynamic and the negotiation of its directionality, transition emphasizes the (strategic) passage from one state of affairs to another. Transition, therefore gives the abstract deliberations on transformation more practical leverage. To that effect, chapter 7 operationalizes the conceptual considerations for empirical research of a degrowth transition. It starts out by taking a look at interventions in practice. The second section, then, turns towards degrowth as scholarly and activist debate that can inform transformative strategies. In doing so, it elaborates the notions of degrowth practice and degrowth politics. Finally, the third section passes over to the study's methodology by proposing a 'diverse logics perspective' in order to research a degrowth transition.

Interventions in practice

Transformation, from a practice-theoretical perspective, is a nonlinear and complex process revolving around the emergence, stabilization, and decline of practices and their broader constellations. Practices are anchored in bodies, artefacts, and things, stabilizing over time and space through habitual and repetitive performances. While accounting for the relative stability and path dependency of social institutions, a perspective on the recurrent enactment of practices stays sensitive and open to change (see above). It is through the grounding of sameness and otherness in the routinized movement of practice that practice theory captures the performativity and contingency as well as the repetitiveness and materiality of social phenomena (Hillebrandt, 2016; Schäfer, 2016a).

Targeted interventions can destabilize individual practices and their alignments and, in doing so, catalyze change. Spurling and McMeekin (2015) and Shove et al. (2012) suggest different 'intervention framings' into practice (see chapter 3). While these framings are concerned with policy specifically, interventions can occur in different areas and have other initiators apart from policy-makers, such as social activists, eco-social entrepreneurs, and civil society in general. Still, the aforementioned proposals provide an entry point to consider interventions in practice. By and large, the 'intervention framings' outlined in chapter 3 can be grouped into two broad categories. First, interventions that target individual practices and revolve around changing their elements or substituting practices as a whole. For instance, changing the materials of driving by switching to electric cars, or substituting driving with cycling by promoting the latter. Second, interventions that target nexuses of practices. For instance, by changing practices associated with driving such as work and grocery shopping, or by supporting communities that take up low-carbon lifestyles that include cycling.

Intervention on the level of individual practices expresses itself either as the reconfiguration of practices' elements or the shift towards other practices entirely. Both aspects are closely related (at what point does a practice become a different practice?) and require some reflection on the typing of practices, an issue that I will turn to below. A change of the elements of mobility practices – say, their materials such as, for instance, the substitution of combustion engines with electromotors, or the conversion of car lanes into cycling paths – can modify driving practices or support the replacement of driving by cycling. A focus on individual practices and their elements, however, neglects the wider constellations and formations practices are embedded in and thus the power that transpires through practices' alignments. Incumbent economic and political institutions, for which automobile and fossil industries are 'system-relevant', are likely to prevent a fundamental shift away from carbon-intensive and car-based mobility patterns. Policy interventions that support a shift in driving practices, for instance through subsidies of electric cars, still ignore a range of other issues that surround electromobility such as the extraction of conflict materials. Consequently they, too, stabilize rather than transform incumbent constellations of practices, ranging from car-centered urban planning to human rights violations. A substitution of driving by cycling, one the other hand, addresses some of these issues more profoundly but runs the risk of remaining particularistic.

While specific practices or their elements are entry points for intervention, a perspective on transformation cannot be restricted to practices in isolation. Spurling and McMeekin (2015, p. 88) – to stick with the example of mobility – explore how mobility interlocks with other practices such as working, shopping, or leisure. In doing so, they consider interventions that change the patterns of mobility practices such as e-shopping and working from home. An intervention framing that transcends the reconfiguration of isolated practices and attends to the ways in which (multiple) shifts affect practices' broader nexuses provides a perspective for wider change. In order to formulate a degrowth transition research agenda, however, this approach needs further development for three reasons. First, the interventions required for a transition beyond growth-dependence are considerably more comprehensive than the reconfiguration of nexuses around, say, mobility practices. Second, a perspective on more profound realignments of social practice requires the awareness of power relations. A degrowth transition is likely to be met by antagonism and resistance. Accordingly, central impulses, at least at an early stage of transition, presumably originate from outside of formal politics and economy. Third, due to the previous points, intervention requires a more profound and radical framing, that means a plausible conception of how practices' alignments can fundamentally change.

Towards a degrowth transition

Interventions in practices and their alignments – for instance in patterns of mobility or relations of production, consumption, and exchange – require political articulations and the collective enactment of positivity. That means interventions premise an (at least temporary) fixation of values, ideas, relations, and identities (see chapter 4). Transformation, consequently, develops a directionality. So far, however, this part follows a broad notion of emancipatory politics without a more concise definition of its parameters and their consequences for social change. To address this disjuncture, I return to the etymologically grounded differentiation between transformation and transition which was developed in chapter 3. While transformation foregrounds the ontology of social dynamics and its politics – issues that the previous chapters explore – transition is concerned with goal-oriented and purposive change. To push this work along more practical lines, the remainder of this chapter integrates the considerations around growth outlined in part I with deliberations on transformation, formulating a research agenda around a degrowth transition and strategy.

Degrowth, thereby, provides a program that is broad and flexible enough to maintain a transformative politics and tangible enough to devise strategies and guide transitional dynamics. It combines a range of imaginaries, principles, practices, and institutions of socio-economic organizing, centering around well-being, justice, and sustainability instead of accumulation and profit. Kallis (2018, p. 118ff.) proposes nine principles that capture the political articulations and fixations of sustainable degrowth. First, degrowth is based on the vision of an egalitarian and classless society without exploitative economic relations. Second, degrowth envisions processes of direct democracy through assemblies at different levels that substitute and complement more abstract forms of representation. Third, production, trade, and consumption in a degrowth society are regionalized and localized as well as reduced through reuse and recycling. Fourth, communities share resources, work, infrastructures, knowledge, and space by organizing them as commons. Fifth, prosperity and wellbeing are defined primarily through healthy relationships rather than material possessions. Sixth, in contrast to the logic of return on investment, resources are also used for 'unproductive expenditures' for the sake of aesthetics and pleasure instead of gain. Seventh, care work is valued as collective responsibility and purpose that is evenly distributed and not skewed along gender or class lines. Eight, degrowth economies are constituted through diverse forms of work, exchange, and organization. And ninth, land, labor, and value are decommodified.

Degrowth's principles, by and large, are in line with other alternative approaches that convene around the notions of postcapitalism and commons (see chapter 2). The principles' scope and openness, thus, render them suitable to guide transitional practice in line with the political and ethical coordinates established in part I. A perspective on a degrowth transition in practice, however, requires criteria through which appropriate interventions, movements, and strategies can be identified. Two questions arise: *what patterns of activity need to be established and conventionalized to translate degrowth's principles into practice?* And *how can degrowth practices shift social alignments towards a degrowth trajectory?* As a matter of course, these questions cannot be answered without empirical evidence. At the same time, there is a need for methodological-analytical guidelines that facilitate the gathering of empirical material on such a complex issue. Answering both questions, consequently, will remain a task throughout the following chapters. In order to pave the ground, this next section develops preliminary notions of 'degrowth practices' and 'degrowth politics' for subsequent chapters to build on.

Degrowth practices and politics

Degrowth's principles enroll and touch upon diverse dimensions of social co-existence including work, mobility, housing, production, and consumption. Each area contains numberless (partially overlapping) activities that can be more or less in line with degrowth's principles. To single out particular practices that activate transitional dynamics is problematic for two reasons. First, the relation of, say, consumption, mobility, and driving shows that the typing of practices significantly differs with respect to its frame of reference. While driving is a type of mobility and a type of consumption, the latter are increasingly comprehensive categories. The question, then, arises, how can practices be typified? Second, most practices that are associated with degrowth, such as cycling – 'socialism can only arrive on a bicycle' (Jose Antonio Viera Gallo) – do not challenge growth-based economies per se. Both aspects need further deliberation.

Practices are generally described through the use of everyday verb forms such as driving, cycling, repairing, and sharing.

> Practices [...] can be identified when action is considered a cultural technique. Only an observer can typologize practices into individual forms. Practices are (like complex actions or discourses) an observer's scheme, namely one identifying formal patterns, which means ways of doing. For a start, observers draw on a rudimentary individuation through everyday verb forms (running, counting...) (Hirschauer, 2016, p. 60, author's translation).

Everyday verb forms, however, are too general a template to characterize degrowth practices. Cycling, for instance, can substitute driving. But it can also occur in the context of a global championship for which cyclist fly around the world. Or repair – another practice that is frequently discussed with reference to postcapitalist economies (Baier et al., 2016) – can contribute to material sustenance, reduce resource consumption, or be a source of revenue and accumulation. Degrowth practice, therefore, can only be a relational notion that takes into account how practices relate to their context (see above). A preliminary definition, therefore, might describe degrowth practices as *conventionalized patterns of activity that translate degrowth's principles into practice*.

To take effect on social alignments in a magnitude that would constitute a degrowth transition, furthermore, degrowth needs to devise political strategies. Politics, from a practice theory perspective, transpire through practices that "explicitly or implicitly attend to, question, or put to the test [...] the plenum of practices itself or slices and aspects thereof" (Dünckmann and Fladvad, 2016, p. 29). In other words, politics express the (deliberate) interference with practices' broader alignments. Dünckmann and Fladvad (2016) describe politics as "the practice of changing the rules of practice". This entails two moments: first that of reflexivity and second that of relatedness. Practices, consequently, are political when they consciously relate back to the plenum of practices (*reflexivity*) and, however minutely, direct the plenum of practices or slices thereof (relatedness).[1] Degrowth politics, then, is the *practice of changing the rules of practice to support parallel and mutually enforcing processes of cultural and institutional change in line with degrowth's principles* (see also Adler, 2017). Degrowth politics, like degrowth practices, however, cannot be defined in the abstract. The next section turns towards considerations around an empirical research agenda of degrowth transition.

Operationalization: the diverse logics perspective

The book's ambition to trace possibilities and constraints of a degrowth transition poses a major empirical challenge. This section concretizes and operationalizes the foregoing conceptual considerations around a degrowth transition in practice and points towards the study's methodology. As the foregoing section on degrowth practices and degrowth politics, it leaves some loose ends that require empirical insights. Parts III and IV, subsequently, turn towards the generation and presentation of empirical data, before part V revisits unresolved issues in light of the empirical grounding.

Transformative geographies enroll a vast number of diverse sites linked in complex webs of practices that enter relationships of dependence, causation, obstruction, enablement, and prefiguration. Broadly speaking, there are two strategies of how research can mobilize its limited resources to account for this complexity – limited in the sense that it cannot look at all places at all times. On the one hand, research can focus on a particular object, practice, or relation across and between different places and times. This often means taking a sectoral focus, for instance, tracing a specific crop, practices of farming and agricultural value chains. On the other hand, it can look at the complex interplay of objects, practices, and relations in a specific geographical context. For instance, the interdependencies within a community or neighborhood. The former approach enables the researcher to gain insights into the effects, tendencies, and interdependencies across dispersed sites. It can, however, only make limited assertions about the processes and interdependencies outside of the relations in focus. The latter approach, in turn, works to capture the complexity of relations in place. It can, however, only make limited assertions about the relations beyond that specific geographical and temporal context. Of course, there are also numerous combinations of both strategies.

---

1   My use of the notions of reflexivity and relatedness, here, differs from Dünckmann and Fladvad's use. It is, nevertheless, inspired by their conceptualization of political practices.

Empirically, this work follows the latter approach, capturing the breadth and scope of transition in place. The sites it researches, however, convene multiple practices that link to a temporal and spatial 'elsewhere' (see chapter 6). Transformative processes enroll diverse geographies beyond place which a perspective on degrowth transition needs to take into account. Conceptually, therefore, the work requires sound tools that allow it to grasp practices' relations beyond their sites of enactment. The remainder of this section develops a concept to trace practices' relatedness beyond place in three steps. First, it contemplates ways to 'structure' the diversity of practices' relatedness by analytically separating different realms of social life that enable a clearer perspective on transition. Second, it reintegrates this perspective with a flat and processual ontology that is wary of emphasizing structuredness. Finally, it develops the notion of 'diverse logics' to trace practices' various forms of relatedness across time and space (Schmid, 2018).

Structured Diversity

Social theorists have structured society into 'systems' (Luhmann, 1998, 2015), 'institutional orders' (Thornton et al., 2012), and 'worlds' (Boltanski and Thévenot, 2006). Without being able to discuss the extensive conceptual arguments behind the respective theories, I use them as inspiration to systematize diversity. Following Luhmann's system theory, Roth and Schütz, for instance, identify ten function systems of society: the political system, economy, science, art, religion, the legal system, sport, the health system, education, and mass media (Roth and Schütz, 2015). Thornton et. al. conceptualize the inter-institutional system made up of the institutional orders of family, community, religion, state, market, profession, and corporation. And Boltanski and Thévenot's society is constituted through six different worlds of common use: the inspired world, the domestic world, the world of fame, the civic world, the market world, and the industrial world. Each of these approaches opens avenues to distinguish different realms of social life. Yet the language of 'systems', 'institutional orders', and 'worlds' cannot be integrated smoothly with practice theories' ontological assumptions (see chapters 5 and 6).

To integrate a structured notion of diversity, as inspired by perspectives on systems, institutional orders, and worlds, with a flat and processual ontology, I return to the discussion of power and scale. Above, I have conceptualized power as a relational category that emerges from practices' alignments. While hierarchies exist *in practice*, they are not a pre-given quality of space itself. All practices and their larger nexuses are situated on the same plane of reality. Hierarchies in practice that unfold in a non-hierarchical spatiality confront practice theory with the challenge of operationalizing scale. In response, Nicolini (2013, p. 213ff.) proposes the metaphor of 'zooming'. Iterative zooming in and out enables a focus on practices' constellations and patterns without recourse to a layered reality. Zooming in on (possibly degrowth) practices exhibits their components and interrelations, but also the differences and tensions within and across activities in specific times and places. Zooming out, on the other hand, enables the researcher to expand the scope and track broader connections and interactions of practices across time and space.

Zooming, the way it is adopted here, is not primarily about the integration of increasingly larger swaths of practices forming complexes and constellations – a perspective that risks reintroducing a sort of layering as problematized with respect to the notion of 'large social phenomena' in chapter 6. But neither does zooming neglect fundamental differences in the density, coherence and structuredness of practices. Instead, it enables the researcher to identify the ways in which practices hang together forming patterns and alignments and thus constituting the relations of power other activities are embedded in. In other words, zooming links (observable) activities in specific geographical contexts to the 'elsewhere' these activities are always linked to, conditioned by, and formative of. It provides a frame to trace practices' relatedness beyond their immediate context while refraining from layered conceptions of space.

While it is a challenge to obtain detailed knowledge about a particular context or specific relation, it is virtually impossible to capture all the activities and sites a given practice is connected to. As a consequence, there is a need to abstract from the actual complexity of practices' relatedness. To consider practices' broader context – a prerequisite for a perspective on power and societal transformation – this work takes inspiration from the aforementioned attempts to structure diversity. It squares attempts to distinguish different realms of social life with the insights of empirical work. In addition, the work draws on a broad body of literature to generate an (inevitably selective and homogenized) picture of the space that constitutes the study's outside (and thus its practices' 'elsewhere'). Combining an empirical and context specific perspective with more abstract and structured conceptions of social co-existence enables this book to link degrowth-oriented activities to the broader alignments they are embedded in. It allows the work to identify and analyze patterns in the relatedness of practices which are alternately stabilized, challenged, and transformed through the activities it observes empirically.

Diverse logics

Patterns in the relatedness of practices (logics) are the central perspective this book develops and uses to identify and analyze transformative geographies. A 'diverse logics perspective' looks at the different ways practices hang together, rather than focusing on particular practices or practice-formations. This has two advantages with respect to a perspective on transition and a flat ontology. First, by looking at how practices hang together and form patterns, the diverse logics perspective avoids attributing transformative potential to single practices or organizations, or denying them such – which in a roundabout way would mean to fall back into categories of structure and agency. Instead, the focus on practices' relatedness foregrounds the effects practices have *in context*. Second, by focusing on patterns in the relatedness of practices instead of constellations, practice-formations, or large social phenomena, the diverse logics perspective avoids the reification of organizations and institutions. Logics describe the ways in which practices hang together rather than the outcome of this congruence. For instance, it identifies practices that connect and interact through calculation and reciprocity rather than tracing the practices that constitute the large social phenomenon of the market. I therefore define 'logics' as *patterns of practices' relatedness* rather than patterns of practices, patterns in practice, or simply practices.

Defining logics as patterns of practices' relatedness, then, means that there is something to be gained from looking at the diverse ways particular practices interact, intertwine, and conspire together. Practices of collaborating, tinkering, documenting, manufacturing, uploading, and repairing can hang together in a way that new (repairable, long-lived, modular, open source) products enter the market and engender a shift towards more sustainable supply chains or a more localized production. The *very same* practices of collaborating, tinkering, etcetera can hang together in other ways, for example generating a community that shares knowledge and support, develops friendships, or disagrees about the role of technology. Furthermore, while the constellation of said practices might shift social relations in one way, they might simultaneously reproduce and stabilize incumbent alignments in another. For instance, in line with technological optimism and imaginaries of decoupling, practice formations around collaboration, repairing, and tinkering might give leverage to green economy approaches.

Figure 2 Social dimensions of transformation

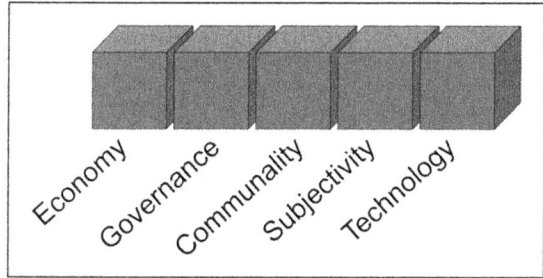

In conversation with empirical data, the study identifies five forms of practices' relatedness: economy, governance, communality, subjectivity, and technology (figure 2). These five patterns, in turn, guide the analysis and interpretation of data.

The identification of patterns or 'logics', therefore, premises further conceptual-methodological considerations. This work follows an abductive approach that links the development of conceptual perspective and empirical data. It is only through the "continuous interplay between theory and empirical observation" (Dubois and Gadde, 2002, p. 559) that the 'diverse logics perspective' evolves, which, in turn, is used to analyze the project's data. For that reason, I will elaborate on the five logics in more detail in chapters 11 and 16, which return to considerations around a structured notion of diversity against the background of the study's methodology and its empirical findings respectively. Chapters 8–10 of Part III, in the meantime, introduce the study's methodology more generally before chapter 11 continues to operationalize the diverse logics perspective for data analysis.

Interlude II: Strategies for transformation

The late Erik Olin Wright (2010) has advanced a theory of transformation that is increasingly influential amongst scholars who search for pathways for radical societal change. Wright's theory of transformation consists of four interlinked components: (1) A theory of reproduction that provides an account of the obstacles to emancipatory transformation; (2) a theory of the gaps and contradictions of reproduction that shows the real possibilities of transformation; (3) a theory of trajectories of unintended social change that specifies the future prospects of both obstacles and possibilities; and (4) a theory of transformative strategies that informs radical practice for building emancipatory alternatives (Wright, 2010, p. 25ff.). Components (1) to (3) resonate with the (practice-theoretical) conceptualization of social dynamics in part II, in conjunction with the analysis and critique of capitalist relations in part I. Taken together, transformation's ontology of social dynamics and its politics, then, pave the way for the development of 'strategies of transformation'. Identifying possibilities and constraints, moments of stability and of change, the dynamics of revolution and counterrevolution, and reformist and revolutionary alternatives raises the question "what sort of collective strategies will help us move in the direction of social emancipation?" (ibid., p. 303).

Wright identifies three forms of transformation he refers to as symbiotic, interstitial, and ruptural (see figure 3). A major difference, thereby, is between the former two which envision transformation through sustained metamorphosis, that is a gradual change, and the latter which is based around "a sharp break with existing institutions and social structures" (ibid., p. 303). Ruptural transformations build on a revolutionary political tradition, confronting capitalist institutions head-on. Marxist-inspired visions of an organized working-class seizing state power to dismantle and restructure its institutions in line with socialist ideals are the "iconic version" (ibid., p. 303) of a ruptural trajectory. Symbiotic and interstitial transformation, in contrast, follow metamorphic imaginaries of change. Instead of a momentous event, transformation is envisioned as a continuous and often inconspicuous process. Symbiotic and interstitial transformations, however, differ fundamentally with respect to their respective relations to incumbent institutions. Symbiotic transformations are processes which address social issues and enhance possibilities for emancipation without challenging capitalist relations directly. Rather, symbiotic transformations "involve strategies in which extending and deepening the institutional forms of popular social empowerment simultaneously helps solve certain practical problems faced by dominant classes and elites" (ibid., p. 305). Interstitial transformations, instead, involve strategies that build alternative forms of social organizations in the "niches and margins of capitalist society" (ibid., p. 303). Instead of confronting or collaborating with dominant political and economic actors, activities following an interstitial path remain outside and often out of sight of capitalist institutions.

Figure 3 Strategic dimensions of transformation

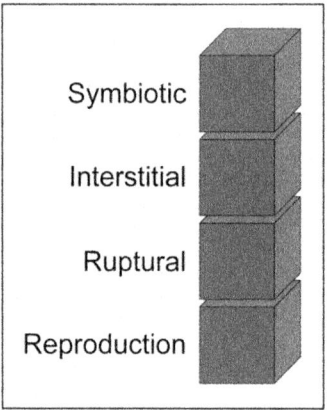

Wright's notion of strategy, however, remains largely implicit. He propounds that, against the background of the knowledge generated through (1) a theory of reproduction, (2) a theory of the gaps and contradictions of reproduction, and (3) a theory of trajectories of unintended social change, collective approaches can be devised to move towards social emancipation. Here, Hardt and Negri's distinction between tactics and strategy helps to sharpen the notion of the latter. Strategy, for Hardt and Negri (2017, p. 15) requires the strategist "to see far, across the entire social field" and entails the "ability to articulate comprehensive long-term plans". This also entails the ability to abstract from particularisms and speak and plan in the name of a general interest. Tactics, in contrast, are based on the immediacy of a spatial and temporal context. It is more an arrangement with and adaptation to given relations of power. This does not mean, however, that tactics are useless. But "only when aligned with the strategic vision can tactical work contribute to the general efforts over the long term" (ibid., p. 15). Strategy, as farsighted course of action, resonates with the notion of (degrowth) politics. Taking reflexivity into account, that is the conscious relation to the plenum of practices, helps to differentiate between patterns of activity with a strategic orientation from more arbitrary or short-sighted ones. Although it is not possible to draw a clear line between tactic and strategy, I argue (in more detail below) that therein lies a key moment for the analysis and justification of pragmatic action and compromise (see chapters 18 and 19).

Each strategy, especially if standing for itself, has strong limitations. Ruptural transformation, in a classic sense as the overthrow of a capitalist state, seems both unlikely and undesirable. Unlikely, because it premises a strong, radical, and coherent opposition capable of confronting and dislodging state power head-on. Undesirable, because its confrontative logics and possibly violent means jar with the ends of social justice and equality. With the immediate consequences likely being negative, furthermore, the issue of counterrevolution arises. That means, if general conditions worsen before improving as a consequence of large-scale disruption – "transition trough" (Wright, 2010, p. 314) – support for radical change might quickly vanish and turn against revolutionary forces.

Interstitial transformations, instead, are rooted in the anarchist tradition that is generally concerned with harmonizing means and ends. The peripheral activities of interstitial transformations in and of themselves, however, might not be able to pose a significant threat to dominant institutions. Symbiotic transformations, building on cooperation, generally exert a greater influence on incumbent social frameworks. Due to their proximity to and compromising with dominant institutions, however, symbiotic activities are likely to be coopted and maybe even help capitalism to overcome its own contradictions and thus ensure its survival. Wright, consequently, envisions an interlocking of all strategies to channel the dynamics towards postcapitalism.

> I think the best prospect for the future in developed capitalist countries is a strategic orientation mainly organized around the interplay of interstitial and symbiotic strategies, with perhaps periodic episodes involving elements of ruptural strategy. Though interstitial strategies, activists and communities can build and strengthen real utopian economic institutions embodying democratic-egalitarian principles where this is possible. Symbiotic strategies through the state can help open up greater space and support for these interstitial innovations. The interplay between interstitial and symbiotic strategies could then create a trajectory of deepening social elements within the hybrid capitalist economic ecosystem (Hahnel and Wright, 2016, p. 103).

There is considerable conceptual purchase in combining Wrights' tripartite strategy with the practice-theoretical perspective on social dynamics developed above. Mapping symbiotic, ruptural, and interstitial strategies onto a practice-theoretical notion of institutions (see chapter 5) opens different pathways for institutional change. In this sense, Wright's typology sheds light on the ways in which changes in practices and practice-formations alter the alignments they are embedded in and thus shift, confront, and substitute social relations (or reproduce them).

Symbiotic transformation, in practice-theoretical terms, describes an alteration through which the overall fabric of practices' alignment stays intact. This is, for instance, the case when consumption practices shift to fair trade and organic food. This shift does not challenge practices' alignment through price and competition but replaces patterns of purely price-driven consumption with such that include ethical considerations (Huybrechts, 2013). Yet, by and large, fair trade and organic food consumption can be well incorporated in competitive markets. Ruptural transformations, in contrast, (partially) break existing alignments through confrontation. For instance, the expropriation and communization of private property or the obstruction of production and trade through blockages (Chatterton, 2006). Here, the alignments of practices of production and exchange through exploitation (of tenants) and externalization (of environmental damage) are interrupted. Interstitial transformations, furthermore, sideline existing alignments by constructing new possibly competing ones. This is less of a confrontational endeavor that, nevertheless, can result in the substitution of existing alignments. Examples, here, include the set-up of parallel arrangements such as time banks and skill-sharing networks that (partially) withdraw from market exchange of labor and services (Seyfang, 2016).

Transformation, or more precisely a degrowth transition, then, is the *change of practice-alignments towards a degrowth trajectory following breaks, substitutions, and shifts of dominant patterns in practices' relatedness*. Chapter 16 below returns to Wright's typology, integrating it with the diverse logics perspective to analyze transformative dynamics in Stuttgart's community economies. In the meantime, chapters 8 to 15 discuss the study's methodology and findings.

Part III: Researching transformative geographies

Outline

Conceptualizing societal change as a complex process revolving around the emergence, stabilization and decline of practices and their broader constellations challenges research to advance an appropriate methodological framework to investigate transformation empirically. Reckwitz (2016, p. 52) reflects on two aspects that set a practice-theoretical methodology apart from discourse-oriented approaches: the 'criterion of the implicitness of meaning' and the 'criterion of materiality'. The criterion of implicitness states that social and cultural forms are highly implicit and substantially (re)produced through a tacit knowledge that is rarely verbalized. Praxeological methodologies face the challenge of comprehending and explicating that which is implicit in non-verbal activities and routines. Practices, furthermore, are inextricably bound up with and transform, bodies, artefacts, and things, calling for an awareness of materiality. Both implicitness and materiality are closely related and require practice-theoretical methodologies to acknowledge the silent, non-verbal, clandestine, taken-for-granted, unconscious and seemingly natural part of social phenomena. Practice theory's aspiration to attend to the implicitness and materiality of socio-cultural formations, then, needs particular conceptual, methodological and analytical tools as well as appropriate reflection in research design. A task this part turns to.

Chapter 8 digs deeper into the implications of the criteria of implicitness and materiality that guide praxeological methodologies. In the vein of aforementioned non-dualistic sensitivity, it conceptualizes implicitness/explicitness and discourse/practice along continua of explicitness and material engagement. Chapter 9, then, translates the general methodological considerations into a research design that guides this work empirically. It schematically presents the iterative unfolding of conceptual and empirical moments and concomitant methods in five steps. Chapter 10 contemplates research as practice, engaging in a critical reflexivity on positionality and normativity. Against this background, I situate this study within action research methodologies. Finally, chapter 11 elaborates on data analysis and coding, tracing the development of the coding schemes that link to the conceptual discussion and the presentation of findings.

Chapter 8: A practice theory methodology

> In practice theory [...] discourse and language lose their omnipotent status.
> *Reckwitz, 2002, p. 254*

Discourse-theoretical perspectives foreground the cultural and social signification of actions and things that can be elicited from both verbal and non-verbal data. From this perspective, the social can be located in regimes of signification (Reckwitz, 2016). For practice theorists, discourse is a specific observational category that centers around the representational side of practices. Practices, characterized by a high degree of implicit and unconscious knowledge, however, exceed representation. The social for practice theorists, then, is located in the recurring patterns of activity that establish, order and uphold social co-existence (see chapter 5).

The criteria of implicitness and materiality, consequently, challenge practice-theoretical research to move beyond language and representation. The explicit surface of written, verbalized or documented qualitative data does not necessarily reflect that which lays beneath in any straightforward manner. Analysis, therefore, demands the researcher to dig beneath the surface of words, sentences and explicit meanings. Naturally, no method can grant the researcher direct access to the tacit dimension of social co-existence. This conundrum can only be approached through methodologically grounded interpretation but never be solved (Reckwitz, 2016).

Discourse- and practice-theoretical approaches, still, are not opposing perspectives but can complement each other. From a praxeological perspective, it would be counterproductive to single out practices that are highly implicit while ignoring practices of representation. To avoid the construction of a false dichotomy between explicit and implicit or material and immaterial practices, it is important to recognize all of these dimensions as constitutive of social phenomena. Practices of speaking are anchored in bodies, make use of a speech apparatus, interact with nervous systems, might involve technological mediation, frequently take direct or indirect reference to physical objects and other bodies, and can profoundly affect subjects and collectives. At the same time, bringing attention to highly implicit and unconscious practices such as breathing can become imbued with meaning – for example in discourses on mindfulness, meditation and yoga.

Representation, therefore, does not stand in opposition to practices' characterization as material and implicit. Instead it can be a more or less prominent part of practice. Repair, for instance, can involve a high degree of reflection, explication and explanation – one of the corner pillars of the phenomenon of repair cafés (Baier et al., 2016) – and still restore the material functionality of artefacts. In other words, while repair practices transform artefacts, they might spread awareness around the wastefulness of modern consumerism and thus be loaded with signification. Nevertheless, a practice theory methodology needs to acknowledge the disparate roles materiality plays in different practices. Talking about repair engages differently with the (material) world than repairing, say, a mobile phone. And representing the possibility of alternative organizational forms is quite different from enacting them (see chapter 4).

Issues around implicitness and materiality pose a fourfold challenge for a practice theory methodology. First, some practices can only be observed but are not explicated by participants. Second, some representational practices lack the counterpart they purport to represent. Third, between aspects one and two, practices exhibit a wide variety of different degrees or forms of explicitness and spread. Fourth, there is considerable interpretative leeway for practices' description, typing and understanding. All four issues require conceptual and methodological reflections. As a first step, I introduce continua of explicitness and material engagement that chapter 10 further operationalizes for the study's research design and analysis. The continua help to grasp practices' differences in material grounding and explicitness without resorting to 'pure' states or dichotomies and instead accepting the "impurities and messiness of the social" (Schäfer, 2016b).

The continuum of explicitness (Hirschauer, 2011, 2016) captures the range of practices' explication from direct expressions to implicit statements and habitual movements. Speaking of a continuum emphasizes that there is no clear-cut difference between discursive practices (or practices of representation) and non-discursive practices. Instead practices involve different degrees of explicitness and can stand in a more or less consistent or contradictory relation to the things they purport to represent. As illustrated by means of examples above, a high level of explicitness does not mean that practices lack a material grounding. Neither, however, does it allow to infer the material existence of that which discursive practices claim. Methodologically, this means that although formal and informal interviewing can be important methods of deducing practices' meanings, the researcher needs to assess the coincidence of practices of representation with observable activities. A first question that a practice theory methodology needs to consider, therefore, is: *how well does the representation correspond to that which is represented?*

Practices, including practices of representation, involve materials (bodies, artefacts and things), but they do so very differently. The continuum of material engagement, hence, does not distinguish material from immaterial practices (which would be oxymoronic) but captures the qualitative differences between practices' material grounding. Practices can differ from each other in the degree to which they involve bodies, artefacts and things, as well as in the form or quality of this involvement. Repairing a phone and talking about repair over the phone might involve quite similar materials, yet there is a fundamental difference in materials' involvement in practices representing repair and practices enacting repair. Whereas, in the latter case, the phone has an "infrastructural relation" (Shove, 2017, p. 158) to repair and stays in the background, in the first instance, repair revolves around the materiality of the phone and radically transforms it. Material involvement, consequently, refers to the *degree to which materials are exposed to the possibility of transformation through their enrolment in practices*. This distinction, again, is not clear-cut and is consequently set up as a conceptual tool in the form of a continuum between materials as a passive backdrop on the one end of the spectrum, and as transforming or transformed protagonist on the other end. A second question that practice theory methodology needs to consider, therefore, is: *how does a practice relate to the materials it involves?*

Taken together, the continua of explicitness and material involvement capture the differences between (1) claiming to advocate more social justice not followed by corresponding behavior, (2) engaging in an exchange on the meaning of social justice within a specific community, and (3) enacting practices of solidarity, mutual help and inclusion. Practices can remain within a discursive realm without taking significant effect on bodies, artefacts and things, as, for instance, the utterance of a detached statement that is not followed by action (1). Practices, furthermore, can be foremost discursive but be part of a cultural transformation. Taking example (2) above, the exchange on the meaning of social justice can be an important part of politicizing economic practice. Third, practices also might involve bodies and artefacts in ways that they are deeply transformed, for instance by sharing food with someone to prevent him from suffering hunger (3).

This distinction sheds light on the epistemic fallacy of community economy's ontological politics (chapter 4) and reiterates the added value of a practice-theoretical perspective. While the disidentification with capitalist social relations can have profound bodily and thus material effects, community economy scholarship lacks the conceptual tools to account for practices' material involvement. It overstates the case that changing the representation of the world equals changing the world itself. A practice theory methodology provides the tools to ascertain that talking about the world is not the world itself, although it is certainly an important part of it.

The continua of explicitness and material involvement allow to capture the (often subtle) differences between narrating, theorizing, planning, and thinking about sustainability on the one hand and building, implementing, and enacting sustainability on the other hand. They provide a heuristic to grasp practices' different forms of involvement with social phenomena such as expressing that repair is important for degrowth economies, explaining how to repair a mobile phone and repairing a mobile phone. In the following, I use the terms 'discursive practice' and 'material practice' when the reference to the respective end of the spectrum supports analytical objectives. Discursive practices, then, are practices with a relatively high level of explicitness. As practices of representation, discursive practices do not allow for inferences beyond the narration itself. Material practices, on the other hand, are practices with a relatively high level of material engagement. Frequently they do not involve explicit moments, but they might be explicated upon request, for example in an interview situation. Discursive and material practices often form counterparts, whereas the former is the explication or narration of the latter. While both are relevant to analyze transformative geographies, they can play quite different roles in the processes of social change. Awareness of the differences between discursive and material practices is crucial for the study's methodological set-up to which the subsequent chapter turns.

Chapter 9: Planning and conducting research on a degrowth case study

> Doing ethnography is like trying to read (in the sense of "construct a reading of") a manuscript – foreign, faded, full of ellipses, incoherencies, suspicious emendations and tendentious commentaries, but not written in conventionalized graphs of sound but in transient examples of shaped behaviour.
> Geertz, 1973, p. 10

Chapter 9 introduces the study's empirical focus and outlines its research approach. Section one, thereby, lays out the case study and its geographical context. Moreover, it details the grounds on which the case study was selected. Section two, then, translates the considerations around a practice-theoretical methodology, presented in the foregoing chapter, into a concrete research design.

The case of Stuttgart

Empirically, the study is based on 24 sustainability-related organizations located in the metropolitan area of Stuttgart. Stuttgart, 6th largest city in Germany and capital of the state of Baden-Württemberg, is located in the southwest of Germany in a prosperous region with a strong industrial sector. The city and region rank amongst the top locations in Germany by per-capita income. Stuttgart, furthermore, has one of the lowest unemployment rates in Germany at around 3% (statistik-bw.de). Automobile industry, engineering, information technology and creative industries are the key economic branches. Although a number of global players such as the *Daimler AG* and *Bosch* have their headquarters in the city and region of Stuttgart, small and medium sized enterprises account for a significant proportion of employment and turnover. In metal production, metal processing and electronics, the bulk of revenue is generated by corporations with sizes between 50 and 500 employees.

Engineering and automobile manufacturing, in turn, is dominated by large enterprises with more than 1000 employees (statistik-bw.de).

Stuttgart's context of medium-sized corporations and industrial imprint is important to understand some specificities of the case on which I reflect below. Stuttgart does not have an established 'alternative milieu' in comparison to more prominent examples in the German context such as Berlin or Hamburg. A notable exception, here, certainly is the opposition against 'Stuttgart 21' – a highly controversial train station reconstruction project which has sparked a lasting, although to date unsuccessful (in the sense that construction continues) protest. To determine how much the mobilization against Stuttgart 21 is a factor in the more recent developments of alternative organizing is beyond the scope of this work. The growing dissatisfaction with the project, at least, was a factor in the 2011 Baden-Württemberg state election which mandated Germany's first Minister-President of the Green Party, later confirmed in the 2016 election. Stuttgart is also the first state capital in Germany with a Green mayor. Aside from a few notable exceptions (see part VI), Stuttgart's Green parliaments, however, are firmly rooted in efficiency and growth-based economic policies. It is outside of these institutions that the study observes and documents a dynamic in activism and eco-social entrepreneurship that addresses a broad range of issues around social inequality and environmental unsustainability and creates a network of alternative organizing. This network is at the center of the study's empirical focus.

The network

The case study comprises 24 sustainability-oriented organizations (see tables 1 to 3 and figure 4). The organizations vary with respect to their economic orientation, legal form, degree of institutionalization, mode of financing and, on a more methodological note, the depth to which they feature in the study's data collection. The selection of the 24 organizations is a methodological decision. Beyond these organizations, a number of individuals and groupings feature prominently in Stuttgart's community economy but were not considered explicitly in order to maintain a manageable sample. 3 of the 24 organizations, on the other hand, were not available for interviewing or participant observation (see tables 1 to 3). Due to their importance in the case, however, they are included through secondary accounts, informal interviewing and desktop research.

An activist group provided the primary access point into the field in spring 2016. Well-connected in the local context, the group helped to establish contacts for an initial sample. Ten interviews and a first round of participant observation traced out the field and generated further contacts through snowballing (Morgan, 2008). In addition to snowballing, the study's sample was broadened through an extensive mapping of and outreach to sustainability and, in particular, degrowth-oriented organizations in the local context of Stuttgart.

A handful of organizations feature prominently as central nodes in Stuttgart's community economy network, and/or are of outstanding relevance for a number of participants and groupings. Figure 4 illustrates the interconnectedness between the organizations that are part of the case. Mind, however, that the illustration is not based on systematic network analysis but on cross-referencing from interview data (see chapter 11). Rather than being a quantitatively grounded representation of the interconnections in Stuttgart's community economy, it reflects the work's perspective on the case study. Some organizations that appear peripheral in figure 4 have ties to organizations that are not included in the empirical sample. Furthermore, the illustration might miss or underestimate links that are beyond the primary focus of data collection. Still, despite the lack of a systematic network analysis, the figure indicates important links that parts IV and V carve out in more detail.

A considerable proportion of participants in this case study are employed by, have contact to, or receive support from technically oriented enterprises. Consequently, there are interconnections between some alternative organizations and (traditional) enterprises that transpire through an exchange of skills, an exchange of materials and through interorganizational cooperation. Considering the case study's context, therefore, is important in at least four ways. (1) Specialized knowledge and skills enable a semi-professional operation of some alternative organizations, providing a broad availability of skills and knowledge that are shared within the larger community. (2) Material support through more solvent enterprises helps some alternative organizations to operate. (3) Cooperation with traditional enterprises, for example through commissions or team building events, provides a further source of revenue with which sustainability-related practices can be cross-subsidized. (4) Last but not least, and on a more speculative note, the broader community can be characterized by a pragmatic and non-dogmatic take on issues of sustainability and economic growth. In conversations and interviews, this was repeatedly attributed to the technology-oriented context by the participants themselves.

As a matter of course, local political and administrative institutions, in addition to the economic context, also have an effect on Stuttgart's community economy. The same is true for supralocal institutions, which, however, cannot be investigated empirically within the scope of the study and instead find consideration as practices' temporal and spatial 'elsewhere' (see part II). Local administration, planning and governance, in contrast, are selectively incorporated in the study's empirics. For reasons of scope, however – and this work is decidedly not a broad analysis of the institutional framework – the focus is on a small number of representatives within governmental institutions who are particularly progressive in their activities and

140 Making Transformative Geographies

Figure 4 Stuttgart's community economy

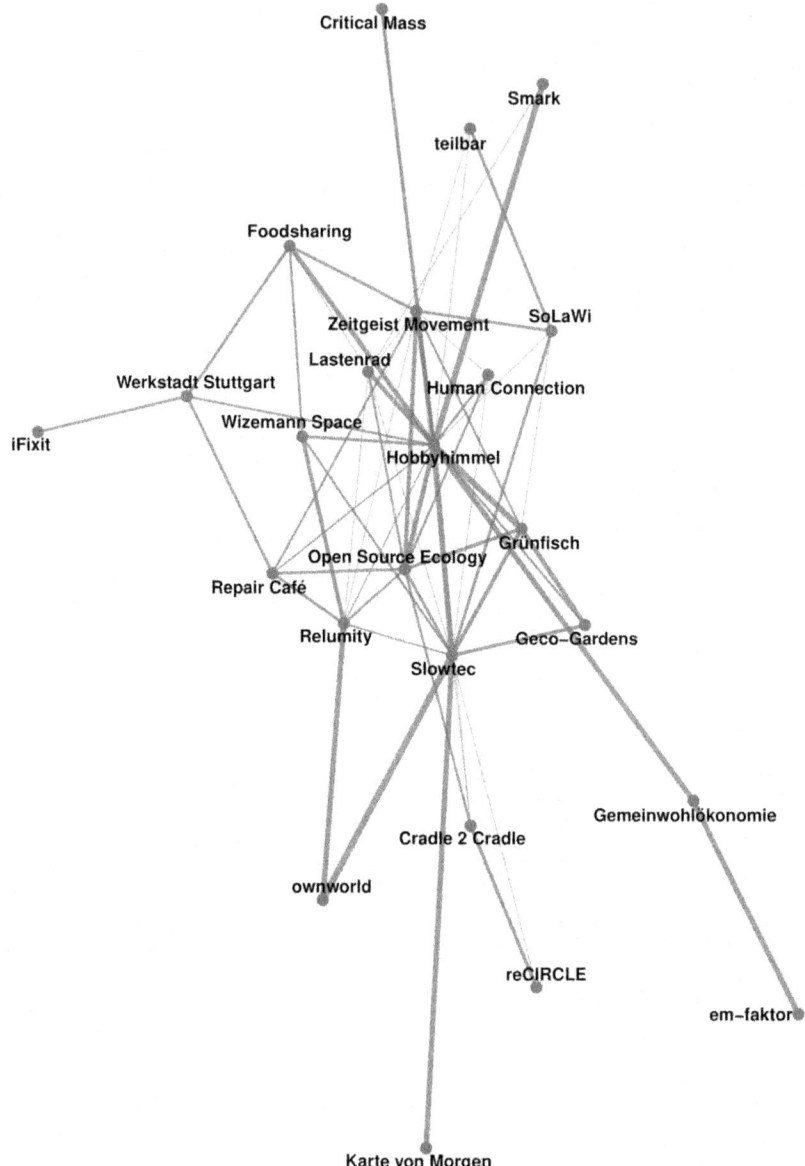

partially show links to the network of Stuttgart's community economy. The study includes three interviews with key individuals from Stuttgart's city council and administration (see table 3), as well as participation in and observation of political events around issues of sustainability with profiled attendees from local and state politics.

Table 1 List of organizations with for-profit legal form

Organization	Description	Data
Slowtec GmbH	Development of sustainable technologies in software and hardware sectors	1-5
ownworld GbR	Development of off-grid, self-sufficient house (ownhome)	1-5
Geco-Gardens GbR	Development, construction and sale of vertical garden systems	1-3;5
reCIRCLE (Elithro UG)	Implementation of reusable take away scheme	1-2
Smark GmbH	Fully automated sale of regional and organic food	1-5
Relumity – Technologie Transfer Initiative GmbH	Development, production and sale of sustainable and reparable LED lights	1-4
Wizemann Space GmbH	Co-Working and event space	1-3
iFixit GmbH	Platform for repair manuals and sale of tools	1
em-faktor – Die Social Profit Agentur GmbH	Agency offering fundraising, CSR, campaigning and branding services to social profit organizations	1-2

Table 2 List of organizations with non-profit legal form

Organization	Description	Data
Human Connection gGmbH	Development of a non-profit and sustainability-oriented social media website	1-2
Werkstadt Stuttgart e.V.	Association organizing free exchange of repair services and skills on a regular basis	1-2
Lastenrad Stuttgart e.V.	Project promoting car-free urban mobility; provision of a free cargo bike lending system	1-3
Hobbyhimmel (Verein zur Verbr. Offener Werkst. e.V.)	Open workshop, providing low-threshold access to high-tech and low-tech tools and machinery	1-5
Grünfisch e.V.	Associating building and operating aquaponics	1-3;5
Solidarische Landwirtschaft (Verein zur Förderung der Sol. Landw. Stuttgart e.V.)	Consumer-producer cooperative for organic agriculture	1-2
teilbar e.V.	Library of things	1-2

Table 3 List of local groups, projects and institutional representatives

Organization	Description	Data
Gemeinwohlökonomie [Economy for the Common Good]	Group advocating a common good oriented economy	1-3; 5
Open Source Ecology	Association working towards an open-source economy	1-3
Zeitgeist Movement (local group)	Movement advocating a resource-based economy	1-3
Cradle to Cradle (local group)	Association promoting a circular economy	1-2
Foodsharing (local group)	Association organizing against food waste	1-3
Repair Café	Project organizing free exchange of repair services and skills on a regular basis	1-3
Critical Mass	Regular campaign for more bicycle use and better cycling infrastructures	1
Karte von Morgen	Development of map tool to support sustainability and joint action	1
City administration Stuttgart		5
City planning Stuttgart		5
City council Stuttgart		5

Case study selection

Reasons for selecting this case study include (1) a pragmatic orientation of most participants, (2) the focus on localization of productive processes by a significant number of organizations and (3) coherence and connectedness within the case. (1) By pragmatic orientation I mean that most participants are not concerned with political affiliations or particularistic perspectives and have a relatively undogmatic, technical and analytical take on sustainability. Although, at times, this stance turns into a naive techno-optimism and managerialism (see part IV), pragmatic, here, does not imply a post-political orientation. Rather, pragmatic refers to the tendency that most organizations and activities are not overly shaped by a particular partisan standpoint. This pragmatic orientation translates into a tendency to test and experiment with organizational forms, technologies and other economic practices, rendering the case quite dynamic and multifaceted.

(2) The localization of productive processes, here, is part of a broader set of attempts to reduce dependency on globally sourced and produced goods through sufficiency-oriented technologies, open source modular construction; and, likewise, local design, construction, assembling, maintenance and repair. While there

are both elaborate schemes and a long tradition of (re)localization in some sectors such as food production (in particular in form of community-supported agriculture), housing (for instance housing cooperatives) and community-oriented activities (spaces for encounter and support), the substitution of global value chains around durable consumer goods poses a significant challenge to degrowth perspectives. In contrast to food, housing and community spaces – all of which are highly important and pertinent foci for degrowth perspectives – there are few localized alternatives for durables such as electronics or clothes. A range of technological and social innovations, however, provide compelling prospects to build viable alternatives for a localization of productive processes. The work, consequently, puts a particular focus on technology-oriented organizations for which Stuttgart constitutes a conducive context for the reasons detailed above.

(3) Connectedness, furthermore, constitutes a third reason for the selection of this case study. Stuttgart's landscape of alternative organizations and actors presents a middle ground between the extremes of a strong community orientation on the one hand and fragmentation and dispersal, that means little connectedness between actors and organizations, on the other hand. In other words, while a 'community' or network around alternative economies is emerging, it is not closed off and thus open to different people, practices, and perspectives including that of research.

All three aspects – pragmatic orientation of participants, the focus on local production and repair, and the organizations' connectivity – speak to the thrust of this study to investigate degrowth transitions with a particular focus on enabling and limiting factors. Pragmatism, by and large, translates into variegated processes of negotiation and compromise, shedding light on the possibilities and constraints of practicing alternative economies within a given institutional framework. Local production and related practices, moreover, attend to crucial questions around the rescaling of globalized value chains that pertain to a majority of everyday goods. Connectivity amongst the organizations, finally, opens a perspective beyond isolated undertakings that focus on an exclusive audience and provides a perspective on cooperation between and beyond alternative organizations and projects.

Research design

The research design reflects foregoing deliberations on a practice-theoretical methodology, in particular by attending to different levels of explicitness and material involvement. Using a combination of desktop research, interviewing, group discussions and ethnography, the study combines methods that focus on representational practices with such that foreground observation. The reasons for doing so are fourfold. First, to capture both discursive and non-discursive practices, providing insights into the translation of narratives and strategies into practice. Second, to scoop out the advantages of the different methods that lay particularly in the high explicitness of interviewing – allowing systematic access to much information within relatively short time – and the high material engagement of participant observation – allowing for deeper insights into practices that are not, or only partially explicated. Third, to account for discrepancies between verbalized accounts and actually observable practices. Fourth, to make up for some – but by no means all – of the shortcomings of the respectively other methods.

The different methods build on each other and can be expressed in a five-step succession. Table 4 gives an overview of the different stages of this study's methodological approach and how they relate to different levels of explicitness and material involvement. Presenting the methods as five-step succession reflects the study's methodological coherence, but is not a strictly chronological representation. Due to the dynamics of empirical work – including difficulties in the availability of interview partners, differences in organizations' accessibility for participant observation, the chronology of events, the generation of new insights, conceptual and methodological (re)considerations and shifting priorities – the actual research process was more fragmented.

Table 4 Research methods and methodological coherence

	Method	Explicit./Mater.	Description
1	Desktop research	Medium level of explicitness; difficult to draw conclusions for material engagement.	Digital research is used to scout interesting organizations, prepare further steps of data collection and amend information, e.g. through tracing the development of individual organizations over time (newsfeed, current information on homepage).
2	Semi-structured exploratory interviewing	High level of explicitness; Difficult to draw conclusions for material engagement.	This stage of empirical data collection establishes contact to the organizations' protagonists, provides an overview of the organizational landscape and connections between organizations, provides insight into different narrations of sustainability and into the strategies to address sustainability-related issues.
3	Participant observation	Both low and high level of explicitness; deeper insights into material engagement.	Participant observation allows the researcher to experience the everyday practices that constitute the various organizations. The researcher develops a tacit knowledge of the communities' practices beyond the insights generated through interviewing.
4	Focus groups	High level of explicitness; explication of tacit knowledge that was acquired during ethno-graphic fieldwork.	This stage questions, validates and amends the data collected through interviewing and through ethnographic methods. It also enables insights into the dynamics of the community. Furthermore, the focus group serves as a means to disseminate preliminary findings and initiate, consider, and prepare further collaboration towards sustainability
5	Semi-structured follow-up interviewing	High level of explicitness; explication of tacit knowledge that was acquired during ethno-graphic fieldwork.	The last stage serves four purposes: explication, validation, deepening and update. Besides allowing for further elaboration of emergent themes of prior stages of data collection as well as their validation, in-depth interviewing is used to collect updated information to provide a longitudinal perspective.

Furthermore, each step has to be seen as contextualized within a broader movement between theory, empirical insights and methodological deliberations. In contrast to the linear structure of (academic) writing, the research process behind it is best characterized as iterative and cyclical. Instead of moving from theory to methodology to data collection, this research project developed through a flexible and contingent process in which theory, methodology and empirics interact and cross-fertilize. Action researchers, along these lines, stress iterative cycles of action and reflection to allow theory and (research) practice to inform each other (Kemmis and McTaggart, 2005). I elaborate on the study's relation to action research methodologies below. At this point, however, the iterative development of theory, methodology and fieldwork are of importance. The research design, as presented in this section, is not a preconceived framework but an emergent result of said iterations. While the separate steps in table 4 complement each other from an ex post perspective, one needs to keep in mind that this succession was not established from the outset. The remainder of this section explores the five methods individually before it puts them in relation to each other.

Stage 1: Desktop research

This research uses the internet as a tool to collect information as well as interact with participants at a distance (Markham and Stavrova, 2016). Due to profoundly different methodological and ethical implications, the latter is discussed below in the context of participant observation. In the following, desktop research refers to use of internet technology to collect information and, in doing so, to prepare and assist other means of data collection – for instance interviews and participant observation – as well as to amend, validate and revise collected data. Initially, desktop research allowed a first overview of organizations' objectives, structure, financing, legal form and other basic information, if provided online. This was helpful in assessing the organizations' suitability for further empirical investigation, preparing for interviews and following up on information provided through formal and informal interviewing. At a later stage of the study, desktop research allowed to track organizations' development through their internet presence or newsletters. Desktop research plays a role throughout the project, but it is most prominent in the initial phase of this study.

Stage 2: Semi-structured exploratory interviewing

In rendering stories, descriptions and intentions visible, interviews capture foremost that part of social phenomena with a high level of explicitness, privileging narratives and meanings over habits and affects. In this study, semi-structured exploratory interviews were used as entry point into the case study and were crucial for the selection process for follow-up research (see subsequent sections). By exploratory, here, I mean that the interviews are rooted in a certain curiosity expressed through an openness towards the conversational trajectories. All exploratory interviews were informed by a flexible guide composed of questions based on preliminary research foci and the desktop research preceding the interviews. The main objective of this stage was to gain insights into practitioners' narratives on alternatives and the strategies pursued to translate these into organizational practice. In addition, interviewing complemented participant observation, which is quite resource intensive. Triangulating interview data with ethnographic data enabled a broadening of the scope beyond what would have been possible with participant observation alone. Nevertheless, the study exercises caution to avoid the conflation of verbal accounts with actual practice when working with different kinds of data (see chapter 11).

The initial set of exploratory interviews looked at ten sustainability-related organizations. Like all subsequent interviews, they were conducted with founders or main representatives of the respective organization. On occasion, two or more interviewees were present. Through this first sample, more contacts became available. Ten more organizations were explored in detail through interviewing during the course of the project. Some, however, only during later stages. Reasons for this delay include difficulties getting hold of interviewees and the dynamic development of the case. Aside from new information that brought organizations into focus which were overlooked by desktop research, or which did not seem relevant at the time, some organizations consolidated only after the initial stage of the project. Still, not all organizations relevant to the study were available for formal interviewing. Some compelling examples, therefore, were included through informal interviewing – discussed in the next section on participant observation – and digital research (see table 4). Depending on relevance, accessibility and availability, furthermore, some of the organizations interviewed during stage two were further explored using ethnographic methods, which the subsequent section turns to.

Stage 3: Participant observation

Ethnographic participant observation is, in a way, the 'natural' method for practice-theoretical perspectives (Reckwitz, 2016). It allows to capture the 'silent' (part of) practices – for example, the supposedly irrelevant, the taken-for-granted, the clandestine, the ineffable, the routinized or the unconscious. According to DeWalt and Dewalt (2011, p. 1), "participant observation is a method in which a researcher takes part in the daily activities, rituals, interactions and events of a group of people as one of the means of learning the explicit and tacit aspects of their life routines and their culture". Participant observation is often used synonymously with ethnography, whereas the latter, however, refers more generally to a research approach or strategy that aims at "understanding and representing how people – together with other people, non-human entities, objects, institutions, and environments – create, experience and understand their worlds" (Till, 2009, p. 626). Here, I am concerned primarily with participant observation as particular research method and its connection to a practice theory methodology. Since participant observation is the core method of this research project, I elaborate the methodological deliberations behind it in more detail.

Practice theory's emphasis on implicitness and materiality results in a particular interest in activities themselves rather than their (discursive) representations (Walsh, 2009). Participant observations' orientation towards first-hand data collection; involvement; sensual, emotional, and embodied experience; and a focus on the concrete situatedness of bodies, artefacts, things and their interactions (Balsiger and Lambelet, 2014), allows for a more direct access to the practices of interest than the verbally-mediated data gathered through interviewing. In this respect, participant observation is a key methodological feature of more-than-representational approaches (Cadman, 2009). As outlined above, however, this is not a dualistic juxtaposition. Practices, certainly, are not devoid of meaning. Rather, meaning is socially produced in, through, and with practices, but it does not necessarily exist in the form of explicit (verbalized) knowledge. Participant observation allows to inquire into both explicit and tacit knowledge as well as the materiality of practice.

According to Robson (2009, p. 314), a "key feature of participant observation is that the observer seeks to become some kind of member of the observed group". Experience becomes a prime means of observation. In stark contrast to the passive observer advocated in "pure observation" approaches (Walsh, 2009, p. 77), the self and her bodily experiences become an active part of observation. Through that, the researcher acquires a deeper, so to speak *more-than-conceptual* knowledge of the situation. At the same time, this deep involvement challenges the researcher to extract herself from the situation, critically reflecting her observations and possibly readjusting the methodological approach. Participant observation, consequently, moves between theory-driven and field-driven moments. Through this iterative movement between theoretical reflection and observations, an understanding emerges that "begins with a set of connected ideas that undergo continuous redefinition throughout the life of the study until the ideas are finalized and interpreted at the end" (Schensul et. al. 1999, cited in Balsiger and Lambelet, 2014).

The researcher develops an intuitive understanding for practices, interactions, possibilities, constraints and obstacles. The explication of tacit knowledge, however, remains a major challenge. It requires repeated questioning of one's own positionality (chapter 10) as well as a systematically developed framework for analysis (chapter 11).

In more practical terms, observation and participation premise access to the sites where practitioners and organizations work and act. Informal conversations, before and after interviews, helped me to build relationships of trust, explain the project's background and discuss possibilities for further engagement. The transition from interviewing to participant observation, thereby, was not always clearcut. Observation inevitably is a part of being present at the sites where organizational activities literally 'take place'. Systematic documentation and thus a more formal form of participant observation set in when I started volunteering at the open workshop *Hobbyhimmel* in spring 2017.

Hobbyhimmel is an 'open workshop' that provides low-threshold access to different work areas equipped with tools and machinery. It was the primary locale for participant observation in the present study. The workshop's accessibility, spatial set-up, informal atmosphere and its central role for a wide range of sustainability-related initiatives rendered it a promising 'site' for observation. Site, here, refers to both the workshop as a specific place or locale of human activity, as well as the relatedness of practices (including their materials and meanings) which travel through the workshop (see chapters 5 and 6). In this sense, the workshop is both a spatial context in which sustainability-related practices transpire (and can be observed), as well as a nexus of practices that extends in time and space and which participant observation can trail and follow.

The workshop, consequently, was the study's primary entry point for an ethnography on sustainability-related practices and organizations. As a locale in which practices materialize, the workshop provided access to a range of other organizations such as *Relumity*, *Foodsharing*, *Lastenrad*, *Smark* and *Grünfisch* (see figure 4). And as a site through which sustainability-related practices travel, it links to other close and distant places. Participant observation, then, moved with the practices to other locales (on condition that they were spatially and temporally accessible). Although not all sites link directly to the workshop, there are numerous connections that I discuss in part IV. Additional sites of observation, then, were scattered across Stuttgart – including the *Wizemann Space*, the Züblin Parkhaus, Stuttgart main station, and various offices and worksites – and beyond Stuttgart in Isingen, Mannheim, and Berlin. The forms of participation, thereby, varied significantly across these different settings and situations. They included active collaboration on operational and organizational processes, the acquisition of trade skills and abilities to operate machinery, taking part in correspondence, participating in various events (such as trade fairs, interorganizational meetings, workshops and panel discussions), informal interviewing, visits to projects sites and off-topic conversations.

> **Digression: Informal interviewing**
> Informal interviewing is a significant part of participant observation (DeWalt and De-Walt, 2011). In general, it is closer to casual conversations than formal interview settings, but differs from non-research conversations for at least two reasons. First, informal interviewing is generally guided by a particular interest of inquiry. Second, it is documented in some form after the conversation. According to DeWalt and DeWalt (2011), informal interviewing can be classified along two continua: the degree of control through the researcher and the uniformity of questions to different informants.
>
> In the context of the present study, informal interviewing served two main purposes. First, to generate meaningful insights beyond more formal interview situations. And second, to collect information from participants that were not available for formal interviewing. Both objectives were approached through targeted questions as well as non-controlled conversations. A specific subtype of the latter was the involvement in chat and email exchanges.
>
> Chat and email exchanges allow one to converse with practitioners at a distance (Markham and Stavrova, 2016). This includes newsletters, newsfeeds on social media as well as group chats and group email exchanges. Whereas the former two are non-reciprocal and are considered above as part of desktop research, the latter involve interactions among several people including the researcher. Although no systematic analysis was conducted, the daily exchange of information through chats and emails provided additional insights and filled the gaps between visits.

Participant observation raises a number of methodological issues that include questions of reliability, interpretative bias, generalizability, and representativeness (Walsh, 2009). While there is well-founded critique of methodologies that uncritically assume any of the above as gold standard of good research (Flyvbjerg, 2006), they provide important food for reflection on participant observation's challenges and shortcomings. More so than standardized methods, participant observation leaves much leeway for interpretation and subjective impressions. This freedom challenges the researcher to be transparent about her assumptions, proceedings, and positionality. In the sense of aforementioned iterative cycles of action and reflection, the critical assessment of one's own position and practices needs to accompany the research process throughout. Transparency, moreover, includes the representation of the study's results as situated and contingent. While a lack of generalizability and representativeness does not make qualitative non-standardized methods less scientific, again, a critical reflexivity and an appropriate caution have to go along with analysis, discussion and conclusion. I return to issues of positionality and research ethics in more detail in chapter 10.

Stage 4: Focus groups

The study used focus groups as a means to question, validate, and amend the data collected through interviewing and ethnographic methods. Focus groups allow the researcher to passively absorb and actively take part in thematic discussions. The reasons for including focus groups in the research design are fourfold. First, focus groups provide deeper insights into the dynamics of the community. Second, focus groups allow for the validation of preliminary findings, as well as the development of a more nuanced perspective. Third, they function as a means of dissemination. While this study did not apply participatory methods in a strict sense (see chapter 10), it sympathizes with the general sensitivities of participatory action research and attempted to allow for a deeper involvement of participants in the research process. The fourth point, which is closely related to the third, is that focus groups serve as means to initiate, consider, and prepare further collaboration by creating a space for exchange amongst practitioners.

Two focus groups with different audiences and orientations were part of this project. The first focus group addressed all four objectives listed above. Aside from the collection of additional data and the verification of preliminary findings, a main concern was to explore possibilities of action and collaboration amongst the participating organizations. All objectives were communicated to the participants in advance. Due to the limited capacities of a focus group discussion only selected organizations were present (*Hobbyhimmel*, *Slowtec*, *Relumity*, *Smark*, and *ownworld*), all of which matched at least two of the following criteria: (1) financial independence and/or a pragmatic financing strategy through a business case, (2) significant correspondence with degrowth principles, and (3) connections to the emergent community.

A second and more streamlined focus group revolved around cooperation within the open workshop. In a group of 20 participants involved with the open workshop, we explored the strengths and weaknesses of *Hobbyhimmel*'s organizational set-up. The two main outcomes of this discussion were deeper insights into the internal structure of the workshop, which is based on self-management (see part IV), and reciprocal learning about ways to improve it.

Stage 5: Semi-structured follow-up interviewing

Semi-structured follow-up interviews allow researchers to address pertinent issues in greater depth. In this study, they served four purposes: the explication of tacit knowledge, the validation of preliminary findings, an update on recent developments, and the broadening of contextual insights. Besides allowing for further elaboration of emergent themes of prior stages of data collection and their validation, in-depth interviewing was used to collect updated information to provide a longitudinal perspective. My involvement with some organizations spanned over a period of more than two years. Due to the fact that the majority of organizations were less than 4 years old at the commencement of empirical work, the documentation over a two-year-period captured a significant timespan in the organizations' development.

In the context of this study, in-depth interviewing has similar advantages and disadvantages as exploratory interviewing (see above). It differs, however, in that it focuses more specifically on pertinent aspects that emerged in the course of data collection. Two types of follow-up interviewing were conducted. First, additional interviews with organizations that were part of exploratory interviewing and/or participant observation. And second, interviews with city employees and political representatives to follow-up on issues around regulations, support, and cooperation.

Integration of different methods

Broadly speaking, the methodological set up of this study moves from explicit to implicit and back to explicit inquiry. Figure 5 schematically illustrates the temporal unfolding with respect to the levels of explicitness the different methods capture.

Desktop research moves within a rather narrow range. Although it provides a low-threshold access to information, it is limited by the information presented on organizations' web pages. The information provided is generally strongly limited and important questions are not explicated. Nevertheless, desktop research provides a useful grounding for semi-structured exploratory interviewing. Interviewing, then, allows for the explication of further details of interest to this study by the interviewees. Rather than being a purely verbal exchange, interviews also entail a number of non-verbal elements that further the development of tacit knowledge. Participant observation, then, increasingly drills down into the organizations' everyday practices. It stretches over a wide range of explicit and implicit moments of inquiry – from informal interviewing to passive observation – and allows the researcher to develop a deep knowledge of the case. The focus group spaces the long phase of participant observation and allows explication of some of the observations in a more formal setting. It also covers a broad spectrum of explicit and implicit aspects, for instance by enabling the researcher to gain insights into the group dynamics. Semi-structured follow-up interviewing, again, takes many observations to a more explicit level and helps the researcher to validate or reinterpret the data. In doing so, it sets up data analysis, which is not just about systematic evaluation of data but also the explication of tacit knowledge on part of the researcher.

Figure 5 Level of explicitness across different stages of inquiry

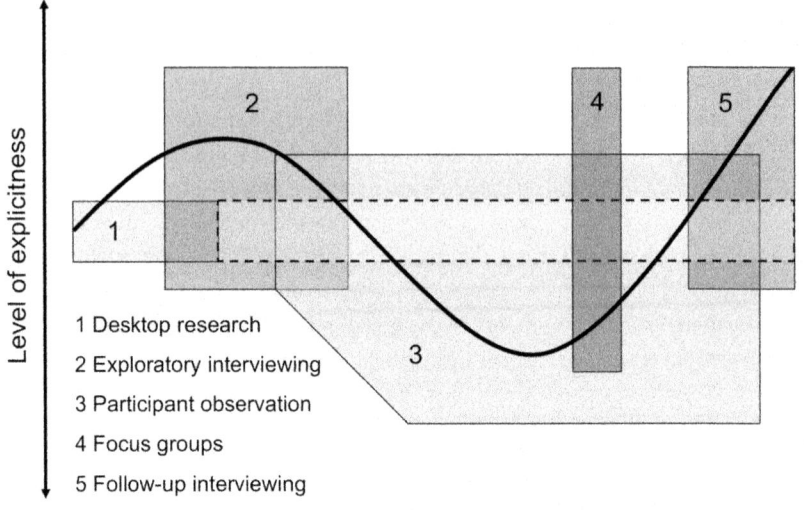

Chapter 10: Research as practice

> PAR is not the only resource that might produce empowering effects, but more than most, its epistemological orientations and practical techniques can provide mechanisms with which to reflect on its own situatedness and potentially domineering effects.
> *Kindon et al., 2007, p. 24*

Practice theory and community economy scholarship both emphasize the situatedness of knowledge production. A practice-theoretical perspective, as a matter of course, extents to the practice of research itself, acknowledging that doing research is highly contextual. Viewed as practice-as-entity, research is a historically and geographically shaped pattern of activities which encompasses particular, methods, forms of knowledge, pieces of writing and institutional frameworks. As performance, research takes place in concrete spatio-temporal settings and is carried out by differently positioned subjects. Community economic thought, furthermore, draws attention to the politics and ethics inherent in the research process. Maintaining that how we present the world has profound effects on the world itself, Gibson-Graham (2014, p. 148) highlight the perils associated with a "'strong theory' [that organizes] events into understandable and seemingly predictable trajectories". Instead of rehearsing an already known reality, community economy scholars call for emancipatory research that centers around difference and possibility.

After presenting methodological considerations with an outward focus in chapters 8 and 9, this chapter turns inward and reflects on questions of politics, ethics, and positionality. It addresses two issues in particular. First, the research politics the study is based on and that inform its methodology. And second, the study's research ethics, including the role of the researcher. The next section turns to literature on participatory action research to outline the coordinates of a reflexive and emancipatory notion of research, before section two considers questions of positionality and self-reflection.

Participatory action research

Participatory action research (PAR) challenges hierarchical and extractive forms of research and rethinks 'traditional' modes of data collection, knowledge production and research objectives (Kindon et al., 2007, 2009). PAR does not so much refer to a particular method (although there arguably are methods more suited for PAR than others) as to a way of approaching research accompanied by corresponding methodological reflections. Within the diversity of approaches, two characteristics of PAR stick out: collaboration and politics.

PAR is participatory both in the sense that the researched participate in the research process – shared knowledge production – and that the researcher participates in communities' activities. PAR challenges the (strong) separation of researcher and researched and aims at collaboratively generating relevant and emancipatory knowledge for the stakeholder community (Pant, 2014). Within participatory approaches, there are numerous different shades of research for, with and by the researched group (Kindon, 2010). Questioning the power-relations of traditional research models, then, PAR opposes imperial, hierarchical and extractive modes of knowledge production. It criticizes claims to neutrality or objectivity of orthodox social science, maintaining that "it serves the ideological function of justifying the position and interests of the wealthy and powerful" (Kemmis and McTaggart, 2005, p. 560). Instead, PAR acknowledges the politics inherent in research. Its conceptual proximity to poststructural, feminist and postcolonial theories makes PAR sensitive to power relations, alternative ways of knowing, and (institutionalized) oppression while explicitly pursuing an agenda of emancipation and empowerment (Kemmis and McTaggart, 2005; Kindon et al., 2007, 2009). PAR builds on a critical theory that is grounded in a fundamental suspicion of the very categories with which traditional theory operates (Horkheimer, 1937). Critical theory questions the status quo of social relations and maintains that a more just society can be built.

Methods-wise, most PAR approaches are flexible and pragmatic. Non-standardized and qualitative methods are usually chosen over structured and controlled means of data collection (Pant, 2014). Common methods include storytelling, collective action and participatory mapping or diagramming (Kindon et al., 2007). Appropriateness is determined by methods' usefulness for the political and emancipatory agenda rather than by hegemonic scientific standards. Yet, this does not imply that PAR approaches dispense with systematic research procedures or are synonymous with "sloppy social science" (Bradbury-Huang, 2010, p. 104). Reflexivity, transparency and comprehensibility are all the more crucial throughout data collection and analysis.

Participant observation, often including participation, does not automatically make participatory action research. Participation in ethnographic terms centers around the researcher's bodily involvement in everyday practices, generating an understanding through sensual, emotional and embodied experience. Participation in terms of PAR, in contrast, is a means of collectively addressing social injustice and working towards emancipation and empowerment. While ethnography does not exclude political engagement, participation for action researchers is "explicitly oriented toward social change" (Kindon et al., 2009, p. 90). PAR might just serve as a token if the research lacks collaborative emancipatory engagement and power is not equally shared amongst researcher and researched (co-researchers) (Pant, 2014).

This study draws selectively on PAR methodologies, which requires a critical examination. Although the study involves participants through explicit invitation of feedback on data analysis – for instance through focus groups and follow-up interviewing – it does not engage in actual co-production of knowledge. The community has no direct power over the interpretation of findings and the researcher retains full responsibility over analysis and output. Furthermore, participants' involvement differs significantly. While in active exchange with some participants, others are only involved passively through more traditional methods such as interviewing.

Reasons for a more selective recourse to PAR lie in the nature of the case study and the concomitant assessment of case-specific methodological adequacies. Although diverse social groups are involved, the community is composed predominantly of white males with a degree in higher education who 'voluntarily' engage in alternative economic practices. While the "goal of PAR is to fundamentally transform social relations – helping those with less power and fewer resources get more of the same" (Pant, 2014, p. 584), the present study's empirical engagement is not with a marginalized community in the general sense. Rather than "changing their own situation" (ibid., p. 585), this book is concerned with how the community works to change social and ecological relations more broadly. The social and environmental injustices that the study examines are spatially and temporally dispersed. In lieu of working with and presenting the perspective of a disadvantaged community, the focus is on groups who choose to involve themselves with said issues. In addition, a deeper involvement of the community is limited by the severe time constraints of many protagonists. Some work several jobs or long hours in their respective organization, leaving little capacity to function as co-researchers.

From this follows a particular interpretation and selective adaption of PAR principles. While practicing an active and politically motivated involvement in the community, a rather traditional separation between researcher and researched prevails. Therefore, the term 'action research' appears more adequate to characterize the projects' methodology. Nevertheless, a number of elements blur the boundaries, such as my collaboration on the organizational set-up of the workshop, different forms of cooperation and support for some organizations, and recurring discussions of findings with the main protagonists of the study. Furthermore, the question of how research and activism can cooperate was repeatedly raised and discussed.

Beyond PAR's grounding in critical theory and the connected politicization of research, PAR is also important for this study's methodology in terms of its movement between action and reflection (see chapter 9). Kemmis and McTaggart (2005, p. 563f.) describe the process of PAR as "spiral of self-reflective cycles" consisting of planning, acting, observing, reflecting, and revising the plan before starting the cycle anew. PAR's spiral captures well the iterative movement between action, reflection, and constant readjustments this study follows.

Furthermore, recurring moments of reflection emphasize the contingency of research itself and invite a perspective on the practices of research, which are always linked to other social relations. The "reflexive-dialectical view of subjective-objective relations and connections" (Kemmis and McTaggart, 2005, p. 573) is a strong point of contact between practice theory and participatory action research methodologies. While practice theory, here, refers to a conceptual perspective that locates the social within the continuous movement of practice, PAR provides the corresponding methodology that acknowledges the mutually transformative moments of research practices, community, researcher, and broader context. From a practice-theoretical point of view, the practices of action research can be understood as "meta practices that help to construct and reconstruct the first-level practices they are investigating" (Kemmis and McTaggart, 2005, p. 574). In this sense, critical research that supports emancipation and change in everyday practice is a vital part in a transition towards degrowth. Practice theory and participatory action research, then, are potential allies in their work for social change through their common focus on reflexivity and processuality.

Positionality and self-reflection

Research is always a view from somewhere. Geographers possess a rich conceptual vocabulary to reflect on the spatial implications of the fact that knowledge and its production is always "situated" and "positioned" (Rose, 1997, p. 308) – which does not imply that it is always made use of. Famously, Donna Haraway refers to the illusion of universal knowledge that is not produced and disseminated from a particular spatial, temporal and social position as "god trick" (Haraway, 1991, p. 189). Recognizing that the practices of research are always enacted from specific (social) locations has profound implications for both their normative orientation and for the role of the researcher. After reflecting on the study's research politics in the preceding section, this section examines the researcher's positionality and the importance of research ethics.

Positionality is a twofold process that closely interlinks the position of the researcher with respect to relatively stable social categories such as "race, nationality, age, gender, social and economic status" (Rose, 1997, p. 308) one the one hand, and the political and ethical positioning she performs on the other. Although both moments of situatedness interpenetrate, we might speak of an 'outwards' and a 'towards' movement of positioning. Race, nationality, age, gender, social and economic status, while some categories are more fluid and navigable than others, are brought 'towards' the researcher through discursive and material practices of subjectification and identification. Subjects, however, do not remain passive and reach 'outward', negotiating the situatedness of self as well as their positioning in relation to others. In order to guide the reflection, I will first consider how I am positioned within the web of practices that constitute the research case (towards) and second, how I am positioning myself throughout the research process (outwards).

Socioeconomic injustices go beyond class differences and include north-south relationships, gender relations and nationalities. As a white, male researcher with German nationality and from a non-precarious background, I am speaking from a relatively privileged position. Sensitivity to intersectionality (Al-Hindi, 2017) is particularly important if situated rather advantageously. This includes the consideration of who can 'speak' (Spivak, 2011) and who is only heard as 'noise' (Rancière, 1998) when alternatives are conceived and proposed. Working with a community that in itself consists of relatively privileged individuals, positionality is not a primary concern with respect to the power-relations between researcher and researched (see above). All the more important, however, is a continuous awareness of intersectionality with respect to the study's conceptualization and interpretation. Here, its grounding in community economy scholarship helps to maintain an openness towards difference and contingency.

Still, research, as outlined above, is never value free and thus requires disclosure of and reflection on the political and ethical positioning it is grounded in. After detailing the book's normative stance in the discussion of degrowth and postcapitalism (see chapters 1 and 2), I reflect on its concrete implications for research practices in the following. Driven by the action research sensitivity to "prioritize the pursuit of justice [...] as the primary aim of research" (Masuda, 2017, p. 1), I started this project with a strong sympathy for the emancipatory thrust of community economies. Consequently, there was a certain risk of exaggerating the significance of specific organizations or practices. The scoping study and the initial stage of interviewing, along these lines, were informed by the search for innovative and subversive practices that can be interpreted as harbinger of postcapitalist economies. Remaining sympathetic to a focus on possibilities (see part II), giving more prominence to restraints in the study's conceptual framework helped me to develop a more critical and distanced position. Nevertheless, this book remains in the spirit of what Esper et. al (2017, p. 671) call "critical performativity" which refers to "scholars' subversive interventions that can involve the production of new subjectivities, the constitution of new organizational models and/or the bridging of these models to current social movements".

Critical performativity needs to navigate a twofold tension. First, the danger of going native. And second, the influence of lasting relationships beyond systemic data collection. Going native refers to the immersion of the researcher in the community by which he loses his "critical external perspective and [...] unquestioningly adopts the viewpoints shared in the field" (Flick, 2014, p. 315). As a consequence, critical performativity becomes uncritical participation. Ethnographic methodologies in general and action research in particular hinge upon meaningful relationships amongst researcher and community members. To that effect, the researcher has to navigate the tension between emotional and practical proximity on the one hand and critical distance on the other. Due to the travel involved in getting to the sites of fieldwork, empirical work usually lasted one to three days and was spaced by one to two weeks in between field visits. This allowed me to move not only in physical space but also in emotional and conceptual space. In addition, the iterative research design between phases of empirical work and critical reflection supported this movement.

Aside from knowledge creation, meaningful relationships and friendships beyond any instrumental research objective are a valuable outcome of my ethnographic fieldwork. While much ethnographic literature discusses immersion and trust in the context of building rapport and strategic relationships, this instrumental view is ethically questionable. Participatory action research methodologies, in contrast, support a critical reflection on extractive and instrumental relationships. In this respect, I appreciate the tension that arises from having built close relationships and take it as a gratifying challenge rather than a dilemma that diminishes the value of research. For me, this also entails a certain indebtedness to the protagonists of this study who have taken much valuable time to share information and introduce me to their organizations. In the sense of mutual help, I try to remain at their disposal for requests and seek an exchange also beyond the actual empirical fieldwork. Amongst other things, this pertains to information gathered and analyzed in the course of the study that might support the organizations.

Of course, the continuous involvement raises the question: what new information is documented and considered in the data analysis? Taking a rather pragmatic approach to this issue, I documented information that seem to be relevant up to the beginning of the final coding (see below). After that, new developments are not considered in the systematic analysis. Nevertheless, they continue to shape my (tacit) knowledge and might therefore, at least indirectly, influence further analysis and discussion. Chapter 11, now, turns towards data analysis in more detail.

Chapter 11: Data analysis

> Coding is a cyclical act.
> Saldaña, 2009, p. 8

Materiality and implicitness challenge data analysis to work with empirical evidence that is only partially explicated. Ethnographic and action research methodologies that are in line with practice theory's conceptual focus emphasize the researcher's direct engagement to develop a tacit understanding of practices, subjects, organizations, and their relations and interactions. A major methodological challenge, therefore, is the explication of tacit knowledge acquired through ethnographic fieldwork. The systematic documentation of participant observation in field notes is an important part of this process. Another part is the analysis itself. Coding, as analytical practice, guides the process of explication and combines the explicit or already explicated data (primarily interview transcripts and field notes) with the researcher's embodied knowledge.

This chapter develops a code framework in conversation with the study's conceptual grounding. After introducing coding as analytical practice that allows for a systematic engagement with empirical data, section one gives an outline of the coding frames. The subsequent section, then, elaborates on three frames that guide further data analysis. It traces their development by establishing links to the empirical data (part IV) and the study's conceptual grounding (part II). The third and last section fuses the different coding frames into a complex framework that guides the main data analysis and transitions to the presentation of findings.

Coding and coding frames: an overview

Coding is an analytical practice in which the researcher systematically works through her material to identify patterns, ideas, events and features of interest to the research inquiry (Benaquisto, 2008; Saldaña, 2009; Till, 2009). In coding, the researcher assigns words or short phrases (codes) to portions of data, which summarize or qualify their relevance and link related segments of data. Coding can be used with a broad range of different materials – such as interview transcripts, field notes, articles, photographs, or paintings – and for a broad range of research designs, from explorative to focused. Importantly, coding itself is already an interpretative act and thus a "transitional process between data collection and more extensive data analysis" (Saldaña, 2009, p. 4). By putting data in conversation with the researcher's (tacit) knowledge, the study's conceptual approach and its specific research interest, "coding generates the bones" (Charmaz, 2006, cited in Saldaña, 2009, p. 8) of further analysis.

Coding and the development of a coding structure do not follow a strict chronological order. In light of the abductive research design of this work, practices of data collection, analysis and interpretation interweave. In doing so they "affec[t] each other and, through their mutual impact, they help contribute to more rigorous conclusions." (Cope, 2010, p. 442). As a consequence, "the process of developing the coding structure for your project is one that is inevitably circular, sporadic and, frankly, messy [...] coding involves reading and rereading, thinking and rethinking, and developing codes that are tentative and temporary along the way, even during an on-going research project" (ibid., p. 445).

A coding frame emerges from, and provides a connection among, different codes. Depending on whether the approach is rather deductive or inductive, the coding frame is developed from theory or grounded in empirical data itself. This study's abductive reasoning develops its coding frame through the iterative movement between theory and empirical data. At first, the study uses three distinct frames that focus on different aspects of the research question (see table 5), namely diversity (1), implicitness and materiality (2), and normativity (3). In addition, one coding frame goes beyond the more streamlined analysis and captures a range of recurring themes (4).

Coding frame 1 (CF1) focuses on the issue of complexity and translates the considerations of chapter 7 on a structured notion of diversity (that allows grasping patterns in practices' relatedness) into an analytical tool. CF1 develops through provisional coding (Saldaña, 2009), starting with a pre-formulated list of codes which are based on the study's conceptual framework and literature review as well as the researcher's knowledge developed during fieldwork. Successive rounds of coding refine CF1 to comprise five patterns of practices' relatedness – economy, governance, communality, subjectivity and technology – that guide further analysis (see table 6).

Coding frame 2 (CF2) focuses on the issues of implicitness and materiality, simplifying the continua of explicitness and material involvement for analytical purposes. CF2 develops through process coding which uses gerunds and is therefore particularly attentive to practices and processes (Saldaña, 2009, p. 77). This coding frame, furthermore, operationalizes the study's interest in possibilities and constraints. Consequently, it consists of two modes of practices – practices of representation and material practices – and four moments in the implementation of alternative practices – alternatives, enablement, constraints and compromise (see table 7).

Coding frame 3 (CF3) focuses on the issue of normativity and builds on CF2. It accounts for different understandings of sustainability and alternatives (see part I). CF3 modifies CF2 by focusing on activities that are in line with degrowth principles (see chapter 7) while maintaining the same code structure (see table 9).

Coding frame 4 (CF4), finally, includes a wide range of topics that speak to the research question and develops through open coding (Till, 2009). Open Coding is a "form of brainstorming, whereby the researcher revisits materials in order to think about possible ideas, themes and issues" (Till, 2009, p. 629). In contrast to coding frames 1 to 3, CF4 has no internal congruence and is simply a collection of topics that are relevant to the study's broader interest. CF4 is not part of the more streamlined analysis, but highlights and introduces additional topics.

Table 5 Coding frames

Coding Frame	Coding Technique	Focus
CF 1: Diverse logics perspective	Provisional Coding	Structuring the diversity of alternative practices and narratives thereof
CF 2: Implicitness and Materiality	Process Coding	Distinguishing between different levels of explicitness and material engagement
CF 3: Degrowth Transition	Normative Coding	Modification of CF2 to accommodate for issues of normativity
CF 4: Grey Codes	Open Coding	20-30 codes that refer to issues of general interest

From conceptual framework to coding frames

Coding frame 1: the diverse logics perspective

Logics are patterns of practices' relatedness, or, in other words, different ways that practices hang together and interact. Chapter 7 advances a 'diverse logics perspective' (DLP) as an analytical tool to grasp practices' relations beyond their sites of enactment. The DLP is particularly important with respect to the study's ambition to investigate a degrowth politics of place beyond place (part II) while following a research strategy that foregrounds the complex interplay of objects, practices and relations in a specific geographical context. The DLP supports the empirical tracing of practices' trajectories that travel through the sites of research but extend beyond the moments and places of fieldwork. In doing so, the DLP operationalizes Nicolini's (2013) notion of zooming, which calls on the researcher to expand the scope and track broader connections and interactions of practices across time and space. Furthermore, the DLP highlights the different ways in which the diverse practices that constitute Stuttgart's community economy themselves hang together.

Provisional coding used emergent categories which were inspired by the different approaches to structure societal diversity outlined in chapter 7. In conversation with conceptual deliberations and empirical insights, the categories were merged, split, cut out and sharpened, not least through the repeated coding of small parts of collected data. The complete process spanned over more than two years and included versions with up to ten different logics that emerged through these iterative processes of theoretical considerations and provisional (re)coding. For reasons of scope, I will not elaborate on the development in detail. For an earlier version see Schmid (2018). Table 6, below, shows the conclusive version of the DLP used for the final rounds of coding and analysis. It comprises five logics: economies, governance, communality, subjectivity, and technology.

Table 6 Codes of the diverse logics perspective (CF1)

Code	Description
Economy	Economy captures practices' relatedness through moments of creation, exchange, reciprocity, comparison, and sustenance. It is particularly visible in production, consumption, exchange and distribution.
Communality	Communality captures practices' relatedness through moments of togetherness, interdependence, contestation, and collective identity. It is particularly visible in practices of support, participation, non-violent disagreement, competition, negotiation, and group-formation.
Governance	Governance captures practices' relatedness through moments of rule, domination, power, control, and norms. It is particularly visible in bureaucratic practices, law (enforcement), policing, politicking, and violence.
Subjectivity	Subjectivity captures practices' relatedness through imaginaries, meanings, theories and concepts on the one hand, and habits, affects, feelings and experiences on the other hand. It is particularly visible in practices of explaining, analyzing, sense-making as well as practices of judgement and (self-) positioning.
Technology	Technology refers to practices' relatedness through infrastructures, documents, machines, tools, substances, and other artefacts. It is particularly visible in practices based on (modern) technological innovations such as instant messaging, nuclear energy, electro mobility, 3D printing, and living in a smart home.

Different rounds of coding – which I detail in the last section of this chapter – apply the codes of the diverse logics perspective to passages that are of interest for this study's inquiry. This does not mean that segments are always coded with all the CF1 codes that can be associated with it (which is often more than one). Rather they are coded with the CF1 code(s) most relevant with respect to the research question. Still, frequently multiple codes are used, for instance economy and technology, to focus on the intersection of different logics. In particular, the code 'compromise', which is part of CF2 often contains a trade-off between several dimensions of practices' relatedness.

Coding frame 2: narrating alternatives and material engagement

Narrations of sustainability and their materialization in practices are of central interest to this study. In order to operationalize the distinction between talking about and imagining alternatives on the one hand, and transforming bodies, artefacts and things according to particular notions of sustainability on the other hand

– a distinction that is conceptually challenging (see chapter 8) – the continua of explicitness and material involvement need to be translated into a coding frame. This section traces the development of coding frame 2 by means of the categories outlined in table 7.

Table 7 Combination of two modes of practices with four moments of transformation

	Alternatives	**Enablement**	**Constraints**	**Compromise**
High level of explicitness	Narrating alternatives	Narrating constraints	Narrating enablement	Narrating compromise
High level of material engagement	Practicing alternatives	Encountering constraints	Encountering enablement	Negotiating compromise

The rows in table 7 distinguish between practices of representation with a high level of explication on the one side and practices with a high level of material engagement on the other side. The first row of codes – 'high level of explicitness' – pertains to data that records or documents 'discursive practices' (see chapter 8). That means, practices which narrate perceived, potential, theoretical, or hypothetical alternatives without allowing inference of the actuality of the activities they describe. The second row of codes – 'high level of material engagement' – applies to data that recounts or records 'material practices'. That means actual, observed and experienced practices in which materials do not solely have an 'infrastructural relation' but are exposed to the possibility of transformation (see chapter 8). This admittedly rather coarse separation provides a heuristic to capture whether data refers to potentials, ideas, possibilities, wishes, fears, and thoughts related to sustainability on the one hand. For instance, an interviewee describing the idea of an open source business model. And observation notes that document practices that materialize in and transform bodies, things, and artefacts on the other hand. Such as the implementation of an open source business model. Different kinds of data, in particular interview transcripts and observation notes, are treated separately at first and only later reintegrated through triangulation (see below).

The columns of table 7 above detail the different aspects of transformation: alternatives, enablement, constraints and compromise. 'Alternatives' refer to practices which differ from common (often unsustainable and unjust) forms of conduct (I detail below the difficulties of the normativity involved). 'Constraints' refer to restrictive moments complicating the implementation of alternatives. Meaning, contextual factors, conditions and organizational practices that impede the translation of ideals into practice. 'Enablement' refers to enabling moments facilitating the implementation of alternatives. That is, contextual factors, conditions, strategies and organizational practices that support the translation of ideals into material practice. And 'compromise' refers to trade-offs between possibilities and constraints. Meaning, the forced, pragmatic, or strategic weighting of some forms of alternative conduct over others.

Analogous to the distinction between a high level of explicitness and a high level of material engagement with respect to alternatives in general, the coding structure distinguishes between the narration and encountering of enablement, the narrating and encountering of constraints as well as deliberation and negotiation of compromise. That means the codes capture potential (narrated) enablement, constraints, and deliberations on trade-offs on the one hand. And material and observable possibilities, constraints, and negotiations on the other hand. Again, of course, this is a coarse distinction that abstracts from the complexity and continuity of the actual spectrum. Table 8 summarizes the codes as used in the coding process.

Table 8 Codes of process coding (CF2)

Code	Description
Narrating alternatives	Codes sections that express how the organization and its practice differ from the business-as-usual that is considered to be unsustainable or unjust.
Narrating constraints	Perceived, potential, theoretical or hypothetical contextual factors, conditions, strategies and organizational practices that impede the translation of ideals into practice
Narrating enablement	Perceived, potential, theoretical or hypothetical contextual factors, conditions, strategies and organizational practices that support the translation of ideals into material practice
Narrating compromise	Perceived, potential, theoretical or hypothetical trade-off between possibilities and constraints
Practicing alternatives	Codes sections documenting the enactment of practices that differ from business-as-usual
Encountering constraints	Actual, material, experienced contextual factors, conditions, strategies and organizational practices that impede the enactment of sustainability-related practices
Encountering enablement	Actual, material, experienced contextual factors, conditions, strategies and organizational practices that support the enactment of sustainability-related practices
Compromising	Actual, material, experienced trade-off between possibilities and constraints.

Coding frame 3: strong sustainability

Sustainability is a highly contested concept and therefore difficult to use as descriptive category for coding. Coding frame 2, consequently, runs into a number of difficulties revolving around different notions of sustainability. In particular, divergences between the orientation of interviewees' or participants' notion of sustainability on the one hand and the study's grounding in postcapitalist and degrowth scholarship on the other. Consequently, CF 2 needs further development and sharpening in accordance with the study's normative orientation (part I). I call this process *normative coding*, since it adds an evaluative dimension to coding (see figure 6 and table 9).

Figure 6 Normative coding

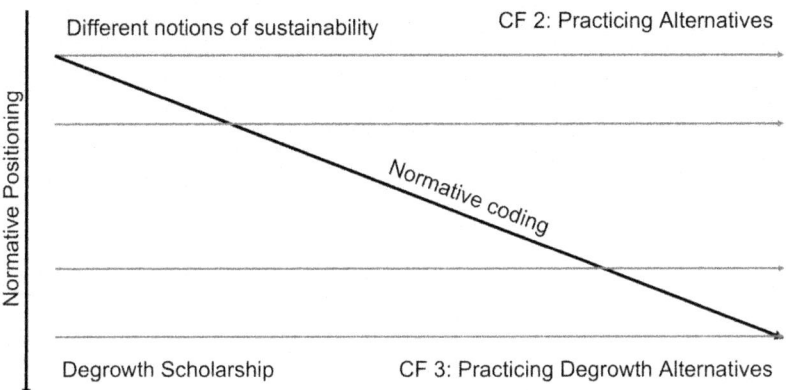

Normative coding aligns the codes of CF 2 with degrowth principles (see chapter 7). 'Practicing degrowth alternatives', consequently, codes sections that document practices that are relevant from a degrowth perspective. 'Encountering constraints' codes segments that document actual, material and experienced contextual factors, conditions, strategies or organizational practices that impede the enactment of degrowth-oriented practices. Analogous, 'encountering enablement' codes segments that document actual, material and experienced contextual factors, conditions, strategies or organizational practices that support the enactment of degrowth-oriented practices. Finally, 'compromising' refers to actual, material and experienced trade-offs between possibilities and constraints for degrowth-oriented practices. Coding frame 3, therefore, builds on and replaces the second-row codes of CF2 (see tables 7 and 9)

Normative coding links to the reflections on positionality and normativity in chapter 10. This specification of coding frame 2, then, adds a selective layer over the coded materials. In doing so, the codings of CF3 highlight material engagement that is relevant from a degrowth perspective. It specifies research question (a) of *what practices follow from and accompany critiques of unsustainable social relations* (see introduction) to *what practices follow from and accompany postcapitalist and degrowth critiques of unsustainable social relations*. The same goes for research question (b) *how do facilitating and constraining moments become relevant in sustainability-related practice* (see introduction), which is further specified to ask *how do facilitating and constraining moments become relevant in degrowth-oriented practice?*

Table 9 Codes of normative coding (CF3)

Code	Description
Practicing degrowth alternatives	Practices of alternative economizing that are relevant from a degrowth perspective
Encountering constraints	Actual, material, experienced contextual factors, conditions, strategies and organizational practices that impede the enactment of degrowth-oriented practices.
Encountering enablement	Actual, material, experienced contextual factors, conditions, strategies and organizational practices that support the enactment of degrowth-oriented practices
Compromising	Actual, material, experienced trade-off between possibilities and constraints for degrowth-oriented practices

Triangulation and final coding

As a consequence of applying multiple methods (see chapter 9), analysis includes different forms of data that require a careful distinction. Interviewing captures primarily practices of representation that provide insights into the perception of, as well as the thoughts and motivations behind, practices but are limited as to the depth of the conclusions that can be drawn beyond the narration of alternatives. Data from participant observation, instead, captures both practices of representation (for instance through informal interviewing) and observable practices, which are then documented and explicated by the researcher. It allows for inferences about material practices. This study combines different methods for several reasons (see chapter 9), including the ability to cover both practices of representation and material practices and to collect comprehensive data in face of the study's limitations (such as temporal and financial resources and difficulties to access sites of practices' enactment).

Coding frame 2 takes the different forms of data into account by differentiating between discursive and material practices. It does, however, treat both sets of data separately – explicated data from interviews and focus groups versus documentation of participant observation. Data analysis cannot simply lump together interview data with data from participant observation. This final section of chapter 11, therefore, reflects on two issues. First, how can data analysis triangulate interview and observation data? And second, how does that translate into coding? To find answers, this section turns to the role of tacit knowledge for data analysis and outlines a systematic procedure through several rounds of coding. Table 10, below, summarizes the different coding phases.

Aside from information explicated in interview transcripts and field notes, the acquisition and development of tacit knowledge is an important pillar for data analysis. Tacit knowledge entails, for instance, the ability to assess and contextualize data. The capacity to judge the validity, accuracy and relevance of information becomes a crucial methodological tool. Inferring practices solely from the observation of their performance severely limits the ability to collect relevant information. Observation, therefore, transcends mere visual witnessing – 'I only believe what I see with my own eyes' – and becomes a method that combines visual input, experience, intuition and secondary evidence to build a coherent case. Consequently, there is much potential in bridging the gap between different kinds of data in order to illuminate the activities of interest.

To ensure a systematic procedure and maintain awareness of the limitations of data triangulation, this study structures the coding process in three phases with different foci. The first coding phase focuses on the narration of alternatives, enablement, constraints and compromise. It codes all interviews including the focus group transcript that all exhibit a high level of explication but do not allow for any conclusions pertaining to material involvement. Coding, at this first stage, combines CF1 (see table 6) with the first-row codes of CF 2 (narrating alternatives, narrating enablement, narrating constraints and narrating compromise) (see table 7). Subsequently, a second round codes the field notes from participant observation. In doing so, it adds information on the activities observed and documented during fieldwork. Coding, at this second stage, combines CF1 with the whole of CF2.

The final (main) coding entails a double shift that includes both triangulation and normative coding. For one thing, it substitutes the second-row codes of CF2 (practicing alternatives, encountering constraints, encountering possibilities and compromising) for the CF3 codes of normative coding (practicing degrowth alternatives, etcetera; see table 9). For another thing, it applies the codes that infer a high level of material engagement to all data, including interview transcripts. The final coding is aware of and attentive to the limitation of interview data, but squares the data with insights from participant observation and other methods to ensure that the interviewees' claims and accounts correspond to actual practice. In my judgment, I rely on tacit knowledge about the participants and their surroundings, general insights into the context, informal interviews, the triangulation of multiple accounts, empathy and trust.

Table 10 Different phases of coding and interpretation

Phase	Process	Coding Frame	Data
I	Coding and interpretation	CF1 and CF2 (first row)	Interviews and focus group
II	Coding and interpretation	CF1 and CF2	Participant observation
III	Coding and interpretation	CF1 and CF2 (first row) and CF3	All data
IV	Interpretation	CF1 and CF3	All data

By integrating all forms of data – from interviewing, observation, desktop research and focus groups – the final coding provides a comprehensive picture of alternatives, enablement, constraints and compromise. To get here, the distinction between representation and material engagement, as emphasized by coding frame 2, has been crucial. In particular, by sensitizing analysis for different kinds of methods and the data they create. The primary concern of this study, however, is not the difference itself between representing and practicing alternatives but the actual implementation of alternatives. Hence, rather than detailing the divergence between (a) what participants say that should be done, (b) what participants say that they do, and (c) what the researcher observes in practice, the study focuses on the enactment of alternatives while emphasizing the importance of being aware of different levels of explication and material involvement in researching transformative geographies.

Consequently, the final analysis (phase IV) is set up to trace the study's interest in practicing degrowth alternatives, encountering constraints, encountering enablement and compromising respectively. In doing so, it drops CF2 which has been an indispensable step for data analysis but deflects the study's main focus. The final step in data analysis, then, is an interpretation of the data coded with coding frames 1 and 3 as applied to all data. It combines CF1 and CF3 to set up a perspective that links diverse forms of practices' relatedness with the different moments in the implementation of alternative practices. The ensuing perspective structures the wealth of data into a number of related categories that support a more detailed understanding of a degrowth transition. Alternatives, for instance, become visible with respect to economies, governance, communality, subjectivities and technology. In the same vein, constraints, enablement, and compromise are specified by different foci on practices' relatedness. As a matter of course, this is a purely analytical move to capture different moments in the complex process of transformation. Part IV builds on this possibility and uses it as a position from which to present the work's findings.

Part IV: Stuttgart's community economy

Outline

Part IV presents the study's findings. It structures into four chapters – alternatives, constraints, enablement and compromise – that travel from the investigation of practices that are deliberately different from growth-based and capitalist institutions, to moments that constrain and enable these alternative practices, and, finally, to the navigation of trade-offs. This arc of suspense ensues from the research questions that guide this book (see introduction) and which chapter 11 translates into coding frames.

Chapter 12 on alternatives traces the study's findings on practices that deviate from and challenge prevailing forms of economic, political, cultural and technological conduct. In doing so, it sketches the landscape of Stuttgart's community economy. Chapter 13 on constraints, then, presents aspects that either curb the organizations directly or limit the effects of their practices for a degrowth transition. Aside from constraints, the study also uncovers a number of factors that facilitate Stuttgart's community economy. To that effect, chapter 14 on enablement identifies institutional arrangements and infrastructures that support organizations in their orientation towards a degrowth transition. Chapter 15, lastly, turns to compromise. In light of diverse constraining and enabling factors, organizations have to trade off between different priorities and develop tactics to navigate transformative geographies.

Where useful and applicable, the diverse logics perspective, established in part II and further operationalized in part III, structures the main body of the ensuing chapters. On occasion, however, the findings include topics that do not fit neatly with the perspective on practices' relatedness through economy, governance, communality, subjectivity, or technology. Rather than a rigid categorization, the diverse logics perspective provides a supportive orientation which remains flexible enough to accommodate other insights.

To illustrate the study's findings, the following sections use interview quotes and excerpts from participant observation side by side. Despite of the study's ethnographic thrust, quotations are included in the presentation of findings for two reasons. For one thing, they capture discursive practices that, after all, are important to the book's epistemological interest (most pointedly captured by the logic of subjectivity). For another thing, the quotations often entail quite nuanced, trenchant and memorizable formulations that represent the observable material practices well. Against the background of part III's detailed discussion of different kinds of data and their triangulation, the quotes are selected carefully and do not stand for themselves. Interview data is squared with insights from participant observation and other methods to ensure that interviewees' claims and accounts find correspondence in actual practice (see chapter 11).

Of infidels and agnostics

This introductory section traces respondents' different objectives and economic philosophies. The organizations that are part of this study were selected due to their opposition to linear, profit-oriented economies as expressed in their public appearance, their self-positioning and as well as their practices (see chapter 9). It is thus of little surprise to encounter a range of alternative orientations and practices in the aforementioned sense. A central precept of all organizations is a critique of self-referential notions of economic practice, that means economizing for economy's or growth's sake. Yet the points of criticism and consequences taken differ amongst the participants and organizations

> It's not that one does business in such a way that people are better off. Rather, at the moment, it is the case that one does business because one does business. And because there are a few people who earn a lot of money with it. Or simply because there is money lying around that wants to be capitalized. That is, of course, a rather obscure starting position. And to get away from that is our goal, of course, no question (I_E02a).[1]

A central driver for all organizations is the sense of doing something meaningful and addressing social and environmental issues. While the organizations experiment with different legal forms and modes of financing, there is a tendency to engage in market-oriented practices in order to be financially self-sufficient while focusing on non-monetary objectives. The majority of participants have a long-standing involvement with the voluntary sector but struggle with the precariousness of their engagement. Indeed, while a number of organizations are based on non-monetary engagement and some rely on public funding and/or private donations, much of the innovative organizing explored in this book explicitly emerges from the need to devise (at least partially) financially independent organizations.

> I need something that works, that can finance itself. But this doesn't mean it has to be a maximization of profits, rather a maximization of meaning (I_E01a).

A (partial) financial independence provides the participants with some autonomy to pursue ethical goals while sustaining themselves and their organizations. Its thus for both personal reasons – making a living, receiving a return or appreciation – and for politico-economic reasons – autonomy of decision-making, having resources at disposal – that some take an entrepreneurial approach to activism. At this, the need for diverse strategies and trade-offs prevails (see chapter 15).

---

1   All direct quotes were translated from German to English by the author. Wherever possible, quotations are translated literally while considering contextual and cultural specificities, metaphors and potentially misleading formulations.

> Everything that is dependent on external sources of money is not sustainable in the long run. Because then you always work for someone else or regularly hold out a tin cup, begging and so on. You just can't act freely. That means you are always dependent. And that's just not stable (I_A01a).

Describing the case at hand in terms of (eco-)social entrepreneurship, however, oversimplifies the trade-off between an economic orientation on the one hand and ecological and social objectives on the other hand. The monetization of ethical activities is a means rather than an end. In other words, while the discourse on social enterprises exhibits a certain thrust to integrate (eco-)social objectives with the (seemingly) given set-up of market-oriented organizing (see chapter 3), the extraction of revenue from social or ecological engagement, here, is perceived primarily as (often rather ambiguous) means of building alternative and independent organizations within a capitalist economy.

> I need a shell, a space. A space in which economic activity is possible within the existing system. But within, that space is organized differently (I_E01a).

This is, however, not to obscure that the organizations differ with respect to problem diagnosis, causal attribution, strategies and goals on the one hand and realization on the other. Most protagonists problematize a growth-based capitalist economy and some firmly emphasize the urgency to establish economic arrangements that renounce a focus on growth. Yet, others discuss social and environmental sustainability without reference to economic (de)growth or explicitly subscribe to growth agnosticism, instead problematizing the linearity of current economies and the lack of implementation of the technological possibilities at disposal.

> [Our organization] does not express any preference at all. If we [as society] want further growth, then it is a good idea to do this within a circular economy. And if we want to focus more on sufficiency strategies, then we should still organize what we still consume in cycles. In any case, this is a concept that embraces both [growth and degrowth] and does not prefer one over the other (I_E08).

Furthermore, opposition against economic exploitation and growthmanship does not translate into practice in any straightforward way. Numerous external and internal constraints as well as the wealth of possibilities in prefiguring, shaping and promoting alternatives – let alone the diverse ethics and perspectives that accompany alternative practices – render the sites of alternative economizing colorful, creative and contradictory. Chapters 13 and 14 below take a close look at constraints and enablement respectively. Here, in a more general sense, it is important to note the multiple shades of dissonances between consideration and application, beliefs and realization, sayings and doings. Note the qualification towards the middle of the following statement:

> [...] that you don't say: 'consume more so that we earn more' but rather communicate: 'do you really need this or can you do without it?' And because it's important that we consume less and consume even less resources ... That's not possible by buying more sustainable things but rather you have to refrain from many things. This is what we try to live. *And as soon as we have the opportunity*, we want to integrate that into our business model. And maybe that really is a step in the right direction, if you really try to buy from small manufacturers that are right around the corner, because that saves resources again ... that one decides not to focus on ever more consumption (I_E06a, emphasis added).

This quote is emblematic for the relation between ideas and concepts on the one side and the 'realities' of a capitalist economy on the other. During the first half of the quote, the interviewee subscribes to ideas of degrowth and infers therefrom a need to not only sell more sustainable products but also avoid unnecessary sales. Sufficiency, however, in the sense of consuming less, turns out to run against his organization's interests and, at the end of the day, is not practicable if the organization is to sustain. *Smark*, the organization the interviewee represents, runs fully automated supermarkets that sell local and organic food. To navigate this contradiction, the organization has to translate sufficiency into something that works economically. While *Smark* focuses on purchasing its foodstuff from local farmers, the imperative of reaching a particular level of sales prevails. Like other companies, *Smark* stimulates sales through low-threshold marketing measures, for instance on social media. Furthermore, the company markets its automation technology to investors who do not necessarily share an orientation towards sustainable consumption. The flash of degrowth ideas, then, vanishes quickly in the sea of practical constraints and makes it quite difficult to tell apart the actual ideals and values from adjustment and compromise. Even in cases where the overall orientation is clearer, the coherent integration of sustainability in organizational practices remains a constant challenge. The subsequent chapters show different priorities and strategies how organizations navigate the challenging landscape of community economies and do (or do not) contribute to a degrowth transition.

Chapter 12: Alternatives

> We create the reality within our possibilities, not wasting our energy on establishing boundaries. Rather we focus on change itself and not on the problems.
> (F_01)

Alternatives refer to doings and sayings that deviate from and challenge explicit and implicit norms and prevailing forms of economic, political, cultural and technological relatedness amongst humans and with the more-than-human world. As detailed above, this neither implies that alternatives are a second choice (White and Williams, 2016) nor that alternatives' capacity and significance for human sustenance is subordinate to more common and strongly institutionalized forms of relatedness (see chapter 6). From a diverse economies perspective, alternative economies are "(1) [p]rocesses of production, exchange, labor/compensation, finance, and consumption that are intentionally different from mainstream (capitalist) economic activity" as well as "(2) an alternative representation of economy as a heterogeneous and proliferative social space" (Healy, 2009, p. 338; see chapter 2). Acknowledging the sites of Stuttgart's community economy as heterogeneous spaces where diverse practices meet and interrelate, the book's interest in alternativeness is not restricted to practices' relatedness through moments of creation, exchange, reciprocity and material provision (what has been referred to as the logic of economy) but also through modes of governance, subjectivities, communality and technology. This chapter covers the findings on alternative practices across these different dimensions.

Slow technology – supporting sufficiency and subsistence

One way of meeting the challenges that *Smark* faces (see above) is the use of technological means to attain a competitive advantage which, in turn, increases the organization's capacity to focus on sustainability-related issues.

> Our goal is, with our business model, to make everything – that means both the products and the logistics behind them – more sustainable. And to achieve this, in part, by automating many processes and simply making them leaner in order to save resources (I_E06a).

Technological innovation, here, occupies an ambivalent position. It is, as is generally the case, a means to gain a competitive edge. This advantage, however, is not meant to maximize returns but to facilitate more sustainable modes of distribution and consumption. Both, by making them more easily available – *Smark*'s fully automated supermarkets are opened 24/7 – and by saving costs, allowing the small organization to survive in a highly competitive food retailing industry.

In other cases, the application of technology is accompanied more explicitly by a broader critique of growth-based economies. A number of organizations take a very conscious, deliberate, emancipating and subversive approach to technology, making it clear that a focus on technology alone does not suffice. In contrast to smart cities, homes, grids and other forms of smartness usually associated with the green economy, a reflexive use of technology emerges: 'slow technology'. Most prominently, *Slowtec*, reflects this awareness in its very name. *Slowtec* describes its mission as follows:

> We develop sustainable technologies that support humans in their development and living and grant long term quality of life – that means also that of future generations – while maintaining a holistic view of human needs and our basis of existence: our earth (slowtec.org, author's translation).

Slowtec is a team of engineers who develop, construct and program soft- and hardware products that support sustainability-related practices. This includes, amongst others, the programming of feedback control systems for solar energy production, the development of automated irrigation systems, the set-up of digital databases and geographic information systems and the construction of decentralized and independent water and energy systems. Technology, for *Slowtec*, is not just a passive backdrop for its business activities or a means for accumulation, but a possibility to further alternative ways of living and economizing if applied wisely. Technology, thereby, is anything but value neutral. Rather, the organization continuously reflects on the upsides and downsides of technology, considering its kind, size, origin and application. In developing and marketing technologies, *Slowtec* raises the question:

> How much technology is needed to be meaningful for people and society and when is it too much? (I_E01a)

Slow technology, however, is not to be mistaken for low technology. All technology-oriented enterprises in this study operate with state-of-the-art software and hardware such as automated system control, 3D printing or photovoltaics, to name only a few. But these technologies are predominantly applied to support sufficiency and subsistence rather than overly technologized livelihoods. One of *Slowtec*'s projects is the *Krautomat*, a partially automated indoor herbage growing system. The product is designed to support year-round autonomous growing of foodstuff. As in many cases, however, a number of factors hamper the full realization of development and production so that the project died before being ready for the market (see chapter 13).

A reoccurring theme with respect to sufficiency and subsistence-oriented technologies is the creation of circular flows of water, energy and nutrients. *Grünfisch* is an association that develops and constructs aquaponics systems. Integrating fish farming with plant growing, *Grünfisch* generates partly closed nutrition cycles, eliminating the need to add fertilizers. In a running system, fish food is the only input and crops the only output.

> The basic ideas, here, simply are circularity and self-sufficiency. And also decentralization. These are ideas that come together in aquaponics. Of course, also connected to a personal interest in nature. But I find that so exciting in terms of the ecological cycle that you can grow things, even here on the roof, which is a totally dead environment. But you make life. You are bringing life here (I_A02).

Geco-Gardens is a small venture that constructs and markets vertical garden systems that are based on a similar principle as aquaponics but with lobworms. The worms decompose organic kitchen waste, releasing nutrients that fertilize the plants in the system. Solar panels provide the energy to circulate the water for nutrient transportation. *ownworld* goes one step further in integrating energy, water and nutrient cycles into a building – the *ownhome*. The *ownhome* is a small stand-alone house constructed to minimize resource consumption through a combination of technology-aided sufficiency and efficiency strategies. Water and energy needs are fully covered by solar energy and rainfall, both harnessed and processed through state-of-the-art technologies to provide electricity and clean water respectively. Used water, furthermore, is circulated and treated through constructed wetland and UV disinfection to provide for raw water and (if treated through reverse osmosis) for drinking water. In addition to energy and water a third focus is on food production and the nutrient cycle.

> Last but not least, the cycle of nutrients should also be brought to life. For this reason, there is a modern urine-diverting dry toilet. The nutrients, which are taken from the earth through the cultivation of food and transformed into high-quality fertilizers by the human organism, are returned to the natural nutrient cycle. (ownworld Flyer, author's translation)

After my first visit to the *ownhome* I noted:

> The project is primarily driven by a desire for a modest but comfortable lifestyle that is socially and ecologically just and allows for more freedom and time wealth. The basic idea is to be independent of the provisioning of water and energy and to some extent food. This, then, leads to an increased financial independence and independence from participating in unsustainable practice (B_E05a).

The use of technology, here, differs fundamentally from the techno-optimism and managerialism of green-growth approaches. Rather than contributing to capital accumulation, technology supports sufficiency and subsistence-oriented practices in a modern world. Technology, then, is a means to withdraw from spaces of capitalist economizing. In that way, organizations like *Slowtec*, *ownworld* and *Geco-Gardens*, in particular, use technology to increase autonomy with respect to everyday needs.

> Actually, that is what this is all about. That one tries to establish a lifestyle that does not fit into the system. That you say: I try to do as much as possible by myself. And in my case to produce as much food as possible in different gardens: at home, in the city, with the Geco-system, with aquaponics. And, of course, if you do something like that, then you put your working time directly into the product without the use of money (I_E04).

Other projects are less focused on the development and spread of new (highly sophisticated) tools and instead advocate for a shift to alternative and possibly simpler technologies. *Critical Mass*, for instance, is a monthly event where a large group of cyclists gather to obstruct traffic and protest the transport political focus on automobility. Depending on the season, a few hundred up to 2000 cyclists claim Stuttgart's streets to demonstrate that more inclusive and sustainable mobility technologies already exist.

Unlocking a sustainable local economy

Sufficiency and subsistence-oriented technologies are important parts of a localized and sustainable economy. Nevertheless, while sufficiency- and subsistence-oriented technologies reduce the need (or desire) for consumption, other needs and wants prevail that cannot be fulfilled locally and sustainably. In response, a number of organizations seek to establish non-exploitative relations of production and exchange through fair sourcing of materials, just working conditions, durable and repairable products, accessible knowledge and appropriate institutional arrangements. Many participants turn to debates on social entrepreneurship and degrowth for inspiration but are disappointed by the lack of tangible outcomes these movements have hitherto failed to produce.

But what is catastrophic, of course – and you can't fool yourself with that – is that with respect to concepts like the post-growth economy, there's hardly anyone who has a tangible product. And that was our claim. To bridge the gap and say: we somehow have a great theory here, that's nice, but nobody has a product for it. Nobody has any tangible suggestions as to what something like this could look like as an economic system (I_E02a).

As a consequence, some organizations try to translate degrowth principles into practice by integrating considerations around social justice and ecological sustainability into design, production and distribution. Longevity, reparability, circularity, modularity and open source, for instance, become an elementary part in product design. The production process, furthermore, is shifted towards fair sourcing of resources and fair working conditions. For degrowth-oriented organizations, then, this means not only to reflect on the role of technology and social needs (see previous section) but also on the question what is produced and for whom. In doing so, some practitioners

[...] intend to change and positively influence the ways in which electrical products are currently produced. And positive in the sense that society and nature are the focus (I_E02a).

Relumity, for instance, is an eco-social startup that engages in the development, production and sale of repairable lamps. *Relumity*'s orientation is grounded in a critique of the wastefulness of mainstream product-design that largely ignores longevity and reparability. The realization that common light bulbs cannot be repaired and deliberations around the possibility to do so motivated the founders to conceive an alternative. Financed primarily through a crowdfunding campaign, *Relumity* developed, produced and sold a few hundred private-use household lamps called *Relumity #LED1*. *Relumity #LED1*'s design is based on longevity, modular design, open source and reparability. Aside from being exchangeable, some of the lamp's parts are easily available (such as the Petri dish used for coverage), or are designed for local (re)production (such as the 3D-printed outer shell).

In addition to the development of novel products that internalize degrowth principles, other organizations set up infrastructures that enable individuals to engage in sustainability-related activities. Repair, local production and sharing – practices closely associated with degrowth (see chapter 17) – require corresponding material and social arrangements. The open workshop *Hobbyhimmel*, which is also the primary site for this study's fieldwork (see chapter 9), constitutes a social and material infrastructure that provides the means for said activities.

Hobbyhimmel is a publicly accessible facility equipped with high-tech and low-tech tools and machinery. Different work spaces, including woodwork, metalworking and a FabLab (fabrication laboratory) area, enable individuals and organizations to engage in sustainability-related practices such as making, repairing, recycling, hacking and sharing. *Hobbyhimmel* is also a community of close to 50 people – with highly different degrees of involvement – who work collectively and on a voluntary basis to provide low-threshold access to this 'productive infrastructure'. During opening hours from Monday to Sunday, 47h per week, every person can use the spaces for a small fee starting at 2€/hour and capped with monthly options between 20 and 35 Euros, depending on the scope of usage. Conventional hand tools and electric machines, thereby, can be used by everyone, whereas larger machines require a safety briefing or a corresponding certificate. Furthermore, the workshop houses a number of degrowth-related events and projects such as 'repair cafés'.

Repair cafés are regular meetings that coordinate the spatiotemporal proximity of materials, competences and meanings to enable community-supported, decommodified repair (Schmid, 2019b). Stuttgart has several repair cafés, two of which are part of this study. One repair café is hosted by the open workshop itself and is a member of the *Repair Café International Foundation*. Another related repair café is organized and hosted by the association *Werkstadt Stuttgart e.V.*

Offline repair related organizing has an online counterpart in repositories for repair manuals and digital design files. *iFixit* hosts an online collection of repair manuals and sells corresponding specialty tools and spares. The organization operates its sole European branch office in Stuttgart and, on occasion, supports local repair-related events. In this vein, various forms of repair-related organizing that include non-monetized repair events, accessible permanent work spaces, reparable products and cultural interventions interlock within and without the local context (Schmid, 2019b).

Sharing is another pillar of Stuttgart's community economy. Sharing – as the collective usage of resources according to particular rules that apply to all participants (see chapter 17) – both supports the reduction of resource consumption through a more efficient utilization of products and provides a low-threshold access to products and services. Aside from its 'openness', that is accessibility, the open workshop reduces the need for individual ownership of tools and machinery.

> An elementary topic is the sharing of things. If in the workshop, for instance, 300 people have used the same jigsaw during the last two and a half years, we have saved 299 jigsaws. They didn't have to be produced; they didn't have to be shipped. So, this whole ecological footprint from the raw materials to the production, packaging, shipping, disposal at the end ... Yes, all this was omitted because it was not necessary, because the 'resource' jigsaw was used efficiently (I_A01b).

Sharing, at times, is part of a more comprehensive commoning of resources, which means the collective ownership and administration of goods, ideas, or infrastructures (see chapter 2). Although organizations' legal form, generally, does not formally accommodate commoning, *Hobbyhimmel*, *Lastenrad*, and *teilbar* constitute organizations that integrate several principles of a commons.

Lastenrad Stuttgart e.V. is an initiative that coordinates, administers and maintains a free cargo-bike lending system. After online registration, everyone can book and use one of the organization's cargo-bikes for up to three days at a time. Originally launched and financed with project money, the initiative continues to operate with volunteers and on donation basis. *Lastenrad* has several lending stations scattered throughout the city, one of which is *Hobbyhimmel*.

teilbar coordinates a common pool of goods that can be borrowed. Again, everyone, after registration, can take part and access articles of daily use without payments. Organizing goods and infrastructures as (partial-) commons decommodifies access and thus makes resources available to individuals and organizations outside of monetized economic relations.

A politics of pragmatism

Alternative forms of economic organization go hand in hand with alternative forms of governance. This is reflected both in the organizational set-ups and in the ways protagonists interpret and engage with institutional regulations. Most organizations, thereby, are not confrontational but rather pragmatic in the conduct of their everyday activities. Although, in many cases, statutory provisions and regulations severely strain organizational resources and leeway (see chapter 13), they are rarely a primary focus of organizations' activities. That means, most protagonists are less concerned with an overly political approach to change laws and regulations than with the development of practical and tangible solution to social and ecological issues. While not all share the same visions, solution-focused pragmatism guides the activities of most organizations.

This pragmatism goes hand in hand with fairly undogmatic ways. Although most members of and contributors to the eco-social enterprises in this study have indeed fairly articulate critiques of socio-ecological injustices, there is much caution towards ideologically driven practice.

> What is very important to me: neither I nor the people from our team are dogmatists. It's not about – and that's something that bothers me a bit in post-growth economics – that we say what it is supposed to be like. Instead, we criticize the current situation and want to use our concepts to initiate a debate on that subject (I_E02a).

Interestingly, many participants do not perceive their practices to be political at all, which can be generally attributed to a narrow understanding of politics as confined to the sphere of formal political institutions. Nevertheless, there is a broad dissatisfaction with the incompatibility of current administrative practices and the organizations' values and goals (see chapter 13). Some organizations, after all, explicitly challenge political and bureaucratic institutions that lack an adequate consideration of forms of entrepreneurship that are geared towards social and ecological concerns rather than profits. *em-faktor* and the *Economy for the Common Good*, for instance, demand a more sophisticated consideration of non-profit-oriented organizations in legal frameworks; in particular, a reformulation of the criteria defining common-interest organizations and of the taxation laws associated therewith.

> We have published a 'social profit manifesto'. Behind this term lies the claim that the non-profit law should be reshaped as well as the vision that companies in general should be measured by their impact and not by their financial profits. Keeping with English, the best term would actually be 'social-impact organization' (I_E03).

> One of the main demands of the Economy for the Common Good is that companies with a favorable Common Good balance pay different taxes (I_L01).

em-faktor already bases its cooperation with other enterprises on ethical principles rather than vacuous legal categories. *em-faktor – Die social profit Agentur GmbH* is a communication agency offering campaigning, fundraising, corporate social responsibility and branding services. Customers and partners are primarily organizations with a social or environmental purpose. Although legally registered as for-profit organization, *em-faktor* prioritizes non-monetary objectives. The organization is audited by the *Economy for the Common Good* (*ECG*) and shows a close association, in terms of content as well as personnel, with the local *ECG* group. *ECG* is a transnational organization comprising over 100 local chapters working towards an economic model that values enterprises according to their contribution to the common good instead of financial profits. A central demand of the *ECG* is to change legal frameworks in accordance with public interests to create favorable conditions for organizations that solve (over those that cause) social injustices and environmental destruction. It sees a key leverage for transformation in charity law and taxation systems.

In Stuttgart, the *ECG* has successfully introduced their agenda into communal politics. The municipality of Stuttgart pioneered the *Economy for the Common Good* by auditing four city-owned enterprises: the *Hafen GmbH* (operator of Stuttgart's harbor), *Stuttgarter Wohnungsbaugesellschaft* (building association), *Stuttgarter Entwässerungsbetrieb* (dewatering operation) and the *Eigenbetrieb Leben und Wohnen* (social services). After an initial audit, the latter two continued with the detailed *ECG* auditing process.

Trust-based economies

A number of organizations and groups in Stuttgart's community economy experiment with non-hierarchical structures and trust-based cooperation. Inspired by alternative organizational forms that are grounded in principles of self-management – as, for instance, advanced by the writings of Frederic Laloux (2014) and the insights of *Holacracy* (Robertson, 2015) – these organizations evenly distribute (decision-making) competences and responsibilities. In lieu of control mechanisms, particular decision-making procedures are in place which all participants must abide by. Furthermore, a flexible system of roles that the individual participants assume ensures that responsibilities are clearly defined and transparent. By engaging in self-management, these organizations cultivate a form of togetherness that dispenses with control and command.

> From an organizational point of view, there is no boss. I am the official managing director. That's what I have to be because of the GmbH [for-profit legal form]. But within the company, the people who take part decide, not me. This requires certain principles: transparency, trust and so on. But there is also the question of how we can set up the company so that it works under these conditions (I_E01a).

Trust does not only play an important role for the internal conduct of specific organizations but also with respect to cooperation across organizations and the larger community. Interorganizational sharing, volunteering and collaboration frequently takes place without formal frameworks (such as contracts and commissions) and the exchange of value-equivalents. Instead, it involves high degrees of trust. Trust, thereby, is not simply premised on close personal acquaintance but is based around shared meanings, common goals, and forms of belonging. By and large, two related tendencies or forms of trust interweave. First, the trust in a common cause. And second, the trust in each other. The 'trust-based economy' that emerges has many facets, some of which are quite elusive for empirical research. In the following, I attempt to trace different ways in which trust characterizes (certain parts of) Stuttgart's community economy.

Volunteering is an important cornerstone for most organizations. That means, many participants contribute to one or more organizations practically or financially, creating a network around common values, solidarity, trust, and mutual help. The sense of contributing to a meaningful endeavor is a central driver in Stuttgart's community economy. Important thereby is that people's engagement is often based on the confidence that the community continues to work for common ideals. Trust, therefore, is closely connected with a shared sense of contributing to a greater cause.

> At the moment, there is a very strong trust-based cooperative cooperation, I call it. That means, you recognize and perceive the value of the other's idea and take from it something like an immaterial value by participating in the realization of the idea. That is an interesting intrinsic motivator that I notice here. But as I said, it is a highly subtle and latent dynamic which is not entirely accessible to me. But it feels very human (I_E02bii).

> There is something that connects us, this common sense or common suffering under the present conditions. And there we try to find new ways in our organizations. And, of course, we become more successful by saying: we network, we exchange and support each other and inspire each other with respect to these points (F_01).

Trust-based relations also shape the practices of more market-oriented organizations. Reciprocity and trust, here, partly substitute for the exchange of value-equivalents and the conclusion of contracts and other forms of formalized agreements. Interestingly, the absence of measurements, compensation and legal binding contracts does not forestall reliability. Many highly implicit rules are in place and enable the community to plan without the recourse to formal agreements.

> Furthermore, there are no control mechanisms, no contracts ... so all these instruments for planning security are lacking. Instead, it [reliability] comes about almost naturally (I_E02bii).

Trust, in this sense, is a prerequisite for organizations to engage in decommodified exchange; that is, the transfer of goods and services not based on the calculation of equivalents (in a monetary or non-monetary sense) but on shared values, solidarity, and mutual interest. *Relumity*, to name one example, provided light installments for the *ownhome* project free of change for confidence in a common cause and the project's ability to contribute to it. Partially decommodified exchange, along these lines, can lead to synergies and help organizations with limited resources to get various forms of support through shared information, practical assistance, or the provision of equipment. Barter, furthermore, helps small organizations to circumvent complex regulatory frameworks and expenses on licenses and taxes. While trust is an important lubricant for community-based and informal economies, more strongly formalized relations, of course, continue to play an important role. Economic relations based on trust, at any rate, require time in order to build confidence on a personal level – both within and without organizations.

Whereas these examples testify trust within and across a small number of organizations, other communities set up trust-based and solidary relations in larger groups. The *Solidarische Landwirtschaft Stuttgart*, a community-supported agriculture scheme, for instance, is premised on the principle, 'everyone to their needs and to their abilities'. *Solidarische Landwirtschaft* is a consumer-producer cooperative for organic agriculture which is based around sustainable and equitable local food production and consumption. Annual bidding rounds, in which each participant makes an offer that she considers appropriate, are repeated until a set amount is collected that covers operation costs for the next year. Production is undertaken by a farmer with support from members of the cooperative. The yield, then, is distributed according to individual needs and preferences. Again, the whole scheme hinges upon the trust based in other participants in order to function well. So far, key protagonists have not reported any stark misbalances in the project.

Cultivating subjects for other worlds

Alternative forms of togetherness go hand in hand with a shift away from calculating, competing, self-involved, and insatiable subjectivities (see chapter 4). Most organizations in this study implicitly and explicitly aim to cultivate forms of trust, solidarity, and mutual help through their practices. This is premised, amongst other things, on the notion that alternative forms of economizing do not only require different sets of rules and agreements but also different subjects who embody social justice and equity. Cooperative, solidary, and self-managed organizational structures are based on individuals who responsibly accept and contribute to non-hierarchical forms of togetherness that work without coercion. At the same time, involvement in an alternative organizational set-up nurtures individuals' abilities for respectful and deliberate social interaction. The absence of instructions necessitates responsibility and reflection on part of the individual.

> The mindset that people in the company have is very important to me (I_E01a).

> When I [as member of the organization] start to think differently and acquire tools, so to speak, to be able to judge for myself what is going on here, then I am on the right path (I_E01a).

Aside from their actual material input, which is rather limited (see chapter 13), alternative organizations prove that different kinds of products, economic relations, legal frameworks, and forms of togetherness are indeed possible. *Relumity*'s repairable, durable, non-proprietary and sustainably sourced light bulb *Relumity #LED1*, for instance, is meant to demonstrate:

> Hey, guys, it's working. You can build such products. It is possible (I_U02a).

Pushing the boundaries of what is perceived as feasible and providing first-hand experiences is key in cultivating alternative subjectivities. This is also a main focus of commons-based projects such as *teilbar*.

> It is important that there are many such projects in the neighborhood in which people participate and realize: there is something that is sustainable and which works a bit differently. So that they practice and understand that there is something else, a different logic. And that they can, and should, behave differently than in the usual exchange logic. And that makes it easier for society [to change towards a commons-based economy] if a larger part of society knows something like that, so that expectations shift accordingly (I_A07).

Learning that there is an alternative to the current mode of social organization encourages individuals to cultivate different practices. The *Repair Cafés*, for instance, challenge the normality of replacement by (re)instituting the normality of repair. Not feeling alone in doing something about social and environmental injustices is crucial for many in order to retain or to regain hope.

> And quite often, yes, when it comes to environmental destruction, resource exploitation or even egocentrism in society, lack of sustainability ... these big issues, many people feel very helpless and have the feeling that they can't do anything. Yes, they find that quite terrible, it makes them downright depressed to some extent. And I think that comes from a feeling of helplessness. And this can be counteracted by initiatives that show what can be done. I believe that repair cafés are very important in such a change because they start where each individual can start. This shows a little bit what each individual can do for himself, what is feasible (I_A03).

Challenging hopelessness is a key aspect in the development of alternatives. Many individuals who are dissatisfied with the current situation are transfixed with the overwhelming 'power' of capitalism. This is a central aspect that Gibson-Graham seek to dismantle – the disidentification with a unified and all-powerful system (see part II). Community economy projects, such as repair initiatives, then, are an integral part of liberating discourses and subjectivities from paralysis.

The same goes for the (self-)understanding of organizations. *em-faktor*, for instance, addresses the fact that organizations that contribute considerably to social and environmental well-being and justice – actually mitigating some of the worst 'externalities' of capitalist enterprises – are called 'non-profit organizations'. An excerpt from *em-faktor*'s social profit manifesto reads:

> You are the biggest employers in the country and you shape the society in which we live in the most diverse ways. With your work, you create considerable social values every day. Your goal is not a monetary gain, but the profit for the people in our society ... We all benefit from your work. Through your commitment you make our world more humane. You are not fillers of our society. You don't have to apologize that money multiplication is not part of your organizational DNA.

Therefore, do not let yourself be described as 'non-profit organizations' anymore. You are a social profit organization! (spo-manifest.de)

Chapter 13: Constraints

> I am not an optimist ... not at all. I just have the 'big defiance'. That's the only thing that keeps me alive.
> (I_L01)

While a range of alternative practices can be observed, they are severely constrained and sidelined by numerous constraints that I will elaborate in this chapter. Set within monetized growth-based and profit-oriented economies, neoliberal forms of governance, and a materialist consumer culture, sufficiency- and subsistence-oriented practices jar with many social norms and institutions. Although sustainability has long entered public and political discourses, it often translates into practices of greenwashing and politicking. Actually sustainable activities, thereby, are notably limited by prevailing forms of economic, political, cultural and technological relatedness.

Consuming to save the planet?

Hobbyhimmel houses a large number of activities that neither replace unsustainable practices nor contribute to the generation of possibilities to do so in the future. Instead, the workshop's productive infrastructure enables individualized forms of consumption that add on to and even exacerbate existing forms of consumption. 3D printing, laser cutting and to a lesser extent also woodworking and metalworking are resource intensive leisure activities which do not necessarily contribute to a more sustainable future. On one occasion, I noted into my fieldwork diary:

> There is great potential for sustainable practices and you can see time and again how it is used by different organizations and individuals. Today, however, was very telling for the overall situation. Most people in the workshop worked on projects that are not really linked to sustainability. One person constructed a handbag out of wood using the laser-cutter, based on a template he found online. He cut thin wood into a specific pattern thereby making it flexible. In the woodwork area, two people built a board game that is going to be a present (B_A01).

At least two caveats apply, therefore, when considering degrowth practices. First, it is difficult to say which of these practices replace less sustainable ones. If, for instance, the manufacturing of a handbag and a present (as on the day of the journal entry above) replace buying a handbag and buying a present, the workshop actually contributes to the localization of production. In many conversations with visitors of the workshop, however, productive practices were reported as additional activities that do not necessarily replace other forms of consumption. Second, it is ambiguous how the resource input for local production – energy use of machines, material input, the individual purchase of materials, the waste through unsuccessful attempts and the transport to and from the workshop – relates to that of large-scale global production networks. From a resource perspective, the comparison of local production and global value chains can be quite ambiguous (Petschow et al., 2014).

In a similar vein, products like *Geco-Gardens*' vertical farm systems, *Slowtec's Krautomat*, and *ownworld's ownhome* are designed to contribute ecologically and pedagogically to a degrowth transition. At the same time, however, for some, these products constitute yet another purchase – not replacing less sustainable practices but adding on to existing consumption patterns. A prospective customer of *ownworld*, for instance, wanted to purchase an *ownhome* as vacation home. Missing the intention behind the project, collaboration was declined.

The consumption of 'green' technologies in and of itself – including products or infrastructures created with a genuine intent to further sustainability-related issues rather than generating profits – does not contribute to a degrowth transition. Only in conjunction with a shift in subjectivities and broader economic alignments, so it seems, do technologies unfold their potential to catalyze sustainable practice.

Money makes the world go 'round

Despite high levels of trust in the community and numerous examples of demonetized productive relations, money is still a central concern for all organizations. On an organizational level, payments for rent, equipment and, where applicable, services and employees require a stable revenue through donations, institutional funding, market activities, or a combination thereof. On an individual level, most practitioners need to earn a living. In particular, organizations that are not based on voluntary work – which constitutes a restrain itself (see below) – need to generate a living wage for the participants.

> Well, it has to pay off on some level. I can feel it somehow. I have to make a living, too (I_E01a).

> I'd like to be everywhere, all the time. I did that before. I founded initiatives and so on. But the bank account was empty and the rent had to be paid. Well, then one can consider to live without money, but then I would have to get out of Stuttgart and live somewhere on the field. That doesn't work either (F_01).

As a consequence, the focus of a large number of organizations shifts away from alternative projects and towards paid commissioned work. Many projects that are promising in social and ecological terms are uncompetitive and unviable in economic terms, thus remaining inchoate, being canceled, or succumbing to market demands. *Slowtec*'s *Krautomat*, for instance, started out as open source project. But without marketing, the project did not generate enough return to remain viable. As a consequence, *Slowtec* decided to discontinue development and search for individuals or organizations that want to advance a more market-based business case within particular boundaries set by the developers.

Scant financial resources, in general, characterize large parts of the organizational landscape in this study. Giving and barter, as exemplified above, partially compensate for this lack. However, only insofar as the respective needs can and want to be fulfilled within the community. Aside from a limited number of goods and services available within the community, financial pressure reduces organizations' leeway for participation in non-monetary economies. While barter is a possibility to confront the lack of resources, it draws much needed capacities away from commodified exchange on which organizational subsistence is premised. The fact that most organizations face the same issues hampers the community economy as a whole since each organization has to carefully household with its resources and capacities. Projects that do not receive long term support – or do not want to rely on external funding – are particularly pressured to withdraw from non-paid work and friendly turns and develop a business case that finances their everyday operations.

> We quickly have great customers who agree with us when it comes to our ideals. But unfortunately, it is often the case that they are in the same situation saying: we lack the financial resources. Because, perhaps, they are themselves in the process of establishing themselves or they want to save the world and that is not necessarily something which is financed well in our society (I_E01c).

Organizations, in this way, are forced to adopt an entrepreneurial mind-set, which, for some, goes against the ideas they attempt to convey. Actors who refuse to adapt to the rules of business and commerce face severe financial and practical restraints. Although there is a widespread excitement for the *ownhome*, for instance, the project does not generate much material output. Turning the idea into a marketable product that creates revenue would require the development of a detailed business plan and the acquisition of investment money. All of this goes against the grain of unconditional and equitable non-commodified economizing.

What is missing [at ownworld] from my point of view is one who takes a more entrepreneurial approach. Which means that he takes care of the steps it takes for a customer to get from enthusiasm to the finished product; that he [the buyer] is accompanied in the purchasing process; what is needed for it; the formalities and so on (I_E01c).

Organizations that actually do formulate and implement a business case often face a market that is flooded with cheapened products based on socially and environmentally externalized costs. *Relumity*, for example, faces multiple competitive disadvantages in the production of *Relumity #LED1*. Costs for fair wages, sustainably sourced materials and a local production that tries to avoid long distance shipping add up to an amount that is far beyond that for conventional lamps.

It is a sad fact that all these great products and great initiatives rely on specific demand. That means, customers pay extra to buy a fairly traded product or a product that is manufactured responsibly. Because the point is to include the costs for reasonable working conditions and environmental costs in the price of the product. And then one should not forget that many of the projects are also certified. And this is another absurdity on top. Because the certification causes further costs which, again, you have to pass on to the customer. This means that you produce a fair product and then you are punished for it economically with additional costs – apart from the fact that the product is already more expensive if you do not externalize costs. That's totally schizophrenic. You are trying to do something good and, as a consequence, you are being punished financially. That is the situation we are in (I_E02a).

If you don't want to take part in this game, you are not competitive. It's impossible! Not that we're looking for competition, but that is what is demanded from us (I_E02bi).

In the face of this skewed situation, investors and administrative institutions demand cost externalization. The disregard for social and environmental justice, therefore, is a de facto requirement for market participation. Organizations that want to follow an entrepreneurial path without compromising their objectives reach an impasse. *Geco-Gardens*, for instance, refuses to outsource production, which causes severe financial restraints that can only be compensated through an additional source of income (see below).

The consultant, when I was at this consultation at the city of Stuttgart, said that I will not be able to avoid cheap production (I_E04).

Even in cases where cost disadvantages can be incorporated into the business case, the availability of fairly sourced materials and upstream products remains a limiting factor. *Relumity*, who put much effort into investigating the possibilities of setting up a fair and short-distance value chain, are still compelled to source parts of their lamps from outside of Europe for a lack of regional and even continental options. Without alternatives, *Relumity* obtains electroluminescent diodes (LEDs) from Japan. The reason for this choice is that the organization assumes the working conditions to be better than in other Asian countries – which remains speculative on the part of *Relumity*, having no capacity to assess the conditions on site.

For-profit policy

The dissonance between existing legal forms and organizational set-up is a reoccurring issue. A mixture between economic activities and the orientation towards social and ecological objectives that most organizations exhibit is not appropriately considered in the binary of for-profit and non-profit legal forms. Engagement in market activities and purposes not considered charitable by the revenue code make it difficult for eco-social enterprises to gain non-profit status, which would grant them tax benefits to partially compensate for prioritizing socio-ecological issues over profits. Furthermore, the non-profit status can be revoked up to three years in retrospect. This poses a high risk in the financial calculation of small organizations.

For most organizations, legal competences and responsibilities also jar with their internal set-up. In particular, non-hierarchical and self-managed organizations find no adequate representation in a corresponding legal structure. While cooperative organizational forms would be most suited, there is a high threshold for small eco-social start-ups to register as cooperative. In particular, the financial burden for the legally prescribed membership in an auditing association as well as the costs for the annual audit prove to be big financial burdens.

All these factors make it difficult for eco-social enterprises to find an adequate legal form. In an early stage, some divert a considerable fraction of their scarce resources to the exploration of advantages and disadvantages of different legal forms. In the open workshop – a particularly difficult case for its combination of volunteer work, partially donation-based financing structure, internal self-management, engagement in commercial activities to cross-subsidize low-threshold access of private and sustainability-related use, and risk associated with (heavy) machinery – a group of volunteers took up the topic. The following observation notes show some of the difficulties such as the lack of clear information about liability and financing.

> The 'legal form group' is stagnating. Finding a suitable legal form is proving to be very difficult. Information on income and earning opportunities is still vague. Various sources are unable to provide clear and committed information on liability and financing. At the moment, forming an association seems to be the best solution. Also, a hybrid of an association that is the sole shareholder of a GmbH [Ltd.] is conceivable (B_Vo1b).

Despite these difficulties, most organizations find a workable solution to deal with external relations such as issues of liability and financing. Dissonance between legal form and organizational set-up, however, can also cause internal problems. For-profit organizations are generally structured hierarchically, with the manager as bearer of ownership rights and/or decisional power. Due to the precarious finances of ecologically and socially driven enterprises (see above), the collaboration entails risks and sacrifices, particularly at the early stages. Hierarchical legal forms make it very difficult to adequately compensate and provide security for (early) collaborators. In one case, these difficulties translated into a personal disagreement that ultimately led to the separation of collaborator and organization. The following field notes render visible the full complexity of the conflict.

> T. has a problem with the fact that L. still has full decision-making power, while L. does not want to give it up until the company is 'firmly on course'. He is willing to give up parts of it as long as he still retains the majority and exactly this is the point of contention: T. does not want L. to have sole decision-making authority. The problem is very multifaceted and seems to be composed of different aspects: (1) The company is still a bit precarious when it comes to finances. This means that it is not possible, yet, to fully concentrate on the things that should be the focus of the company. Many compromises are still necessary. (2) T. does not contribute to the organizations' revenue (yet). In principle, this is not a problem because his activities fit with the company's ideals. However, against the background of the still precarious financial situation, this contributes to the tensions. (3) Connected to the foregoing point, L.'s activities earn the bulk of the company's revenues. The rest is not self-sustaining (yet). (4) The organization as GmbH [Ltd.] is covered by L.'s private loans. He, therefore, is in debt and is reluctant to transfer business shares. (5) The legal form of the GmbH, in this context, is unsuitable for the enterprise (B_G19).

In cases where legal constructs are available to respond to specific needs, they are often difficult to realize for small organizations with limited temporal, administrative, and financial resources. Advisory and notarial costs and the need to acquire in-depth knowledge eat into small budgets and draw much needed resources away from day-to-day operations. The result is a general uncertainty and dissatisfaction with the status quo, easily projected onto the organization or other members thereof.

Similar issues exist with regulatory frameworks. The volume of statutory provisions poses a number of difficulties for small eco-social enterprises. Two intertwined problems cause (in some cases existential) difficulties. First, regulations are oversized for small, experimental and eco-socially oriented organizations. Second, it is difficult to obtain clear, case-specific and binding information about the legal situation. Even though counselling programs are available for (some) organizations, they are generally only of limited help. Many organizations face contradictory information. Regulations and administrative responsibilities are not clearly evident and located on different levels – European, national, federal, communal – which further complicates the situation. When I asked if there are any programs or authorities that start-ups can approach to inquire, one responded remarked:

> There is a bunch of them and everyone says something different (I_E04).

Another complained in more general terms:

> Bureaucracy is definitely an issue. Incredibly so. Current politics puts a lot of obstacles in the way of start-ups. There are many people who don't dare or don't take the risk because the costs are too high. On the other hand, if you make a mistake, something that you don't pay attention to – which can easily happen because it's a giant regulatory maze for start-ups – then you've got back-payments which, in the worst case, can cause bankruptcy (I_E08).

Organizations that go about their business without penetrating the jungle of regulations can face lengthy and expensive processes of formal approval. *Hobbyhimmel*, for instance, carried out interior work without the respective permits. The retrospective approval cost over 1000 Euros and took far over half a year for completion. *ownworld*'s water provision and disposal systems, which make both fresh water provision and sewage hook-up superfluous, pose an even more complex issue. The conversion of rainwater is only permissible under particular circumstances, especially in cases where there is no other source of water. The recycling of grey water is not foreseen at all in regulatory frameworks. Furthermore, a sewage hook-up is compulsory for inhabited properties. All these regulations become moot, but are not dropped, in the case of *ownhome*'s closed water system. Administrative competencies for these questions are on different levels and, despite sustained efforts and professional measurements of water quality, there are still not results at the time of writing.

The tragedy of (artificial) scarcity

Economic and administrative constraints intersect with and have an effect on interpersonal relations. The need to prioritize (well-) paid commissioned work renders non-monetized community economies a privilege pursuable in times of stable resources. Mutual help, then, is often second to financial consolidation. Participants, in this respect, turn away (from) alternatives to secure their own 'survival' and well-being as well as that of their organization. While mutual help and solidarity, as portrayed above, are important pillars of the community, they are of limited relevance in the organizations' daily conduct. Service-oriented organizations that earn their money through the sale of working time diminish their source of income directly through engagement in non-commercial exchange. As a consequence, they (need to) carefully weigh the voluntary work invested in non-monetized projects. Associations and projects that are largely demonetized and based on volunteer work are thus put in an asymmetrical relationship since most of them do not command the financial means that are required to engage in formal market exchange. Spaces of non-monetized transfer, then, remain strongly confined and with it the alternative (economic) practices of these organizations.

Slowtec, for instance, commands a range of programming and development skills that are extremely valuable for other organizations within the community. For a lack of financial leeway, however, they have to decline requests even from projects they are enthusiastic about.

> It's a social problem that people simply don't have time to help each other. They have so much on their hands that they don't find the time (I_P01).

Scarcity of time finds its counterpart in a scarcity of appreciation and respectful conduct. Individuals and organizations that engage in non-monetized economic relations and mutual help, in spite of the financial and legal difficulties associated with it, generally still expect a form of reciprocity. In lieu of monetary compensation, then, other forms of appreciation are important to sustain mutuality. In cases in which exchange relationships are perceived as misbalanced and non-reciprocal, non-monetized economies break down. Organizations, especially if entrepreneurially oriented, then, resort to monetized exchange instead.

> I need some kind of gain. The gain does not have to be financial, sometimes a thank-you is enough. For example, I did all the technology for the organization. And the thank-you was: the email doesn't work, why does this not work? Why does that not work? And that's just incredibly exhausting. You put energy into it, even pay for it yourself and the only thanks you get is: this doesn't work. I said to myself, this can't be it, this has to work more economically somehow (I_E01a).

Me, myself, and I

Reciprocal relationships hinge upon appropriate structures, principles, and cooperative subjectivities. Organizations that depart from formal and hierarchical relations need to find a suitable mode of cooperation. Unequal input between individuals, inchoate structures, vague commitments, and ineffective collaboration remain constant challenges, especially in the context of self-management.

Self-management is unfamiliar to most subjects and thus something that first has to be learned and incorporated. For example, despite several discussions in team meetings and repeated attempts to shape *Hobbyhimmel*'s internal structure according to principles of self-management, recurrent issues such as unclear responsibilities and over- or underdeveloped individual initiatives prevail. In particular, the allocation of 'roles' that attribute clear responsibilities to individuals remains partial and inconsistent, as the following notes I took testify.

> The significance of roles remains somewhat unclear. Not even the focus group could clarify this issue despite repeated emphasis. This seems to be a key element which is still missing. Many find it difficult to engage with this form of organization and frequently fall back into 'old' patterns: waiting for instructions or relying on someone else to take care of an issue (F_02).

Aside from organizations' internal structuring, trust and mutuality play also an important role in their daily business. Control, in general, is not only undesirable for some organizations from an ethical and educational point of view, it would also exceed their capacities. This means that the functioning of many organizations depends on individual sincerity and adherence to basic codes and rules. In the open workshop, for example, machines can be accessed without direct control and usage is accounted for mainly on a trust basis. For volunteers of *Hobbyhimmel* the competences are still more far reaching, including permanent access to the workshop space. Responsibility, then, is not only relevant for the organization's proper functioning but also with respect to safety and questions of liability.

A number of organizations report egoistic behavior and a (false) sense of entitlement by users. This ranges from lack of appreciation all the way to – albeit astonishingly few – cases in which individuals exploit the respective project. *Hobbyhimmel*, for instance, has had a number of cases in which commercial users try to circumvent the higher industrial rate by passing for a private visitor. The cargo bike initiative, in turn, reports a significant fraction of users that use the complementary service without appreciating the work behind the project, nor its social and environmental objectives.

> From people's feedback I get the feeling that many of those who write mails or call don't understand what we're doing here. They see that the cargo bike is for free, that's it. Anything else they don't care about (I_V04).

In general, many lack an understanding of the (economic) difficulties that eco-social organizations face. Internalized costs to ensure fair and (possibly) regionalized production, non-exploitative supply chains and preferably recyclable and innocuous materials are reflected in a higher price for sustainable products – for example *Slowtec's Krautomat* (before the project was terminated), *Relumity's Relumity #LED1*, or *Geco-Gardens'* vertical farms. They do not fit with a bargain mentality and are frequently met with incomprehension, while, of course, others are excluded on an economic basis through high costs.

Another problem is the lack of knowledge or awareness of the issues and possibilities surrounding sustainability-related activities. Infrastructures such as the open workshop facilitate a number of alternative practices but are also used for adverse purposes (see above).

> The people who use this here rarely have this train of thought [about sustainability]. Only between 10 and 20 percent of the users use the workshop for reasons like: 'I'm saving resources', 'I don't need to buy the device', 'I can manufacture a spare part', or 'I can rebuild the thing to last longer' (I_A01a).

Apart from the participants or 'non-participants' that clash with the organizations' values and codes, there is the behavior of individuals who are both familiar with and sympathetic to novel forms of non-hierarchical relatedness and still regress to individualistic and counterproductive patterns. This rather elusive issue is best exemplified by self-observation as noted in the reflections on a bad day of fieldwork in the workshop.

> I have tried to bring the board into a cloud shape with the jigsaw. That didn't work. I probably used a saw blade that was too thick, which then got too hot when I tried to cut the curve. Because this was very unpleasant for me, I put the singed saw blade back into the suitcase and put the board in the pile of the waste wood. These are exactly the users the workshop doesn't need. On top of that, I didn't charge myself for the usage. That wasn't intentional, but it's a bad sign that people might be behaving the way I did even though they think the project is very good and actually support it … so somehow harming the project or exploiting it without actually wanting it or wanting anything bad, on the contrary … (B_V01p).

Deeply engrained patterns of egocentric behavior also reside in individuals who positively respond to alternative practices and organizations. Frequently, subjects who feel very strongly about alternative approaches loose critical distance. This occasionally results in a strong identification with particular labels or projects and a rejection of possible allies. In the present study, this was largely the case with some smaller initiatives rather than with enterprises, the latter of which generally had a more 'undogmatic' approach (see above). Different forms of identification with particular projects or labels range from consequential rejection of specific practices to vanity and self-importance.

Chapter 14: Enablement

> We were able to benefit greatly from the entire infrastructure. The same way, we have used it again for the current project ... we can draw on the machines that are already there and that we can simply use without having to procure them ourselves.
> I_E06a

Despite numerous constraints, Stuttgart's community economy shows alternative forms of economic, political, cultural and technological relatedness. This section identifies institutional arrangements, strategies and scopes of action that support the organizations' objectives and enable their engagement in degrowth-oriented activities under the given socio-economic conditions.

Supportive infrastructures

Hobbyhimmel's productive infrastructure catalyzes a number of alternative practices and supports individual and organizational endeavors in local production, repair, maintenance, coordination and other sustainability-related activities. The open workshop cross-subsidizes private users and eco-social enterprises through profitable business activities such as hosting team-building events and commercial users. With *Hobbyhimmel* being financially self-sufficient, eco-social organizations can use the workshop free of change, at a discounted rate, and/or outside of normal opening hours. Almost all organizations in this study exhibit ties to the workshop (see figure 4), including *Relumity*, *Smark*, *Lastenrad*, and *Grünfisch* who use *Hobbyhimmel*'s infrastructure for their projects – some more frequently (and fundamental to their functioning) than others.

> We support others who say 'we do not accept the status quo'. They are people from all kinds of different projects ... And they all do something within their area of focus, an action or a business or whatever. And we can support them in doing that (I_A01b).

Some eco-social enterprises use the workshop to produce (parts of) their products or infrastructures locally without the need to acquire and own the means of production. *Smark*, for example, used the workshop to manufacture parts for their first automated store. *Relumity*, furthermore, realized the production of the casings for their *Relumity LED#1*, a lamp for household use, in the open workshop. This is not only to avoid long-distance shipping but also to test and ensure the local capacity for maintenance and repair:

> I can actually say that the spares are locally available. Not necessarily as tangible objects, but they can be produced [by means of 3D printing] and reproduced locally. The materials are available and the means of production are available through the open workshop (I_E2bii).

Organizations that are mainly engaged in non-commercial activities, too, use the workshop for construction, repair, prototyping or simply as a meeting space. *Grünfisch*, for instance, built some of their aquaponics systems in the workshop. And *Lastenrad* regularly services their bikes in the workshop. In turn, the broad community of activists and eco-social entrepreneurs supports the workshop through volunteering, donations in kind and dissemination of its concept.

Beyond the material space of the workshop, supportive infrastructures are in place in a more metaphorical sense. Most organizations that are part of this study are interconnected (see figure 4) and form a pool of common resources, including skills, knowledge, contacts and a workforce that can be tapped into in case of need. Similar supportive networks exist also beyond place. For instance, the communities that develop and provide open source software and hardware products that sustainability-oriented organizations (and others) can use. Almost all initiatives both work with open source software (and sometimes hardware) and, in turn, contribute to the pool of open source products. *Lastenrad*, for instance, uses an open source software that significantly facilitated the set-up a digital booking system.

> This booking system also plays a key role. It was developed by people in Cologne. Commons booking is an open source tool that all cargo bike initiatives in Germany use (I_A04).

Open source hardware products are less widespread. Above all, because, in contrast to software, they generally constitute rivalrous goods. This, however, changes rapidly in times of 3D printing. *Open Source Ecology* (OSE) is a global movement that develops and advocates open source hardware products. A particular focus, thereby, is on replicability through standardization, structurally identical parts and new production methods. Although there is no instituted local group in Stuttgart, some individuals have close ties with the German-wide *OSE* association. One of the products developed locally – using the workshop space of *Hobbyhimmel* – is a mobile hydroponic system. This and other open source products significantly lower the threshold for individuals and organizations to access and build on existing knowledge.

Digital infrastructures, furthermore, open up new possibilities for alternative forms of organizing that catalyze transformative processes. Participants frequently refer to the role of networking tools and "digital multipliers" (I_L04). Commercial social media, however, aim for the maximization of user time spent in digital environments. Tools particularly designed for social change, instead, facilitate sustainability-related organizing. The *Karte von Morgen* [map of tomorrow] and *Human Connection* are two projects with a thrust towards networking for eco-social transformation. The *Karte von Morgen* is a participatory mapping tool that collects and rates sustainability-related initiatives and enterprises. It provides a quick orientation for individuals and organizations over options for more sustainable consumption and, more indirectly, provides possibilities for building alternative networks. The latter, then, is explicitly addressed by *Human Connection*. *Human Connection* is a social network that brings together sustainability-related information and action. As non-profit and based on donations, the network is committed to social and environmental concerns rather than advertising and maximization of user time. A range of different functions (not all of them implemented at the time of writing) facilitates online coordination for offline activism. This includes the linking of posts with further information, appropriate organizations, and fitting discussion forums.

Sustainability-related business models

Internalization of costs through fair sourcing and equitable working conditions, the focus on non-profitable issues and areas, and the engagement in non-monetized transfer tilt the economic playing field to the detriment of eco-social enterprises. Nevertheless, there are business models which partly compensate for this disadvantage. Durable products, for example, lend themselves to contracting models. That means the customer no longer purchases the product but a service. The hardware required to deliver that service – for example light – remains in the contractor's ownership who is responsible for its continuous performance. Longevity, then, is in the interest of the service provider to minimize expenditure. *Relumity*, in this manner, engages in light contracting in a business-to-business context, thus internalizing durability into the business case.

> Generally, this is an incredibly attractive way for us to market our products. Because we know that our extremely durable products don't need to be repaired very often and we therefore save maintenance costs (I_E02a).

Furthermore, there are opportunities to generate revenue through projects that are in line with the enterprises' values. Increasing awareness of climate change leads to public and private investments in energy transition and other adaptation and mitigation measurements. While these commissions in and of themselves do not challenge current social and economic alignments, they also do not jar with the organizations' objectives. These commissions, then, provide opportunities for sustainability-related business.

> This project is about the energy transition, an information campaign. And that's something we support 100 percent. And we got a commission to develop the software (I_Eo1b).

In addition, commissions from other eco-social enterprises and associations provide an opportunity to conciliate financial revenue with non-financial objectives. As outlined above, most eco-social enterprises are low on funds themselves. But sourcing goods and services from other eco-social enterprises whenever possible creates internal relations that strengthen these organizations.

> The Karte von Morgen [map of tomorrow] project has now, so to speak, become an official commission for us. It's a relatively small job, but this way I can now work with a befriended company. That's actually quite nice, because basically that's what we want to push. The project fits thematically and is not in competition with our working time. So far, it has mostly been the case that I had to do work on projects like this on the weekend. But slowly work and activism combine (I_Eo1b).

Aside from compatible commissions, advance payments and donations are a major enabling factor for organizations' activities. Crowdfunding is a means to acquire the funds for implementing a project or starting a business. Several organizations which are part of this study, including *Relumity*, *Geco-Gardens*, and *Human Connection*, have used reward-based crowdfunding. That means the backers receive a form of compensation, generally a product or service produced or provided through the endeavor which the crowdsourced money supports. Crowdfunding can also be donation-based. Donations in general remain an important financial source for most associations and groupings in Stuttgart's community economy, including some of the more market-oriented organizations.

Institutional support

Different forms of institutional (mostly monetary) backing are important for a large number of organizations from the sample. Innovation vouchers, founder's stipends, living labs, research projects and various forms of earmarked subsidies considerably broaden individuals' and organizations' room for maneuver. Innovation vouchers, for instance, are a relatively simple and accessible way to receive a partial reimbursement of research and development costs. This, however, requires that the company is solvent enough to advance the full expenditures.

> One can apply for each [type of] innovation voucher once a year. And if you're not stupid ... compared to other funding measures this is really easy in terms of bureaucratic burden. Because we can't afford to spend time on applications that are 50 pages long. But right now, the innovation vouchers are indeed of help (I_E01c).

Other forms of state-institutional sponsorship schemes can create similar leverages. Stuttgart is the first major city in Germany to have a commissioner for urban gardening. Urban Gardening schemes in Stuttgart receive assistance both in finding appropriate spaces as well as through a subsidy of gardening related expenses. Another example is the support of private organizations in the *Economy for the Common Good* audition process. Again, it is unique amongst major German cities that private enterprises receive a 50% subsidy to get certified by the *ECG*. Although dwarfed in comparison with other subsidies, institutional support contributes to a growing niche of alternative enterprises. This last example, however, was too close to the conclusion of data collection, not allowing for the documentation of any substantial observable effects. *Hobbyhimmel* and *em-faktor*, the two organizations from the study's sample audited by the *ECG*, went through the certification process prior to the launch of the subsidy scheme.

One city council member resurfaces in different contexts as key force for a progressive political agenda. Her role in aforementioned *ECG* audits of city-owned companies as well as the support for private enterprises' common good audit is quite prominent. The engagement of an individual politician, here, set the ball rolling for a number of official commitments and institutional measures that address several of the foregoing issues around non-profit regulations and systematic disadvantages for eco-social enterprises in a capitalist market economy. For sure, these are small steps but in a promising direction. While generally disenfranchised with communal- and politics on other administrative levels, a number of interviewees have singled out this council member as a powerhouse for (small) institutional change.

> We are very lucky to have this huge support in the city council. Above all, the support is from a city councilor who has been fully committed to using her possibilities in the city council and who has managed to get some municipal companies to do the common good balance now. And the project continues. There are more subsidies for the companies to develop further ... and private companies get a subsidy for their first balance from the office of economic development (I_L01).

Importantly, the intentions behind these measurements are largely compatible with a fundamental shift away from growth-dependent economies, as the following quote from the city councilor testifies.

> A basic issue that we have is that we live in a growth paradigm and that everyone always thinks he has to grow everywhere and the systems are designed in such a way that you actually have to grow, if you are a stakeholder, in order to survive. Even if you may not want it at all ... And this is certainly the biggest social innovation we need in the next few years: economies, economic systems, evolutionary changes to go beyond growth, or at least a decoupling of the two (I_S03).

Due to the multiple constraints mentioned above, the coalition between institutional actors on the one hand and eco-social entrepreneurs and activists on the other is still small. Nevertheless, first small steps in a progressive direction are taken.

In community we trust

Trust is the lubricant that facilitates mutual support within and across eco-social organizations. Trust in other collaborators, in their collective capacity and in the worthiness of their cause is a key factor that motivates and enables many activities. Despite a number of financial and legal constraints (see above), community economies work through the dedicated engagement of a number of individuals who belief both in the possibility of transformation and in others that share their commitment.

> It's almost like the humus on which the whole thing can grow. The social context is, perhaps through its nature or setup of form, thoroughly permeated by trust. So, there is a high concentration or a high dose of trust in this contact (I_E02biii).

Mutual trust facilitates collaboration without the need for immediate payback. For example, when *Relumity* supplied the light installations for the *ownhome* prototype, the transfer of materials and labor would have been much more difficult on a commission base (in terms of finances and formalities). Instead, the conviction that the *ownhome* project pushes a similar agenda and does not exploit the support enabled the cooperation. Furthermore, trustful relationships can be multipliers in the pursuit of common objectives. The experience of past collaborations and mutual sympathy allows participants to put trust in each other's judgement. Relying on the experience and appreciation of others facilitates the challenging search for collaborators who share the same values.

Organizations that take a leap of faith by basing their activities on confidence often experience a return in times of need. One example is *Hobbyhimmel*'s counter service (1-2 persons who oversee the workshop during opening hours and provide support for users). Frequently, there are gaps in the shift schedule. Nevertheless, the workshop has not remained closed for a single day during more than two years of data collection. Although the workshop's supervision is organized on a voluntary basis, there is an extremely high reliability and a corresponding trust in the collective. More generally, therefore, trust is also an enabler in the sense that individuals are convinced that others will continue to make sacrifices and challenge obstacles to further common goals around sustainability, which, in turn, increases their own willingness.

Relations based on trust, however, do not imply the absence of disagreement and of a need to compromise. Collectively agreed-on and transparent rules and procedures, thereby, help to avoid misunderstandings and ensure fair negotiations. *Slowtec*, for example, does not have positions with defined tasks for which one is employed, but a number of more and less enticing roles that have to be assumed to ensure the organization's functioning. Here, substantial coordination is required to balance both the allocation of different functions and duties and to cover all necessary activities. Setting up and cultivating appropriate procedures is a continuous learning process. Collected experiences and input from other groups advance the establishment of appropriate structures. Not unlike trust, the cultivation of these relations cannot be forced but need to grow organically. Once they are established, however, they are an important enabler of alternatives modes of (economic) organization.

> I notice that it is incredibly important that we have a structure. And perhaps even more structure than a normal [hierarchically structured organization], so that we can communicate at eye level (I_E01b).

Trusted subjectivities and devotion

The trust invested in individuals can fundamentally change the parameters of togetherness. At the same time, when communities invest trust in individuals, it does something to the subjects involved. On many occasions, I observed interesting dynamics and processes of reinforcement in groups – both towards more or less cohesion – depending on the investment or withdrawal of trust. These shifts are highly implicit and only partially available to conscious reflection. But the fact that trust repeatedly came up in formal and informal discussions attests its importance for community economies.

> What does that do to the subjects? If they are trusted all of a sudden and given responsibility. What is their answer? What possibilities do they have? They can hardly answer with distrust; they were given an advancement of trust. It does

> something with them. And I think this is a crucial point which I think is very good and that, in this way, a transformation can take place within existing organizations (F_01).

Trust in each other and the mutual cause is a fundamental moment in transformative practice. A particular driver of this are individuals who are highly dedicated to their project or organization. While the protagonists of eco-social organizations would not be able to pursue their objectives without the help of engaging contributors, it is important to reflect on the dedication, readiness, and capacities the former bring in. Most organizations in this study exhibit key personalities who have an essential role in the set-up and shaping of their organization. Often, this goes hand in hand with great personal risk and devotion. In the end, this requires someone who is so deeply invested in the project that work becomes vocation.

The founder of the open workshop, for instance, quit his job to devote three years full time to the project. He used the first year to plan the project and find an appropriate location. In the following two years, he spent more than the regular working week to implement his idea and consolidate the workshop. In other organizations, similar engagement has proved crucial in establishing a relatively stable organization despite of the various constraints. Some of the economic and governmental disadvantages organizations face (see above) are thus compensated by strong engagement.

Commitment alone, however, does not suffice and has to be accompanied by new ways of thinking. Although eco-social organizations do not necessarily break explicit rules, they frequently transgress the boundaries of 'business-as-usual'.

> One transgresses 'the usual' several times in such a process, or almost regularly one should say. Because the novelty of these qualities [here: reparability] could only be brought about by new ways of thinking, a new understanding of the necessity of these qualities. And then, derived from it, also new abilities in the provision of these qualities (I_E02biii).

Breaking with "mental infrastructures" (Welzer, 2011) entails a high degree of reflexivity about routines and norms and the ability of their questioning. Subjects challenge conditioned behaviors and finally unlearn them while cultivating other – alternative – routines. On occasion, the departure from 'normal' ways of doing things clashes with the mainstream and seems odd or out of place. This makes setbacks and the relapse into old patterns a regular part of (personal) transformation.

Chapter 15: Compromise

> If I were to follow my idealism 100% then I may have my idealism but no team and no enterprise and consequently no effect.
> (I_E01b)

Alternative practices are frequently sidelined by the 'reality' of financing, markets, growth-centered governance structures, habits, competitive forms of social intercourse and egocentric subjectivities. Yet, organizations and individuals continue to encounter possibilities through trust, innovation, chance, devotion, inventiveness and institutional support. Together these factors – and there are many more that this study did not uncover or which I had to neglect for reasons of space – constitute a diverse playing field on which transformative geographies unfold. Degrowth practices and politics, then, exist as ambiguous, contradictory, and often unclear patterns of activity that navigate the complex field of possibilities and constraints through trade-offs, impulse decisions, and long-term strategies. This last section sketches findings pertaining to the compromises organizations make. That means, the ways they anticipate, fight, embrace, and respond to incumbent practices and institutions which they find themselves exposed to and embedded in.

Trade-off

Organizations that financially depend on sales and paid commissions have to enter commercial relationships with others. Potential business partners, however, might not share the same value set, or, in fact, engage in activities that counteract the principles of sustainability and justice. For a lack of 'allies', eco-social enterprises compromise by doing business with individuals and organizations of different degrees of compatibility. *Slowtec* is a particularly conspicuous example when it comes to the assessment of commissions that do not fit the organization's ideals. The organization has rejected a number of inquiries in areas that are socially or environmentally problematic or, from the point of view of its members, unnecessary. On the other side, *Slowtec* also accepts commissions that are controversial from a degrowth perspective such as the cooperation with an automobile enterprise, which also included a transcontinental flight of one of the members. *Slowtec* makes these compromises very consciously, weighting (environmental or social) costs against the possible (future) impact of their organizational activities.

> They pay normal industry prices and that enables us, again, to work here in the team for a few months. I know about them [the negative effects of my practices] and deliberately make a compromise. If I were to follow my idealism 100% then I may have my idealism but no team and no enterprise and consequently no effect. And, I'm afraid, it will continue this way for a little longer (I_E01b).

Similar to commissions, there is no black and white when it comes to the sourcing of materials, the purchase of products, or their design, construction and sale. While most organizations strive to be as 'fair' and 'sustainable' as possible, budget constraints, time constraints and a lack of availability (for instance of upstream products) repeatedly causes them to opt for choices that are less expensive, less time-consuming or simply available at all. *Relumity*, for instance, put much effort in setting up a fair and local supply chain. For a lack of regional, national and even continental alternatives, *Relumity* decided to obtain electroluminescent diodes (LEDs) from Japan for reasons that the working conditions are likely to be better than in other Asian countries (see above). Others have to trade off due to financial restraints. *Hobbyhimmel*'s audition report for the *Economy for the Common Good* reflects the rationality behind these compromises as follows:

> As a startup with high investments and running costs as well as a very limited start-up budget, it was not always possible to go for the best option with respect to the common good. However, we consider for each purchase decision whether there are better, more meaningful alternatives and whether these lie within the financial possibilities (D_A01b).

Compromise between availability, costs and ideals is a recurrent issue beyond the few examples mentioned. *Relumity, Slowtec, Smark, Hobbyhimmel, Geco-Gardens* and others constantly have to compromise in their sourcing of materials. This is particularly conspicuous with respect to electronics where affordable continental let alone regional alternatives hardly exist. Without trade-offs, however, none of these organizations would be able to operate.

Alternative income sources, charity projects, and social tariffs

Volunteer work and mutual support are important pillars of Stuttgart's community economy. On the one side, many organizations are financially weak and depend on (or are significantly disencumbered by) non-monetized support. On the other side, organizations face payments for rent, equipment and, where applicable, for services and employees and thus require a stable revenue through donations, institutional funding, market activities or a combination thereof.

Factoring out labor costs significantly eases the financial pressure. This, however, is in itself problematic and in some cases boarders on (self-) exploitation. There is, of course, a distinction to be made between different organizational types. A first type comprises associations, which are based on volunteer work in principle. A second type are organizations that hover between volunteer work and the ambition to commercialize their activities in order to be self-sustaining. And a third type are organizations that manage to cover operations, including labor costs. Individuals who contribute to organizations that fall into the former two categories generally have alternative income sources. Some are employed by universities or hold similar jobs with enough flexibility, enabling them, to some extent, to combine their entrepreneurial activities with other responsibilities. Others have paid day jobs with reduced working hours to allow for both a modest income and enough time to invest in (for them) more meaningful activities.

Organizations that are not a side or leisure activity for their protagonists need to generate at least a minimum wage for some or all participants. This, however, often leaves little leeway for engagement in non-monetized economies that do not 'pay off' financially (see above). Yet, the ideas most eco-social entrepreneurs want to work on and the organizations they seek to cooperate with often lack the financial means to pay regular wages. Trapped within these tensions, some organizations implement 'social tariffs' and/or focus their volunteer work to maintain oversight.

> We call it seven-days-project. That means, so to speak, we donate seven working days per year to an organization and we work completely free of charge (I_E03).

em-faktor compounds its voluntary engagement into a 'seven-days-project' in which the whole organization devotes seven working days to a charitable project. The selection of a project often emerges from personal ties or from within the local context. The local group of the *Economy for the Common Good* – of which *em-faktor*'s manager is a member – for instance, was the addressee of a seven-days-project in which *em-faktor* designed and printed a brochure for the association. Apart from controllability, a condensed voluntary engagement also creates better visibility. *em-faktor*, in this sense, draws on their seven days project for marketing purposes.

Slowtec has social tariffs at about half the normal rate for charitable projects. The decisive factor, here, is not the organization's legal form but their purpose and financial situation. The fact that many of *Slowtec*'s potential partners would qualify for reduced rates, however, further strains *Slowtec*'s finances. Commissions from the *Karte von Morgen* project, for instance, are calculated with the social tariff. In addition to significantly lower rates, there are issues with the project's liquidity and its ability to render account of their project-based money. In sum, that means that *Slowtec* works for a reduced rate that, in addition, is only paid partially. This exchange is based on the trust that the project can pay the bill at a later stage.

Lower rates and more focused voluntary engagement are a frequent compromise between financial requirements and social purpose. In the case of *Slowtec*, a significant shift occurred from earlier attempts to cross-finance decommodified work with a small number of well-paid commissions to a severe limitation of their non-monetary engagement. A more structured take on volunteering and support, now, helps to trade off between financial requirements and a social focus. On one occasion, I noted:

> Seems like Slowtec has matured and become more 'realistic'. This does not necessarily mean that they are compromised on any level, but that there is simply not enough room to maneuver in the long run for decommodified support. Maybe there is also a kind of dissatisfaction with the lack of entrepreneurialism of other organizations (B_E01f).

Diversified business and Trojan Horse?

Smark started out with the slogan: 'Our goal is to make sustainable consumption the easiest. For us this means throwing all principles overboard'. This slogan appeared on the main page of their internet presentation, followed by a range of impressions from local farmers – fields, happy animals, scenic views. A few months later, the front page greets the visitor with a picture of a shipping container that has been redesigned as fully automated supermarket, headlined 'the supermarket 4.0 – 500 Products. 24 hours. 15m2'. According to *Smark*'s new internet presentation, the organization's goal has shifted: 'Shopping at any time. Spontaneously. Simple. Offline and Online'. Scrolling down, one is presented with various advantages of fully automated supermarkets – any references to local food and sustainability one searches in vein. What happened?

Rewind to early 2018. *Smark* just opened a second store in the west of Stuttgart. Like their first store, the veneer is made of recycled wood, this time from an old garden shed from Stuttgart-Botnang. The food for sale is organic and local, supporting a range of small brands and farmers. The organization has one member who scouts suppliers that fit *Smark*'s vision of sustainable food consumption. Since mid-2018 the store also carries fruits and vegetables that are sold on a trust-base. *Smark* aims to expand further, both to spread the concept and to reach a size that can sustain the organization economically – at this time the founders still depend on support through a subsidy program. With respect to potential investors they state:

> You have to explain it very plausibly that it is also economical and that, possibly, investors can get a return. And for us, the issue is that we have to make some com-

promises when it comes to our idealism. That means we wouldn't get anything if we just said: we're only interested in making sustainable consumption the easiest. So, of course, in addition it has to be economical. And here we simply have to make a bit of a compromise and try to make it profitable. Because otherwise we won't get any investors, it won't be attractive for them. Because nobody has that kind of money to fool around. Or probably very few (I_E06b).

Rewind to late 2017. *Smark*'s *Kesselkiste*, their first project, located at Stuttgart main station, has been running for a few months. The technology is still prone to failures, requiring frequent site visits and technical support. At this point, the founders invested over three years fulltime into the development of the technology. Funding came through a stipend called 'EXIST', which aims to support innovative technology-oriented or knowledge-based start-ups. Technology, from the outset, was a means to create more efficient processes which grant the organization a competitive advantage. This way, the more expensive regional and organic products gain in attractiveness.

In early 2019, this very advantage – at least on the surface – is turned into a means to generate profits. Still, it holds true that *Smark*'s elaborate technology requires high investments. The discursive shift from sustainability to technology has to be seen as adjustment to the requirements of potential investors whose primary interest lies in revenue rather than fair sourcing and ecological food production. *Smark*'s approach, then, resembles a Trojan Horse (the automated supermarket) that is used to reshape food retailing from within (making local and organic products easily available).

In spring 2019, the internet presence changed again, this time asking the visitor to choose whether she is interested in *Smark*'s products or *Smark*'s technology. Selecting the former transfers the visitor to scenic images and the promise: 'Regional and sustainable purchasing. Around the clock. Every day'. The latter links to *Smark*'s technology-based business approach: the supermarket 4.0.

Self-restriction

In contrast to *Smark*, *Slowtec* deliberately does not allow any classic investments. Instead *Slowtec* focuses on 'organic growth'. This is a compromise in so far, as it makes investments in materials and development work as well as the recruitment of additional contributors much more difficult and the organization vulnerable to delayed payments, back taxes, unforeseen costs and delays in the work process. In the past, *Slowtec* was under severe financial strain several times. This does not only compromise their charitable orientation (see above) but also complicate planning. Nevertheless, the enterprise is autonomous in its management and registers annually increasing turnovers. If continuing along this trajectory, *Slowtec* generates increasing leeway for activities in line with its social and environmental values and objectives.

In a similar vein, many protagonists compromise when it comes to their own income and merit. The founder of *Hobbyhimmel*, for instance, invested three years and much of his savings into the project without getting any returns. Similarly, many volunteers and entrepreneurs live on the breadline, paycheck to paycheck, and on mini-jobs they hold in addition to other activities. Of course, there are significant differences between individuals. Some are supported by their partners, parents or through savings from previous occupations. Others deliberately challenge themselves to live minimalist lifestyles. Nevertheless, their financial precariousness brings with it a general insecurity. One protagonist seriously worried about retrospective payments for several months' worth of health insurance – due to an administrative issue with the legal form of his company affecting his insurance status – which would pose a severe financial challenge to him.

Grey zones

Regulatory frameworks and statutory provisions – including construction regulations, requirement of permits, questions of liability, taxation and charges, accountancy, data privacy, health regulations and employment laws – often complicate the conduct of small organizations. Most organizations lack the appropriate resources to learn about regulatory frameworks in detail and comply. Although they are generally non-confrontational in their dealings, many organizations intentionally and unintentionally transgress statutory provisions.

A common 'compromise' lies in an intentional lack of knowledge. Due to organizations' limited resources as well as ambiguous information from public institutions, it is often not quite clear what full compliance would look like, let alone how it could be translated into practice. Smaller and larger 'grey zones' provide opportunities for a rather lenient interpretation. Examples, which I will not elaborate in much detail, include the deliberate omission of applying for permits and thus evading the administrative expenditures that come with it. Another strategy is the avoidance of costs and bureaucracy by organizing the transfer of goods as donation and not as sale. Generally, there is a concrete suggestion over the amount which is 'expected' to be donated, making the transaction relatively predicable nonetheless.

It is important to stress that these strategies are not born out of malevolence or negligence. In most cases the full compliance would strain organizations' capacities to a level that can cause severe pressure, financial and otherwise, and might even imperil their subsistence. Said strategies, therefore, are alternately forms of self-protection, protest or mitigation – and sometimes all at the same time.

Self-management

Direct democracy and consensus-based decision-making are lengthy processes that can be quite paralyzing for organizations. While some set priority on inclusiveness and participation and accept the difficulties that come with it, others prefer and depend on more lean and efficient processes of decision-making. The forms of self-management practiced by *Slowtec*, *Hobbyhimmel* – and in a less structured way by some other organizations in the sample – are forms of compromise between trust and control, participation and flexibility, individual responsibility and organizational capacity. The strategies of *Holacracy* and Laloux's *Reinventing Organizations* are empirically based and refined tools that provide practicable approaches to self-management. Instead of consensus, they are based on consent. That means, decisions are not made unanimously (in the sense that everyone has to fully agree) but on the basis that no one vetoes or resists that which is to be decided.

Although *Slowtec* and *Hobbyhimmel* are 'self-managed', they still have a manager or chairperson. This apparent contradiction, again, is a compromise. First, between their legal form – for-profit enterprise [GmbH] in the case of *Slowtec* and registered association [e.V.] in *Hobbyhimmel*'s case – and the ideals of non-hierarchical organizing. And second, although the manager has equal rights and duties in everyday operations, she functions as a 'last resort' in case of conflict or emergency. This, in many ways, is deemed necessary due to the various constraints of and threats to organizational processes such as financial straits and individual troublemakers.

Non-confrontative confrontation

Alternative projects can be unappealing to those who are unfamiliar with and skeptical of their values, purposes and objectives. To invite "reluctant subjects" (Gibson-Graham, 2006, p. 23), some organizations act as Trojan Horse for spreading alternative practices (see above). The workshop, for instance, is compatible with a wide range of different lifestyles and attitudes. Yet, its material set-up subtly confronts attendees with issues around resource use, waste, planned obsolescence, car-centered mobility, economic growth and others through placards, flyers, books and conversations. The latter being quite important: as meeting place for diverse individuals that would not meet otherwise, the workshop often houses informative but also controversial exchanges, exposing visitors to sustainability- and degrowth-related discourses.

In communicating its purpose, *Hobbyhimmel* draws on appealing messages including its easily accessible workspace, flexible payment options, opportunities to realize creative projects, and the support through its team and other users. At the same time, the organization refers prominently to pertinent social and environmental issues such as overconsumption and planned obsolescence. The workshop, in this vein, is advertised as a meaningful solution to these issues, as can be seen in the following excerpt from a flyer:

> The problem: 1,5 earths are required to cover our current resource consumption. 2030 it will be two planets. That these developments are increasingly problematic is already clear to most people. More and more people want to contribute to change but do not know how they can do so [...] Our solution: We want to bring the problems and causes to light and point out possibilities how everyone can contribute to change. The open workshop, for us, is a central tool to do so, for it combines and realizes important approaches such as sharing economy, open source, co-working, post-growth and commons [...] What we have attained: Hundreds of projects, repairs, and work pieces have been realized. In most cases, the user would not have been able to do so [without the workshop]. Either for a lack of space, equipment, knowledge, or the possibility to engage in noisy and messy activities. The uniformly positive feedback from different sides encourages us to continue (D_A01e).

This way, the workshop and other organizations 'nudge' reluctant subjects to engage with more critical topics. Degrowth narratives, furthermore, are accompanied by corresponding practices. The workshop prominently houses projects related to plastic reuse, upcycling, post-fossil mobility and urban gardening. These practices and projects appear prominently as showcases at public appearances and to users of the workshop. With its unimposing appearance and communication, the workshop manages to subtly expose subjectivities to issues and solutions around sustainability and degrowth.

Interlude III: Of transition

Transition is tricky business, for "as soon as we begin to deal with what comes next, we enter the terrain of speculation, conditionality and advocacy, as well as hope and imagination" (Chatterton, 2016, p. 405). It is therefore important to reflect on some fundamental issues before discussing the possibilities and insights the study's findings might yield.

First, the evidence collected is, of course, limited by the study's temporal, spatial and contentual scope. Although I was in the field for over two years, remaining in contact even beyond, the context of a dissertation project and the rhythms of academia require a temporal demarcation and caesura in empirical engagement. The data therefore allows only a glimpse into Stuttgart's community economy between 2016 and 2018. On the other side, this has been a quite turbulent and exciting period with a promising dynamic. Data interpretation, therefore, is driven by a certain hopefulness that this momentum continues.

In spatial terms, too, my perspective is limited to the urban area of Stuttgart, apart from some notable exceptions. Multiple ties point to dispersed organizations, localities and sites. Although these links occasionally took me outside of Stuttgart, other sites do not feature prominently in this study's findings since they remain too fragmented and underexplored. Most important, however, is my focal restriction to a small number of eco-social enterprises and organizations, only a few of which I could explore in greater depth to understand their intricate workings, rationales and practices. While other organizations are covered rather superficially, I also had to leave out a large number of possible allies for a degrowth transition – individuals, groups and enterprises – that I did not have sufficient time for or access to.

Second, an orientation towards what comes next involves numerous normative decisions. In contrast to representations of the present, the turn to possible futures leaves little leeway to escape into apparently neutral descriptions. Moving towards the discussion of this study's findings, it is important, therefore, to reiterate its orientation towards the values and principles associated with a degrowth transition (detailed in chapters 2, 7, and 10). Writing about the future, furthermore, draws on – and speaks to – different imaginaries and practices and is thus a part of transformative politics itself. Of course, there is more to transformation than its discourses (see chapter 4). This book gives a prominent place to the materialities that both enable and constrain transformation. Nevertheless, it presents itself to the reader as *text* and is thus, for now, part of the discourse on transformation to which it hopes to contribute.

Third, uncertainty often becomes prescription. Individual examples of how transition *could* unfold quickly become instructions on how it *should* unfold, forgetting about the specific contextualities of different sites and practices. It is therefore important to note that this book does not devise a specific and uniform strategy for transition. It does, however, aim to contribute to transformative knowledge and capacity, around which strategies can develop. Despite the need for critical reflection, the diverse findings on alternatives, possibilities, constraints and compromises bring about both evidence and inspiration how a degrowth transition might, and already does, unfold in practice. The findings demonstrate how organizations answer to difficulties and seek compromise to advance their values and objectives despite numerous obstacles (which are often similar across different sites). Although the organizations' tactics do not provide hard and fast rules of how to realize transformative projects, they inspire possible actions and solutions.

Before discussing my own interpretation of the data and making inferences on what might follow for transformative geographies, some protagonists of this study shall get a chance to speak for themselves. To that effect, this interlude closes part IV with an excerpt from a focus group discussion that propounds a particular imaginary of change. The general thrust of this discussion did not only inspire some of the interpretations that follow, but also gives a deeper insight into the community's dynamics and some of the aspects that drive it.

On an evening in mid-October ten of us sit around the meeting table in Slow Villa – as the building that houses *Slowtec*'s shared bureau and living spaces is nicknamed – discussing the preliminary findings of this research. In the second half of our nearly three-hour conversation, the topic shifts to transformation. I asked the participants to reflect on the role of community and mutual help for their activities. The following discussion ensued:

> T.: Well, yes, it has already been mentioned that there is something that connects us, this common sense or common suffering under the present conditions. And there we try to find new ways in our organizations. And of course, we become more successful by saying: we network, we exchange and support each other and inspire each other with respect to these points. Because everyone can bring his or her own strengths to these new approaches. And this ... recently we talked about spots of change. [We imagined that] there are spots within these organizations and that they grow from the inside [of organizations] and then cross over. Then, somehow, more cooperation comes about. Also with the customers, with whom

a higher level of trust can be established. And that's how it spreads, without us having to take to the streets and demonstrate hard-core: We need different laws here and there. Instead, we create the reality within our possibilities, not wasting our energy on establishing boundaries. Rather we focus on change itself and not on the problems.

S.: I would also say that it becomes quite apparent, here, this 'not being against something' but creating an alternative, something better that replaces the old. There is a quote somewhere from a clever person who once said that. I think it was Buckminster Fuller. And that's what I see here. Of course, you can try for five years to push through a new legal form [more appropriate for eco-social enterprises] in politics and convince everyone, and, and, and, and. Or you adapt until enough people actually do something different under the guise of a limited. And then, at some point, other people get the hang of it and say: hey, then we would actually need a different legal form which has to be created first. And then everyone says: finally, now we can switch. It's very similar for us, we also say: there is nothing that really fits our organization. First we had a sole proprietorship and now the association. But it still isn't the right form. But spending much time dealing with this doesn't lead us anywhere. Simply do it [that which is the purpose of your organization]. And what I wanted to say about trust: I think it's quite good that we, most of us here, know each other well and also work together and exchange ideas. And that trust increases as a result. And when I tell H.: I know someone who can do it in such and such a way and with whom I have had contact before. Then the network expands much faster than if he would now simply go to L. and say: hey, I heard you were doing something with lamps. Then he may think: hmm does he also want to do something with lamps? That means [many questions remain unanswered]: Where does the person come from? What's his background? But if he knew that we work together or I had known him for 2 years, then you would just know that he fits in terms of orientation. I think this [trust] broadens the network of actors and I think that's important.

R.: Or at some point you have reached a limit and you are in a bubble. That's the danger I see.

H.: That's what I have addressed in the interview, because I believe that we cannot scale this culture of trust at will. So there's a limit, I say, to human capacity. Or perhaps a social capacity. That doesn't mean it can't work across the board. But at some point, it has to become fragmented. It can't be monolithic, I think.

S.: No, but that will come about automatically.

H.: It will become [fragmented] automatically due to the spatial component.

S.: But also through the differences in orientation. Every one of us has a different focus, right? That's why ... but what do you mean by bubble? That we live in our own world or what?

R.: Yes, we all agree here.

S.: I wouldn't say that (laughs), let's go into detail.

R.: Let's go into detail, exactly. But on the surface, we all go into a similar direction, the way I see it. We want to change something. We want to be self-organized. We don't want to maximize profits, but perhaps we want to do business a little more sustainably. That's a common goal and the problem is that if I go to the next bar now and tell them what I want to do, it's a completely different world. And that's a different bubble. That's the bar bubble.

(everyone talks at once)

R.: And now the question is, how can our bubble be stretched so far that we even connect to the bar bubble. Or do we want that at all?

S.: Well, I think it's not bad at all [that we have our own bubble] because then you don't feel so alone in this world. Rather you think: there are a few others who are just as crazy and who put in a lot of work and receive little in return. Yes, indeed, I think that's rather positive.

R.: That's positive in any case.

S.: Yes, I agree... and everybody has the possibility to become part of this bubble. And we have so many interfaces. It's not like we only do business internally and say: ok, I only get food from the Krautomat and you only build it for us and then it would become a bubble at some point. But we have so many external relationships with the pub world.

U.: And it's more like the growing spots again.

S.: Exactly, we become bigger spots, with connections. And when someone from the pub world says: I'm interested in something with cultivation and blablabla, then I say: Why don't you go to Slowtec? And then your bubble gets bigger ... or your spot. From this point of view, I see that as a positive. It might be that at some point a negative bubble ...

R.: Nah, I see it positively. I see everything positively (laughs). I only see ...

S.: Bubble sounded so negative for me ...

R.: No, the bubble as a risk, not as a status quo or something. So rather as risk actually.

S.: As distinction?

T.: There are a lot of these bubbles. At the same time there is probably a bubble in Leipzig and in Berlin (laughs). But that's wonderful. And I think that this image of networking, there is something to it. If there are these bubbles, if they get bigger and then melt together, then maybe we have a big bubble and you say this is bad now. But then, maybe, we already made a transformation. But we have to keep looking anyway.

Part V: A degrowth transition in practice

Outline

Stuttgart's community economy comprises diverse practices that constitute capitalist, alternative-capitalist, and non-capitalist forms of labor, enterprise, transactions, property, and finance. Guided by a combination of different moments in the enactment of alternatives – practicing alternatives, encountering constraints, encountering enablement, and making compromises – and the diverse logics perspective on practices' relatedness through economy, communality, governance, subjectivity, and technology, the previous part structures this diversity and traces the different ways in which alternatives materialize empirically. The challenge at hand, now, is to map these diverse practices onto the complex unfolding of social dynamics and to interrogate their relatedness beyond place for the possibilities of a degrowth transition, a task this part turns to.

The foregoing interlude closes with a long excerpt from a focus group discussion on transformation. The participants imagine organizations as spots or bubbles that might grow and connect to eventually transform societal relations more broadly. This is a powerful imaginary frequently evoked throughout literature on transformation, for instance as 'autonomous geographies' (Pickerill and Chatterton, 2006), as 'interstitial spaces' (Wright, 2010), as 'Halbinseln gegen den Strom' [peninsulas against the current] (Habermann, 2009), or as 'seeds of change' (Seyfang, 2014).

But do the empirical insights of this study support such an imaginary? In order to formulate a tentative response to the research question how community activism and civic engagement can shift transformative geographies towards a degrowth trajectory (see introduction), this part integrates empirical material with the rich thematic and conceptual groundwork expounded in parts I to III. Before I outline the structure of this part in more detail, I ought to reiterate the study's take on transformative geographies.

Social dynamics, from a practice theory perspective, unfold as nonlinear and complex processes revolving around the emergence, stabilization and decline of practices or practice formations. Practices hang together and form larger nexuses, complexes and constellations, such as degrowth-oriented organizations, city councils, or markets. Power, thereby, is not a property of individual people, organizations, and institutions but resides in practices' alignments. That means, power emerges from the different ways the (innumerable) practices that constitute social phenomena relate to each other. This perspective both decenters the power of capitalism and the notion of capitalism as homogenous entity, while remaining attentive to the coercion that transpires through practices' alignment with the interests of capital (see chapter 6).

Parts I and II show that although capitalist forms of production, transfer, and governance are not the only way in which economic practices hang together – as the diverse economy perspective maintains – they enroll and align a significant fraction of economic activities. Take, for instance, the production of a smartphone, which connects practices of "salvage accumulation" (Tsing, 2015, p. 63) of materials like lithium and tantalum with practices of assembling the phone under inhumane working conditions (Marchant, 2018) and a highly disproportionate surplus appropriation (Kenneth et al., 2011). The individuals and communities affected by these exploitative practices, the enterprises that attempt to internalize costs, as well as the individual consumer faced with the decision what phone to buy have little leverage over such a constellation. Their practices appear to be conditioned from 'elsewhere' (see chapter 6). Yet, practices of fair sourcing, repairing, open source design, fair working conditions, equitable allocation of surplus, and ethical consumption that transpire through the infrastructures of open workshops like *Hobbyhimmel*, the skill-sharing and help in the *Repair Cafés*, the modular design of products like *Relumity #LED1*, the repair manuals of *iFixit*, and diverse non-profit business models, open perspectives onto the possibility of different alignments. This raises a number of questions for the possibility and form of a degrowth transition which this part explores in more detail.

The first question revolves around a politics of place beyond place. Empirically, this study captures the complexity of relations around alternative economies in place. Thematically, however, it aims to explore transformative geographies beyond place. The study's empirical focus on place, then, limits its ability to trace social and material relations beyond the geographical and temporal context of Stuttgart. Or, to be more precise, beyond the sites it covers empirically. A perspective on transformative geographies, therefore, requires thorough conceptual and methodological tools to grasp practices' relations beyond their immediate context. On a basic level, this entails two intertwined aspects: a notion of the broader context and a concept of practices' relatedness beyond place. Throughout this work, I address both.

Part I takes a general look at growth-based economic, political, and cultural institutions in the Global North. It considers diverse economic practices; capitalist cheapening; sustainable consumption; and non-capitalist forms of production, transfer, and surplus allocation. Engaging in a comprehensive literature review and trailing the various constellations and actors involved in the struggles over economic and political conditions, it paints a broad picture of the dynamics within which the work of transformation is set. Part II, then, extends the perspective on transformation conceptually. It develops a detailed argument how practices hang together, align and materialize, but also how they shift and change. On this ground, Chapter 7 operationalizes practices' relatedness through the 'diverse logics perspective' that systematizes the practice-theoretical notion of 'zooming' (Nicolini, 2013). It develops the notion of 'logics' as *patterns in the relatedness of practices*, setting up an approach that focuses on the ways practices hang together. In doing so, it foregrounds shifts and ruptures in practices' incumbent alignments, their reproduction, and the reinforcement of alternative alignments – opening a perspective on changing power relations and the materialization of postcapitalist possibility.

Parts III and IV elaborate on this analytical framework methodologically and empirically in a dialectical manner: while the diverse logics perspective guides analysis, empirical insights develop and refine it (see chapter 11). Against this background, the ensuing discussion on transformation is grounded in rich empirical data from a specific site squared with the many sided (or 'sited') and conceptually grounded insights beyond place. Chapter 16, with this in mind, (re)turns to the question of a *politics of place beyond place* and combines the study's conceptual and contextual insights with its empirical findings, sketching the tendencies and possibilities of a degrowth transition.

The second question revolves around the constitution of degrowth practices and degrowth organizations. The empirics of this study show a broad variety of practitioners and organizations that engage in sustainability-related activities. Tracing different forms of practices' relatedness in and beyond place does not suffice to capture the possibilities for a degrowth transition. Consequently, the study needs to develop a conceptually grounded understanding of practices and organizations that work towards a degrowth transition. Rather than singling out particular practices or organizational forms, chapters 17 and 18 propose more nuanced perspectives on degrowth practices and organizations. Chapter 17 develops a notion of degrowth practices as *conventionalized patterns of activity that reflectively relate to practices' broader alignments in ways that found the assumption that these activities have an effect in line with degrowth's principles*. Chapter 18, then, contextualizes the notion of degrowth practices by looking at different types of organizations – symbiotic, interstitial, and pragmatic – which, each in their own way, incorporate degrowth-oriented activities.

The third question revolves around possible leverages that further a degrowth transition. The profound changes required to veer current societal trajectories away from deepening crises premise a widespread dissemination of degrowth practices and organizations. Yet incumbent alignments compel degrowth-oriented organizations and actors to compromise, watering down much activity oriented towards radical change. Despite the difficulties to identify, let alone single out particular approaches and lines of action, chapters 19 and 20 discuss the possibilities of a strategic orientation. Rather than losing themselves in the hybridity, contingency, diversity, and processuality of transition, they trace the development of possible avenues to further a degrowth transition. Chapter 19 develops the notion of 'hybrid infrastructures' while chapter 20 identifies particularly viable socio-spatial degrowth strategies.

Chapter 16: Sketching a degrowth transition

> To some, our examples will seem like insignificant islands, to others, inspiring seeds of the future, grassroots innovations that will flourish into something more significant ... Maybe they are glimmers of hope that have always shone in dark times, the seeds under the snow waiting for better times.
> *Chatterton and Pickerill, 2010, p. 488*

Degrowth convenes a number of theoretical and practical approaches that seek to abandon economic growth and related narratives of development, innovation, and progress as guiding principles of human co-existence. Instead, degrowth proposes a reflective recalibration of economic, political, and social institutions to support a temporally and spatially equitable, sustainable, and dignified survival of human and non-human species (see chapter 2). What is at stake from a degrowth perspective, then, is not only a downscaling of economic parameters (in a narrow sense) but the ideology of progress across all social domains: technological innovation, self-enhancement, community development, and political expansion, all of which are regularly modelled on a notion of (ecological) evolution. A degrowth transition, therefore, exceeds economic degrowth and includes all dimensions of social life including politics, culture, identity, and technology (Schneidewind, 2018; see chapter 7).

Stuttgart's community economies, as the findings in part IV show, confront and erode incumbent alignments of practices on multiple fronts simultaneously. The lens of the 'diverse logics perspective' sheds light on different practices that gnaw away on the apparent verities of growth, innovation, enhancement, development, expansion, and evolution. Degrowth-oriented organizations, however, do not blindly oppose, say, technological progress, but subject technological innovation to critical reflection and politics (Kerschner et al., 2018). Similarly, although a number of organizations deliberately forgo profits and expansion due to the ways they align practices of sourcing, management, production, work, and sale, they do not withdraw from market exchange altogether. The community's activities, consequently, interfere with incumbent alignments of practices in quite different ways.

In connection with the introductory deliberations of this part, this chapter subjects three issues to further exploration and discussion. First, a degrowth transition entails a large-scale shift in economic, political, and cultural practices. But how do the findings of a place-based study map onto the fundamental, dispersed, and far-reaching changes a degrowth transition implies? Second, the patterns that constitute Stuttgart's community economy relate very differently to incumbent alignments and include many practices that reproduce and reinforce rather than shift, rupture, or replace them. Against this background, which activities are transformative and how so? And third, contradictions and tensions, here, do not only emerge between transformative activities and growth-based institutions, but also between the different dimensions of a degrowth transition. How do the different social dimensions of transformation relate to each other?

All three issues are closely imbricated and can only be addressed together. This chapter combines the two typologies developed above (see figure 7). First, on patterns in practices' relatedness, that is *social dimensions of transformation* (see chapters 7 and 11; figure 2). And second, on different forms of practices' interference with incumbent alignments, that is *strategic dimensions of transformation* (see interlude II; figure 3). Both typologies were developed in response to the need to account for the relation between place-specific activities and spatially more dispersed nexuses of practices and are thus sensitive towards questions of spatial extent (see part II).

The five perspectives on practices' relatedness – economy, governance, communality, subjectivity, and technology – that informed the coding process (see chapter 11) and supported the presentation of findings (see chapters 12 to 15), shed light on different dimensions in which a degrowth transition can (and has to) unfold. Symbiotic, interstitial, and ruptural transformation as well as reproduction, furthermore, lay out four modes how practices relate to broader alignments (see interlude II). Structured by the diverse logics perspective and different modes of transformation, the remainder of this chapter aims to sketch a degrowth transition. It is guided by the question: what could a degrowth transition look like in the light of this study's empirical findings? The first section sets the ground by referring back to the context of this research, situating the findings in place. The subsequent sections each explore transformative dynamics along one perspective on practices' relatedness – economy, governance, communality, subjectivity, and technology. For each perspective, I briefly set the scene by reflecting on issues outlined in parts I and II. I then square the respective social dimension with the findings in part IV and consider moments of symbiotic, interstitial, and ruptural transformation that the data reveal. While this chapter builds on the study's findings, it discusses them rather superficially to set up a perspective on the width and breadth of a degrowth

Figure 7 Social and strategic dimensions of transformation

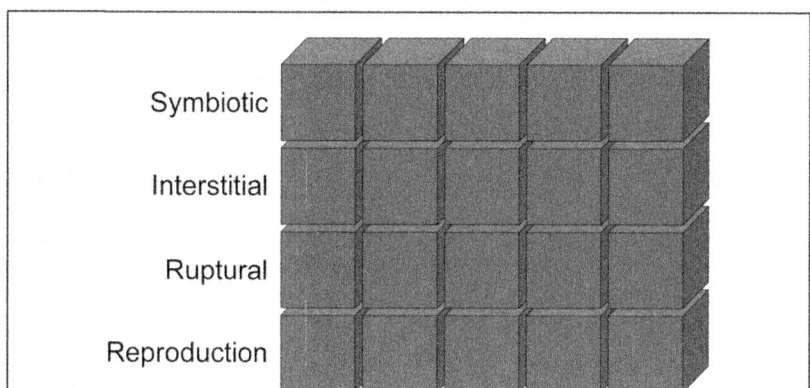

transition. The ensuing chapters (17 to 20), then, dig deeper into the practices, organizations and strategies involved.

Stuttgart's politics of place beyond place

Chapter 9 situates the case study in the relatively prosperous and industry-oriented context of Stuttgart. It reflects on the context's particularities and possible consequences for research on degrowth economies. Aside from conducive factors for technologically oriented alternative organizations – such as specialized knowledge and skills, material support, and selective cooperation with industrial companies – Stuttgart is also relevant as a site of globalized production and consumption. With a number of the world's leading companies in automobile and high-tech industries, such as *Bosch, Daimler, Porsche, IBM, Siemens,* and *Mahle,* most of whom have their head-quarters or important subsidiaries in the metropolitan area, Stuttgart links and commands considerable flows of resources, materials, and money.

Stuttgart, therefore, is not just a site affected by practices' elsewhere, but it is also origin and commander of global relations. Massey (2008, p. 15, emphasis in original), along these lines, raises the crucial question: "if the reproduction of life in a place, from its most spectacular manifestations to its daily mundanities, is dependent upon poverty, say, or the denial of political rights, elsewhere, then should (or *how* should) a 'local' politics confront this?" In Stuttgart, similar to Massey's London, the prosperity of place depends on innumerable relations to other places. Flows of capital, workers, resources, products, directives, documents, and knowledge are entangled with salvage accumulation, dispossession, displacement, oppression, exploitation of workers, cheapening of natures, and other forms of ecosocial injustices (see chapter 1).

A politics of place beyond place, consequently, starts *in* place. Changes in the patterns of provisioning, sourcing, exporting, commanding, and many others are important elements of a degrowth-oriented politics (see chapters 6 and 7). Although the organizations that feature in this study are not the global players that leverage global value chains, some of their practices interfere with incumbent alignments and provide plausible links and orientations for a degrowth transition. Putting the practices of Stuttgart's community economy in relation to the institutions that characterize growth-based societies, thereby, shows how their activities collide with, shift, replace, rupture, and reproduce broader alignments.

Needless to say, Stuttgart's organizations and activists certainly do not make a degrowth transition by themselves. But while changes in one place do not allow for the inference of a broader transformation, they do not exclude, indeed rather promote, similar dynamics unfolding in other places. Putting local transformation into relation with practices' broader alignments, then, opens a perspective on the possibilities of a *politics of place beyond place in many places*. Some of the practitioners that feature in this book, therefore, are important pioneers who provide the ground for critical scholars, activists, politicians, planners, and entrepreneurs in various places to ally and affect change. The remainder of this chapter collects, systematizes, and interprets the degrowth-oriented dynamics of Stuttgart's community economy.

Economy

The logic of economy captures practices' relatedness through moments of creation, exchange, reciprocity, comparison, and sustenance. It is particularly visible in practices of production, consumption, distribution, and appropriation. Incumbent institutions align said practices in ways that support the accumulation of capital, for instance through a focus on exchange value, rates of productivity, wage dumping, and the externalization of costs. Or in the words of Patel and Moore (2018), a cheapening of work, nature, and lives (see chapter 1).

Degrowth criticizes that economic practices aligned through exchange value and productivity counteract social and environmental justice and imperil community, democracy, wellbeing, and ecosystems. Just and sustainable economies require an end of exploitation and the (re)embedding of economic practices into democratic and solidary value systems. Production and exchange ought to align through usefulness, equity, and sustainability instead. Degrowth scholarship proposes the localization and regionalization of productive activities; the organization of resources as commons; the sharing of work, resources, space, knowledge, and skills; and the decommodification of land, labor, and value as coordinates of a degrowth economy (Kallis, 2018; see chapters 2 and 7). Productivity, measured in monetary terms, then, gives way to expenditures that enrich pleasure and well-being. Such an economy draws on diverse ways of organizing economic relations which elude quantification and supplant markets as prime mechanism for allocation.

The study's findings, however, show that organizations run into difficulties if they do not align their practices through exchange value, rates of productivity, wage dumping, and the externalization of costs. Short and fair value chains based on regionalized production and assembly are uncompetitive beyond a small group of idealists and lifestyle consumers. *Relumity* and *Geco-Gardens*, for instance, face severe restrictions by refusing to base production on offshoring and cheap sourcing. To compensate (at least partially) for financial restraints, most organizations in this study accept low returns (and thus precarious wages or no compensation at all), despite much engagement that is often considerably beyond a regular working week. Making compromises in the face of such limitations, practitioners and organizations also reproduce incumbent economic alignments. Aside from drawing on and upholding non-transparent and possibly exploitative value chains, market pressures bring organizations to engage in marketing- and sale-related activities. In lieu of aggressive marketing and focus on exchange value, organizations like *Smark*, *Relumity* and *Geco-Gardens*, of course, offer products and services that target social and environmental needs and are not reducible to artificial need creation. Notwithstanding, these organizations attempt to win customers to sell their products and services to and, in doing so, align with a competitive logic that clashes with degrowth principles (see chapter 7).

In combination with symbiotic and interstitial transformative practices, however, their orientation also contains shifts and substitutions that are conducive to a degrowth transition (see figure 8). A selective cooperation with organizations that share similar values partially substitutes for competition and introduces elements of reciprocity into economic practice. Furthermore, their products and services expand the availability of ethical alternatives, to some extend compelling competitors to realign their practices. *Smark*'s (original) slogan 'to make the purchase of sustainable food the easiest one' expresses this tendency well. In doing so, these organizations introduce different elements and practices to the (local) economy. The findings show that a number of organizations indeed engage in local production and sourcing, draw on alternative materials and organizational forms, and put an emphasis on use values. These practitioners and organizations are guided by the question whether a product or service is socially and environmentally useful rather than the question whether it can be sold on a market.

Figure 8 Transformation of practices' economic relatedness

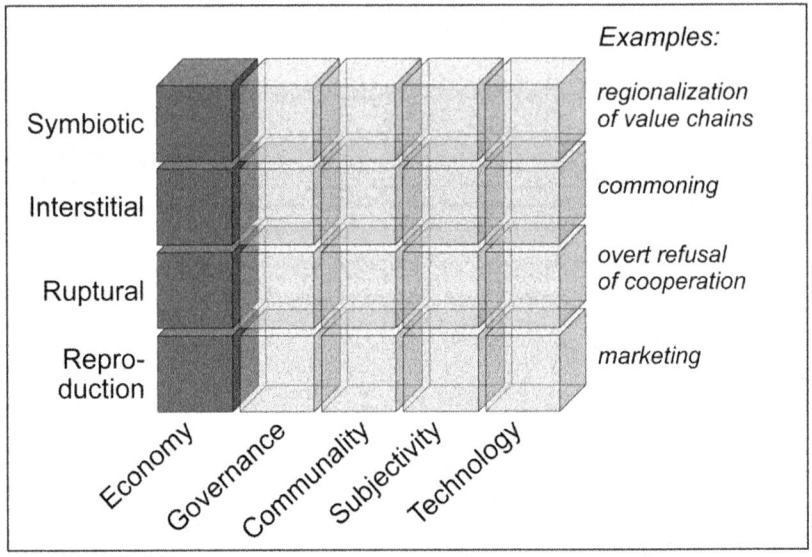

Some organizations' practices, thereby, relate symbiotically to incumbent economic alignments, shifting them towards more sustainable trajectories. *Smark*, for instance, sources regional and organic products from local farmers and sells them through a fully automated supermarket, supporting the shift towards a more sustainable food consumption. *Relumity*, in turn, sets up a more regionalized and transparent value chain for lightbulbs, which they sell in a business-to-business context.

Furthermore, some organizations' practices relate interstitially to economic alignments, substituting for unsustainable practices. For instance, *Hobbyhimmel* and the *Repair Cafés* provide spaces in which people engage in repair practices, (partially) replacing the purchase of new products. *Lastenrad* and *teilbar* provide cargo bikes and other goods that can be used free of charge, setting up a commons that substitutes individual ownership and introduces relations of sharing.

Since most organizations in this study focus on setting up alternative spaces, there are few examples of practices that relate rupturally to incumbent institutions and oppose economic alignments. Marginal cases are organizations like *Slowtec* or *em-faktor* that refuse to cooperate with enterprises which engage in destructive business practices. By detailing that refusal, *Slowtec* and *em-faktor* oppose and confront capitalist enterprises with their exploitative business activities. Oppositional tendencies, however, are very moderate and remain the exception.

Governance

The logic of governance captures practices' relatedness through moments of rule, domination, power, control, and norms. It is particularly visible in bureaucratic practices, law (enforcement), policing, politicking, and acts of violence. In a growth society, much of regulation and control aligns with capital accumulation. Examples include regulation – supporting private property and enclosure of social and natural commons, for instance through patents or mining rights – policing – for instance through police repression, intimidation and the use of excessive force at protests, such as those against Stuttgart 21 or more recently the anti-G20 protests in Hamburg (Haunss et al., 2017) – and politicking – the inadequate and insufficient legislation to respond to social and environmental issues and the denial of more fundamental examination of their root causes (see chapter 1). Bureaucratic practices, furthermore, fail to sufficiently support and encourage civic and economic engagement for social and environmental justice and to protect initiatives that do not align with market demands. Current German non-profit law, for instance, excludes political engagement for freedom, social justice, and autonomy.

Degrowth seeks to reorient the logic of governance towards democratic forms of decision-making as well as participatory and polycentric forms of control. Practices, then, should be aligned in ways that foster equality; care for disadvantaged individuals and groups; prevent socially and environmentally harmful practices; encourage dialogue and non-violent communication; and protect the commons through, for instance, redistribution of wealth, fair wages, transparency, more possibilities for participation, and the strengthening of local politics. Foremost, that would mean to sever social norms and rules from capital accumulation. Bureaucracy, law, norms, and police work, from a degrowth perspective, should align through equality, participation, non-violence, non-coercion, and care.

The findings, however, show that most organizations face a number of bureaucratic challenges ranging from inadequate legal forms to disproportionate administrative expenditures. *Slowtec, em-faktor*, and *Relumity*, amongst others, bear the same tax burden as extractive enterprises although their focus is primarily socially and environmentally motivated. Furthermore, some of the organizations that are possibly entitled to tax exemptions do not attempt to acquire non-profit status for fear of revocation and retrospective tax payments. In addition, high bureaucratic expenditures and unreliable institutional support can threaten the existence of small organizations like *reCIRCLE*. Nevertheless, a perspective through the lens of governance sheds light on a number of activities that shift, substitute, and oppose the ways practices relate through rule, control, and administration (see figure 9).

em-faktor's thrust to judge organizations and enterprises by their social and not by their monetary profits, as declared in the 'social profit manifesto', chimes in with claims by the *Economy for the Common Good* to reform charity laws and taxation. In response to these and other impulses, the work of the Green Party in Stuttgart's city council to audit city-owned enterprises engenders small governmental shifts towards a different evaluation of economic activity. Although these changes are superficial and relate largely *symbiotically* to present institutional alignments, the claims of the *Economy for the Common Good* in itself challenges capitalist institutions. The ECG seeks to tame markets through common-good-oriented taxation, maximum income, limits to personal assets, restrictions on heritages etcetera, essentially abrogating capitalism's unlimited drive for accumulation.

As with practices' economic relatedness, however, few activities relate rupturally to incumbent alignments of practices through governance. This is mainly due to the fact that there is little focus on protest movements in this study. There are, however, exceptions in the sample. *Critical Mass*, for instance, actively disrupts traffic and thereby challenges the political protection and privileging of automobility. A number of individuals from organizations like *Hobbyhimmel* and *Lastenrad* participate in these events and the organizations themselves support them. In addition, organizations like *Slowtec* relate *interstitially* to bureaucracy and law by setting up an outer shell that corresponds to legislative practices while prefiguring other forms of governance internally. Practices of self-management, non-contractual cooperation, and mutual support remain outside of the sphere of influence of legislation at first. In some cases, however, alternative practices merge into a twilight zone with respect to taxation and control. In this vein, some organizations seek ways around administrative boundaries by ignoring regulations, deliberately remaining uninformed, and navigating legal grey areas.

By and large, however, the practitioners and organizations in this study cooperate with bureaucratic and state institutions. In the face of the consequences of non-compliance, for instance with taxation laws, organizations have little leeway for opposition. For the most part, non-compliance is out of question and thus not part of organizations' reflection or strategy. Despite various disagreements with legislative and policing practices, the confrontation of state institutions remains largely symbiotic with few tendencies outside of formal political practices. Partial withdrawal from state practices poses a greater challenge to organizations and individuals than the (partial) disengagement from markets. Building non-commodified value chains, for instance as community-supported agriculture, hinges primarily on sufficient input of non-market resources and work. In contrast, taxation, policing, and regulatory frameworks affect organizations irrespective of their organizational set-up. It remains a major challenge to change governance to en-

Figure 9 Transformation of practices' relatedness in governance

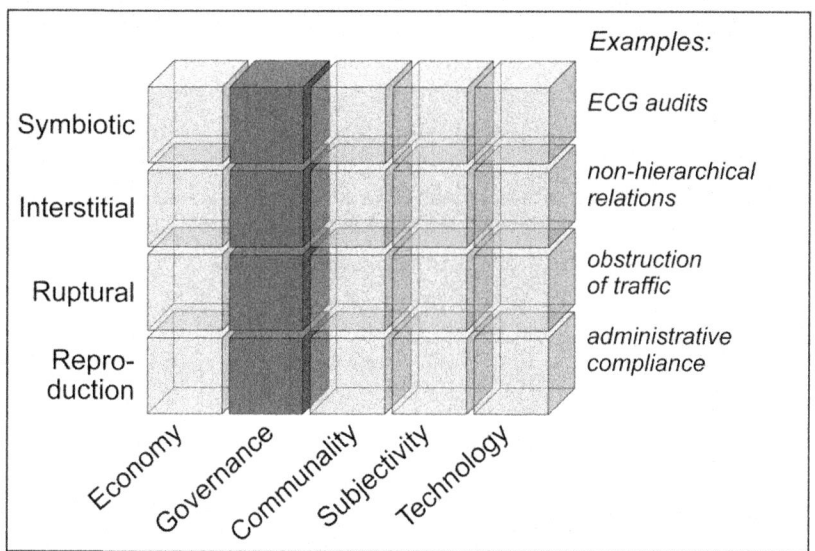

courage rather than discourage non-market and common-good-oriented forms of organization.

Communality

The logic of communality captures practices' relatedness through moments of togetherness, interdependence, contestation, and collective identity. It is particularly visible in practices of support, participation, non-violent disagreement, competition, negotiation, and group-formation. In contrast to the foregoing logics of economy and governance, it is more difficult to speak of a prevalent alignment. Generally, however, incumbent economic, political and social institutions foster instrumental and calculative relations rather than appreciation, reciprocity, and solidarity. Neoliberalism models central areas of social life – like education, care, and politics – on the market, which revolves around self-interest and competition (W. Brown, 2015; Ratner, 2019). In connection with the dismantling of solidarity-based welfare systems, individuals' interests are pitched against each other, creating a 'dog-eat-dog society'. Interpersonal ties in many areas of social life – such as work, public life, academia, social media, and sometimes even acquaintances – are shaped by self-centeredness, superficiality, and opportunism, as a consequence.

Neoliberal discourse, furthermore, veils interdependencies through individualist ontologies, responsibilization, and the naturalization of egotistical behavior (W. Brown, 2015). Instead of reflecting on togetherness as being-in-common – the notion that being is always being *with* another – political and public discourses frequently instrumentalize a common-being – a common substance or identity around which togetherness is set-up – such as, for instance, in the agitation against migration.

Scholarship on alternative economies maintains that human existence is fundamentally interdependent (Gibson-Graham, Cameron, et al., 2013; see chapter 4). The ways in which humans organize and depend on each other, furthermore, is the object and outcome of negotiation and disagreement (Dikeç, 2015; Rancière, 1998). Degrowth seeks to cultivate practices that align through co-dependence and democratic participation. Cooperation replaces competition as central principle of organizing societal relations (Bollier and Helfrich, 2012; Meretz, 2015). Degrowth-oriented togetherness, in this sense, fosters practices' alignment alongside trust, reciprocity, solidarity, and non-violent communication rather than competition, extraction and managerialism.

The findings, however, show that organizations which attempt to build relations of trust, mutual help, and solidarity within and without their groupings face a number of challenges. *Slowtec*'s practices of self-management, for instance, are at odds with legal and economic frameworks they face. More generally, the non-instrumental and voluntary support between different participants and organizations is limited by financial, temporal, and legal restraints. For a lack of time and resources, many participants partake in the competition for sales or funding instead of devoting time to their moral priorities around social and environmental justice. Solidarity beyond place is even more difficult, since fairly sourced materials and sustainably produced goods are often not available or not affordable. Many organizations are therefore involved in possibly exploitative commodity chains.

Nevertheless, the study abounds with examples of practices that affirm trust and support rather than extraction and calculation (see figure 10). A focus of many organizations revolves around products or activities that cultivate and maintain equitable relations to other humans and non-humans rather than extracting value from them. Sourcing of (more) fairly traded and sustainable products and materials is one way this materializes.

In the face of the limitations of linear value chains, however, a number of organizations go one step further and attempt to close the loops of resources, energy, nutrients, or water. In doing so, *Cradle to Cradle*, *reCIRCLE*, *ownworld*, *Grünfisch*, and *Geco-Gardens shift* practices of living, food production, and consumption from linearity and extraction towards circularity and co-dependence. *Cradle to Cradle*'s practices, thereby, have a largely *symbiotic* relation with incumbent institutions, even considering the possibility of accelerating consumptive cycles. *ownhome*'s energy, water, and nutrient cycles, in contrast, substantially *substitute* for consumptive practices, affirming the dependence of human sustenance on natural flows.

ownworld, furthermore, is part of a larger community with *Relumity*, *Slowtec*, and others that cultivate practices of mutual help and trust. Although decommodified exchange is severely limited by financial, temporal, and legal restraints, a number of practitioners and organizations foster *interstitial* spaces of trust-based economizing. Concomitant with the affirmation of interdependence, the organizations' practices also politicize production, distribution, and consumption. *Hobbyhimmel* and the *Repair Cafés*, for instance, draw attention to the politics of planned obsolescence and short production cycles, broadening the opposition against these pillars of growth-based economies.

Figure 10 Transformation of practices' relatedness in communality

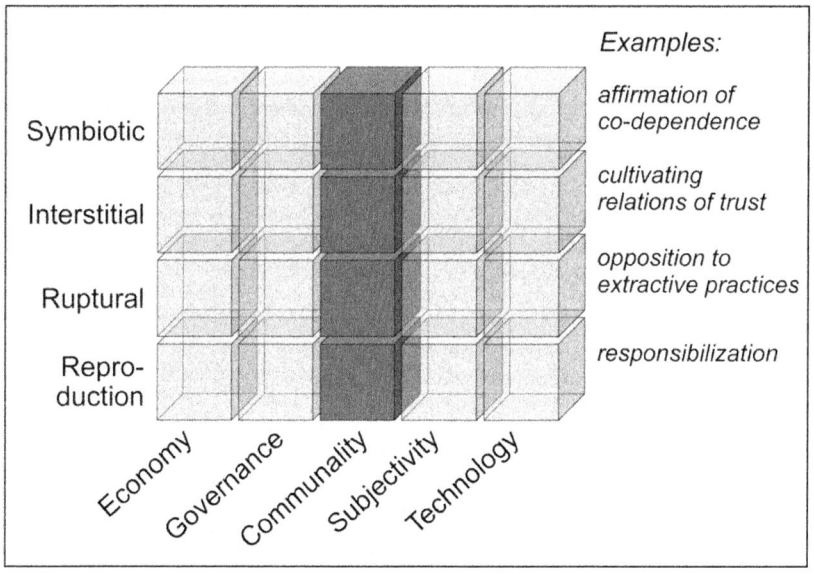

In contrast to alternative alignments of economy and governance, which are often rife with compromise, the enactment of trust is quite consistent. Despite stark limitations of decommodified relations, there is a strong sense of togetherness between many of the practitioners and organizations, not least because some individuals are members and supporters of multiple organizations. Community-based care, however, raises a number of questions around responsibilization and the privatization of welfare. Substituting dismantled welfare systems through social enterprises not only exempts state institutions from responsibility, but also transfers welfare from democratically legitimized institutions to private entrepreneurs. Degrowth scholars and activist, therefore, need to avoid that autonomy, entrepreneurship, and decentralization revert to competitive (communality) and extractive (economy) tendencies.

Subjectivity

The logic of subjectivity captures practices' relatedness through imaginaries, meanings, theories, and concepts on the one hand, and habits, affects, feelings, and experiences on the other hand. It is particularly visible in practices of explaining, analyzing, sense making, as well as practices of judgement and (self-) positioning. In capitalist societies, 'mental infrastructures' (Welzer, 2011) are largely geared to competition and growth. Media, educational, and political discourses align to a significant degree with narratives of progress, in particular economic growth and technological innovation, and largely ignore limits to growth, the unlikeliness of absolute decoupling, and the imperialist basis of prosperity in the Global North (Brand and Wissen, 2017; Jackson, 2017; see chapter 1). Individuals, thereby, are pushed to succeed and keep up with social advancement rather than engage critically with social and environmental issues. It is individuals' responsibility to act as 'homines oeconomici' and entrepreneurialize themselves as human capital (W. Brown, 2015). Organizing society around calculative individualists fosters uncompromising, self-centered and ignorant subjectivities, valued in terms of success and focused on self-enhancement. Like with other forms of practices' relatedness, alternative alignments exist but are discouraged rather than fostered by incumbent economic, political and social institutions.

Postcapitalist and degrowth approaches emphasize the need to develop empathy, altruism, and joyful doing in order to establish a socially and ecologically sustainable economy. Community economy scholarship, in particular, focuses on subjects' disidentification with capitalism as central lever for transformative geographies (Gibson-Graham, Cameron et al., 2013; see chapter 4). In the same vein, degrowth and other approaches to alternative economizing challenge the naturalization of self-centered rationalism and the ideology that markets divert egoism towards common good, while acknowledging that social institutions based on individualism reproduce such behavior (Kallis et al., 2018; Muraca, 2013; Habermann, 2012; Raworth, 2017; Schneidewind and Zahrnt, 2014).

Empathy, respect, and altruism are, in some ways, the antithesis of capitalist competition. In a social environment where people are required to assert themselves against others, many are overwhelmed by a lack of coercion and control. At the same time, alternative economic projects are vulnerable to egoistic and exploitative behavior. Calculative, ignorant, and self-centered subjectivities jar with alternative forms of economizing and decision-making on numerous fronts, ranging from incompatible attitudes to difficulties in adapting to non-hierarchical co-operation.

Although the individuals that participate as supporter or customer in Stuttgart's community economy are generally cooperative – and overly asocial behavior is rare – incidents of (voluntary or involuntary) damaging occur at times. Most difficulties, however, are due to deep-seated attitudes and habits that clash with organizations based on voluntary participation, autonomy, sufficiency, and principles of solidarity. *Slowtec* and *Hobbyhimmel* that both experiment with self-management experience reluctance and insecurity of subjects to adapt to non-hierarchical forms of work and decision-making. Many protagonists, furthermore, align strongly with a focus on efficiency and optimization of their own practices and that of their organizations.

All these aspects, of course, apply to people who actually participate in the projects and organizations featured in this study. On a more speculative note, these and other reasons, such as lack of awareness about social and environmental issues and the inability to engage in alternative practices, also prevent others from participating.

Subjectivity, however, is not only a key premise for transformative practice but also a site of transformation itself (see figure 11). Hardt and Negri (2017, p. 224) note "subjectivities are radically transformed by their participation in political organizing and political action". Along these lines, the study identifies a number of practices shifting, substituting, and rupturing incumbent alignments of subjectivity. Most prominently, trust features in this book both as catalyzer of community economies and as challenge to subjectivities which are accommodated to distrust, control, and hierarchy. *Interstitial* spaces of trust-based economizing, therefore, not only substitute for extractive and competitive relations (see logic of communality above), but they also change the identities, attitudes, and affects of those involved. In particular, the experience that things can be done differently is a strong leverage and encouragement for further alternative practice. It produces "resonance", in the words of Hartmut Rosa (2016, p. 736, author's translation) which "keeps alive the notion and desire for a different form of world relationship". Put simply, it gives subjects hope that collective efforts can bring about positive change (Gibson-Graham and Community Economies Collective, 2017; Kallis and March, 2015; see also chapter 4).

Participation, for instance as volunteer or visitor of the open workshop, also exposes individuals to doings and sayings related to social and environmental issues, which they might not encounter otherwise. This confrontation can lead to *shifts* and in extreme cases also *ruptures* in judgments, sense-making, and (self-)positioning vis-à-vis social, economic and environmental relations. Besides emotional and cognitive competences, the involvement with alternative organizations also enhances practical skills for a degrowth economy. Repair, for instance, which I will discuss in detail below, is a crucial element of sufficiency and subsistence as is cultivated by organizations like *Hobbyhimmel* and the *Repair Cafés*.

Figure 11 Transformation of practices' relatedness in subjectivity

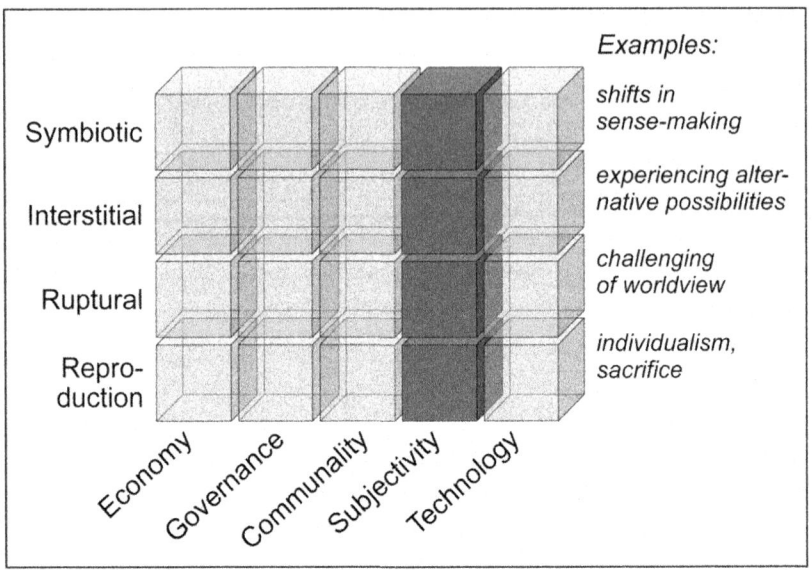

In some ways, however, practitioners and organizations reproduce incumbent forms of subjectivation. Although, in line with the findings on commonality, subjectivities largely deviate from exploitative and self-centered forms of relatedness, some tendencies like (self-) optimization and responsibilization prevail. Individuals, for instance, take on large workloads, sacrificing themselves for the cause. While this is admirable, it is also problematic insofar as it puts disproportionate pressure and responsibility on individual subjects. Aside from reproducing individualistic tendencies, the formation of groupings around exposed individuals are more vulnerable, for instance, if that person leaves or pushes the organization into a different direction.

Technology

The logic of technology refers to practices' relatedness through infrastructures, documents, machines, tools, substances, and other artefacts. It is particularly visible in practices based on (modern) technological innovations, such as instant messaging, nuclear energy, electro mobility, 3D printing, and living in a smart home.

A growth-based economy appropriates technology as a means to increase capital accumulation. Incumbent institutions align technology-focused activities alongside increased productivity, creation of new markets, mass production, and convenience. As a consequence, technological development is primarily driven by the demand to increase competitiveness and accelerate production-consumption cycles. Innovation, against this background, does not prioritize social and ecological needs but responds to profit opportunities. Furthermore, negative effects such as ecological destruction, social alienation, and the increase of vulnerability and dependence are frequently ignored, downplayed, or willingly accepted.

Alternative approaches show a range of divergent positionings towards technology. The spectrum ranges from visions of a fully automated luxury communism (Bastani, 2018; see chapter 2) to anarcho-primitivism, which seeks to return to a pre-agricultural society (Huber, 2015). Degrowth scholarship, in general, proposes a localization and regionalization of markets, the strengthening of subsistence economies, and a reduction in material consumption through sufficiency and voluntary simplicity (Demaria et al., 2013; Kerschner et al., 2018; Paech, 2012). Degrowth, thereby, opposes the naive techno-optimism of the green economy discourse which holds tight to business-as-usual forms of economic practice for the unlikely prospect of an absolute decoupling of resource consumption and economic growth (Jackson, 2017). However, this does not mean that degrowth opposes technological development as such. Technology, rather, is subject to reflection and debate about its appropriateness and usefulness. Technology can well materialize in ways that facilitate degrowth's aspiration for subsistence and sufficiency – for example through off-the-grid tiny houses – and regionalized value chains – for example through 3D printing. By and large, degrowth seeks to align technology-related practices alongside usefulness, autonomy, emancipation, and preservation.

The findings show that organizations which are technologically oriented face a number of contradictions. Many technologies, in particular those that include electronic components, rely on resources and upstream products, the extraction and production of which is not clearly traceable and is likely to include social exploitation and ecological damage. *Hobbyhimmel*'s productive infrastructure, *Relumity*'s lamps, *Slowtec*'s *Krautomat*, *Smark*'s fully automated supermarket, *Geco-Gardens*' vertical farm systems, and *ownworld*'s *ownhome*, to name the most prominent technologies in this study, all depend on input that is partially beyond control of the provider and producer. Nevertheless, all these products and infrastructures catalyze and support sustainability-related practices, such as localized production, sustainable consumption, repair, and self-sufficiency. It is therefore a difficult calculation – ethically and materially – to trade off sustainability-related products against the conditions of their sourcing and production.

Technology-related practices, therefore, are an important dimension of a degrowth transition (see figure 12). *Smark*'s automated supermarket, for instance, makes regional and organic food available 24/7 in central places such as Stuttgart's main station, contributing to a *shift* in practices of food consumption. *Hobbyhimmel*'s productive infrastructure, furthermore, enables a range of practices around local fabrication, upcycling, maintenance, and repair that partially *shift* relations of production and *substitute* for consumption. Equally so the *ownhome* which, by closing electricity water and nutrient cycles, provides amenities few people in the Global North would voluntarily do without while significantly reducing the footprint of its occupants. These and other technologies occasion interstitial spaces that allow individuals and communities to withdraw from a number of exploitative and unsustainable practices. Technology, to that effect, interacts closely with other dimensions of practices' relatedness.

Figure 12 Transformation of practices' technological relatedness

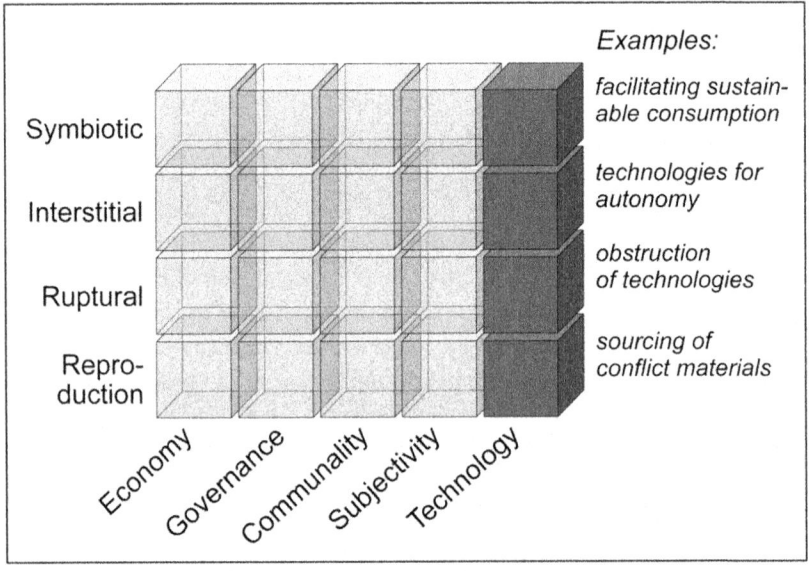

The community's practices also relate *rupturally* to incumbent alignments of technology. *Critical Mass*, say, deliberately obstructs car mobility and advances (well-tried) non-fossil and resource-sparing mobility technologies. Still, novel technologies and technologically mediated relations also reproduce incumbent alignments around consumption and convenience. The organizations have limited leverage over the use and application of their products and infrastructures and the practices linked thereto. Using *Hobbyhimmel*'s infrastructure to 3D-print resource-intensive gadgets or buying the products of *Slowtec* and *Relumity* as "positional goods" (Hirsch, 1995) and repurposing them counter the degrowth effects of these technologies. It is clear from this data that technology can support an orientation towards degrowth but only in connection with political, economic, and cultural moments. The same is true for all dimensions of practices' relatedness discussed in this chapter. Economy, governance, communality, subjectivity, and technology closely hang together, an issue the following section turns to.

A multifaceted transition

Processes of social change towards degrowth trajectories consist of a complex interplay of different logics and modes of transformation. The preceding sections square diverse forms of practices' relatedness with different strategies of intervention. Both perspectives, thereby, shed light on the possibilities and constraints of a degrowth transition. On the one hand, the diverse logics perspective brings various areas of change into view. Tracing transformative dynamics across economy, governance, communality, subjectivity, and technology shows that transition unfolds in multiple arenas of social co-existence that can both reinforce and jar with each other. The development of technologies, for instance, can support sustainability-related practices while reinforcing extractive value chains and competition for market shares. Shifting economic practices towards fair sourcing can counteract salvage accumulation while underlining individual responsibility and leaving wrongheaded regulatory frameworks in place.

On the other hand, a perspective on different modes of transformation shows how sustainability-related activities shift, substitute, confront, and reproduce incumbent alignments. It sheds light on the strategies and possible leverages of alternative practices. Drawing on different strategies allows enterprises and practitioners to address and navigate conflicting challenges and objectives. Combining symbiotic with interstitial forms of intervention, for instance, enables organizations to subsist while partially substituting for unsustainable practices.

Transition manifests simultaneously through various moments in practices' relatedness and through different strategic orientations, all of which degrowth scholarship must attend to. Joining perspectives on transformation's social and strategic dimensions renders visible the full complexity of transition and its tensions. It is only from such a comprehensive view that possible trajectories of change can be drawn.

It is clear that a degrowth transition must entail change across all dimensions of social co-existence and employ different modes of transformation. There is no singular leverage point for transition. Some approaches tend to overemphasize a single dimension that should be the focus of transformative practice. The postwork strand of postcapitalist thought, for instance, imagines technological process as a way out of capitalism (Chatterton and Pusey, 2019; see also chapter 2). Community economy scholarship, in contrast, places much emphasis on subjectivities and communality while neglecting issues of power and governance (see chapter 4). And Marxist thought traditionally revolves around governance and a narrow conception of economy without adequate consideration of subjectivity and communality. Furthermore, Marxism counts on ruptural transformation while neglecting the merits of symbiotic and interstitial strategies. In doing so, it overemphasizes antagonism, leaving little leeway for imagination and diversity (see chapter 2). This chapter's analysis suggests that, if to occur, a degrowth transition is likely to entail simultaneous shifts, substitutions, and oppositions[1] across diverse forms of practices' relatedness, which gradually realign towards postcapitalist ends.

The general insight that transition is multifaceted, however, is of limited use without closer examination of what this entails for research and activism on transformative geographies. Thus far, this chapter has discussed various ways in which changes in practices' relatedness lead to changes in socio-spatial relations more broadly. To unravel these connections, the subsequent chapters zoom in on the practices and organizations that are relevant for a degrowth transition. In doing so, chapters 17 and 18 further develop the notions of degrowth practices and degrowth organizations respectively (see chapter 7). Chapters 19 and 20, then, zoom out again, trailing concrete degrowth strategies.

---

1 Ruptural transformative strategies remain largely outside of the study's empirical focus. Against the background of chapter 16's analysis, social movements engaging in antagonistic and oppositional practice appear to be an important potential ally for Stuttgart's community economy. A point to which I return in chapters 19 and 20 and the conclusion.

Chapter 17: Degrowth practices

> In a degrowth society, everything will be different: different activities, different forms and uses of energy, different relations, different gender roles, different allocations of time between paid and non-paid work and different relations with the non-human world.
> D'Alisa et al., 2015, p. 4

Discussing degrowth practices in the context of a degrowth transition in practice, as sketched above, raises a crucial question: are degrowth practices those practices that are in line with degrowth's principles or those practices that work towards a degrowth transition? Depending on the definitional thrust, degrowth practices comprise quite different activities. Marketing, for instance, including the building of a memorable brand, the printing and distribution of promotional material, and the allowance of discounts, jars with degrowth's principles of sufficiency and self-determination. Yet it can create an important leverage for sustainability-oriented organizations within a marketized environment.

A host of other practices such as local production, ethical purchasing, cooperation in community-based initiatives, and volunteer engagement, on the other hand, are in line with degrowth principles but not necessarily bound up with a degrowth agenda. Although these activities stand for a shift in practice, they do not automatically address or challenge the growth-based economy. Lacking a more radical orientation, then, activities that were initially oriented towards social and environmental justice are frequently integrated and indeed seized and appropriated by incumbent institutions (Kenis and Lievens, 2015; see chapter 1). Aside from creating new sources of revenue, it is "really capital's only feasible path … to embrace the autonomous and cooperative potential of workers, recognizing that this is the key to valorization and increased productivity, and at the same time, try to contain it" (Hardt and Negri, 2017, p. 143).

Degrowth, consequently, needs to be wary of the pseudo-solutions of green capitalism. Green(ed) practices and progressive politics appear to address social and environmental issues while leaving the foundational institutions of capital in place. This poses a great challenge for critical scholarship to assess and evaluate the capacity and role of sustainability-related practices for transition. Žižek (2018), on that note, flips Marx's 11th thesis on Feuerbach, claiming that the point is to reinterpret the world self-critically instead of engaging in hasty action. Žižek does not advocate for a withdrawal from action but for the critical attention to "false activity" (ibid., p. 394). Taking this warning seriously from a practice theory perspective means to pay attention to practices' meanings. Or more precisely, as I will argue below, its politics. *Hobbyhimmel*, for instance, was indeed set up with the intention to provide an infrastructure for a degrowth transition. The practices of local production, repair, volunteering, upcycling, and others that constitute the workshop on an everyday basis, however, link to degrowth's broader agenda only to a limited extent.

Circling back to the question of activities' congruence with degrowth principles versus their orientation towards a transition, then, unveils a crucial moral and strategic decision. The difference between coherence and tactics translates into a focus on the end – a degrowth society – on the one hand and on the means of a transition thereto on the other hand. The (tendentially anarchist) notion of prefiguration demands congruence between the two while (often Marxist) visions of a revolution suggests that the end justifies the means. The discrepancy between means and ends has been subject to much debate and, simply speaking, constitutes a major divide between anarchism and Marxism (Harvey, 2015; Springer, 2017; see chapter 2). For the present purposes, the juxtaposition of means and ends sheds light on the spectrum of strategies available to degrowth which, in turn, inform the notion of degrowth practices. Chapter 16, above, advances a perspective beyond this chasm and proposes a more pragmatic stance combining different strategies of transformation (Wright, 2010). A non-dogmatic pragmatism premises both: goal-orientation (ends) and reflection about the possibilities to get there (means). Instead of putting means and ends into a specific relation a priori, the adequacy of this relation itself needs to be part of a degrowth politics.

Degrowth politics comprise moments of reflexivity and relatedness (see chapter 7). Reflexivity, thereby, refers to practices' reflective relation to the plenum of practices. Degrowth practices, consequently, involve motivations, intentions, and knowledge that align with degrowth principles. Relatedness, furthermore, refers to the interaction of practices with other practices. That means, degrowth practices, in some form, bear on the way other practices interrelate and align. Defining degrowth practices through a notion of politics, rather than on the base of everyday verb forms like repairing, sharing, or volunteering, helps to avoid aforementioned limitations. A degrowth politics, then, captures those activities that work towards a degrowth transition – both with respect to their orientation (is there an underlying critique of a growth-based economy and a motivation to change it?) and with respect to their effect (do practices support a degrowth transition even if they are not directly aligned with degrowth principles?).

Degrowth practices, in this sense, are *conventionalized patterns of activity that reflectively relate to practices' broader alignments in ways that found the assumption that these activities have an effect in line with degrowth's principles*. To determine practices' relatedness, I have developed the notion of logics which is based on the idea that practices are bound together through different patterns such as economy, governance, communality, subjectivity, and technology (see chapters 7 and 11). The previous chapter outlines the basis of empirical data on how a degrowth transition along these lines might unfold. Following up, this chapter zooms in on individual practices and traces their role for a degrowth transition. It discusses two practices that feature prominently in the degrowth debate – repair and sharing – reflecting on their consideration as degrowth practices.

Repair

Repair is a key practice in the context of a degrowth transition (Bertling and Leggewie, 2016), while aligning, at times, with incumbent institutions. Service, maintenance, and repair are established sectors, for instance in the car industry. Repair itself is as old as the human use of tools – when something breaks, people either repair it, build it anew, or do without it. Maintenance, moreover, is repair's prospective counterpart. In a growth-based economy, however, repair and maintenance might get in the way of capital accumulation (Packard, 2011). If products last too long, consumption decreases. Planned obsolescence, labor division, and the complexification of production, in turn, are tendencies that shorten product cycles and reduce the repairability of products (Bertling and Leggewie, 2016; Packard, 2011). Simultaneously, the decision whether to repair something is increasingly guided by economic viability, ousting other reasons such as resource conservation. Instead of being the rule, repair has become the exception as, for instance, in cases of high sentimental value of a broken object.

Some organizations in Stuttgart's community economy, including *Hobbyhimmel* and the *Repair Cafés*, push the importance of repair in a world in which replacement has become the norm. In lieu of economic viability, they emphasize the relevance of repair for empowerment, pleasure, and sustainability. From a practice theory perspective, these alternative meanings are crucial to trace repair as degrowth practice. The open workshop in general and the *Repair Cafés* in particular, then, are sites that integrate repair's elements – materials, meanings, and competent bodies – to facilitate the enactment of repair. Besides advancing meanings and motivations that emphasize repair's role for social change, the organizations provide access to the materials repair practices require – from simple hand tools to special tools for proprietary fasteners and even 3D printers to manufacture spares. Furthermore, repair requires capable bodies that can perform repair practices. Since many subjects do not possess the respective competences, the *Repair Cafés* coordinate the physical co-presence of skillful subjects.

Still, this does not make all repair-related activities in the context of these organizations degrowth practices. Activities driven by cost saving, for instance, do not necessarily align with degrowth principles. This, of course, does not render these activities altogether unimportant for a degrowth transition. Focusing solely on meanings would mean to neglect repair's tendentially favorable environmental record irrespective of the intentions behind it. Key, here, is that a number of repair activities indeed *do* reflect on the role of repair for degrowth economies (or comparable ideas). But how is it possible to separate between political and non-political repair practices? Does it make sense to do so? And do any of the repair practices have an effect beyond place? Naturally, there is no black and white. This is where the diverse logics perspective can help to trace tendencies, which, in turn, shed light on the role of repair for a degrowth transition.

The five social dimensions of repair as advanced by the diverse logics perspective carve out repair's different intentions, effects, and politics (figure 13). Technologically, repair challenges the construction of difficult-to-repair products. Along with a turn to repair, repair-friendly products like *Relumity #LED1* engender a shift in practices of production, design, construction, and sale that align technologically through reparability and longevity. In terms of practices' economic relatedness, repair can reduce consumption, primarily if accompanied by the motivation to save resources. Repair, in this sense, prefigures subsistence and sufficiency-oriented degrowth economies. In cases where repair does not replace new purchases, this effect, of course, is absent.

Governance, then, sheds light on the power relations and policy effects of these emergent forms of repair-related organizing. Activism linked to the phenomena of repair cafés and open workshops increasingly challenges the lack of considerations of repair and reparability in policy and regulation. Regarding community, the *Repair Cafés* foster spaces of encounter, which also has political consequences. In communication with others, repair becomes an object of reflection; subjects exchange repair-related knowledge; and, on occasion, previously non-political repair activities are politicized. Intellectually and physically, repair changes subjectivities, including awareness and valuation of objects and the acquisition of repair-related competences. Subjects who are able to and value repair (and maintenance) over replacement, in turn, are crucial protagonists in all of the above.

Repair activities, consequently, move between different degrees of reflexivity (conscious relation back to the plenum of practices) and relatedness (however small direction of the plenum of practices or parts thereof), whereas both aspects do not necessarily need to correlate. Depending on the meanings that accompany repair

Figure 13 Social dimensions of degrowth-related repair

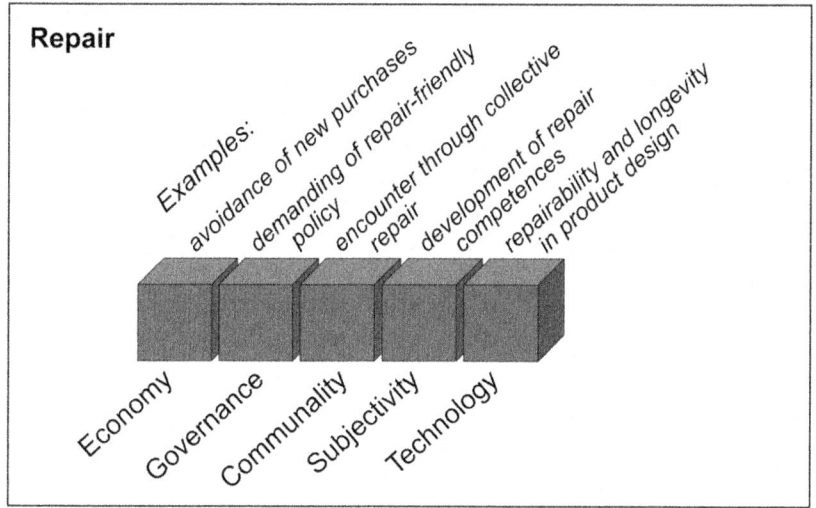

activities and the ways in which these activities relate to other practices, repair, indeed, constitutes a degrowth practice. This, however, cannot be an either/or distinction but rather an orientation for examining the role of repair activities for a degrowth transition. At the end, as with all activities, each individual enactment of repair is idiosyncratic. But through *Hobbyhimmel*, the *Repair Cafés*, and many other sites of repair, patterns of activity are conventionalized that challenge the culture of replacement and prefigure other forms of practice. They do not always carry the radical meaning of degrowth, but, in particular when they do, they are important stepping-stones towards a degrowth society.

Sharing

Practices of sharing feature prominently in different strands of the debate on alternative economies. The sharing economy, in particular, is a buzzword that appears far beyond the confines of alternative discourses. As a consequence, a wide spectrum of activities are lumped together under said label, ranging from decentralized and deregulated forms of neoliberal value production to non-monetary schemes of local production and consumption (Cohen and Muñoz, 2016; Martin, 2016b; Richardson, 2015). The breadth of practices considered as 'sharing' necessitate a critical discussion of definitional issues (Frenken and Schor, 2017). This, however, is not the place to drill holes in the sharing economies argument. What I am interested in, rather, is the relevance of sharing practices for a degrowth transition.

Sharing, here, refers to *individuals and organizations collectively using resources according to particular rules that equally apply to all participants*. Sharing, in this sense, is close to the notion of commoning (Kallis, 2018, p. 119), but might involve formally private ownership and monetary exchange as long as the surplus value is returned to the community or spent on community-related expenditures. For-profit sharing schemes, in turn, such as many car-sharing or workspace-sharing projects, constitute forms of renting rather than sharing against the background of this definition.

Sharing activities are a pillar of a number of organizations in the empirical sample of this study. *Hobbyhimmel*, for instance, constitutes a form of sharing of tools and machinery. Although the use of the workshop is monetized, all revenues flow back to cover for the workshop's maintenance and operating costs, which are, in addition, cross-subsidized through the yield from commercial users and donations. *Lastenrad* and *Foodsharing* constitute non-monetary sharing schemes and might be described as food and mobility commons respectively. Moreover, knowledge and skills, rather than artefacts or things, are shared. One such example is *iFixit*'s online repository of repair manuals, another the skill-sharing in repair-related events such as the *Repair Cafés* (see above).

Like repair, sharing in itself does not constitute a degrowth practice as defined above. Many acts of sharing in the organizations mentioned do not necessarily align with degrowth principles. Jointly using a highly energy-intensive infrastructure such as a 3D printer, for instance, does not automatically mean that all related activities are degrowth-oriented. And of those that are – say, the printing of spare parts for repair – only some activities reflexively relate to practices' broader alignments. Nevertheless, sharing, like repair, has material effects regardless of intention. In conjunction with a more reflective and critical orientation in organizations that politicize sharing, these activities, then, partially link to degrowth politics. *Hobbyhimmel*, for instance, explicitly relates the provisioning of a shared productive infrastructure to degrowth principles. To some extent, even individual enactments of sharing that do not include political motivations and intentions support the degrowth-related agenda of the organizations they participate in. Nevertheless, the organizations themselves are generally ambiguous in their relation towards degrowth principles – an aspect that I discuss below in the context of degrowth organizations.

The diverse logics perspective, again, supports an assessment of different manifestations of sharing and their relation with other activities (figure 14). Technologically, sharing furthers the potential of internet-based tools in optimizing the utilization of goods and services. Digital commons such as *Commons Booking*, a plugin that *Lastenrad* uses, or *iFixit*'s collection of repair manuals, constitute important resources for other sustainability-related practices such as repair and fossil-free transportation (see above).

Economically, sharing intensifies the use of individual commodities and/or creates opportunities for non-commodified access. Sharing, in this sense, prefigures economies based on access and common ownership rather than private ownership. Policy, thereby, is often in the way of sharing, such as the lack of supportive legal forms and regulatory frameworks that fit the needs of non-monetized or partially monetized sharing schemes. Although the increasing participation in sharing economies puts pressure on policy to respond, governing institutions are slow in adapting to and encouraging sharing practices. Government-supported projects such as *teilbar* constitute only small institutional steps. Still, sharing economies more broadly loosen norms around private ownership.

With regard to community, the sharing practices observed in this study generally involve a great amount of trust and dedication, contributing to the cultivation of convivial forms of togetherness. Sharing of tools in the workshop, for instance, does not involve deposit or specific checks but is largely based on trust. Based on the volunteer work of individuals who build and maintain these organizational forms, sharing is a central part in the creation of solidary communities. Being involved in sharing food, tools, skills, knowledge, and other things, furthermore, affects subjectivities. An important leverage for degrowth transition, therefore, is individuals' experience with access- instead of ownership-based economies. Sharing, therefore, unties the strong emotions (fear, security, entitlement) that are linked to private property, encouraging individuals to experiment with different property situations.

Zooming in on degrowth practices shows that it is anything but straightforward to define activities which are effective in terms of a degrowth transition. The analysis above highlights two challenges in identifying *conventionalized patterns of activity that reflectively relate to practices' broader alignments in ways that found the assumption that these activities have an effect in line with degrowth's principles*. First, in terms of reflexivity (conscious relation back to the plenum of practices) there are various depths of practices' deliberations and intentions to address institutionalized exploitative and unjust relations. Intentions, furthermore, do not have any direct link to practices' material effects. Second, in terms of relatedness (however small direction of the plenum of practices or parts thereof), the difficulties of assessing the effects of contextually embedded activities on broader relations of power prevail. Across-the-board statements that single out, say, practices of repair, sharing, or cycling, therefore, fall short. The notion of degrowth practices is bound to be a contextual one.

The analytical perspective built throughout this book provides a valuable tool to approximate degrowth practices and assess their diverse effects on practices' broader alignments. Aside from repair and sharing, a host of other practices could

Figure 14 Social dimensions of degrowth-related sharing

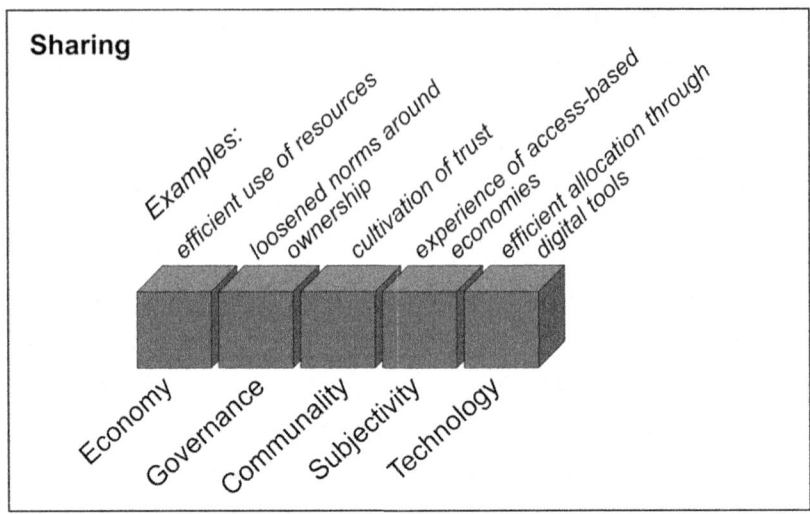

be explored piece-by-piece, including (local) fabrication, product development, participation, enjoyment, caring, helping, giving, volunteering, and (non-hierarchical) management. For reasons of scope, however, this book limits itself to the exemplary discussion of repair and sharing above. Instead, it zooms out from the perspective on individual practices and explores the role of complexes of practices – as organizations – for a degrowth transition. A perspective on organizations has a crucial advantage over that on individual practices. It contextualizes activities, providing a broader and more coherent picture of links and trade-offs between practices which for themselves are difficult to evaluate with respect to their role in a degrowth transition. Chapter 18, to that effect, goes on to develop a notion of degrowth organizations.

Chapter 18: Degrowth organizations

> It is my contention that the starting point
> for a more equal and sustainable economy
> should be small business.
> *Parker, 2017, p. 420*

Organizations are "constantly in the process of becoming" and thus constitute "dynamic, multiple, performative and open-ended" (Pallett and Chilvers, 2015, p. 151) complexes of practices, or, in other words, practice formations embedded in broader nexuses of practices. Analogous to the question of degrowth practices, degrowth organizations are not a matter of black-and-white painting. Although similar difficulties apply for the definition of degrowth organizations as for that of degrowth practices, there is a crucial advantage of the former notion over the latter. Looking at practice formations, the focus is not so much on specific patterns of activity – such as sharing or repair – but on a number of interrelated practices. That means, in contrast to the notion of degrowth practices, (degrowth) organizations already contextualize possibly degrowth-oriented activities.

For instance, *Slowtec*'s decision to accept a commission from a company in the automobile sector in order to cross- subsidize other activities appears far removed from degrowth's principles. Considering the fact, however, that *Slowtec*'s choice is to compromise or perish puts another complexion on things. Decisions like this enable *Slowtec* to operate as an enterprise that furthers sufficiency and subsistence-oriented technologies. Compromising constitutes a key leverage to enable transformative practices, arguably more so than a consistent adherence to degrowth principles (see above). Compromising itself, then, might be considered a degrowth practice. *Slowtec* relates reflectively to practices' broader alignments in deliberately weighting advantages against negative consequences and align their activities accordingly. In doing so, *Slowtec* is able to engage in activities, say the work on the *Karte von Morgen* mapping tool, for strongly reduced rates, which, again, have an effect in line with degrowth's principles

A few points, however, need further exploration. In the case of *Slowtec*, motivation and intend are well reflected and communicated. At the time of research, all members of *Slowtec* identify with a degrowth agenda and align organizational practices accordingly. In a small organization with little assets, like *Slowtec*, the link between revenues and potential output is straightforward. Despite limited resources, *Slowtec* engages in projects like *ownhome* or *Karte von Morgen* that are fully congruent with degrowth principles. But how can a perspective on degrowth organizations account for more divergent motivations and meanings? How can it trace the dispersed and ambiguous effects of organizational practices? And how can it distinguish compromise from cooptation? The remainder of this chapter approaches these questions by developing a typology of organizational 'ideal types'.

Wright's (2010) typology of symbiotic, ruptural, and interstitial transformations provides an orientation to differentiate between different types of organizations (see interlude II). Symbiotic transformations are processes that address social issues and enhance possibilities for emancipation without challenging capitalist relations as such. Ruptural transformations are based around "a sharp break with existing institutions and social structures" (ibid., p. 303), confronting capitalist institutions head-on. And interstitial transformations involve strategies that build alternative forms of social organization in the "niches and margins of capitalist society" (ibid., p. 303).

The organizations in this study differently draw on and combine these strategies. A closer look at the different orientations of the organizations in this study identifies three ideal types, which I refer to as symbiotic, interstitial, and pragmatic. Symbiotic organizations, as the name says, follow largely symbiotic strategies and show a high degree of integration in and collaboration with incumbent institutional frameworks. Interstitial organizations, in contrast, attempt to implement alternative social and technological relations more consistently and tend to be wary of compromise. Ruptural strategies, Wright's third mode of transformation, lacks an organizational pendant in this study. Since most organizations are goal-oriented, few of their strategies and practices are directly oppositional (see chapter 16). This work only briefly touches on the collaboration of eco-social organizations and social movements, which is beyond its scope but constitutes promising terrain for further research (see conclusion). Instead, I distinguish organizations that follow the pragmatic combination of symbiotic and interstitial strategies as third ideal type – pragmatic organizations.

Symbiotic organizations

Symbiotic organizations' practices align for the most part with dominant state and market institutions and they have a high readiness to collaborate with policy-makers and for-profit businesses. Organizations of this type that are legally speaking for-profit enterprises, generally, have a clearly defined business model that is particularly geared towards a specific social or environmental issue and/or particular goods and services. Associations that can be characterized as symbiotic, typically have a specific focus on a well-defined and rather particular social and environmental problem. Financially, some symbiotic organizations face common challenges of start-ups, small enterprises, and associations while others find quite lucrative market niches in the green or social economy (see chapter 3). Due to their alignment with incumbent institutions and their often particularistic focus, symbiotic organizations, in general, are susceptible to integration and cooptation.

Not all enterprises and associations that address a social or environmental issue, however, are symbiotic. Symbiotic organizations follow a symbiotic strategy, which, drawing on Hardt and Negri's aforementioned notion of strategy, implies that they 'see far into the social field' (see interlude II). In addition to tactics, that is the reaction to the immediacy of a spatial and temporal context, strategic organizations orient their activities towards long-term plans. Symbiotic organizations, then, address social issues *and* enhance possibilities for emancipation, but doing so without confronting or seriously challenging capitalist relations as such. Rather, symbiotic organizations revolve around "strategies in which extending and deepening the institutional forms of popular social empowerment simultaneously helps solve certain practical problems faced by dominant classes and elites" (Wright, 2010, p. 305).

From the study's empirical sample, *em-faktor* best exemplifies a symbiotic organization (see figure 15). Its services in branding, fundraising, campaigning, and corporate-social-responsibility largely align with a (competitive) market economy. *em-faktor*'s practices are primarily geared towards the marketing of sustainability-related activities. While *em-faktor* works for a broad range of foundations and charitable organizations, its portfolio also includes businesses (or foundations related to businesses) for whom social and environmental justice do not constitute a focus of priority. Pertaining to the former, improved marketing can be an important factor in gaining a higher visibility and spread. Pertaining to the latter and to the many shades in between, *em-faktor* contributes to greenwashing. Furthermore, a strong emphasis on market-based tools for change neglects the limitations of branding, fundraising, campaigning, and corporate-social-responsibility in the context of a degrowth transition.

Still, *em-faktor*'s objectives and practices are not shortsighted. Orienting on the principles of the *Economy for the Common Good* and addressing profound issues around the notion of financial profit as economic goal, measurement, and legal base, *em-faktor*, indeed, both integrates and supports degrowth-oriented practices. In contrast to those of interstitial and pragmatic organizations, however, they are more difficult to spot through layers of more conventional activities.

Symbiotic organizations like *em-faktor*, consequently, are very difficult to place and evaluate with respect to a degrowth transition. From a moderate perspective, symbiotic organizations are important for a degrowth transition for at least two

Figure 15 Social and strategic dimensions of em-faktor's practices

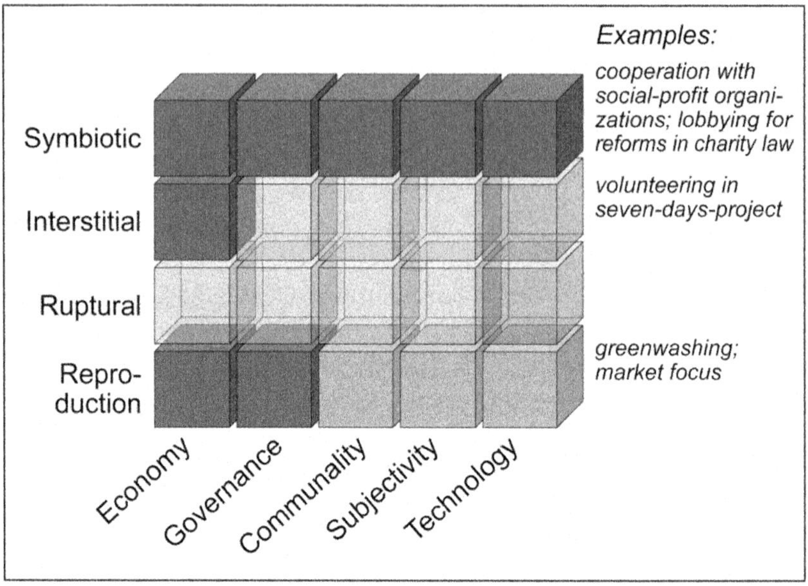

Symbiotic — Examples: cooperation with social-profit organizations; lobbying for reforms in charity law

Interstitial — volunteering in seven-days-project

Ruptural

Reproduction — greenwashing; market focus

Axes: Economy, Governance, Communality, Subjectivity, Technology

reasons. First, symbiotic organizations bridge the gap between mainstream and alternative economic practices and can mediate between the two. That means, they provide low threshold points of entry or contact to businesses and policy-makers outside of alternative spaces. Second, by being connectors, symbiotic organizations are more likely to receive funding (as associations) or generate revenue (as enterprises), thus acquiring resources to further other sustainability- and possibly degrowth-related activities. A radical perspective, thereby, might criticize that symbiotic organizations leave the overall fabric of practices' alignments intact. Due to their proximity to and compromising with dominant institutions, symbiotic organizations may even help capitalism to overcome its own contradictions and thus ensure its survival.

Interstitial organizations

Interstitial organizations, in contrast to symbiotic organizations, largely withdraw from state and market spaces and follow a prefigurative strategy. They attempt to build alternatives outside of dominant alignments of practice. In doing so, these organizations seek to prefigure solidary, non-exploitative, and non-hierarchical institutions. Interstitial organizations, therefore, are wary of compromise and cooperation with incumbent institutions and instead practice alternatives as coherently as possible. Organizations of this type are mostly constituted as non-profit or are (voluntarily or involuntarily) loose groupings without legal form. Most have to work with strongly limited resources due to their withdrawal from monetized and marketized practices.

Analogous to symbiotic organizations, not all organizations that disengage from state and market institutions and create interstices do so strategically and in line with degrowth principles. Interstitial organizations, in the way the notion is used here, engage in prefigurative politics – the experimental anticipation of sustainable and just social relations in the here and now.

ownworld, for instance, follows a largely interstitial strategy (see figure 16). The *ownhome* is a tool to (partially) withdraw from market practices and lead a more sustainable lifestyle. A combination of efficiency and autonomy enables the inhabitant to significantly reduce his resource consumption. However, there is little focus on dissemination and growth of the project due to the rejection of an expansive logic. Prefiguring an economy of unconditional giving and mutual solidarity, rather than equivalence-based exchange, the project does not develop a business model and thus lacks the financial resources that would allow for greater flexibility – for instance pertaining to the legal issues *ownworld* faces (see chapter 13). The consequential adherence to (degrowth) principles, here, has a two-edged effect on transformative geographies. On the one hand, the *ownhome* attracts many visitors and thus spreads the idea and knowledge about self-sufficient housing. On the other hand, for lack of a business case and due to numerous legal issues, it is very challenging for those interested to actually acquire their own *ownhome*.

Interstitial organizations can be a flagship for degrowth economies by adhering consistently to degrowth principles, for instance by rejecting the participation in competitive markets and the expansive logic of 'upscaling' and 'impact'. For the very same reasons, interstitial organizations generally lack resources and aspiration to spread and disseminate their technologies and social innovations. This has quite ambiguous effects for the role of interstitial organizations in transformative processes across different logics. The consequential enactment of degrowth principles can be quite compelling for subjects to experience alternative forms of (economic) being-in-common. In line with Gibson-Graham's focus on resubjectivation (see chapter 4), interstitial organizations make a strong case that things can be done differently, challenging individuals and communities to rethink personal and political relations. On the other hand, however, a limited concern and capacity for pushing change across other social dimensions more decisively – for instance setting up a business-case to make resource-low housing available to a broad audience – weakens the transformative potential of interstitial organizations.

Figure 16 Social and strategic dimensions of ownworld's practices

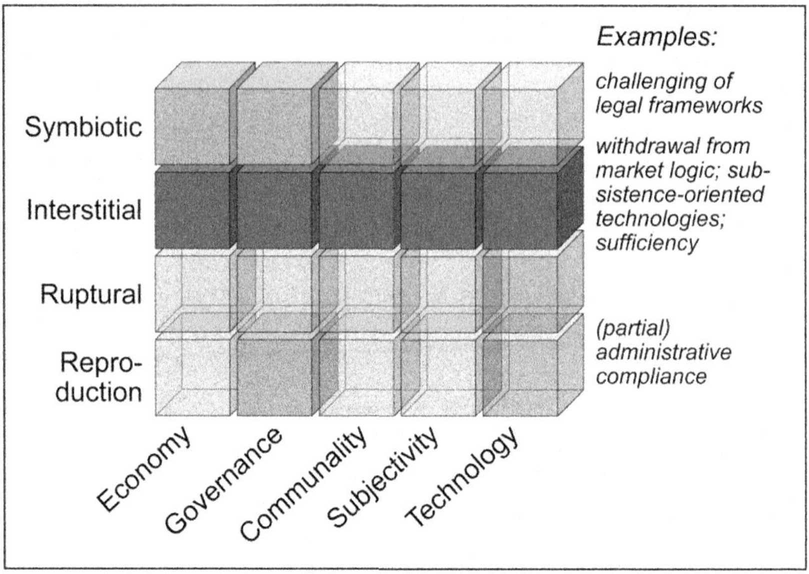

```
                                    Examples:
                                    challenging of
   Symbiotic                        legal frameworks
                                    withdrawal from
                                    market logic; sub-
   Interstitial                     sistence-oriented
                                    technologies;
                                    sufficiency
   Ruptural
                                    (partial)
   Repro-                           administrative
   duction                          compliance

   Economy  Governance  Communality  Subjectivity  Technology
```

This is not to say that the transformative potential of interstitial organizations is limited to a shift in subjectivities. For instance, as of the end of 2018, collaborators and sympathizers of the *ownhome* founded an association that supports and links individuals who seek to practice a just lifestyle. The *SoBaWi* [community-supported construction][1] is designed to enable participants to acquire their own *ownhome* while avoiding cooptation and integration into capitalist circuits of value. The association, however, was founded only after this study's empirics and might well face similar restraints that have been observed with respect to other interstitial organizations. With this in mind, pragmatic organizations offer another perspective.

Pragmatic organizations

Pragmatic organizations participate in market practices and cooperate with state institutions but do so very selectively. In contrast to symbiotic organizations, this

---

1   SoBaWi is short for German 'Solidarische Bauwirtschaft' which can be translated as community-supported construction. The abbreviation stands in reference to SoLaWi, the German abbreviation for community-supported agriculture.

cooperation is quite cautious of integration and cooptation. And, in contrast to interstitial organizations, pragmatic organizations are less consequential in prefiguring degrowth economies – although this remains an important characteristic. The focus shifts from prefiguration – where the means align with the ends – towards compromising – where means are reflectively employed to pursue a transformative strategy. Pragmatic organizations acknowledge the ways in which their stability, reach, and scope hinge on their ability to relate pragmatically to material constraints and, at least partially, align with dominant economic and bureaucratic institutions.

Even more so than symbiotic organizations, pragmatic organizations differ from enterprises and associations that solely address social or environmental issues without following an emancipatory agenda. In reflectively combining and balancing interstitial and symbiotic strategies, pragmatic organizations are thoroughly oriented towards transformation. In contrast to symbiotic organizations, which include but do not revolve around a transformative strategy, pragmatic organizations build transformative objectives deep into their organizational set-up.

Slowtec exemplifies a pragmatic organization that develops a business model and positions itself in the market while remaining cautious not to imperil the organization's ends. *Slowtec* cooperates with a range of businesses, some of which correspond better to their values than others. In doing so, its members reflect on the up- and downsides, making deliberate compromises. As a consequence, *Slowtec* is independent of external funding and although it draws on subsidies, it does not hinge on their support. Free of investors and public institutions, *Slowtec* operates as an independent organization. As much as possible, *Slowtec* tries to prefigure alternative forms of design, production, exchange, and management. Yet, always cautious not to imperil the organization's existence, in particular its financial basis, over idealism.

Pragmatic organizations like *Slowtec* navigate a thin line between symbiotic and prefigurative strategies (see figure 17). Like symbiotic organizations, they are prone to integration and cooptation, for instance when making too many compromises. Like interstitial organizations, they face resource limitations if not making compromises which allow them to leverage more radical activities. Nevertheless, following a fairly undogmatic, flexible, and yet critical strategy sets up pragmatic organizations to prepare the ground for more fundamental changes. In combining different strategic logics of transformation, pragmatic organizations are likely to play a pivotal role for a degrowth transition. Wright (2010) himself sees the interplay of different strategies, in particular interstitial and symbiotic, as the best prospect for a transformation (see interlude II). Elsewhere he elaborates that:

> Through interstitial strategies, activists and communities can build and strengthen real utopian economic institutions embodying democratic-egali-

Figure 17 Social and strategic dimensions of Slowtec's practices

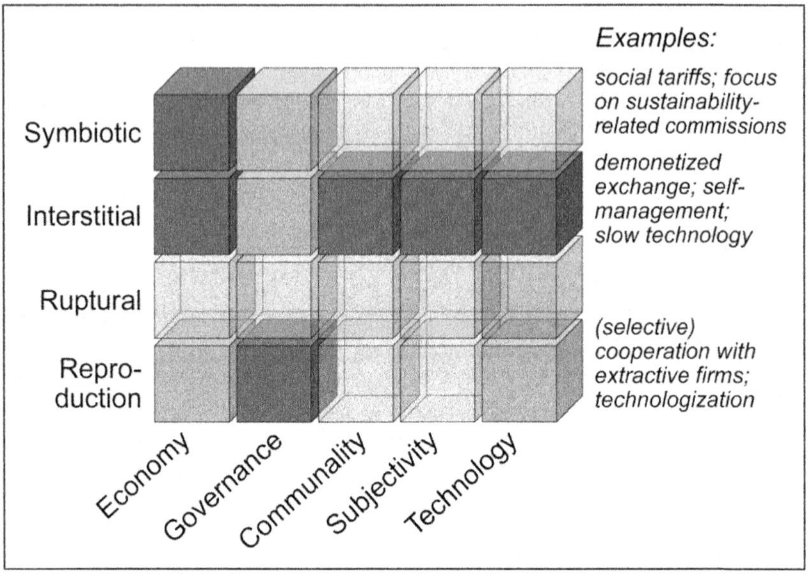

	Examples:
Symbiotic	social tariffs; focus on sustainability-related commissions
Interstitial	demonetized exchange; self-management; slow technology
Ruptural	
Reproduction	(selective) cooperation with extractive firms; technologization

Axes: Economy, Governance, Communality, Subjectivity, Technology

tarian principles where this is possible. Symbiotic strategies through the state can help open up greater space and support for these interstitial innovations. The interplay between interstitial and symbiotic strategies could then create a trajectory of deepening social elements within the hybrid capitalist economic ecosystem (Hahnel and Wright, 2016, p. 103).

Pragmatic organizations, in this sense, are hybrid configurations that integrate symbiotic and interstitial strategies. For themselves, of course, they have limited effect with respect to a degrowth transition. However, they constitute important anchor points for other organizations to connect to and join in. The strategic hybridity of pragmatic organizations that enables them to sustain within the current institutional landscape while orienting towards a radical emancipatory transformation opens an avenue towards a more comprehensive (supraorganizational) strategy. The next chapter, now, zooms back out and links the discussion of degrowth practices and organizations to a broader strategy around transformative infrastructures.

Chapter 19: Degrowth strategies

> To equate movements with strategy means that the movements already have (or can develop) adequate knowledge of the social reality and can plot their own long-term political direction.
> *Hardt and Negri, 2017, p. 18ff.*

Alternative economies, as both the discussion in part I and the empirical findings show, consist of a broad variety of activities and relations. There is no sharp dividing line to the growth-based capitalist economy that degrowth-oriented organizations oppose, substitute, and cooperate with. Community economy scholarship, in particular, eschews depoliticizing tendencies of a ready-made alternative blueprint (see chapters 3 and 4). Instead it emphasizes the diversity of economic practices that differently align and stabilize, forming institutional nexuses around solidarity, sustainability, and justice, as well as such around growth, expansion, and capital. Practices, as conventionalized patterns of activity, overlap, interfere, oppose, modify, and reproduce each other, constituting a complex mesh of hybrids between capitalist relations and alternative forms of economizing.

Above, I discuss the difficulties of singling out specific practices or organizations from this composite playing field as degrowth practices and degrowth organizations while affirming the effort of analytically sharpening both notions. On a similar note, transition necessitates a close reading of opposing and compliant tendencies to avoid simplified analyses and the jumping to conclusions. Transition processes are set within the concrete spaces of social co-existence and unfold with and from the everyday practices of social reproduction. Transitional dynamics, therefore, are always the result of socio-spatial struggles and negotiations and emerge through a complex dynamic of resistance and cooptation, politics and submission, endeavor and coercion, and conditioned and conditioning moments. As a consequence, transition does not move in straightforward, defined, or predictable ways but through destabilizing and restabilizing movements and counter-movements.

Hybridity, contingency, diversity, and processuality, however, should not veil possibilities, risks and responsibilities and preclude the development of forceful strategies for a degrowth transition. This book demonstrates at length the insufficiency of simply acknowledging diversity and complexity (R. Lee, 2016; Jonas, 2016; see in particular chapters 2, 4 and 7). Detailed analyses of the outsides and insides of organizations, institutions, and actors need to run with the complexities of transformative geographies, rather than surrender to them. Hardt and Negri (2017, p. 20), along these lines, call for "strategic movements" that have or develop knowledge of the social reality, long-term visions of co-existence, and capacities to engage in material politics. In this sense, the present chapter brings the discussion of the possibilities of a degrowth transition (chapter 16) and the zooming in on degrowth practices (chapter 17) and organizations (chapter 18) full circle by zooming back out in order to develop a degrowth strategy. It proposes the creation of 'transformative infrastructures' through a 'politics of hybridity' as key components of such a strategy. The subsequent thoughts bring together the various conceptual and empirical insights of this book into a coherent proposal of how a degrowth transition in practice might unfold.

Transformative Infrastructures

Degrowth-oriented practices and organization, as the study shows, jar with incumbent institutions on multiple fronts, making the shift of societal trajectories away from current patters of profound unsustainability a major challenge. In response, the development and conventionalization of alternative practice alignments opens an avenue for transformation. Numerous authors emphasize the importance of hubs around which transformative practice can build and from which it can eventually erupt to affect broader change. Longhurst (2015, p. 192f.), for instance, describes "alternative milieus" as spaces providing "ontological security" – practical resources, norms, and moral support for experimentation that encourage individuals to escape dominant routines and cognitive frames. Scholars working on (strategic) niche formation and management as well as 'upscaling', although often with a considerably narrower focus than degrowth, identify various factors that allow grassroots initiatives and innovations to form and disseminate (Seyfang and Haxeltine, 2012; Loorbach et al., 2017). And Hardt and Negri (2017, p. 36), in a more abstract sense, imagine the building of "constituent potential" – accumulated capacity for resistance and action – that can release in form of collective struggle.

Common to these approaches is their emphasis on a form of capacity or 'materialized possibility', that is configurations or practice-alignments which provide (more) conducive conditions for alternative (read: socially just and ecologically sustainable) activities to develop and stabilize. A degrowth transition, following this imaginary, is the process of accumulating capacity to eventually abandon growth-based socio-economic trajectories in favor of a degrowth society. Regardless of whether the crossover itself is imagined as an abrupt shift or a smooth transition, and whether it occurs in time to avoid (further) social and ecological breakdown, transformative strategies that spring from this perspective revolve around building arrangements that catalyze practices in line with degrowth principles. Following this focus on the materialization of configurations that underlie transformative practices, it is helpful to draw on the concept of infrastructure.

Infrastructure, according to Boyer (2018, p. 226), can be understood as an "'energopolitical' process [that] allows something to happen". That is, infrastructures store energy or potential which is then released to enable or conduce particular processes. With respect to transition, this means looking at (and advancing) the ways degrowth practices and organizations build configurations and arrangements which increase the potential for further (and possibly more deeply aligned) degrowth-oriented activities. Against the background of an infrastructural degrowth strategy, transformative work is to enter in and materialize as transformative infrastructures. But how does the static connotation of infrastructure fit in with a practice-theoretical perspective on transformation?

Larkin (2013, p. 329) defines infrastructures as "matter that enable the movement of other matter". Reading this definition with three different emphases advances of a notion of infrastructure that prepares the ground for the further development of a strategy around it. First, infrastructures are *matter* that enable the movement of other matter. Taking matter in a broad sense, the first emphasis highlights infrastructures as materializations of social dynamics. Social performances stabilize over time and space through inscription into bodies, artefacts, and things, institutionalizing patterns and relations (see chapter 5). Second, infrastructures are matter that *enable* the movement of other matter. The second emphasis focuses on the conditioning side of infrastructures. Practices stabilize in material configurations that catalyze certain activities. Infrastructures, then, are the material grounding of possibility, enabling or conditioning specific practices. Third, infrastructures are matter that enable the *movement of other matter*. Activities that ensue from infrastructures' enablement do something. That means they have effects on the world. Infrastructures might catalyze activities that shift, rupture, and realign incumbent institutions or such that reproduce and stabilize the status quo.

The constituent 'infra', thereby, indicates that infrastructures themselves form the (material) background of practices. For Shove (2017, p. 158) things have an "infrastructural relation" to a practice when they are necessary but not interacted with directly. Shove names a range of examples including power grids, harbors, pylons, kitchens, homes, and oxygen supply. Her notion of infrastructural relation, however, can be extend to most artefacts, depending on how they are enrolled into practice (see chapter 8). Infrastructures, furthermore, are not limited to artefacts and things. Also, capable and knowledgeable bodies form supportive structures by providing skills, abilities, and expertise. *Transformative infrastructures*, thus, are *material and social nexuses that constitute the enabling backdrop of degrowth-oriented practices*.

Building transformative infrastructures (or reclaiming and appropriating existing ones), then, means setting up material (for instance *Hobbyhimmel*'s workspace) and habitual (say, the acquisition of repair competences) patterns that 'store' the energy of transformative work. Strategy, thereby, is relevant in a twofold sense. First, in mobilizing the resources and energies that are required to build transformative infrastructures. And second, in orienting infrastructures to enable particular processes and activities. Discussing symbiotic and interstitial approaches with respect to both aspects highlights the advantages of combining both strategies (see chapter 18).

Interstitial strategies attempt to build infrastructures that conduce practices which are closely aligned with degrowth principles. The focus, here, is not solely on enabling degrowth-oriented activities, but also on avoiding to facilitate such that are not in line with degrowth principles. A case in point is the reluctance of *ownworld* to build a business case around the *ownhome* and thus loosen control over how it is used – for instance as an additional commodity and means to generate revenue and not as infrastructure to withdraw from capitalist circuits of value while leading a resource-poor lifestyle. Flows of energy to and from incumbent alignments, then, are largely prevented. Interstitial strategies, as consequence, often fail to mobilize enough resources to 'scale up' and stabilize their endeavors, but they remain quite consequential in avoiding cooptation and integration.

Symbiotic strategies, on the other hand, try to find synergies between transformative activities and those in line with incumbent institutions. By doing so, they can mobilize energy and resources, which would not have been accessible to them otherwise, in order to build (potentially transformative) infrastructures. *emfaktor*'s organizational set-up, for instance, gives leverage to (partially) degrowth-oriented practices and practice formations, but only by remaining closely bound up with formal commissions and market-oriented practices. A drawback, then, is that symbiotic infrastructures generally remain too closely linked to business-as-usual to dissociate from the institution of capital (see above).

As with respect to pragmatic organizations, their combination of interstitial and symbiotic strategies opens a possible avenue for an infrastructural degrowth strategy. Setting up infrastructures that are aligned with interstitial objectives – which means they are congruent with degrowth principles – yet allow for 'energy flows' to and from incumbent alignments, could be a way to build and store increasing transformative potential. This would be premised, of course, on the influx, for instance monetary resources to build and maintain a transformative infrastructure, being greater than the outflux, say the use of the infrastructure for endeavors that go against the grain of degrowth. The interplay of different strategies and the deliberations and trade-offs involved therein, however, need further examination in the following.

Politics of hybridity

The empirical material of this work identifies a number of organizations that integrate different strategies and catalyze further degrowth-oriented practices. Aside from *Slowtec*, which exemplifies well the compromising and trading off between symbiotic and interstitial strategies (see chapter 18), the open workshop *Hobbyhimmel* stands out as site that supports a number of degrowth-oriented practices and organizations. Examples include repair and maintenance, for instance of cargo bikes; local fabrication of products like *Relumity #LED1*; diverse sharing practices; and the exchange of sustainability-related information and skills (see chapter 14). In this vein, the workshop constitutes an infrastructure for degrowth practices. To be able to do so, the workshop cross-subsidizes low-threshold access to workspaces for private users and sustainability-related projects through revenues from commercial services.

Hobbyhimmel's infrastructure, however, also enables a multitude of less desirable practices around individualized consumption and resource intensive leisure activities. Only part of the practices in the workshop actually further a degrowth agenda (see chapter 17). Moreover, the workshop has limited control over the value chains that enter its material set up of tools, machinery, resources, parts, and construction materials. In combination with the financial restraints that condition the workshop's procurement, its material infrastructure is deeply rooted in possibly exploitative and extractive practices. From a degrowth perspective, the infrastructure of the workshop is a hybrid between degrowth practices and practices that align with capitalist institutions.

Hybridity is nothing out of the ordinary. A diverse economies perspective on social enterprises shows that most organizations are driven by a wide range of motivations and engage in a number of more-than-capitalist practices (North, 2016; Huybrechts and Nicholls, 2012). Moreover, the very notion of social entrepreneurship builds on the idea of hybridity (see chapter 3). Social enterprises combine different institutional logics by blending an economic orientation with social values. Hybridity, then, stems from trading off and balancing resource acquisition and social mission, resulting in strategies such as "compromising, avoiding, denying and manipulating [...] to respond to competing external demands [...] and deleting, compartmentalizing, aggregating and synthesizing to cope with internal identity struggles" (Doherty et al., 2014, p. 427).

There is, however, a crucial difference between the sort of compromises made by social enterprises and cognate organizations on the one side – we might refer to them as "alternative-additional" organizations (Jonas, 2016, p. 7) in the sense that they operate alongside rather than challenging capitalist institutions – and the compromises made by degrowth organizations on the other side. In discussing the breadth and possible pitfalls of social entrepreneurship, chapter 3 criticizes the restriction of transformative agency to market-mediated activities. Social entrepreneurship, generally, takes economic institutions, in particular markets, as given. Degrowth organizations, in contrast, work towards a profound transformation of the institutional context in which they are set. This is, of course, not always a clear-cut distinction (see chapter 18).

Alternative-additional organizations and degrowth organizations, therefore, differ with respect to how hybridity is implemented in the organizational conduct. For the former, hybridity is a coping tactic that enables them to link their social mission to incumbent institutions. Degrowth organizations also employ different tactics in response to the contradictions between their values and the instituted alignments they face. In contrast to alternative-additional organizations, however, degrowth organizations have (lower case p) political aspirations and work towards institutional change in line with degrowth principles. Hybridity, in this case, is not solely a coping tactic but embedded in political and strategic deliberations and trade-offs.

'Politics of hybridity', in this sense, refers to the *reflexive compromising in individual or organizational activities in the name of a desired future which accepts the substantiation of exploitative and unjust social relations*. Needless to say, such a politics can be as dangerous as it can be effective. For this reason, many theories of transformation, in particular anarchist-inspired writings, emphasize prefiguration. A prefigurative politics contests the temporal continuation and legitimation of power relations for the prospect of radical change in the future and thus a "politics of waiting" (Springer, 2014a, p. 407) or a "transitional stage" (Price, 2012, p. 34). Advocates of a strongly prefigurative approach to transformation, consequently, are wary of pragmatism and compromise. Understandably so, as the acceptance and justification of injustice and unsustainable practices also pave the way for a greened and CSR-clouded economy that continues to exploit lives and natures.

Prefiguration, however, also limits organizations' capacity to engage in transformative work (see above). A lack of well-established alternative relations of production, transfer, and financing can coerce organizations to compromise with respect to funding, governance, sourcing, and control over the appropriation of their products. A pressing question, then, is how to weigh the (in)consequences of compromise against the prospects for societal change?

Viewing compromise in the context of a degrowth strategy around transformative infrastructures, I argue, is key in evaluating hybridity. Hardt and Negri's (2017) distinction between short-term tactics, based on the immediacy of the spatial and temporal context, on the one side, and a more prospective strategy, guided by long-term visions and plans, on the other side, links hybridity to degrowth politics. Strategic compromise entails the abstraction from particularistic interests and carefully weights its diverse effects. Mapping these considerations around hybridity onto the concept of degrowth politics (see chapter 7) highlights two criteria for a 'degrowth politics of hybridity' and a possible foundation for its justification: reflexivity and the production of constituency.

The first of the two criteria for political practices is that they consciously relate back to the plenum of practices (reflexivity), which, in the context of a degrowth transition, means that the carriers of these practices have "adequate knowledge of the social reality and can plot their own long-term political direction" (strategy) (Hardt and Negri, 2017, p. 18ff). Taking seriously the critique put forth by aforementioned position of a prefigurative politics means that strategic compromises carefully balance means and ends. Hybridity, against this background, is the outcome of conscious trade-offs. When *Hobbyhimmel* host teambuilding events for for-profit companies or enables users to use a 3D printer to manufacture action figures, it does so primarily to be in the position to cross-subsidize low admissions, spread a do-it-yourself mentality, and address a broad audience. On an organizational level, these trade-offs are deliberate.

The second of the two criteria for political practices is relatedness. Degrowth politics change the rules of practice to support processes of institutional change in line with degrowth's principles (see chapter 7). A central aspect of a 'degrowth politics of hybridity', then, are its effects. This is comparatively easy to answer in cases where practices have apparent positive social and ecological influences, for example when a product gets repaired. In many cases, however, the effects are more diffuse and immediate unsustainabilities have to be weighed against (vague) prospects for societal change. For instance, when the members of *Slowtec* engage in the development of automated irrigation systems or the construction of decentralized and independent water and energy systems, they do so in the assumption that these technologies further more (self) sufficient and resource poor lifestyles and contribute to sustainability and social justice in the long run. In the short run, however, there is much compromise around sourcing of materials, cooperation with capitalist enterprises, and diversion from the organization's foci and ideals.

Hybridity, against this background, differs significantly across different organizations. From blindly perpetuating existing injustices and forms of exploitation, all the way to being part of a transformative strategy, carefully weighting varying effects and future prospects. Differentiating between different forms of hybridity is particularly important to tell apart organizations that challenge instituted forms of injustice and unsustainability from those that remain rooted in green and social economies, not being able to drill down to the root causes of environmental and social issues. This is not to deny legitimacy to organizations that lack a transformative strategy. There are numerous reasons for compromise without a strategic vision, such as the provision of immediate help, the alleviation of grievances, and the lack of access to appropriate resources and knowledge. Caution, however, must be exercised when injustices and unsustainabilities are blindly accepted in the name of compromise and pragmatism.

Injustices and exploitation of human and non-human lives can never be fully justified. In the context of economic institutions which are fundamentally based on the appropriation of human and ecological relations elsewhere, however, it is virtually impossible not to live at the expense of others (Brand and Wissen, 2017; Patel and Moore, 2018; see part I). Not engaging in compromise, against this background, is impossible for most degrowth-oriented organizations. Hybridity, therefore, has to be checked in how far it enables further degrowth-oriented practices. Or, in other words, how it contributes to building potential for a transformation away from injustices and unsustainabilities.

Hybrid infrastructures

Compromising, as the partial substantiation of exploitative and unjust social relations, is both a slippery ground and a reality for most degrowth-oriented organizations – in particular for those labeled 'pragmatic organizations' above. Acknowledging the difficulties associated with compromise, this section draws together foregoing deliberations on transformative infrastructures and politics of hybridity to formulate a degrowth strategy.

Transformative infrastructures are *material and social nexuses that constitute the enabling backdrop of degrowth-oriented practices*. Mobilizing resources and energies to build transformative infrastructures and aligning infrastructures to enable specific processes and activities, however, often requires *reflexive compromising in individual or organizational activities in the name of a desired future which accepts the substantiation of exploitative and unjust social relations*.

One way to approach the difficult question of how to justify compromise is to square the immediacy of prefiguration with the prospects of transition. Solely focusing on the here and now goes against the grain of a strategic orientation towards emancipatory transformation. Subordinating the present to a vague prospect of a just future, in turn, provides a dangerous legitimation of injustices. A degrowth strategy around transformative infrastructures, therefore, checks a 'politics of hybridity' for its effects in producing "constituency" (Hardt and Negri, 2017, p. 36). In other words, it assesses degrowth-oriented practices and organizations in terms of their capacity to build potential for further emancipatory action.

'Hybrid infrastructures', then, are *material and social practice formations that constitute resources for degrowth practices and organizations while still depending on and thus sub-*

stantiating social relations that jar with degrowth's principles. They actualize possibilities for different forms of economizing while grounded in the materialities of dominant practice alignments. Akin to what Longhurst (2015) calls 'alternative milieu' and Habermann (2009) refers to as 'Halbinseln gegen den Strom' [peninsulas against the current], they are anchors around which degrowth practices can thrive. On the other side, however, hybrid infrastructures are rooted in practices that partake in the 'repetition' of exploitative and unjust social institutions (Schäfer, 2016a). They simultaneously challenge and reproduce dominant socioeconomic alignments.

A politics of hybridity, in this view, constitutes an important strategy for a degrowth transition. Hybrid infrastructures are the results of strategic compromises, providing stepping-stones for more radical change. They build and store potential for a degrowth transition that might erupt as radical realignment of practices. Hybrid infrastructures materialize postcapitalist possibility and, in doing so, integrate pragmatic and hopeful approaches. A strategy around a politics of hybridity, then, deliberately accepts the ethical challenges of pragmatism in the hope that it contributes to the building of a more just future – an expectation which inevitably remains speculative.

Chapter 20: Transformative geographies and socio-spatial strategies

> The strategic power of the multitude is the only guarantee.
> *Hardt and Negri, 2017, p. 280.*

Transformations are profoundly spatial processes. The argument of this book, accordingly, develops around the close imbrication of space, politics, and transformation. It advances the notion 'transformative geographies' to describe the *spatial struggles and negotiations over just and sustainable forms of (more-than-) human co-existence materializing in antagonistic, divergent, adjusting, and synergistic practices of everyday (re)production*. Space is thus relevant in different ways. In addition to the book's conceptual argument, which is spatial throughout, the geographical dimensions of change are explicitly captured in interlude I by what Jessop et al. (2008) call a 'territory, place, scale, and network research agenda'.

Place-based, scalar, and networked forms of spatiality are conceptually grounded in a practice-theoretical perspective in the course of the book's theoretical discussion. Place locates practices in concrete spatio-temporal contexts where chains of activity intersect through the co-presence of bodies, meanings and materials (see chapters 4 and 5). A perspective on networks, moreover, broadens the view to capture the close interrelatedness of activities, bodies, ideas, and locales across space. It considers the people, ideas, and goods that travel through places, connecting them to other close and distant sites.

Social relations, however, are spatially uneven and differently structured. Although the relational perspective inspired by the book's practice-theoretical approach abandons concepts of a layered reality, it retains the notion of scale. Thinking scale through a site-ontology, then, acknowledges that practices are always conditioned by a temporal and/or spatial 'elsewhere' (see chapter 6). Hierarchy, consequently, is not a pregiven quality of space but emerges through diverse alignments of human activity unfolding on a single plane of reality. Thinking about social structures in terms of practice-alignment also shapes the ways in which the book conceives of the spread, diffusion, expansion, dissemination, or 'growth' of sustainability-related practices. Transformation, or more precisely a degrowth transition, then, is the *change of practice-alignments towards a degrowth trajectory following breaks, substitutions, and shifts of dominant patterns in practices' relatedness.*

Thus far, the focus has been on a spatial conceptualization of transformation. This section, however, goes one step further and considers how different forms of spatiality can be mobilized in the context of degrowth strategies. In other words, it returns to the discussion of territorial, place-based, scalar, and networked forms of socio-spatial relatedness and links them to the foregoing insights on transformation's social and strategic dimensions. Exploring transformation through a 'territory, place, scale, and network research agenda' deepens the alignment of strategic orientation and social dimensions which are attuned through common spatialities. For reasons of scope, I single out three insightful examples in the following: networked interstitial strategies for economic transformation; territorial ruptural strategies for transformations in governance; and place-based symbiotic strategies for transformations in communality. In addition, I suggest further links between social, spatial, and strategic dimensions of transformation.

Networked interstitial strategies for economic transformation

From production in its transnational corporations to the most mundane patterns of its citizens' consumption, Stuttgart's diverse economy depends on innumerous relations to other places. Flows of capital, workers, resources, products, directives, documents, and knowledge generally elude individuals' and organizations' control and are entangled with salvage accumulation, dispossession, displacement, oppression, exploitation of workers, cheapening of natures, and other forms of eco-social injustices and ecological destruction in place and elsewhere (see chapter 1). In response, a number of organizations (attempt to) set up regionalized and more just value chains that maintain transparency throughout production, transfer, and consumption. *Smark* and *Solidarische Landwirtschaft*, for instance, coordinate the production and distribution of local organic foodstuff and demonstrate what more equitable and sustainable food networks could look like.

Products like mobile phones or light bulbs, however, require a significantly more complex input than locally grown food. In particular natural resources such as tantalum, tin, or gold rely on translocal value chains. Small eco-social organizations generally lack the means to mobilize, coordinate, and maintain alternative circuits of value that would allow for a dissociation from exploitative and ecologically destructive activities. *Relumity*'s efforts shed light on the possibilities and difficulties of such an endeavor. Still, as I will argue with respect to the networked spatialities of economic relations, interstitial strategies based around alternative spaces of production, transfer, and consumption, provide the most compelling avenue for a fundamental transformation of practices' economic relatedness – that means the ways practices relate with respect to creation, exchange, reciprocity, comparison, and sustenance (see chapter 16). This, of course, does not exclude symbiotic and ruptural strategies, which, however, are less fit to address economies' primarily networked spatialities.

Ruptural strategies are based around a sudden break with incumbent institutions through direct conflict. Confronting growth-based patterns of production, consumption, distribution, and appropriation head on through ruptural strategies, however, is difficult with respect to networks that lack of a clear center to target. Corporations themselves, in particular small and medium sized enterprises, are positioned in economic relations that constrain a shift away from exchange value, rates of productivity, wage dumping, and the externalization of costs. Decentralization, privatization, and marketization have created complex interdependencies and pericapitalist spaces – non-transparent and dispersed economic relations that are simultaneously inside and outside of capitalism (Tsing, 2015). Targeting the conglomerate of transnationally operating enterprises and opaque value chains, therefore, is a diffuse endeavor. This does not rule out the merit in confronting specific corporations which can clearly be held responsible for destructive activities, for instance by impeding localizable practices such as coal mining. Confrontations, however, are primarily symbolic and are more likely to generate effects in terms of governance rather than economy (see below).

Symbiotic strategies, in turn, rely on compromise and cooperation with incumbent institutions. They navigate a thin line between subversion and reinvention of capitalist relations. For symbiotic strategies to work towards a degrowth transition, it is important to have reliable allies and mutual knowledge of each other's intentions. The complexity and vastness of economic networks confronts symbiotic strategies with a non-transparent landscape of possibly exploitative relations of production, transfer, and consumption. Although symbiotic practices can engender (small) shifts, the complexity of globally interlinked economic relations renders a symbiotic change of networked spatialities unlikely. Economic interests, furthermore, seek to prevent fundamental shifts and hold exploitative relations in place. In that respect, symbiotic action risks lending legitimacy to exploitative economies instead of fundamentally altering them. This is not to contradict foregoing deliberations on pragmatic organizations and hybrid infrastructures. Symbiotic strategies play an important role in changing practices' economic relatedness by drawing resources from existing relations. Symbiotic approaches, therefore, provide important tactical elements, but a successful long-term strategy is likely to be primarily interstitial.

Interstitial strategies seek to build transformative networks that replace unjust and unsustainable economic relations. They react to the complexity of exploitative (global) value chains by setting up fair and, where possible, more localized alternatives. By substituting incumbent institutions with "potentially autonomous circuits of cooperation" (Hardt and Negri, 2017, p. 145), interstitial strategies channel energies away from confrontation and corroboration of capitalist economic relations towards building alternative connections and translocal networks, instituting non-exploitative relationships across space. Networks of cooperation, following an interstitial imaginary, can incrementally substitute globalized consumption until "whole swathes of economic life [actually do] move to a different rhythm" (Mason, 2016, p. xv).

While interstitial strategies might be best suited to effect change in practices' economic relatedness, they are insufficient without changes across governance, communality, subjectivity, and technology. These, in turn, center around different spatialities, foregrounding other socio-spatial strategies. Next, I turn to the territoriality of governance.

Territorial ruptural strategies for transformations in governance

Rule, domination, and control, especially when codified in law, manifest primarily through the territorial organization of socio-spatial relations. Stuttgart's activists, organizations, entrepreneurs, and citizens have to abide by regulations that are instituted through nested territorial entities. Communal, regional, state, federal, and supranational governmental bodies issue and enforce laws that govern the everyday conduct in the administrative area of Stuttgart, where most of the study's organizations are based, and beyond. Much of this regulation and control aligns with capital accumulation, for instance by protecting private property (even if obtained illegitimately), issuing inadequate and insufficient legislation to respond to social and environmental issues, and failing to support pro-social and pro-environmental practices.

The *Economy for the Common Good* has achieved modest accomplishments in introducing their agenda into communal politics, bringing the municipality of Stuttgart to audit four city-owned enterprises and subsidize private enterprises to go through the audition process. A progressive administrative step is certainly also Stuttgart's employment of a commissioner for urban gardening who coordinates and supports urban agriculture initiatives. Aside from very few dedicated city councilors and officials, however, there is little evidence for profound economic reforms, let alone a legislative departure from growth-based economies. Stuttgart's legislation, planning, and administration remain firmly oriented towards large-scale industry and economic growth. Furthermore, a number of important issues such as legislation on taxation are beyond the competences of Stuttgart's city council and a matter for state, federal, or European governments.

Developing forceful degrowth strategies to reorient the logic of governance away from capital accumulation and towards democratic, participatory, and polycentric forms of control requires a deeper consideration of its territorial spatiality. Interstitial strategies are best fit to address the networked spatialities of practices' economic relatedness, but they are less promising with respect to the territorial organization of governance. Ruptural and to some extent symbiotic strategies, instead, provide more convincing avenues for a transformation in governance. The following thoughts, however, come with an important caveat. Neither the administrative and legislative practices of (local) governance nor resistance through ruptural strategies are primary foci of this book. As a consequence, territorial forms of spatiality have played a minor role in its argument. Nevertheless, for the purpose of broadening the view and exemplifying the potential of spatially-sensitive transformative strategies, the following paragraphs outline territorial ruptural strategies for transformations in governance.

The territorial spatiality of incumbent governmental institutions stands in contrast to economic networks. Territorially organized control formally excludes interstitial spaces in which alternative alignments of bureaucracy, administration, and policing could evolve. Grey zones around regulation and taxation provide important leeway for eco-social organizations (see chapter 15) but are necessarily limited in scope and are non-generalizable. The possibility of developing alternative administrative practices that exist side-by-side with incumbent institutions and eventually replace them is rather unlikely.

As opposed to the networked spatialities of economic practices, however, formalized governance has a more defined center (or better centers) that can be targeted and confronted. The places from which territorial control emanates can be located quite specifically. Although, of course, there are multiple regulative authorities and often ill-defined responsibilities, the drivers behind incumbent alignments of governance practices can be identified (in the sense that the individuals and processes behind legislative, administrative, and police practices are generally known). It is then possible to hold individuals and groups accountable for legal frameworks that impede the formation of sustainable and just economies while allowing or even conducing exploitation. Ruptural strategies confront governing bodies with the aim to compel them to change legislative and regulative practices. Despite numerous difficulties (some of which I elaborate below), ruptural strategies thus provide a potential route towards profound changes within a short time.

Symbiotic strategies, too, are important with respect to governance. As I discuss below, however, it is helpful to base the considerations on symbiotic strategies around the concept of place. On a highly speculative note, it might be said that ruptural strategies – which are more difficult to ignore than symbiotic ones, since they interrupt the ordinary run of events – are particularly useful for more abstract (read: indirect and disconnected) levels of governance. In the context of more immediate and responsive relations, however, cooperative strategies might be more promising for their ability to create a foundation for exchange and communication rather than an antagonism between protesters and the accused. With this, the next section moves towards the logic of communality.

Place-based symbiotic strategies for transformations in communality

Ruptural strategies can be a powerful addition to the largely interstitial and symbiotic strategies which this study's organizations follow. Particularly with respect to the urgency of transformation in the face of irreversible ecological damage and the crossing of planetary boundaries, antagonisms and sharp breaks with existing institutions must amend the non-confrontational politics of metamorphous transitions. Antagonism, however, has one decisive disadvantage that is not to be underestimated. It separates community in 'us versus them' – those who resist confront others who are held responsible. While a common target can catalyze further mobilization of protesters, it can also cause disintegration and hardened fronts that hamper collective engagement towards a degrowth transition, or even support a counter-movement by generating a (false) shared experience of being wrongfully accused.

Being based around opposition, then, ruptural strategies easily slip into and reproduce contentious and competitive forms of togetherness. Degrowth, in contrast, seeks to foster practices' alignment alongside trust, reciprocity, solidarity, and non-violent communication rather than competition and hostility. In the context of a degrowth transition, ruptural strategies need to be carefully weighed against the potentials of more integrative and reconciliating approaches. A perspective on place helps to sharpen the deliberation between different strategies.

Places, as meaningful locations where historical trajectories arise, interact, stabilize, and change, operate through proximity, socio-spatial embedding, and areal differentiation (Jessop et al., 2008). Proximity, thereby, facilitates the cultivation of trust, reciprocity, and communication – qualities of commonality that are desirable from a degrowth perspective (see chapter 16). These qualities, of course, neither result automatically from proximity nor are they reducible to a local context. Still, attention to local differentiation and interaction opens up possibilities to foster interaction across praxeologically distant but geographically close sites.

Stuttgart, as this study's geographical focus includes multiple sites through which transformative and reproductive practices transpire. The effects of Stuttgart's eco-social organizations on local and translocal alignments of practices, however, dwarfs in comparison to those of big corporations and state institutions. *Slowtec*, *Geco-Gardens*, and *Relumity* are unlikely to affect the global value chains and their command by the likes of *Daimler*, *Siemens*, and *Bosch*. Stuttgart's city and state administrations do not reverse their orientation because of the *Economy for the Common Good*. And *Lastenrad, Foodsharing, Smark*, and *Hobbyhimmel* are in no position to substitute for the city's infrastructures.

But exceptions prove the rule. Located in *Siemens* Street and between buildings of *Bosch* and *Daimler, Hobbyhimmel* indeed attracts individuals, including managers, from these organizations and word has spread across their floors and offices. Learning about alternative enterprises, some individuals reduce or cancel their employment with larger corporations to seek more meaningful work with organizations like *Slowtec*. And some city councilors and state politicians try to implement the demands of *Economy for the Common Good*. All these highly erratic and contingent events are the result of cooperative rather than confrontative relations in place.

Symbiotic strategies and their more inclusive and harmonious practices, however, come at a price. Symbiotic strategies continuously run the risk of being integrated into capitalist relations in ways that stabilize rather than challenge incumbent alignments. In order to be transformative, symbiotic strategies have to point beyond capitalist relations while tactically and selectively drawing on incumbent institutions. Coalitions that work with and within dominant institutions face numerous tactical decisions and compromises. As outlined above, a politics of hybridity is based on reflexivity (see chapter 19). Reflexivity, in turn, premises knowledge about situational dynamics and the motivations of possible allies. Direct contacts, deeper insights into organizational and institutional practices as well as a high level of trust, therefore, are important resources for symbiotic strategies.

Place-based symbiotic strategies, consequently, open a perspective on the formation of local coalitions that work towards a degrowth transition. In the face of the limitations of interstitial and ruptural strategies, cooperation with incumbent institutions is an essential building block of transformative strategies. Like the foregoing perspectives on networked and territorial spatialities, considerations around place help to attune social and strategic dimensions of transformation. Symbiotic strategies, of course, come with a number of limitations also; in particular the issue of cooptation. Place-based symbiotic, territorial ruptural, and networked interstitial strategies, therefore, need to go hand-in-hand.

Putting socio-spatial strategies into perspective

A perspective on transformative geographies reveals the intricate interplay of different strategies, logics, and socio-spatial relations. It affirms that a degrowth transition premises synergies between symbiotic, interstitial, and ruptural strategies in transforming practices' relatedness across economy, governance, communality, subjectivity, and technology through place-based, networked, territorial, and scalar socio-spatial relations. Although this work examines the nexus of diverse forms of practices' relatedness, modes of transformation, and socio-spatial relations by means of a specific case-study, it makes a plausible case that awareness of these different social, spatial, and strategic dimensions contributes to a theory and practice of (degrowth) transition in a more general sense.

The foregoing sections highlight three socio-spatial strategies: networked interstitial strategies for economic transformation, territorial ruptural strategies for transformations in governance, and place-based symbiotic strategies for transformations in communality. These strategies are neither to be understood in isolation nor do they exclude other strategic orientations. Economy and governance, for example, still require forms of cooperation with incumbent institutions and organizations while both governance and communality profit from interstitial strategies that create free spaces to experiment with alternatives.

Technology and subjectivity, furthermore, lend themselves to the formulation of other socio-spatial strategies. Open source soft- and hardware, for instance, which breaks free from commercial interests and is collectively shared and advanced, can unleash immense potential for the creation of alternative networks that compete with incumbent institutions. Blockchain technologies, to name a prominent example, could potentially create parallel currencies that entirely sideline debt-and-interest-based and therefore growth-depended ones. Networked and scalar interstitial strategies provide a promising focus in that respect. Subjectivity, again, demands a rather place-specific focus. The creation of interstitial spaces that provide moral support and encouragement to escape dominant routines and cognitive frames and to experiment with alternatives, is a promising avenue.

These deliberations are meant to bring together social, spatial and strategic considerations to reflect on the question of how community activism and civic engagement can channel transformative geographies towards a degrowth trajectory. Rather than prescribing any strategic line of action, this analysis identifies a number of correspondences between social, spatial, and strategic moments. As much as the different social, spatial, and strategic categories used here are to be understood as analytical tools, the socio-spatial strategies derived therefrom abstract from the complexity of transformative geographies. Nevertheless, the analysis suggests particularly viable foci for the development and pursuit of socio-spatial strategies. These are summarized in figure 18.

Figure 18 Socio-spatial strategies

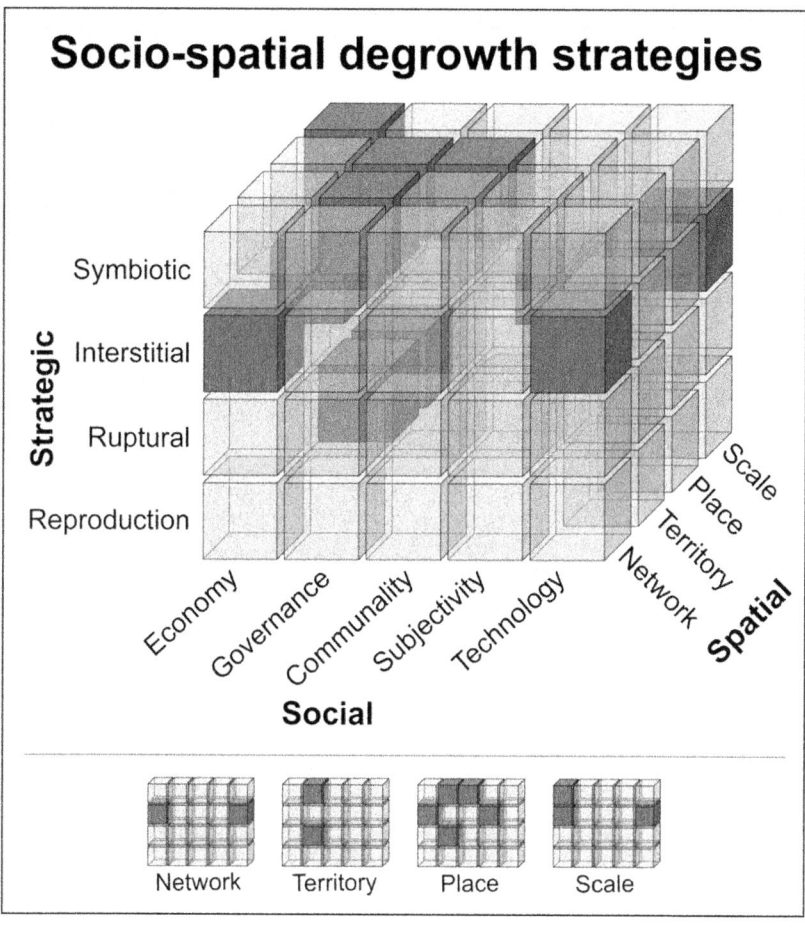

Concluding thoughts on making transformative geographies

> What is politically possible is at odds with what is physically possible, so in a sense, it is the servomechanism-agents of Kapital, not their opponents, who 'demand the impossible' now. Their fantasy of a sustainable Kapitalism carrying on, forever, without burning the planet, is perfectly delirial.
> Fisher, 2018, p. 433f.

Activists, scholars, entrepreneurs, and politicians around the world increasingly take note of the ills of current modes of social organizations and the possibilities of a different future. In 2019, *Fridays for Future* (FfF) have surged from a one-person protest to a global movement within a few months. Worldwide, thousands of school students skip classes (mostly on Fridays) and gather to demand decisive political action against climate breakdown. Aside from students, other groups such as *Scientists for Future*, *Parents for Future*, and *Artists for Future* have formed in support of the school strike for climate.

In the shadows of the protests of FfF, the movement Extinction Rebellion (XR) spreads globally. The movement demands radical social and political change that counteracts the current trajectory of ecocide. Its tactics are to disturb and interrupt business-as-usual through blockages and other non-violent acts of civil disobedience. While FfF and XR unsettle the routines of everyday practices – by skipping school, blocking traffic, and raising awareness of global injustices and radical unsustainability – diverse community projects, social enterprises, and degrowth organizations enact and build alternative forms of togetherness. All these developments are not simply spontaneous agitations but eruptions of long-standing grassroots organizing and dissatisfaction with formal politics. Writing-off social resistance as spontaneous "eclipse[s] and discredit[s] the work, knowledge, and organizational structures that stand behind events of protest and revolt" (Hardt and Negri, 2017, p. 21).

FfF and XR, much like the Occupy Movement in 2011, are flare-ups of a deep-rooted emancipatory struggle over a more just and sustainable form of (more-than-) human co-existence that smolders largely unnoticed in the interstices of incumbent practice alignments. Episodic outbreaks of oppositional work go hand-in-hand with a wealth of symbiotic and interstitial practices, including more sustainable forms of consumption, the decommodification and democratization of economic relations, the cultivation of trust-based and emancipatory alternatives, and the orientation towards sufficiency. Seen on their own, community economies and social movements are easily discounted as niche phenomena and revolutionary fads that will pass by. In the context of postcapitalist resistance, however, they become visible as manifestations and eruptions of the desire for a just future by many. They materialize in manifold alternative practices and organizations that both draw on and add to the capacity for collective struggle. Alongside more established initiatives and organizations, thus, the recent movement against climate change adds to the multifarious "constituent potential" (Hardt and Negri, 2017, p. 36) for transformative geographies.

Transformative work, however, faces many forces that militate against it. Whereas protests against climate change and for sustainability and justice find a broad base in the Global North, the required scope of social and economic restructuring these demands entail is less well understood and supported. Green economy ideologies have created the appearance that a sustainable and just society is just around the corner, solely requiring market expansion to hitherto non-marketized natures and lives, the technological innovation of not-yet-so-smart cities, and some small changes in people's habits. Business-as-usual, then, can continue and capital accumulation can be reconciled with social justice and ecological systems. The deep institutional and emotional entrenchment of growth in modern societies, thereby, becomes ever more apparent in the continuing attachment of mainstream politics and media to an economic system that is based on self-interest and dependent on continuous growth as the best possible way to organize modern societies, despite clear signs to the contrary. This leads large parts of public and political discourse to ignore evidence that makes an absolute decoupling of growth and resource consumption highly implausible and its protagonists to continue employing economic metrics that have limited significance for general social well-being (Jackson, 2017).

Institutional inertia, embodied habits, fear, insufficient knowledge, lack of imagination, and vested interests, thus, thwart emancipatory struggles for a degrowth transition. Hope as important driver for emancipatory action, therefore, does not suffice to navigate the unruly terrain of resistance. Transformation rather requires strategies that develop long-term visions of togetherness, build on the knowledge of possibilities and constraints, and enlarge the ground for postcapitalist practice. Tracing and dissecting the complexities of transformative geographies, this work speaks to the development of visions, alternatives, and strategies around the notion of a degrowth transition. It drills down into the social, spatial, and strategic dimensions of transformation and advances a conceptually and empirically grounded assessment of the possibilities and limitations of community activism and civic engagement for shifting transformative geographies towards a degrowth trajectory. While the book emphasizes the central role of community economies, it shows that shifting societal trajectories away from current patterns of injustice and unsustainability is a task that requires different strategies – symbiotic, interstitial, and ruptural – that work across all areas of social life – economy, governance, communality, subjectivity, and technology – and transpire through different spatialities – place, scale, network, and territory.

Advancing research on transformative geographies

This book integrates different perspectives on and dimensions of transformation, calling forth a comprehensive research agenda on transformative geographies. Acknowledging different modalities of resistance, areas of social co-existence, and transformative strategies puts its argument on a broad base. By taking a distinctly spatial approach to transformation, furthermore, the book sharpens the perspective on transformative processes and their complex geographies. In conjunction with the conceptual and theoretical considerations, the book advances a number of categories and empirically grounded abstractions that provide practical leverage for transformative theory and practice, operationalizing research on a degrowth transition. The following sections summarize the book's central contributions to the growing debate on transformative geographies.

Taking a holistic perspective

In combining different perspectives and emphases, this work advances a balanced and critical discussion that evades the extremes of hopeful naivety, false 'realism', escapist theory, empirical particularism, and one-sided foci on specific areas of social life. It integrates antagonism and imagination as different modalities of resistance (Zanoni et. al., 2017; see chapters 2, 5 and 6); empirical material and conceptual-methodological tools to trace transformative practice (see chapters 7 and 11); economy, governance, communality, subjectivity, and technology as different areas of transformation (see chapters 7 and 16); and symbiotic, interstitial, and ruptural strategies of change (see interludes I and IV and chapter 16). It does so by looking at a broad sample of 24 sustainability-related organizations that exemplify different ideals, strategies, and orientations and, above all, form a comprehensive network that exceeds a focus on individual examples in isolation (see chapter 9). The following paragraphs reflect on the merits of calling on a broad variety of perspectives to approach questions around transformative geographies.

The tension between antagonism and imagination ensues from oppositional and often (partially) essentializing perspectives on 'undesirable' practices, actors, institutions, or economic forms on the one hand, and the (over-) emphasis of plurality, possibility, and openness on the other hand. Against the background of a critical engagement with the respective literatures, the study develops a research agenda around the materialization of postcapitalist possibility. In combining the ontological politics of community economy scholarship (see chapter 4) with practice theory's grounding of social life in conventionalized patterns of activity (see chapter 5), it proposes a relational perspective that acknowledges plurality and becoming while remaining rooted in power relations that transpire through practices' alignments (see chapter 6). The book thus integrates antagonism's opposition to economic practices that reproduce and consolidate unsustainable trajectories with imagination's embracement of the possibilities of diversity.

To trace processes of change, including enabling and constraining moments of transformative practice, then, this study analyses and contextualizes empirical data with abductively developed conceptual, methodological, and analytical tools. These allow the study to advance an empirically grounded perspective of a *(degrowth) politics of place beyond place* by connecting degrowth-oriented practices with their broader alignments (see chapter 7). That means, although the study faces limits in researching practices' relatedness across time and space by focusing on a particular local context, it integrates extensive literature-based knowledge into its argument. Systematically and carefully combining empirical data with a broader contextual view enables the book to trace transformative dynamics beyond place and thus link the study's empirical site to transformative geographies beyond.

Empirically and conceptually, furthermore, the work integrates perspectives on different forms of practices' relatedness (see chapters 7, 11 and 16). By separating economy, governance, communality, subjectivity, and technology for analytical purposes to dissect transformative dynamics, the study shows how change transpires through different areas of social co-existence simultaneously. Tracing transformative processes across different areas and illustrating their close interaction, then, challenges perspectives that attempt to single out specific starting points without acknowledging the entwined interplay of diverse social dimensions. Transformative geographies, consequently, premise an iterative understanding of change that enrolls multiple dimensions of social co-existence.

Radical change also cannot be expected to come about through any single form of transformative strategy. The book develops a case for the creative combination of symbiotic, interstitial, and ruptural interventions into incumbent practice alignments (Wright, 2010; see chapters 3 and 16). For itself, each mode of intervention faces strong limitations. Combining these different strategies, however, creates more leeway for alternative practices, for instance by avoiding co-optation and overcoming resource constraints. Integrating different social, strategic, and spatial dimensions of change, then – the latter to which I turn to below – the study advances a plausible scenario how practices' broader alignments might shift towards a postcapitalist future (see chapter 20).

Last but not least, the book is based on empirical research that draws on a broad sample of sustainability-related organizations (see chapter 9). Covering 24 projects, associations, and enterprises, it explores a variety of thematic foci, models of financing, legal forms, motivations, and strategies. Aside from opening a perspective on the diversity of organizational forms that a degrowth transition enrolls, it emphasizes the importance of inter-organizational links and coalitions. By looking at Stuttgart's community economy more broadly, the study provides valuable insights into the connections between different actors which coalize (not always without drawbacks) for (radical) change (see chapters 12-19).

Operationalizing transformation

A holistic perspective on transformative geographies requires sound concepts to abstract from the complexity of its processes. In response, the book develops a number of conceptual categories and empirically grounded abstractions that operationalize and guide research on transformation. Advancing a number of working definitions around transformation, transition, and degrowth not only gives the study more practical relevance and leverage, it also contextualizes the book within the broad field of sustainability transition research. Against this background, the study assesses a broad range of degrowth-related activities. This section traces the study's contributions in operationalizing transformative geographies.

By developing a number of empirically grounded categories such as the notions of degrowth practices, degrowth organizations, degrowth politics, and the diverse logics perspective, the study advances useful concepts to abstract from the complexities of transformative geographies. It is clear from the empirical and theoretical work of this book that there is no black and white between sustainable/unsustainable and degrowth/business-as-usual trajectories. Organizing knowledge around critical concepts developed in close conversation with empirical data supports our understanding of transformative geographies.

Aside from improving the understanding of transformative processes, said categories also help to assess and devise action in line with degrowth's principles. While acknowledging the hybridity of actually existing transformative practices and practice-formations, the categories allow the study to carve out prospects to successfully navigate the tension between reproduction and integration on the one hand, and isolation, sacrifice, and lack of resources on the other hand. Here, the book takes an explicitly practical orientation and seeks to provide useful knowledge for a degrowth transition.

In addition, the study's operationalization of transformation in line with degrowth principles allows it to articulate a clear normative standpoint and develop its argument accordingly. While the study shows numerous links to existing institutions and symbiotic as well as interstitial forms of transformative practice, it takes a decisive stance against business-as-usual approaches around ecological modernization, sustainable development, and the green economy, all of which ignore the fundamental contradictions of sustainability and social justice with capital accumulation.

Spatializing transformation

Space is the pivot of this book's perspective on transformation in two ways. For one thing, the conceptual argument draws on spatial thought to acknowledge the close imbrication of space, politics, and transformation. It brings together stability, institutional inertia, and materialization with contingency, performativity, and difference into a coherent conceptual framework around the notion of transformative geographies (see chapters 5 to 7). For another thing, the study takes a differentiated view on the geographies of transformation, acknowledging pertinent forms of socio-spatial relatedness (see interlude I and chapter 20). The following paragraphs reflect on the various advantages of thinking transformation spatially.

Linking close and distant sites through a conceptual framework around practices' relatedness, this volume traces a (degrowth) politics of place beyond place. Adopting an explicitly geographical perspective, thereby, allows the book to demonstrate the role of activism in place for transformative processes at large. This way, it overcomes the dichotomization of local and global and develops a non-hierarchical notion of scale (see chapter 6). It shows that practices are always conditioned from a spatial or temporal 'elsewhere'. This 'elsewhere', however, is rooted in sites through which practices transpire and thus always has a place (Massey, 2005, 2008; see chapters 6, 7 and 16). A spatial perspective on transformation, then, allows the book to account for power relations without reverting to a layered reality.

Acknowledging a degrowth politics of place beyond place, furthermore, materializes postcapitalist possibility. In line with the integration of antagonism and imagination (see above), a distinctly spatial approach allows for the conceptualization of a non-hierarchical ontology while accounting for the materiality of social relations. Power and possibility, then, are not opposites, but both emerge from practices' alignments. Practices' alignments, in turn, become visible as contingent yet material formations which can be shifted, ruptured, or substituted but always against the constraints of institutional inertia. Transformative strategies, then, need to develop around both possibilities and constraints.

Space is not only important in conceptual but also in analytical terms. Drawing on Jessop et al.'s TPSN research agenda, the book explores the role of territory, place, scale, and network for transformative geographies. It carves out how transformation unfolds through territorial, place-based, scalar, and networked spatialities. Squaring spatial with social and strategic dimensions of transformative geographies, then, chapter 20 considers how different forms of spatiality can be mobilized in the context of degrowth strategies. Attuning transformative strategies and different social dimensions through common spatialities, it proposes networked interstitial strategies for economic transformation, territorial ruptural strategies for transformations in governance, and place-based symbiotic strategies for transformations in communality as particularly viable socio-spatial degrowth strategies.

Autocritique and potentials for future research

In advancing an innovative perspective on transformative geographies, this book also faces a number of difficulties and limitations that require reflection. These are primarily of methodological and empirical nature. Methodologically, the study encounters several challenges in pursuing a practice theory methodology throughout. Empirically, the study's sample remains superficial with respect to practices' relatedness beyond place, the depth of understanding of the institutional frameworks in which alternative organizations operate, and the integration of potential allies such as social movements. All of the above constitute shortcomings but also open promising areas for future research. Aside from deepening and broadening the study's empirical base, the reflections suggest much potential in a deeper integration of symbiotic and interstitial with ruptural interventions, the detailed elaboration of socio-spatial strategies, and a perspective on local coalitions.

Methodological and empirical limitations

Practice-theoretical perspectives focus on activities that 'actually take place' – which means in a strict sense that they are observable from the researcher's perspective – and the patterns that emerge from their observation. Due to a number of constraints around accessibility and the temporal and spatial dispersion of alternative practices, this study draws on interviewing to complement its ethnography (see chapter 9). As a consequence, the study relies on different kinds of data that it integrates to form a coherent picture of the empirical case (see chapter 11). Yet, in doing so, it cannot avert the partial conflation of representative (discursive) and material practices. Lines blur between concrete practices observed and described on the one hand and more speculative accounts of occurrences and the possibilities of what could be on the other hand. The study is transparent about the collection, handling, analysis, and presentation of data. Nevertheless, it does not implement practice theory's conceptual and methodological principles throughout. While it is practice theory's strength to capture the implicit and material part of social phenomena (Reckwitz, 2016; see chapter 8), the presentation of findings in part IV does not always provide a clear picture of the extent and depth of alternative practices. Expanding the study's expressiveness would require a much more expansive collection of ethnographic empirical evidence.

Within the scope of the project's resources that would have meant to curtail the sample to only a few organizations. Although I reflected on this possibility early on in the research process, I decided to take a broader focus for several reasons. First, limiting the sample to a small selection from the outset would have excluded some compelling examples, the relevance of which only became apparent during the research process. Second, the study's perspective on links between organizations is one of its central contributions to research on transformative geographies. As outlined above, the study provides insights into the connections between different actors which coalize for (radical) change. Third, the foregoing reflection on the study's contributions also highlights the merit of taking into account different thematic foci, models of financing, legal forms, motivations, and strategies. A smaller sample would have limited the study's insights into the diversity of approaches and orientations.

Related with the foregoing critique, the study remains shallow with respect to the description of practices' relatedness beyond place. In the introduction, I reflect on two different strategies to approach research on transformation's complexity with the limited resources at hand. I opt for a perspective on the complex interplay of practices and relations in a specific geographical context while developing conceptual and methodological tools to take into account practices' relatedness beyond place. In this vein, the framework that this study advances links empirical data to its broader context. Adding to its broad focus, then, the study would have profited from an in-depth empirical examination of particular practices' relatedness – for instance 3D printing in the workshop – with broader alignments – say, the sourcing of energy and filaments (material used for 3D printing) and the capacity of local production to replace other forms of consumption.

Contingent on the research question, furthermore, the study comprises limited data on the institutional frameworks in which alternative organizations operate. Although it includes interviews with key individuals from Stuttgart's city council and administration as well as ethnographic data from the participation in a number of political events around issues of sustainability with profiled attendees from local and state politics, it lacks a systematic examination of the institutional context. As a consequence, the book covers economic, political, and social institutions primarily through the lens of eco-social enterprises instead of developing an independent analysis. Such a perspective would be a useful extension of the study's activist-centered approach, enriching the knowledge about constraints and possible leverages for transformative practice.

Future research on transformative geographies

Aside from highlighting the study's limitations, the foregoing reflections open a number of compelling avenues for further inquiry. While this book advances a comprehensive perspective that integrates transformation's social, spatial, and strategic dimensions, it cannot cover the full scope of such an endeavor. Answering some questions, it leaves open others and raises new ones that lay bare potential for future research. This section outlines three prospective areas for investigation: a deeper integration of symbiotic and interstitial with ruptural interventions, the detailed elaboration of socio-spatial strategies, and a perspective on local coalitions.

Adding to the discussion of how symbiotic and interstitial strategies complement each other, a more detailed and empirically grounded integration of ruptural strategies would significantly expand the study's argument. Ruptural strategies only play a minor role in the study's empirics and remain underexplored. By and large, this is due to its perspective on alternative economies rather than on protest movements and resistance. Nevertheless, while symbiotic and interstitial strategies are more 'productive' and thus naturally the key focus of alternative economic organizing, a coherent integration of oppositional activities might prove to be a key leverage for transitional dynamics.

Ruptural strategies are particularly enticing and problematic at the same time. In contrast to symbiotic and interstitial strategies, which generally can be integrated or ignored, ruptural interventions have an immediate impact. Interrupting the ordinary run of events provokes a reaction by those affected and thus forces them to interact, at least partially, with the issues they are confronted with. Extinction Rebellion, for instance, has blocked several of London's traffic hubs in April 2019, affecting 100.000s of people and drawing attention to the threat of social and ecological collapse (Kaufmann et al., 2019). In light of the urgency to counteract the destabilization of ecological systems and to end systemic human rights violations, confrontation seems the right answer. It provides a chance to stop daily routines and business-as-usual and direct attention to issues that are tucked away behind the surface of everyday practice and shoved off to often remote places which bear the costs of the Global North's imperial way of life – materializing in degraded ecosystems, slums, factories, prisons, militarized borders, and contaminated land.

Ruptural strategies, however, can easily backfire. Individuals who are interrupted in their daily routines, for example commuting to or from work, are likely not to show understanding for the 'nuisance'. Instead of engaging more reflectively with the issues raised by protestors, they might reject the cause and reinforce their own stance on principle. Significant parts of mainstream media and politics, which have an interest in maintaining the status quo, do their bit by either ignoring or discrediting such movements and actions. Eventually, confrontation, then, might cause disintegration and hardened fronts that hamper collective engagement towards a degrowth transition or even support a counter-movement by generating a (false) shared experience of being wrongfully accused.

At large, therefore, ruptural strategies must be targeted and affect primarily those groups and individuals who command enough resources to shift or abandon destructive practices. The study's practice-based approach highlights that practices' alignments structure significant parts of human activity. That means that although most people living in the Global North partake in and reproduce exploitative patterns in one way or another, it is important to take into consideration how incumbent alignments of practices constrict their scope of action (a lack of reliable, affordable, and well-connected public transportation, for instance, can force commuters to rely on car-based mobility). And while people in the Global North certainly need to shift to more sufficient lifestyles, the responsibilization of individuals runs the risk of leaving more structural aspects untouched.

Ruptural strategies, consequently, need a careful assessment based on empirical and theoretical insights. Extinction Rebellion, for instance, base their approach on insights from historical examples of civil disobedience. Non-violence has proven to heighten the chance of success and is a core principle for all XR activities (Kaufmann, et al., 2019). Carefully selecting targets for intervention and spreading understanding for the cause on site, furthermore, are ways in which XR cushion confrontation without compromising their action. Against the background of the limitations of ruptural strategies, the best prospect lies in focusing on changes in governance (see chapter 20). One lever, thereby, could be the demanding of legislation that furthers alternative circuits of value and thus broadens the base for interstitial strategies.

Future research, therefore, should focus on creating a deeper understanding of how ruptural strategies can be integrated in a degrowth transition and how different strategies augment each other. Attuning social, spatial, and strategic dimensions of transformation, chapter 20 has started a conversation on particularly viable socio-spatial strategies. In theoretical terms, a more detailed account of the multifarious relations between spatial, social, and strategic dimensions of transformation can push forward research on transformative geographies. Empirically, future research could gather more practical and case-specific knowledge, possibly focused around a particular issue, say charity laws and taxation, to be then integrated into strategic considerations.

A coherent integration of different socio-spatial strategies, furthermore, requires a broad coalition that links potentials, resources, and leverages across economy, politics, and civil society. Bringing together different actors, interests, and institutional logics is challenging both in empirical and conceptual terms. Research can support the theoretical and practical mediation and draw lessons from particular cases to help build local coalitions that drive transformative processes from below.

And yet the question remains, in how far can strategic movements and local coalitions actually shift societal patterns towards a degrowth trajectory? Research can provide practical insights to facilitate and support transformative geographies. Moreover, it can contribute philosophically and argumentatively to expose expedient questions and perspectives. In closing, the book returns to the profound issues of hope and realism it started out with.

A false sense of realism

'Degrowth has a valid point but the demand of and hope for a degrowth transition is unrealistic and naive'. This is how many 'realists' react to degrowth's insights and claims. In spite of the evidence for degrowth practices and the discussion of possible avenues for a degrowth transition, this study's empirical findings cannot refute the critique that degrowth is a long way from becoming a general form of conduct. The compelling examples, inspirational practices, and remarkable individuals and organizations in this book dwarf in comparison to the plethora of practices that reproduce prevalent patterns. Even a reading for difference cannot dismiss the strong limitations of a degrowth transition.

Basing realism, however, on the probability of a particular future to emerge from the current state of affairs is a fallacy. It puts that which is politically probable over that which is physically necessary (Fisher, 2009, 2018). Reality, here, refers to two quite different things. On the one side, the conventionalized and historically and geographically contingent patterns of human activity that make some societal trajectories more probable than others. And, on the other side, the complex and in many ways still poorly understood ecologies human existence is embedded in. A major difference between the two meanings is that while social relations are contingent on a "never-ending process of being together, of struggling over the boundaries and substance of togetherness, and of coproducing this togetherness in complex relations of power" (Gibson-Graham and Community Economies Collective, 2017, p. 5), ecologies extend far beyond human reach. Damages to the webs of life humankind is part of can be irreversible and, as in the case of climate change, nuclear waste, and soil degradation, continue to have grave effects for millennia.

Realism, therefore, refers to vastly different realities. In the sense of the well-known phrase that it is 'easier to imagine the end of the world than it is to imagine the end of capitalism', green growth imaginaries exhibit a twisted sense of reality.

Well in the know of planetary boundaries and the physical constraints that economic activities face, green capitalists cling to economic growth, putting all their money on one horse: technology. Carbon capture and storage, genetic engineering, ever more sophisticated herbicides, asteroid mining, and the terraforming of other planets are only some of the still inchoate technologies that are more seriously considered than an economic restructuring to create an equitable and needs-based economy. Realistic, then, means perpetuating social relations that are based on the competitive maximization of individual profit and realized through the exploitation of lives and natures on an ever-growing scale, at a time when social and ecological systems are on the brink of collapse. All of this on the off chance of a rapid decoupling of economic activity from resource consumption and a miraculous fulfillment of social justice. At the same time, it is naive, from this perspective, to hope for an equitable global distribution of the planet's plentiful resources and the cultivation of relations of trust and solidarity that address basic needs of human beings and respect the complex ecologies they are embedded in. Emancipation, in the context of a green economy, is no longer the struggle to free from oppression and exploitation in order to live in accordance with human and non-human others. Rather it is the imaginary and agenda to disenthrall humans from the constraints of interdependence and deny nature.

Perhaps, humanity's continuation along a growth-based trajectory is indeed more probable than its transition into a degrowth era. But it is by no means more realistic. At the end, 'realism' is meaningless if it does not take into account the physical materiality human life (still) depends on (and will most likely for the foreseeable future). The question, therefore, is not one of probability but of feasibility and desirability. Using realism as an argument to dismiss that which needs to be done to maintain a habitable planet and protect basic human rights is not reasonable but short-sighted. And the belief in a technological miracle over a reflective recalibration of economic, political, and social institutions might even be considered pathological (at any rate cynical).

The overwhelming evidence from social and environmental sciences shows that the continuation along present trajectories cannot be sustained in the long run. In this spirit, Victor (2008) presents us with the choice between degrowth by design or by disaster and Latouche (2009, p. 8) warns that "the alternative really is: degrowth or barbarism". Not changing anything, then, seems to be at least as utopian as advocating radical change. Realism itself becomes a question of politics. "Today a lack of realism", Gorz states as early as the late 70s, "no longer consists in advocating greater well-being through degrowth and the subversion of the prevailing way of life. Lack of realism consists in imagining that economic growth can still bring about increased human welfare, and indeed that it is still physically possible" (Gorz, 1977, quoted in Kallis et al., 2015, p. 1).

Skeptical hope

Unmasking the false sense of realism of degrowth skeptics does not refute their valid objection that incumbent practice-alignments point away from a degrowth trajectory. This book has made an elaborate argument against an overemphasis of possibility and hope that neglects the constraints transformative geographies face. Acknowledging the power relations degrowth-oriented practices are embedded in is necessary to avoid being "vulnerable to caricature and dismissal as a naive, voluntarist reformism that sits comfortably with capitalist modes of diversity and lifestyle choice" (Miller, 2015, p. 366).

With a false sense of realism out of the way, skepticism becomes an important ingredient for the emancipatory struggle against capital. The critical reflection of transformative action prevents premature contentment and the underestimation of the task at hand. Alone, however, skepticism does not provide much encouragement to continue along the rocky road towards a degrowth transition. In conjunction with a critical perspective, hope turns from being a possible pitfall of naivety to a driving force of transformation. Hope can unleash the energy which skepticism channels towards strategic transformative practice.

Strategy entails a far-reaching oversight – both temporally in terms of a vision and spatially in terms of surveying the social field. Knowing the possibilities and constraints for transformative action, strategic movements can align their activities accordingly. To that effect, tracing and dissecting the diverse strategic, social, and spatial moments of transformation supports the development of power and knowledge for a degrowth transition. Degrowth strategies stay true to degrowth's principles in their vision but acknowledge the necessity of and develop the capacities for reflexive compromising under the banner of an emancipatory transformation. Building awareness of possibilities and constraints enables organizations to navigate incumbent alignments of practice in order to expand the potential for radical change. This potential for alternative economic, political, cultural, and technological alignments is already latent in the networks of alternative organizing which prefigure an equitable future.

The cultivation of webs of alternative practices give reason for careful hope. A kind of hope that drives decisive action but does not content with less than radical change. A hope that mobilizes more and more people to build constituent potential that eventually shifts practices' alignments towards a radically different trajectory, oriented on social and ecological needs and balances.

Acknowledgements

This book is based on a PhD dissertation in human geography at the University of Luxembourg, supervised by Christian Schulz and co-supervised by Tim Freytag and Gerald Taylor Aiken. This publication is funded by the Department of Geography and Spatial Planning at the University of Luxembourg.

Parts of this book's argument have been published as research papers. In particular the following chapters include previously published material: Chapters 2, 5, 6 and 7 include fragments from a review article on degrowth and postcapitalism entitled "Degrowth and postcapitalism: Transformative geographies beyond accumulation and growth" published in Geography Compass (Schmid, 2019a). Parts of chapters 5, 6, 7 and 12 to 15 have been published as a research paper entitled, "Structured Diversity: A Practice Theory Approach to Post-Growth Organizations" in Management Revue (Schmid, 2018). Chapters 9 and 12–15 draw on a research paper published in Ephemera entitled, "Repair's diverse transformative geographies – lessons from a maker community in Stuttgart" (Schmid, 2019b). Chapters 4, 5 and 6 draw on a co-authored paper with Thomas Smith (Schmid and Smith, 2020). And chapter 5 includes translated fragments of a contribution of mine to a book chapter on practice theory and space entitled "The Site of the Spatial. Eine praktikentheoretische Erschließung geographischer Raumkonzepte" (Schmid, et al. 2019). The fragments from all papers have been considerable reworked and expanded for the purposes of this work.

In addition to previous publications and financial backing, this work builds on the patience and support of many individuals who I thank for taking the time and energy to help me understand, think, and write about the mechanisms and possibilities of social change. I am greatly indebted to many of Stuttgart's activists, volunteers, eco-social entrepreneurs, and officials who took much of their valuable time to introduce me to their organizations, projects, initiatives, and institutions. Beyond learning about many new and fascinating topics, about encouraging and shocking facts, and about the possibilities and obstacles of real change, I got the chance to develop lasting friendships with inspiring people who I admire for their foresight and courage to challenge our unsustainable lifestyles.

I particularly want to extent my gratitude to Christian Schulz who has been an exemplary PhD-supervisor. Granting me the space and liberties I needed to grapple with the complexities of research, he always provided a guard rail when I ventured too far. He dedicated much time to providing invaluable advice and support. The same goes for Gerald Taylor Aiken and Tim Freytag, who, as co-supervisors, have done a tremendous job. More than once, an inspiring chat with Gerald proved the best antidote when being stuck. And Tim brought me back to a structured and balanced focus when I ran the danger of getting bogged down in details. I also thank Jan-Tobias Doerr who did not only share an office with me but also many valuable thoughts, and Thomas Smith for many inspiring exchanges that are reflected in this work's conceptual framework in particular. I greatly appreciate the support from Mirjam Galley and her colleagues at transcript who have made this publication possible. Furthermore, I also thank Birgitt Gaida and Nils Riach who lent their graphic and programming skills to visualize this work's ideas and some of its data and Anne Lang for her assistance in proofreading.

Lastly, I am very grateful to my parents Rosi and Markus Schmid who have supported me throughout my life, including the ups and downs of my educational path, and to my partner Veronika Pfeiffer who continuously cheered me up and always provided helpful thoughts during the journey of this work.

List of Figures

Figure 1 Spatial dimensions of transformation 70
Figure 2 Social dimensions of transformation 123
Figure 3 Strategic dimensions of transformation 126
Figure 4 Stuttgart's community economy 140
Figure 5 Level of explicitness across different stages of inquiry 154
Figure 6 Normative Coding 169
Figure 7 Social and strategic dimensions of transformation 237
Figure 8 Transformation of practices' economic relatedness 240
Figure 9 Transformation of practices' relatedness in governance 243
Figure 10 Transformation of practices' relatedness in communality 245
Figure 11 Transformation of practices' relatedness in subjectivity 248
Figure 12 Transformation of practices' technological relatedness 250
Figure 13 Social dimensions of degrowth-related repair 257
Figure 14 Social dimensions of degrowth-related sharing 260
Figure 15 Social and strategic dimensions of em-faktor's practices 264
Figure 16 Social and strategic dimensions of ownworld's practices 266
Figure 17 Social and strategic dimensions of Slowtec's practices 268
Figure 18 Socio-spatial strategies 287

List of Tables

Table 1 List of organizations with for-profit legal form 141
Table 2 List of organizations with non-profit legal form 142
Table 3 List of local groups, projects and institutional representatives 143
Table 4 Research methods and methodological coherence 146
Table 5 Coding frames 163
Table 6 Codes of the diverse logics perspective (CF1) 165
Table 7 Combination of two modes of practices with four moments of transformation 166
Table 8 Codes of process coding (CF2) 168
Table 9 Codes of normative coding (CF3) 170
Table 10 Different phases of coding and interpretation 172

References

Acosta, A., & Brand, U. (2018). Radikale Alternativen: warum man den Kapitalismus nur mit vereinten Kräften überwinden kann. München: oekom Verlag.

Adler, F. (2017). Postwachstumspolitiken - Wege, die Landschaften verändern. In F. Adler & U. Schachtschneider (Eds.), Postwachstumspolitiken. Wege zur Wachstumsunabhängigen Gesellschaft. München: oekom Verlag.

Affolderbach, J., & Krueger, R. (2017). "Just" ecopreneurs: re-conceptualising green transitions and entrepreneurship. Local Environment, 22(4), 410–423. https://doi.org/10.1080/13549839.2016.1210591

Aiken, G. (2012). Community Transitions to Low Carbon Futures in the Transition Towns Network (TTN): Community as seen by Transition Towns. Geography Compass, 6(2), 89–99. https://doi.org/10.1111/j.1749-8198.2011.00475.x

Alexander, S. (2013). Voluntary Simplicity and the Social Reconstruction of Law: Degrowth from the Grassroots Up. Environmental Values, 22(2), 287–308. https://doi.org/10.3197/096327113X13581561725356

Al-Hindi, K. F. (2017). Intersectionality. In D. Richardson, N. Castree, M. F. Goodchild, A. Kobayashi, W. Liu, & R. A. Marston (Eds.), International Encyclopedia of Geography: People, the Earth, Environment and Technology (pp. 1–4). https://doi.org/10.1002/9781118786352.wbieg0102

Allen, J. (2017). Power. In D. Richardson, N. Castree, M. F. Goodchild, A. Kobayashi, W. Liu, & R. A. Marston (Eds.), International Encyclopedia of Geography: People, the Earth, Environment and Technology (pp. 1–9). https://doi.org/10.1002/9781118786352.wbieg0581

Althusser, L., & Balibar, É. (1977). Reading Capital (2nd ed). London: NLB.

Amanatidou, E., Gritzas, G., & Kavoulakos, K. I. (2015). Time banks, co-production and foresight: intertwined towards an alternative future. Foresight, 17(4), 308–331. https://doi.org/10.1108/FS-05-2014-0035

Anderson, B. (2017). Hope and micropolitics. Environment and Planning D: Society and Space, 35(4), 593–595. https://doi.org/10.1177/0263775817710088

Anderson, C. (2012). Makers. The New Industrial Revolution. Random House USA.

Andreucci, D., & McDonough, T. (2015). Capitalism. In G. D'Alisa, F. Demaria, & G. Kallis (Eds.), Degrowth: a vocabulary for a new era (pp. 59–62). New York; London: Routledge.

Arthur, L., Keenoy, T., Scott Cato, M., & Smith, R. (2016). Where is the "Social" in Social Enterprise? In D. Fuller, A. E. G. Jonas, & R. Lee (Eds.), Interrogating Alterity (pp. 207–222). New York; London: Routledge.

Asara, V., Otero, I., Demaria, F., & Corbera, E. (2015). Socially sustainable degrowth as a social–ecological transformation: repoliticizing sustainability. Sustainability Science, 10(3), 375–384. https://doi.org/10.1007/s11625-015-0321-9

Avelino, F., & Grin, J. (2017). Beyond deconstruction. A reconstructive perspective on sustainability transition governance. Environmental Innovation and Societal Transitions, 22, 15–25. https://doi.org/10.1016/j.eist.2016.07.003

Avelino, F., Grin, J., Pel, B., & Jhagroe, S. (2016). The politics of sustainability transitions. Journal of Environmental Policy & Planning, 18(5), 557–567. https://doi.org/10.1080/1523908X.2016.1216782

Avelino, F., & Wittmayer, J. M. (2016). Shifting Power Relations in Sustainability Transitions: A Multi-actor Perspective. Journal of Environmental Policy & Planning, 18(5), 628–649. https://doi.org/10.1080/1523908X.2015.1112259

Avelino, F., Wittmayer, J. M., Pel, B., Weaver, P., Dumitru, A., Haxeltine, A., … O'Riordan, T. (2017). Transformative social innovation and (dis)empowerment. Technological Forecasting and Social Change. https://doi.org/10.1016/j.techfore.2017.05.002

Baier, A., Hansing, T., Müller, C., & Werner, K. (2016). Die Welt reparieren: Eine Kunst des Zusammenmachens. In A. Baier, T. Hansing, C. Müller, & K. Werner (Eds.), Die Welt reparieren. Open Source und Selbermachen als Postkapitalistische Praxis (pp. 34–63). Bielefeld: transcript.

Balsiger, P., & Lambelet, A. (2014). Participant Observation. In D. Della Porta (Ed.), Methodological practices in social movement research (First edition, pp. 144–172). Oxford: Oxford University Press.

Barnett, C. (2017). The priority of injustice: locating democracy in critical theory. Athens: The University of Georgia Press.

Bastani, A. (2018). Fully automated luxury communism. London; New York: Verso.

Bathelt, H., & Glückler, J. (2014). Institutional change in economic geography. Progress in Human Geography, 38(3), 340–363. https://doi.org/10.1177/0309132513507823

Bauwens, M., Kostakis, V., & Pazaitis, A. (2019). Peer to Peer: the commons manifesto. University of Westminster Press.

Bauwens, T., & Mertens, S. (2018). Social economy and polycentric governance of transitions. In I. Cassiers, K. Maréchal, & D. Méda (Eds.), Post-growth economics and society: exploring the paths of a social and ecological transition. New York; London: Routledge.

Belina, B. (2013). Raum. Münster: Westfälisches Dampfboot.
Benaquisto, L. (2008). Codes and Coding. In L. M. Given (Ed.), The Sage encyclopedia of qualitative research methods (pp. 85–88). London; Thousand Oaks: Sage Publications.
Bendix, D. (2017). Reflecting the Post-Development gaze: the degrowth debate in Germany. Third World Quarterly, 1–17. https://doi.org/10.1080/01436597.2017.1314761
Berg, L. D. (2009). Discourse Analysis. In International Encyclopedia of Human Geography (pp. 215–221). https://doi.org/10.1016/B978-008044910-4.00420-X
Bergek, A., Jacobsson, S., Carlsson, B., Lindmark, S., & Rickne, A. (2008). Analyzing the functional dynamics of technological innovation systems: A scheme of analysis. Research Policy, 37(3), 407–429. https://doi.org/10.1016/j.respol.2007.12.003
Bertling, J., & Leggewie, C. (2016). Die Reparaturgesellschaft. Ein Beitrag zur großen Transformation? In A. Baier, T. Hansing, C. Müller, & K. Werner (Eds.), Die Welt reparieren. Open Source und Selbermachen als postkapitalistische Prakxis (pp. 275–286). Bielefeld: transcript.
Beveridge, R., & Koch, P. (2018). Urban everyday politics: Politicising practices and the transformation of the here and now. Environment and Planning D: Society and Space, 37(1), 142-157. https://doi.org/10.1177/0263775818805487
Bina, O. (2013). The green economy and sustainable development: An uneasy balance? Environment and Planning C: Government and Policy, 31(6), 1023–1047. https://doi.org/10.1068/c1310j
Binswanger, H. C. (2013). Die Wachstumsspirale: Geld, Energie und Imagination in der Dynamik des Marktprozesses (4., überarb. Aufl). Marburg: Metropolis-Verl.
Binswanger, M. (2009). Is there a growth imperative in capitalist economies? A circular flow perspective. Journal of Post Keynesian Economics, 31(4), 707–727. https://doi.org/10.2753/PKE0160-3477310410
Bloemmen, M., Bobulescu, R., Le, N. T., & Vitari, C. (2015). Microeconomic degrowth: The case of Community Supported Agriculture. Ecological Economics, 112, 110–115. https://doi.org/10.1016/j.ecolecon.2015.02.013
Blühdorn, I. (2017). Post-capitalism, post-growth, post-consumerism? Eco-political hopes beyond sustainability. Global Discourse, 7(1), 42–61. https://doi.org/10.1080/23269995.2017.1300415
Bollier, D. (2015). Commoning as a Transformative Social Paradigm. Retrieved from The Next System Project website: thenextsystem.org
Bollier, D., & Helfrich, S. (Eds.). (2012). The wealth of the commons: a world beyond market and state. Amherst, MA.: Levellers Press.
Boltanski, L., & Chiapello, E. (2018). The new spirit of capitalism (New updated edition). London: Verso.

Bouzarovski, S., & Haarstad, H. (2018). Rescaling low-carbon transformations: Towards a relational ontology. Transactions of the Institute of British Geographers. https://doi.org/10.1111/tran.12275

Boyer, D. (2018). Infrastructure, Potential Energy, Revolution. In N. Anand, A. Gupta, & H. Appel (Eds.), The promise of infrastructure (pp. 223–244). Durham: Duke University Press.

Bradbury-Huang, H. (2010). What is good action research?: Why the resurgent interest? Action Research, 8(1), 93–109. https://doi.org/10.1177/1476750310362435

Brand, U., & Wissen, M. (2017). Imperiale Lebensweise: zur Ausbeutung von Mensch und Natur im globalen Kapitalismus. München: oekom Verlag.

Brickell, K., & Datta, A. (Eds.). (2011). Translocal geographies: spaces, places, connections. Farnham Burlington, VT: Ashgate.

Brown, K. (2014). Global environmental change I: A social turn for resilience? Progress in Human Geography, 38(1), 107–117. https://doi.org/10.1177/0309132513498837

Brown, W. (2015). Undoing the Demos. Neoliberalism's Stealth Revolution. Cambridge: MIT Press.

Buch-Hansen, H. (2014). Capitalist diversity and de-growth trajectories to steady-state economies. Ecological Economics, 106, 167–173. https://doi.org/10.1016/j.ecolecon.2014.07.030

Buch-Hansen, H. (2018). The Prerequisites for a Degrowth Paradigm Shift: Insights from Critical Political Economy. Ecological Economics, 146, 157–163. https://doi.org/10.1016/j.ecolecon.2017.10.021

Burkhart, C., Schmelzer, M., Treu, N., & Konzeptwerk Neue Ökonomie (Eds.). (2017). Degrowth in Bewegung(en): 32 alternative Wege zur sozial-ökologischen Transformation. München: oekom Verlag.

Cadman, L. (2009). Non-Representational Theory/Non-Representational Geographies. In International Encyclopedia of Human Geography (pp. 456–463). https://doi.org/10.1016/B978-008044910-4.00717-3

Caffentzis, G., & Federici, S. (2014). Commons against and beyond capitalism. Community Development Journal, 49(1), 92–105. https://doi.org/10.1093/cdj/bsu006

Carr, C., & Gibson, C. (2016). Geographies of making: Rethinking materials and skills for volatile futures. Progress in Human Geography, 40(3), 279–314. https://doi.org/10.1177/0309132515578775

Cassiers, I., & Maréchal, K. (2018). The economy in a post-growth era. In I. Cassiers, K. Maréchal, & D. Méda (Eds.), Post-growth economics and society: exploring the paths of a social and ecological transition (pp. 1–12). New York; London: Routledge.

Castree, N. (1999). Envisioning Capitalism: Geography and the Renewal of Marxian Political Economy. Transactions of the Institute of British Geographers, 24(2), 137–158. https://doi.org/10.1111/j.0020-2754.1999.00137.x

Castree, N. (2014). The Anthropocene and Geography I: The Back Story: The Anthropocene and Geography I. Geography Compass, 8(7), 436–449. https://doi.org/10.1111/gec3.12141

Chatterton, P. (2006). "Give up activism" and change the world in unknown ways: Or, learning to walk with others on uncommon ground. Antipode, 38(2), 259–281.

Chatterton, P. (2016). Building transitions to post-capitalist urban commons. Transactions of the Institute of British Geographers, 41(4), 403–415. https://doi.org/10.1111/tran.12139

Chatterton, P. (2019). Unlocking sustainable cities: a manifesto for real change. London: Pluto Press.

Chatterton, P., & Pickerill, J. (2010). Everyday activism and transitions towards post-capitalist worlds: Everyday activism and transitions towards post-capitalist worlds. Transactions of the Institute of British Geographers, 35(4), 475–490. https://doi.org/10.1111/j.1475-5661.2010.00396.x

Chatterton, P., & Pusey, A. (2019). Beyond capitalist enclosure, commodification and alienation: Postcapitalist praxis as commons, social production and useful doing. Progress in Human Geography, 27-48. https://doi.org/10.1177/0309132518821173

Coenen, L., Benneworth, P., & Truffer, B. (2012). Toward a spatial perspective on sustainability transitions. Research Policy, 41(6), 968–979. https://doi.org/10.1016/j.respol.2012.02.014

Cohen, B. (2018). Post-capitalist entrepreneurship: startups for the 99%. Boca Raton, FL: CRC Press.

Cohen, B., & Muñoz, P. (2016). Sharing cities and sustainable consumption and production: Towards an integrated framework. Journal of Cleaner Production, 134, 87–97. https://doi.org/10.1016/j.jclepro.2015.07.133

Cope, M. (2010). Coding Transcripts and Diaries. In N. J. Clifford, S. French, & G. Valentine (Eds.), Key methods in geography (2nd ed). London; Thousand Oaks: Sage Publications.

Coraggio, J. L. (2017). Towards a new economics: concepts and experiences from Latin America. In Peter North & M. S. Cato (Eds.), Towards just and sustainable economies: the social and solidarity economy North and South (pp. 15–35). Bristol: Policy Press.

Cretney, R. (2014). Resilience for Whom? Emerging Critical Geographies of Socio-ecological Resilience: Resilience of What, for Whom? Geography Compass, 8(9), 627–640. https://doi.org/10.1111/gec3.12154

Crutzen, P., & Stroemer, E. (2000). The Anthropocene. Global Change Newsletter, 41, 17–18.

Cumbers, A. (2009). Marxism/Marxist Geography I. In International Encyclopedia of Human Geography (pp. 461–473). https://doi.org/10.1016/B978-008044910-4.00710-0

D'Alisa, G., Demaria, F., & Kallis, G. (Eds.). (2015). Degrowth: A vocabulary for a new era. New York; London: Routledge.

Daly, H. E. (1973). Toward a steady-state economy. San Francisco: W. H. Freeman.

Daly, H. E. (1996). Beyond growth: the economics of sustainable development. Boston, Mass: Beacon Press.

Davies, S. R. (2017a). Hackerspaces: making the maker movement. Cambridge, UK; Malden, MA, USA: Polity.

Davies, S. R. (2017b). Characterizing Hacking: Mundane Engagement in US Hacker and Makerspaces*. Science, Technology, & Human Values, 016224391770346. https://doi.org/10.1177/0162243917703464

Defourny, J., & Nyssens, M. (2012). The EMES approach of social enterprise in a comparative perspective. Working Paper, 12(03).

DeLanda, M. (2006). A New Philosophy of Society. Assemblage Theory and Social Complexity. London: Continuum.

Della Porta, D., & Diani, M. (2006). Social movements: an introduction (2nd ed). Malden, MA: Blackwell Publishing.

Demaria, F., & Kothari, A. (2017). The Post-Development Dictionary agenda: paths to the pluriverse. Third World Quarterly, 1–12. https://doi.org/10.1080/01436597.2017.1350821

Demaria, F., Schneider, F., Sekulova, F., & Martinez-Alier, J. (2013). What is degrowth? from an activist slogan to a social movement. Environmental Values, 22(2), 191–215. https://doi.org/10.3197/096327113X13581561725194

DeWalt, K. M., & DeWalt, B. R. (2011). Participant observation: a guide for fieldworkers (2nd ed). Lanham, Md: Rowman & Littlefield, Md.

Dierksmeier, C., & Küng, H. (2016). Qualitative Freiheit: Selbstbestimmung in weltbürgerlicher Verantwortung. Bielefeld: transcript.

Dikeç, M. (2015). Space, politics and aesthetics. Edinburgh: Edinburgh University Press.

Doherty, B., Haugh, H., & Lyon, F. (2014). Social Enterprises as Hybrid Organizations: A Review and Research Agenda: Social Enterprises as Hybrid Organizations. International Journal of Management Reviews, 16(4), 417–436. https://doi.org/10.1111/ijmr.12028

Dubois, A., & Gadde, L.-E. (2002). Systematic combining: An abductive approach to case research. Journal of Business Research, 55(7), 553–560. https://doi.org/10.1016/S0148-2963(00)00195-8

Dufays, F., & Huybrechts, B. (2016). Where do hybrids come from? Entrepreneurial team heterogeneity as an avenue for the emergence of hybrid organizations. International Small Business Journal, 34(6), 777–796. https://doi.org/10.1007/s13398-014-0173-7.2

Dünckmann, F., & Fladvad, B. (2016). The Practice of Changing the Rules of Practice: an Agnostic View on Food Sovereignty. Geographische Zeitschrift, 104(1), 25–49.

Easterlin, R. (1974). Does economic growth improve the human lot? In D. P. Reder & M. W. Reder (Eds.), Nations and Households in Economic Growth: Essays in Honor of Moses Abramovitz (pp. 89–125). New York: Academic Press.

Elden, S. (2010). Land, terrain, territory. Progress in Human Geography, 34(6), 799–817. https://doi.org/10.1177/0309132510362603

Enright, T., & Rossi, U. (2017). Ambivalence of the urban commons. In A. Jonas, B. Miller, K. Ward, & D. Wilson (Eds.), Handbook on Spaces of Urban Politics (pp. 1–22).

Esper, S. C., Cabantous, L., Barin-Cruz, L., & Gond, J.-P. (2017). Supporting alternative organizations? Exploring scholars' involvement in the performativity of worker-recuperated enterprises. Organization, 24(5), 671–699. https://doi.org/10.1177/1350508417713218

Eversberg, D., & Schmelzer, M. (2018). The Degrowth Spectrum: Convergence and Divergence Within a Diverse and Conflictual Alliance. Environmental Values, 27(3), 245–267. https://doi.org/10.3197/096327118X15217309300822

Everts, J. (2016). Connecting Sites: Practice Theory and Large Phenomena. Geographische Zeitschrift, 104(1), 50–67.

Everts, J., Lahr-Kurten, M., & Watson, M. (2011). Practice matters! Geographical inquiry and theories of practice. Erdkunde, 65(4), 232–334. https://doi.org/10.3112/erdkunde.2011.04.01

Faulconbridge, J. R., & Hall, S. (2009). Economics and Human Geography. In International Encyclopedia of Human Geography (pp. 332–337). https://doi.org/10.1016/B978-008044910-4.00279-0

Felber, C. (2018). Gemeinwohl-Ökonomie. München: Piper.

Fickey, A. (2011). 'The Focus Has to be on Helping People Make a Living': Exploring Diverse Economies and Alternative Economic Spaces: Diverse economies and alternative economic spaces. Geography Compass, 5(5), 237–248. https://doi.org/10.1111/j.1749-8198.2011.00418.x

Fischer, A., Holstead, K., Hendrickson, C. Y., Virkkula, O., & Prampolini, A. (2017). Community-led initiatives' everyday politics for sustainability – Conflicting rationalities and aspirations for change? Environment and Planning A, 49(9), 1986–2006. https://doi.org/10.1177/0308518X17713994

Fisher, M. (2009). *Capitalist realism: Is there no alternative?* Winchester: Zero Books.

Fisher, M. (2018). K-punk: The collected and unpublished writings of Mark Fisher (2004-2016) (D. Ambrose, Ed.). London, UK: Repeater Books.

Flick, U. (2014). An introduction to qualitative research (Ed. 5). London; Thousand Oaks: Sage Publications.

Flyvbjerg, B. (2006). Five Misunderstandings About Case-Study Research. Qualitative Inquiry, 12(2), 219–245. https://doi.org/10.1177/1077800405284363

Foucault, M. (2008). The birth of biopolitics: lectures at the Collège de France, 1978-79 (M. Senellart, Ed.). Basingstoke; New York: Palgrave Macmillan.

Frenken, K., & Schor, J. (2017). Putting the sharing economy into perspective. Environmental Innovation and Societal Transitions. https://doi.org/10.1016/j.eist.2017.01.003

Fukuyama, F. (2006). The end of history and the last man. New York: Free Press.

Fuller, D., & Jonas, A. E. G. (2003). Alternative Financial Spaces. In Alternative Economic Spaces (pp. 55–73). https://doi.org/10.4135/9781446220825.n3

Fuller, D., Jonas, A. E. G., & Lee, R. (2016). Interrogating Alterity. Alternative Economic and Political Spaces. New York; London: Routledge.

Geels, F. W. (2011). The multi-level perspective on sustainability transitions: Responses to seven criticisms. Environmental Innovation and Societal Transitions, 1(1), 24–40. https://doi.org/10.1016/j.eist.2011.02.002

Geels, F. W., & Schot, J. (2007). Typology of sociotechnical transition pathways. Research Policy, 36(3), 399–417. https://doi.org/10.1016/j.respol.2007.01.003

Geertz, C. (1973). The Interpretation of Cultures. Basic Books Inc.

Geertz, C. (2003). Thick description: Toward an interpretive theory of culture. Culture: Critical Concepts in Sociology, 1, 173–196.

Geiselhart, K., Winkler, J., & Dünckmann, F. (2019). Vom Wissen über das Tun—Praxeologische Ansätze für die Geographie von der Analyse bis zur Kritik. In S. Schäfer & J. Everts (Eds.), Handbuch Praktiken und Raum. Humangeographie nach dem Practice Turn (pp. 21–76). Bielefeld: transcript.

Georgescu-Roegen, N. (1971). The Entropy Law and the Economic Process. Harvard University Press.

Gherardi, S. (2016). To start practice theorizing anew: The contribution of the concepts of agencement and formativeness. Organization, 23(5), 680–698. https://doi.org/10.1177/1350508415605174

Gherardi, S. (2017). Sociomateriality in Posthuman Practice Theory. In A. Hui, T. R. Schatzki, & E. Shove (Eds.), The nexus of practices: connections, constellations and practitioners (pp. 38–51). New York; London: Routledge.

Gibson, K., Cahill, A., & McKay, D. (2015). Diverse Economies, Ecologies, and Ethics. Rethinking rural transformation in the Philippines. In G. Roelvink, K. St. Martin, & J. K. Gibson-Graham (Eds.), Making other worlds possible: performing diverse economies (pp. 194–224). Minneapolis, Minn.: Univ. of Minnesota Press.

Gibson-Graham, J. K. (1996). The End of Capitalism (as we knew it). A Feminist Critique of Political Economy. Minneapolis; London: Minnesota Press.

Gibson-Graham, J. K. (2006). Postcapitalist Politics. Minneapolis; London: Minnesota Press.

Gibson-Graham, J. K. (2008). Diverse economies: performative practices for 'other worlds'. Progress in Human Geography, 32(5), 613–632. https://doi.org/10.1177/0309132508090821

Gibson-Graham, J. K. (2012). Diverse Economies: Performative Practices for "Other Worlds." In T. J. Barnes, J. Peck, & E. Sheppard (Eds.), The Wiley-Blackwell companion to economic geography (pp. 33–46). Chichester: Wiley-Blackwell.

Gibson-Graham, J. K. (2014). Rethinking the Economy with Thick Description and Weak Theory. Current Anthropology, 55(9), 147–153. https://doi.org/10.1086/676646

Gibson-Graham, J. K., Cameron, J., & Healy, S. (2013). Take Back the Economy. An Ethical Guide for Transforming our Communities. Minneapolis; London: Minnesota Press.

Gibson-Graham, J. K., & Community Economies Collective. (2017). Cultivating Community Economies. Retrieved March 24, 2017, from The Next System Project website: http://thenextsystem.org/cultivating-community-economies/

Gibson-Graham, J. K., Erdem, E., & Özselçuk, C. (2013). Thinking with Marx for a Feminist Postcapitalist Politics. In R. Jaeggi & D. Loick (Eds.), Marx' Kritik der Gesellschaft. Berlin: Akademie Verlag.

Glassman, J. (2003). Rethinking Overdetermination, Structural Power, and Social Change: A Critique of Gibson-Graham, Resnick, and Wolff. Antipode, 35(4), 678–698. https://doi.org/10.1046/j.1467-8330.2003.00345.x

Glassman, J. (2006). Primitive accumulation, accumulation by dispossession, accumulation by 'extra-economic' means. Progress in Human Geography, 30(5), 608–625. https://doi.org/10.1177/0309132506070172

Gorz, A. (1968). Reform and Revolution. The Socialist Register, 5, 111–143.

Graeber, D. (2018). Bullshit Jobs: a theory. London: Allen Lane.

Gram-Hanssen, K. (2011). Understanding change and continuity in residential energy consumption. Journal of Consumer Culture, 11(1), 61–78. https://doi.org/10.1177/1469540510391725

Gritzas, G., & Kavoulakos, K. I. (2016). Diverse economies and alternative spaces: An overview of approaches and practices. European Urban and Regional Studies, 23(4), 917–934. https://doi.org/10.1177/0969776415573778

Gudynas, E. (2011). Buen Vivir: Today's tomorrow. Development, 54(4), 441–447. https://doi.org/10.1057/dev.2011.86

Habermann, F. (2009). Halbinseln gegen den Strom: anders leben und wirtschaften im Alltag. Königstein/Taunus: Helmer.

Habermann, F. (2012). Wir werden nicht als Egoisten geboren. In S. Helfrich & Heinrich Böll Stiftung (Eds.), Commons. Für eine neue Politik jenseits von Markt und Staat (pp. 39–44). Bielefeld: transcript.

Hahnel, R., & Wright, E. O. (2016). Alternatives to capitalism: proposals for a democratic economy. London; New York: Verso.

Hansen, T., & Coenen, L. (2015). The geography of sustainability transitions: Review, synthesis and reflections on an emergent research field. Environmental Innovation and Societal Transitions, 17, 92–109. https://doi.org/10.1016/j.eist.2014.11.001

Hansing, T. (2017). Offene Werkstätten. Infrastrukturen teilen, gemeinsam nutzen und zusammen selber machen. In C. Burkhart, M. Schmelzer, N. Treu, Konzeptwerk Neue Ökonomie, & DFG-Kolleg Postwachstumsgesellschaften (Eds.), Degrowth in Bewegungen. 32 alternative Wege zur sozial-ökologischen Transformation (pp. 236–247).

Haraway, D. J. (1991). Simians, cyborgs, and women: the reinvention of nature. New York; London: Routledge.

Hardt, M., & Negri, A. (2004). Multitude: War and democracy in the age of Empire. New York: The Penguin Press.

Hardt, M., & Negri, A. (2009). Commonwealth. Cambridge, Mass: Belknap Press of Harvard University Press.

Hardt, M., & Negri, A. (2017). Assembly. New York: Oxford University Press.

Hargreaves, T. (2011). Practice-ing behaviour change: Applying social practice theory to pro-environmental behaviour change. Journal of Consumer Culture, 11(1), 79–99. https://doi.org/10.1177/1469540510390500

Hargreaves, T., Longhurst, N., & Seyfang, G. (2013). Up, Down, round and round: Connecting Regimes and Practices in Innovation for Sustainability. Environment and Planning A: Economy and Space, 45(2), 402–420. https://doi.org/10.1068/a45124

Harvey, D. (1982). The limits to capital. Oxford: B. Blackwell.

Harvey, D. (2010). A companion to Marx's Capital (Vol. 1). Verso Books.

Harvey, D. (2011). The enigma of capital: and the crises of capitalism. London: Profile Books.

Harvey, D. (2014). Seventeen contradictions and the end of capitalism. London: Profile Books.

Harvey, D. (2015). "Listen, Anarchist!" A personal response to Simon Springer's "Why a radical geography must be anarchist." Retrieved from http://davidharvey.org/2015/06/listen-anarchist-by-david-harvey/

Haunss, S., Daphi, P., Gauditz, L., Knopp, P., Micus, M., Scharf, M., ... Zajak, S. (2017). No G20. Ergebnisse der Befragung von Demonstrierenden und Beobachtungen des Polizeieinsatzes. Retrieved from https://refubium.fu-berlin.de/bitstream/handle/fub188/23081/NoG20_ipb-working-paper.pdf?sequence=1

Hayden, A., & Wilson, J. (2017). Beyond "GDP" Indicators: Changing the Economic Narrative for a Post-consumerist Society? In M. J. Cohen, H. S. Brown, & P. Vergragt (Eds.), Social change and the coming of post-consumer society: theoretical advances and policy implications (pp. 170–191). New York; London: Routledge.

Healy, S. (2009). Alternative Economies. International Encyclopedia of Human Geography, 3(1), 338–344.

Helfrich, S. (2015). Muster gemeinsamen Handelns. Wie wir zu einer Sprache des Commoning kommen. In S. Helfrich, D. Bollier, & Heinrich-Böll-Stiftung (Eds.), Die Welt der Commons. Muster gemeinsamen Handelns (pp. 36–54). Bielefeld: transcript.

Helfrich, S., & Bollier, D. (2019). Frei, fair und lebendig - Die Macht der Commons.

Henderson, H. (1999). Beyond globalization: shaping a sustainable global economy. West Hartford, Conn: Kumarian Press.

Hendriks, C. M., & Grin, J. (2007). Contextualizing Reflexive Governance: the Politics of Dutch Transitions to Sustainability. Journal of Environmental Policy & Planning, 9(3–4), 333–350. https://doi.org/10.1080/15239080701622790

Hickel, J., & Kallis, G. (2019). Is Green Growth Possible? New Political Economy, 1–18. https://doi.org/10.1080/13563467.2019.1598964

Hielscher, S., & Smith, A. (2014). Community-based digital fabrication workshops: A review of the research literature. Science and Technology Policy Research, (8). Retrieved from http://sro.sussex.ac.uk/49214/1/2014-08_SWPS_Hielscher_Smith.pdf

Hillebrandt, F. (2014). Soziologische Praxistheorien. Eine Einführung. Wiesbaden: Springer.

Hillebrandt, F. (2016). Die Soziologie der Praxis als poststrukturalistischer Materialismus. In H. Schäfer (Ed.), Praxistheorie. Ein soziologisches Forschungsprogramm (pp. 71–94). Bielefeld: transcript.

Hirsch, F. (1995). Social limits to growth (Rev. ed). New York; London: Routledge.

Hirschauer, S. (2011). Sei ein Mann! Implizites Zeigen und praktisches Wissen. In R. Schmidt, W. M. Stock, & J. Volbers (Eds.), Zeigen: Dimensionen einer Grundtätigkeit (pp. 89–104). Weilerswist: Velbrück Wissenschaft.

Hirschauer, S. (2016). Verhalten, Handeln, Interagieren. Zu den mikrosoziologischen Grundlagen der Praxistheorie. In H. Schäfer (Ed.), Praxistheorie. Ein soziologisches Forschungsprogramm (pp. 45–67). Bielefeld: transcript.

Hobson, K. (2016). Closing the loop or squaring the circle? Locating generative spaces for the circular economy. Progress in Human Geography, 40(1), 88–104. https://doi.org/10.1177/0309132514566342

Hobson, K., & Lynch, N. (2016). Diversifying and de-growing the circular economy: radical social transformation in a resource-scarce world. Futures. https://doi.org/10.1016/j.futures.2016.05.012

Hoffman, J., & Loeber, A. (2016). Exploring the Micro-politics in Transitions from a Practice Perspective: The Case of Greenhouse Innovation in the Netherlands. Journal of Environmental Policy & Planning, 18(5), 692–711. https://doi.org/10.1080/1523908X.2015.1113514

Hölscher, K., Wittmayer, J. M., & Loorbach, D. (2018). Transition versus transformation: What's the difference? Environmental Innovation and Societal Transitions, 27, 1–3. https://doi.org/10.1016/j.eist.2017.10.007

Hopkins, R. (2014). Einfach. Jetzt. Machen! Wie wir unsere Zukunft selbst in die Hand nehmen (2nd ed.). München: oekom Verlag.

Horkheimer, M. (1937). Traditionelle und Kritische Theorie. Zeitschrift Für Sozialforschung.

Houtbeckers, E. (2018). Framing Social Enterprise as Post-Growth Organising in the Diverse Economy. Management Revue, 29(3), 257–280. https://doi.org/10.5771/0935-9915-2018-3-257

Huber, M. (2015). Anarcho-Primitivismus: Keine Zivilisation, kein Staat! In P. Seyferth (Ed.), Den Staat zerschlagen! (pp. 259–280). https://doi.org/10.5771/9783845243962-259

Hui, A., Schatzki, T. R., & Shove, E. (2017). Introduction. In A. Hui, T. R. Schatzki, & E. Shove (Eds.), The nexus of practices: connections, constellations and practitioners (1 Edition, pp. 1–7). New York; London: Routledge.

Huybrechts, B. (2013). Social Enterprise, Social Innovation and Alternative Economies: Insights from Fair Trade and Renewable Energy. In H.-M. Zademach & S. Hillebrand (Eds.), Alternative Economies and Spaces. New Perspectives for a Sustainable Economy (pp. 113–154). Bielefeld: transcript.

Huybrechts, B., & Nicholls, A. (2012). Social Entrepreneurship: Definitions, Drivers and Challenges. In C. K. Volkmann, K. O. Tokarski, & K. Ernst (Eds.), Social Entrepreneurship and Social Business (pp. 31–48). https://doi.org/10.1007/978-3-8349-7093-0_2

I.L.A. Kollektiv (Ed.). (2019). Das gute Leben für alle: Wege in die solidarische Lebensweise. München: oekom Verlag.

Illich, I. (1973). Tools for Conviviality. London: Calder and Boyars.

Jackson, T. (2017). Prosperity without growth: foundations for the economy of tomorrow. New York; London: Routledge.

Jacobsson, S., & Bergek, A. (2011). Innovation system analyses and sustainability transitions: Contributions and suggestions for research. Environmental Innovation and Societal Transitions, 1(1), 41–57. https://doi.org/10.1016/j.eist.2011.04.006

Jessop, B., Brenner, N., & Jones, M. (2008). Theorizing sociospatial relations. Environment and Planning D: Society and Space, 26(3), 389–401. https://doi.org/10.1068/d9107

Johanisova, N., Crabtree, T., & Fraňková, E. (2013). Social enterprises and non-market capitals: a path to degrowth? Journal of Cleaner Production, 38, 7–16. https://doi.org/10.1016/j.jclepro.2012.01.004

Johanisova, N., & Fraňková, E. (2013). Eco-social enterprises in practice and theory. A radical vs. mainstream view. In M. Anastasiadis (Ed.), ECO-WISE social enterprises as sustainable actors: concepts, performances, impacts (pp. 110–129). Bremen: EHV Europäischer Hochschulverlag.

Johanisova, N., & Fraňková, E. (2017). Eco Social Enterprises. In C. L. Spash (Ed.), Routledge Handbook of ecological economics: Nature and societ (pp. 507–516). New York; London: Routledge.

Johanisova, N., & Wolf, S. (2012). Economic democracy: A path for the future? Futures, 44(6), 562–570. https://doi.org/10.1016/j.futures.2012.03.017

Johnsen, C. G., Nelund, M., Olaison, L., & Meier Sørensen, B. (2017). Organizing for the post-growth economy. Ephemera: Theory and Politics in Organization, 17(1), 1–21.

Jonas, A. E. G. (2006). Pro scale: further reflections on the "scale debate" in human geography. Transactions of the Institute of British Geographers, 31(3), 399–406. https://doi.org/10.1111/j.1475-5661.2006.00210.x

Jonas, A. E. G. (2016). "Alternative" This, "Alternative" That…: Interrogating Alterity and Diversity. In D. Fuller, A. E. G. Jonas, & R. Lee (Eds.), Interrogating Alterity. Alternative Economic and Political Spaces. New York; London: Routledge.

Jones, A. (2009). Marxism/Marxist Geography II. In International Encyclopedia of Human Geography (pp. 474–485). https://doi.org/10.1016/B978-008044910-4.00711-2

Jones, M. (2009). Phase space: geography, relational thinking, and beyond. Progress in Human Geography, 33(4), 487–506. https://doi.org/10.1177/0309132508101599

Jorgensen, M., & Phillips, L. J. (2002). Discourse Analysis as Theory and Method. https://doi.org/10.1177/0959354301114006

Joutsenvirta, M. (2016). A practice approach to the institutionalization of economic degrowth. Ecological Economics, 128, 23–32. https://doi.org/10.1016/j.ecolecon.2016.04.006

Kallis, G. (2018). Degrowth. Newcastle upon Tyne: Agenda Publishing.

Kallis, G., Demaria, F., & D'Alisa, G. (2015). Introduction. Degrowth. In G. D'Alisa, F. Demaria, & G. Kallis (Eds.), Degrowth: a vocabulary for a new era (pp. 1–17). New York; London: Routledge.

Kallis, G., Kerschner, C., & Martinez-Alier, J. (2012). The economics of degrowth. Ecological Economics, 84, 172–180. https://doi.org/10.1016/j.ecolecon.2012.08.017

Kallis, G., Kostakis, V., Lange, S., Muraca, B., Paulson, S., & Schmelzer, M. (2018). Research on Degrowth. Annual Review of Environment and Resources, 43(1). https://doi.org/10.1146/annurev-environ-102017-025941

Kallis, G., & March, H. (2015). Imaginaries of Hope: The Utopianism of Degrowth. Annals of the Association of American Geographers, 105(2), 360–368. https://doi.org/10.1080/00045608.2014.973803

Karamchandani, A., Kubzansky, M., & Frandano, P. (2009). Emerging Markets, Emerging Models: market-based solutions to the challenges of global poverty. Monitor Group.

Kaufmann, S. K., Timmermann, M., and Botzki, I. (2019). Wann wenn nicht wir*: Ein Extinction Rebellion Handbuch (U. Bischoff, Trans.). Frankfurt am Main: Fischer Verlag.

Kellermann, P. (Ed.). (2011). Begegnungen feindlicher Brüder: zum Verhältnis von Anarchismus und Marxismus in der Geschichte der sozialistischen Bewegung. Münster: Unrast.

Kellermann, P. (Ed.). (2012). Begegnungen feindlicher Brüder: zum Verhältnis von Anarchismus und Marxismus in der Geschichte der sozialistischen Bewegung. Bd. 2. Münster: Unrast.

Kellermann, P. (2014). Begegnungen feindlicher Brüder: zum Verhältnis von Anarchismus und Marxismus in der Geschichte der sozialistischen Bewegung. Bd. 3. Münster: Unrast

Kemmis, S., & McTaggart, R. (2005). Participatory Action Research. Communicative Action and the Public Sphere. In N. K. Denzin & Y. S. Lincoln (Eds.), The SAGE Handbook of Qualitative Research (4th ed., pp. 559–603). London; Thousand Oaks: Sage Publications.

Kemp, R., Schot, J., & Hoogma, R. (1998). Regime shifts to sustainability through processes of niche formation: The approach of strategic niche management. Technology Analysis & Strategic Management, 10(2), 175–198. https://doi.org/10.1080/09537329808524310

Kenis, A., & Lievens, M. (2015). The Limits of the Green Economy. From reinventing capitalism to repoliticising the present. New York; London: Routledge.

Kenneth, K., Linden, G., & Dedrick, J. (2011). Capturing value in global networks. Retrieved from http://pcic.merage.uci.edu/papers/2011/Value_iPad_iPhone.pdf.

Kerschner, C. (2010). Economic de-growth vs. steady-state economy. Journal of Cleaner Production, 18(6), 544–551. https://doi.org/10.1016/j.jclepro.2009.10.019

Kerschner, C., Wächter, P., Nierling, L., & Ehlers, M.-H. (2018). Degrowth and Technology: Towards feasible, viable, appropriate and convivial imaginaries. Journal of Cleaner Production, 197, 1619–1636. https://doi.org/10.1016/j.jclepro.2018.07.147

Kindon, S. (2010). Participatory Action Research. In I. Hay (Ed.), Qualitative research methods in human geography (3rd ed, pp. 259–277). Oxford; New York: Oxford University Press.

Kindon, S., Pain, R., & Kesby, M. (2009). Participatory Action Research. In International Encyclopedia of Human Geography (pp. 90–95). https://doi.org/10.1016/B978-008044910-4.00490-9

Kindon, S., Pain, R., and Kesby, M. (2007). Participatory Action Research Approaches and Methods Connecting people, participation and place. New York; London: Routledge.

Kjeldsen, C., & Ingemann, J. H. (2016). The Danish Organic Movement: From Social Movement to Market Mainstream and Beyond…? In D. Fuller, A. E. G. Jonas, & R. Lee (Eds.), Interrogating Alterity. Alternative Economic and Political Spaces (pp. 175–190). New York; London: Routledge.

Konersmann, R. (2015). Die Unruhe der Welt. Frankfurt am Main: Fischer Verlag.

Krueger, R., Schulz, C., & Gibbs, D. C. (2017). Institutionalizing alternative economic spaces? An interpretivist perspective on diverse economies. Progress in Human Geography. https://doi.org/10.1177/0309132517694530

Kuhn, G. (2005). Tier-Werden, Schwarz-Werden, Frau-Werden: eine Einführung in die politische Philosophie des Poststrukturalismus. Münster: Unrast.

Kunkel, B., & Daly, H. E. (2018). Ecologies of Scale. New Left Review, 109(1), 81–104.

Kunze, C., & Becker, S. (2015). Collective ownership in renewable energy and opportunities for sustainable degrowth. Sustainability Science, 10(3), 425–437. https://doi.org/10.1007/s11625-015-0301-0

Laclau, E., & Mouffe, C. (2001). Hegemony and socialist strategy: towards a radical democratic politics (2nd ed). London: Verso.

Laloux, F. (2014). Reinventing Organizations. Brussels: Nelson Parker.

Lange, B. (2017). Offene Werkstätten und Postwachstumsökonomien: kollaborative Orte als Wegbereiter transformativer Wirtschaftsentwicklungen? Zeitschrift Für Wirtschaftsgeographie, 61(1), 38–55. https://doi.org/10.1515/zfw-2016-0029

Lange, B., & Bürkner, H.-J. (2018). Open workshops as sites of innovative socio-economic practices: approaching urban post-growth by assemblage theory. Local Environment, 23(7), 680–696. https://doi.org/10.1080/13549839.2017.1418305

Larkin, B. (2013). The Politics and Poetics of Infrastructure. Annual Review of Anthropology, 42(1), 327–343. https://doi.org/10.1146/annurev-anthro-092412-155522

Latouche, S. (2009). Farewell to Growth. https://doi.org/10.1111/j.1468-2257.2011.00571.x

Latour, B. (1993). We have never been modern. Cambridge: Harvard University Press.

Latour, B. (2005). Reassembling the social: an introduction to actor-network-theory. Oxford: Oxford Univ. Press.

Lawhon, M., & Murphy, J. T. (2012). Socio-technical regimes and sustainability transitions: Insights from political ecology. Progress in Human Geography, 36(3), 354–378. https://doi.org/10.1177/0309132511427960

Lee, F. (2009). A History of Heterodox Economics: Challenging the mainstream in the twentieth century. https://doi.org/10.4324/9780203883051

Lee, R. (2006). The ordinary economy: Tangled up in values and geography. Transactions of the Institute of British Geographers, 31(4), 413–432. https://doi.org/10.1111/j.1475-5661.2006.00223.x

Lee, R. (2013). The Possibilities of Economic Difference? Social Relations of Value, Space and Economic Geographies. In H.-M. Zademach & S. Hillebrand (Eds.), Alternative Economies and Spaces. New Perspectives for a Sustainable Economy (pp. 69–84). Bielefeld: transcript.

Lee, R. (2016). Spiders, Bees or Architects? Imagination and the Radical Immanence of Alternatives/Diversity for Political-Economic Geographies. In D. Fuller, A. E. G. Jonas, & R. Lee (Eds.), Interrogating Alterity. Alternative Economic and Political Spaces. New York; London: Routledge.

Lefebvre, H. (1991). The Production of Space. https://doi.org/10.1027/1618-3169/a000129

Lefebvre, H. (2014). Critique of Everyday Life. London: Verso.

Leyshon, A., Lee, R., & Williams, C. C. (Eds.). (2003). Alternative economic spaces. London; Thousand Oaks: Sage Publications.

Lietaert, M. (2010). Cohousing's relevance to degrowth theories. Journal of Cleaner Production, 18(6), 576–580. https://doi.org/10.1016/j.jclepro.2009.11.016

Linebaugh, P. (2014). Stop, thief! the commons, enclosures and resistance. Oakland: PM Press.

Lockyer, J. (2017). Community, commons, and degrowth at Dancing Rabbit Ecovillage. Journal of Political Ecology, 24(1), 519. https://doi.org/10.2458/v24i1.20890

Loick, D. (2017). Anarchismus zur Einführung. Hamburg: Junius.

Longhurst, N. (2015). Towards an 'alternative' geography of innovation: Alternative milieu, socio-cognitive protection and sustainability experimentation. Environmental Innovation and Societal Transitions, 17, 183–198. https://doi.org/10.1016/j.eist.2014.12.001

Loorbach, D. (2010). Transition Management for Sustainable Development: A Prescriptive, Complexity-Based Governance Framework. Governance, 23(1), 161–183. https://doi.org/10.1111/j.1468-0491.2009.01471.x

Loorbach, D., Frantzeskaki, N., & Avelino, F. (2017). Sustainability Transitions Research: Transforming Science and Practice for Societal Change. Annual Review of Environment and Resources, 42(1), 599–626. https://doi.org/10.1146/annurev-environ-102014-021340

Loorbach, D., & Rotmans, J. (2010). The practice of transition management: Examples and lessons from four distinct cases. Futures, 42(3), 237–246. https://doi.org/10.1016/j.futures.2009.11.009

Luhmann, N. (1998). Die Gesellschaft der Gesellschaft. Suhrkamp.

Luhmann, N. (2015). Soziale Systeme: Grundriß einer allgemeinen Theorie (16. Auflage). Suhrkamp.

Lunn, J. (2017). Ethics in Geography Fieldwork. In D. Richardson, N. Castree, M. F. Goodchild, A. Kobayashi, W. Liu, & R. A. Marston (Eds.), International Encyclopedia of Geography: People, the Earth, Environment and Technology (pp. 1–9). https://doi.org/10.1002/9781118786352.wbieg0974

Macrorie, R., Foulds, C., & Hargreaves, T. (2015). Governing and governed by practices: exploring interventions in low-carbon housing policy and practice. In Y. Strengers & C. Maller (Eds.), Social practices, intervention and sustainability: beyond behaviour change. New York; London: Routledge.

Malm, A. (2016). Fossil capital: The rise of steam-power and the roots of global warming. London: Verso.

Malm, A. (2018). The progress of this storm: nature and society in a warming world. London: Verso.

Marchant, B. (2018). One device: the secret history of the iphone. New York; Boston; London: Back Bay Books.

Marcuse, H. (1972). Counter-Revolution and Revolt. Boston: Beacon Press.

Markard, J., Raven, R., & Truffer, B. (2012). Sustainability transitions: An emerging field of research and its prospects. Research Policy, 41(6), 955–967. https://doi.org/10.1016/j.respol.2012.02.013

Markham, A., & Stavrova, S. (2016). Internet/Digital Research. In D. Silverman (Ed.), Qualitative research (pp. 229–244). London; Thousand Oaks: Sage Publications.

Marques, P., Morgan, K., & Richardson, R. (2017). Social innovation in question: The theoretical and practical implications of a contested concept. Environment and Planning C: Politics and Space, 496-512. https://doi.org/10.1177/2399654417717986

Marston, S. A., Jones, J. P., & Woodward, K. (2005). Human geography without scale. Transactions of the Institute of British Geographers, 30(4), 416–432. https://doi.org/10.1111/j.1475-5661.2005.00180.x

Martin, C. J. (2016a). The sharing economy: A pathway to sustainability or a nightmarish form of neoliberal capitalism? Ecological Economics, 121, 149–159. https://doi.org/10.1016/j.ecolecon.2015.11.027

Martin, C. J. (2016b). The sharing economy: A pathway to sustainability or a nightmarish form of neoliberal capitalism? Ecological Economics, 121, 149–159. https://doi.org/10.1016/j.ecolecon.2015.11.027

Martínez-Alier, J., Pascual, U., Vivien, F. D., & Zaccai, E. (2010). Sustainable degrowth: Mapping the context, criticisms and future prospects of an emergent paradigm. Ecological Economics, 69(9), 1741–1747. https://doi.org/10.1016/j.ecolecon.2010.04.017

Marx, K. (1852). The Eighteenth Brumaire of Louis Bonaparte. Retrieved from https://www.marxists.org/archive/marx/works/1852/18th-brumaire/ch01.htm

Marx, K. (1981 [1867]). Capital: a critique of political economy (D. Fernbach, Ed.; B. Fowkes, Trans.). London; New York: Penguin Books.

Mason, P. (2016). Postcapitalism. A Guide to our Future. Penguin Random House.

Massey, D. (2005). For space. London; Thousand Oaks: Sage Publications.

Massey, D. (2008). World city. Cambridge: Polity Press.

Masuda, J. R. (2017). Participatory Action Research. In D. Richardson, N. Castree, M. F. Goodchild, A. Kobayashi, W. Liu, & R. A. Marston (Eds.), International Encyclopedia of Geography: People, the Earth, Environment and Technology (pp. 1–6). https://doi.org/10.1002/9781118786352.wbieg0833

Meadows, D. H., & Club of Rome (Eds.). (1972). The Limits to growth: A report for the Club of Rome's project on the predicament of mankind. New York: Universe Books.

Meadows, D. H., Randers, J., & Meadows, D. L. (2004). Limits to growth: The 30-year update (1. printing). White River Junction, Vt: Chelsea Green Publ.

Meretz, S. (2015). Commonismus statt Sozialismus. In Marxistische Abendschule Hamburg (Ed.), Aufhebung des Kapitalismus. Die Ökonomie einer Übergangsgesellschaft (pp. 259–277). Hamburg: Argument.

Miller, E. (2010). Solidarity Economy: Key Concepts and Issues. In E. Kawano, T. Masterson, & J. Teller-Ellsberg (Eds.), Solidarity Economy I: Building Alternatives for People and Planet (pp. 1–12). Amherst, MA: Center for Popular Economics.

Miller, E. (2013). Community Economy: Ontology, Ethics, and Politics for Radically Democratic Economic Organizing. Rethinking Marxism, 25(4), 518–533. https://doi.org/10.1080/08935696.2013.842697

Miller, E. (2015). Anticapitalism or Postcapitalism? Both! Rethinking Marxism, 27(3), 364–367. https://doi.org/10.1080/08935696.2015.1042705

Moore, J. W. (2015). Capitalism in the web of life: Ecology and the accumulation of capital (1st Edition). London: Verso.

Morgan, D. L. (2008). Snowball Sampling. In L. M. Given (Ed.), The SAGE encyclopedia of qualitative research methods. London; Thousand Oaks: Sage Publications.

Morland, D. (2018). Anti-capitalism and poststructuralist anarchism. In J. Purkis & J. Bowen (Eds.), Changing anarchism. https://doi.org/10.7765/9781526137289.00008

Morrow, O. (2019). Sharing food and risk in Berlin's urban food commons. Geoforum, 99, 202–212. https://doi.org/10.1016/j.geoforum.2018.09.003

Moulaert, F., & Ailenei, O. (2005). Social Economy, Third Sector and Solidarity Relations: A Conceptual Synthesis from History to Present. Urban Studies, 42(11), 2037–2053. https://doi.org/10.1080/00420980500279794

Moulaert, F., MacCallum, D., Mehmood, A., & Hamdouch, A. (Eds.). (2013). The international handbook on social innovation: collective action, social learning and transdisciplinary research. Cheltenham: Elgar.

Moulaert, F., Martinelli, F., Swyngedouw, E., & Gonzalez, S. (2005). Towards Alternative Model(s) of Local Innovation. Urban Studies, 42(11), 1969–1990. https://doi.org/10.1080/00420980500279893

Mountz, A. (2018). Political geography III: Bodies. Progress in Human Geography, 42(5), 759–769. https://doi.org/10.1177/0309132517718642

Müller, M. (2015). Assemblages and Actor-networks: Rethinking Socio-material Power, Politics and Space: Assemblages and Actor-networks. Geography Compass, 9(1), 27–41. https://doi.org/10.1111/gec3.12192

Muraca, B. (2013). Decroissance: A Project for a Radical Transformation of Society. Environmental Values, 22(2), 147–169. https://doi.org/10.3197/096327113X13581561725112

Murdoch, J. (2006). Post-structuralist geography: a guide to relational space. London; Thousand Oaks: Sage Publications.

Nancy, J.-L. (1991). The Inoperative Community. Minneapolis; Oxford: Minnesota Press.

Nancy, J.-L. (2000). Being Singular Plural. Stanford: Stanford University Press.

Nancy, J.-L. (2016). The disavowed community. New York: Fordham University Press.

Nicholls, A. (Ed.). (2006). Social Entrepreneurship: New Models of Sustainable Social Change. Oxford: Oxford University Press.

Nicolini, D. (2013). Practice Theory, Work, and Organization: An Introduction. Oxford: Oxford University Press.

Norman, W., & Macdonald, C. (2004). Getting to the bottom of the Triple Bottom Line. Business Ethics Quarterly, 14(2), 243–262. https://doi.org/10.1016/j.ijpe.2012.01.035

North, P. (2014). Ten Square Miles Surrounded by Reality? Materialising Alternative Economies Using Local Currencies. Antipode, 46(1), 246–265. https://doi.org/10.1111/anti.12039

North, P. (2016). The business of the Anthropocene? Substantivist and diverse economies perspectives on SME engagement in local low carbon transitions. Progress in Human Geography, 40, 437–454. https://doi.org/10.1177/0309132515585049

North, P., & Cato, M. S. (2017). Towards just and sustainable economies: the social and solidarity economy North and South. Bristol: Policy Press.

North, P., & Nurse, A. (2014). Beyond entrepreneurial cities: towards a postcapitalist grassroots urban politics of climate change and resource constraint. Métropoles, 32–41.

Noterman, E. (2015). Beyond Tragedy: Differential Commoning in a Manufactured Housing Cooperative. Antipode, 48(2), 433–452. https://doi.org/10.1111/anti.12182

Notz, G. (2011). Theorien alternativen Wirtschaftens. Stuttgart: Schmetterling Verlag.

Nyberg, D., Spicer, A., & Wright, C. (2013). Incorporating citizens: corporate political engagement with climate change in Australia. Organization, 20(3), 433–453. https://doi.org/10.1177/1350508413478585

Nyssens, M., Adam, S., & Johnson, T. (Eds.). (2006). Social enterprise: at the crossroads of market, public policies and civil society. London; New York: Routledge.

O'Brien, K. (2012). Global environmental change II: From adaptation to deliberate transformation. Progress in Human Geography, 36(5), 667–676. https://doi.org/10.1177/0309132511425767

OECD (Ed.). (2011). Divided we stand: why inequality keeps rising. Paris: OECD.

O'Neill, J. (2018). How not to argue against growth: happiness, austerity and inequality. In H. Rosa & C. Henning (Eds.), The good life beyond growth: new perspectives (pp. 141–152). London; New York: Routledge.

O'Neill, K., & Gibbs, D. (2016). Rethinking green entrepreneurship. Fluid narratives of the green economy. Environment and Planning A, 48(9), 1727–1749. https://doi.org/10.1177/0308518X16650453

Ostrom, E. (2010). Beyond Markets and States: Polycentric Governance of Complex Economic Systems. American Economic Review, 100(3), 641–672. https://doi.org/10.1257/aer.100.3.641

Packard, V. (2011). The waste makers. Brooklyn: Ig Publishing.

Paech, N. (2009). Die Postwachstumsökonomie - ein Vademecum. Zeitschrift Für Sozialökonomie, 46(160–161), 28–31.

Paech, N. (2010). Eine Alternative zum Entkopplungsmythos: Die Postwachstumsökonomie. Humane Wirtschaft, 5, 12–15.

Paech, N. (2012). Befreiung vom Überfluss. Auf dem Weg in die Postwachstumsökonomie. München: oekom Verlag.

Painter, J. (2010). Rethinking Territory. Antipode, 42(5), 1090–1118. https://doi.org/10.1111/j.1467-8330.2010.00795.x

Pallett, H., & Chilvers, J. (2015). Organizations in the making: Learning and intervening at the science-policy interface. Progress in Human Geography, 39(2), 146–166. https://doi.org/10.1177/0309132513518831

Pant, M. (2014). Participatory Action Research. In D. Coghlan & M. Brydon-Miller (Eds.), The Sage encyclopedia of action research (pp. 583–588). London; Thousand Oaks: Sage Publications.

Pantzar, M., & Shove, E. (2010). Understanding innovation in practice: a discussion of the production and re-production of Nordic Walking. Technology Analysis & Strategic Management, 22(4), 447–461. https://doi.org/10.1080/09537321003714402

Parker, M. (2017). Alternative enterprises, local economies, and social justice: why smaller is still more beautiful. M@n@gement, 20(4), 418. https://doi.org/10.3917/mana.204.0418

Patel, R., & Moore, J. W. (2018). A history of the world in seven cheap things: a guide to capitalism, nature, and the future of the planet. London: Verso.

Patterson, J., Schulz, K., Vervoort, J., van der Hel, S., Widerberg, O., Adler, C., ... Barau, A. (2017). Exploring the governance and politics of transformations towards sustainability. Environmental Innovation and Societal Transitions, 24, 1–16. https://doi.org/10.1016/j.eist.2016.09.001

Peck, J. (2013). For Polanyian Economic Geographies. Environment and Planning A, 45(7), 1545–1568. https://doi.org/10.1068/a45236

Peck, J., & Theodore, N. (2007). Variegated capitalism. Progress in Human Geography, 31(6), 731–772.

Peet, R., & Watts, M. (1996). Liberation Ecologies. Environment, Development, Social Movements. London; New York: Routledge.

Petschow, U., Ferdinand, J.-P., Dickel, S., Flämig, H., & Steinfeldt, M. (Eds.). (2014). Dezentrale Produktion, 3D-Druck und Nachhaltigkeit: Trajektorien und Potenziale innovativer Wertschöpfungsmuster zwischen Maker-Bewegung und Industrie 4.0. Berlin: Institut für ökologische Wirtschaftsforschung.

Petschow, U., aus dem Moore, N., Pissarskoi, E., Korfhage, T., Lange, S., Schoofs, A., Hofmann, D. (2018). Gesellschaftliches Wohlergehen innerhalb planetarer Grenzen: Der Ansatz einer vorsorgeorientierten Postwachstumsposition. UBA Texte 89/2018.

Petschow, U., & Peuckert, J. (2016). Kollaborative Ökonomie – Potenziale für nachhaltiges Wirtschaften. Ökologisches Wirtschaften, 31(3), 14. https://doi.org/10.14512/OEW310314

Pickerill, J. (2016). Eco-homes: People, place and politics. Zed Books.

Pickerill, J. (2017). What are we fighting for? Ideological posturing and anarchist geographies. Dialogues in Human Geography, 7(3), 251–256. https://doi.org/10.1177/2043820617732914

Pickerill, J., & Chatterton, P. (2006). Notes towards autonomous geographies: Creation, resistance and self-management as survival tactics. Progress in Human Geography, 30(6), 730–746.

Piketty, T. (2017). Capital in the twenty-first century. Cambridge: Belknap Press.

Plumwood, V. (2002). Environmental culture: the ecological crisis of reason. London; New York: Routledge.

Polanyi, K. (2001 [1944]). The Great Transformation: the political and economic origins of our time. Boston: Beacon Press.

Price, W. (2012). The Anarchist Method. An Experimental Appriach to Post-Capitalist Economies. In A. J. Nocella & J. Asimakopoulos (Eds.), The Accumulation of Freedom. Writings on Anarchist Economics. Oakland: AK Press.

Rancière, J. (1998). Disagreement: Politics and Philosophy. Minneapolis; London: Minnesota Press.

Rancière, J. (2004). Introducing Disagreement. Angelaki - Journal of the Theoretical Humanities., 9(3), 3–9.

Rancière, J. (2011). The thinking of dissensus: politics and aesthetics. Reading Rancière, 1–17.

Ratner, C. (2019). Neoliberal psychology. New York: Springer

Rätzer, M., Hartz, R., & Winkler, I. (2018). Editorial: Post-Growth Organizations. Management Revue, 29(3), 193–205. https://doi.org/10.5771/0935-9915-2018-3-193

Rauschmayer, F., Bauler, T., & Schäpke, N. (2015). Towards a thick understanding of sustainability transitions. Linking transition management, capabilities and social practices. Ecological Economics, 109, 211–221. https://doi.org/10.1016/j.ecolecon.2014.11.018

Raven, R., Schot, J., & Berkhout, F. (2012). Space and scale in socio-technical transitions. Environmental Innovation and Societal Transitions, 4, 63–78. https://doi.org/10.1016/j.eist.2012.08.001

Raworth, K. (2017). Doughnut economics: seven ways to think like a 21st-century economist. London: Random House.

Reckwitz, A. (2002). Toward a theory of social practices: A development in culturalist theorizing. European Journal of Social Theory, 5(2), 243–263. https://doi.org/10.1177/13684310222225432

Reckwitz, A. (2003). Grundelemente einer Theorie sozialer Praktiken: Eine sozialtheoretische Perspektive. Zeitschrift Für Soziologie, 32(4), 282–301. https://doi.org/10.1515/zfsoz-2003-0401

Reckwitz, A. (2016). Kreativität und Soziale Praxis. Studien zur Sozial- und Gesellschaftstheorie. Bielefeld: transcript.

Richardson, L. (2015). Performing the sharing economy. Geoforum, 67, 121–129. https://doi.org/10.1016/j.geoforum.2015.11.004

Richters, O., & Siemoneit, A. (2017). Wachstumszwänge: Ressourcenverbrauch und Akkumulation als Wettbewerbsverzerrungen. In F. Adler & U. Schachtschneider (Eds.), Postwachstumspolitiken. Wege zur Wachstumsunabhängigen Gesellschaft (pp. 169–182). München: oekom Verlag.

Robertson, B. J. (2015). Holacracy: the new management system for a rapidly changing world (First edition). New York: Henry Holt and Company.

Robson, C. (2009). Real world research: a resource for social scientists and practitioner-researchers. Malden: Blackwell.

Rockström, J., Steffen, W., Noone, K., Persson, Å., Chapin, F. S. I., Lambin, E., ... Foley, J. (2009). Planetary Boundaries: Exploring the Safe Operating Space for Humanity. Ecology and Society, 14(2). https://doi.org/10.5751/ES-03180-140232

Roelvink, G., St. Martin, K., & Gibson-Graham, J. K. (Eds.). (2015). Making other worlds possible: performing diverse economies. Minneapolis: Univ. of Minnesota Press.

Rosa, H. (2016). Resonanz: eine Soziologie der Weltbeziehung. Berlin: Suhrkamp.

Rosa, H. (2018). Available, accessible, attainable. The mindset of growth and the resonance conception of the good life. In H. Rosa & C. Henning (Eds.), The good life beyond growth: new perspectives (pp. 39–53). London; New York: Routledge.

Rosa, H., Dörre, K., & Lessenich, S. (2017). Appropriation, Activation and Acceleration: The Escalatory Logics of Capitalist Modernity and the Crises of Dynamic Stabilization. Theory, Culture & Society, 34(1), 53–73. https://doi.org/10.1177/0263276416657600

Rosa, H., & Henning, C. (Eds.). (2018). The good life beyond growth: new perspectives. London; New York: Routledge

Rose, G. (1997). Situating knowledges: positionality, reflexivities and other tactics. Progress in Human Geography, 21(3), 305–320. https://doi.org/10.1191/030913297673302122

Rosol, M. (2018). Alternative Ernährungsnetzwerke als Alternative Ökonomien. Zeitschrift für Wirtschaftsgeographie, 62(3–4), 174–186. https://doi.org/10.1515/zfw-2017-0005

Roth, S., & Schütz, A. (2015). Ten Systems: Toward a Canon of Function Systems. Cybernetics and Human Knowing, 22(4), 11–31. https://doi.org/10.2139/ssrn.2508950

Saar, M. (2010). Power and critique. Journal of Power, 3(1), 7–20. https://doi.org/10.1080/17540291003630320

Saar, M. (2014). The immanence of power: From Spinoza to "radical democracy." Voorschoten, Netherlands: Uitgeverij Spinozahuis.

Saldaña, J. (2009). The coding manual for qualitative researchers. Los Angeles: Sage.

Samers, M. (2005). The Myopia of "Diverse Economies", or a Critique of the "Informal Economy." Antipode, 37(5), 875–886. https://doi.org/10.1111/j.0066-4812.2005.00537.x

Schäfer, H. (2016a). Praxis als Wiederholung. Das Denken der Iterabilität und seine Konsequenzen für die Methodologie praxeologischer Forschung. In H. Schäfer (Ed.), Praxistheorie. Ein soziologisches Forschungsprogramm (pp. 137–159). Bielefeld: transcript.

Schäfer, H. (2016b). The transitive methodology of practice theory. Retrieved November 7, 2018, from Practice Theory Methodologies website: https://practicetheorymethodologies.wordpress.com/2016/02/22/hilmar-schafer-the-transitive-methodology-of-practice-theory/

Schatzki, T. R. (1996). Social practices: a Wittgensteinian approach to human activity and the social. Cambridge: Cambridge University Press.

Schatzki, T. R. (2002). The site of the social: A philosophical account of the constitution of social life and change. Pennsylvania State Univ. Press.

Schatzki, T. R. (2003). A New Societist Social Ontology. Philosophy of the Social Sciences, 33(2), 174–202. https://doi.org/10.1177/0048393103251680

Schatzki, T. R. (2008). Social practices: a Wittgensteinian approach to human activity and the social. Cambridge: Cambridge University Press.

Schatzki, T. R. (2010a). Materiality and Social Life. Nature and Culture, 5(2). https://doi.org/10.3167/nc.2010.050202

Schatzki, T. R. (2010b). The timespace of human activity: on performance, society, and history as indeterminate teleological events. Lanham: Lexington Books.

Schatzki, T. R. (2016a). Keeping Track of Large Phenomena. Geographische Zeitschrift, 104(1), 4–24.

Schatzki, T. R. (2016b). Praxistheorie als flache Ontologie. In H. Schäfer (Ed.), Praxistheorie. Ein soziologisches Forschungsprogramm (pp. 29–44). Bielefeld: transcript.

Schatzki, T. R., Knorr-Cetina, K., & Savigny, E. von (Eds.). (2001). The practice turn in contemporary theory. New York; London: Routledge.

Schmid, B. (2018). Structured Diversity: A Practice Theory Approach to Post-Growth Organisations. Management Revue, 29(3), 281–310. https://doi.org/10.5771/0935-9915-2018-3-281

Schmid, B. (2019a). Degrowth and postcapitalism: Transformative geographies beyond accumulation and growth. Geography Compass. https://doi.org/10.1111/gec3.12470

Schmid, B. (2019b). Repair's diverse transformative geographies – lessons from a maker community in Stuttgart. Ephemera: Theory and Politics in Organization, 19(2), 229–251.

Schmid, B., Reda, J., Kraehnke, L., & Schwegmann, R. (2019). The Site of the Spatial. Eine praktikentheoretische Erschließung geographischer Raumkonzepte. In J. Everts & S. Schäfer (Eds.), Handbuch Praktiken und Raum. Humangeographie nach dem Practice Turn (pp. 93–136). Bielefeld: transcript.

Schmid, B., & Smith, T. S. J. (2020). Social transformation and postcapitalist possibility: Emerging dialogues between practice theory and diverse economies. Progress in Human Geography, 1–22.

Schmid, B., & Taylor Aiken, G. (2020). Transformative mindfulness: The role of mind-body practices in community-based activism. *Cultural Geographies*.

Schneider, F., Kallis, G., & Martinez-Alier, J. (2010). Crisis or opportunity? Economic degrowth for social equity and ecological sustainability. Introduction to this special issue. Journal of Cleaner Production, 18(6), 511–518. https://doi.org/10.1016/j.jclepro.2010.01.014

Schneidewind, U. (2018). Die große Transformation: eine Einführung in die Kunst gesellschaftlichen Wandels. Frankfurt am Main: Fischer Verlag.

Schneidewind, U., & Zahrnt, A. (2014). The Politics of Sufficiency. München: oekom.

Scholar, H. (2017). The neglected paraphernalia of practice? Objects and artefacts in social work identity, practice and research. Qualitative Social Work: Research and Practice, 16(5), 631–648. https://doi.org/10.1177/1473325016637911

Schor, J. (2010). Plenitude: The new economics of true wealth. Penguin Press.

Schulz, C., & Affolderbach, J. (2015). Grünes Wachstum und alternative Wirtschaftsformen. Geographische Rundschau, 65(5), 4–9.

Schulz, C., & Bailey, I. (2014). The Green Economy and Post-growth Regimes: Opportunities and Challenges for Economic Geography. Geografiska Annaler, 96(3), 277–291. https://doi.org/10.1111/geob.12051

Scoones, I., Leach, M., & Newell, P. (Eds.). (2015). The politics of green transformations. London; New York: Routledge.

Scott, J. C. (2017). Against the grain: a deep history of the earliest states. New Haven: Yale University Press.

Seidl, I., & Zahrnt, A. (2010). Postwachstumsgesellschaft. Konzepte für die Zukunft. Marburg: Metropolis.

Sekulova, F., Kallis, G., Rodríguez-Labajos, B., & Schneider, F. (2013). Degrowth: from theory to practice. Journal of Cleaner Production, 38, 1–6. https://doi.org/10.1016/j.jclepro.2012.06.022

Seyfang, G. (2014). New economics of sustainable consumption: Seeds of change. Palgrave Macmillan.

Seyfang, G. (2016). Time Banking: A New Economics Alternative. In D. Fuller, A. E. G. Jonas, & R. Lee (Eds.), Interrogating Alterity. Alternative Economic and Political Spaces (pp. 193–206). New York; London: Routledge.

Seyfang, G., & Haxeltine, A. (2012). Growing Grassroots Innovations: Exploring the Role of Community-Based Initiatives in Governing Sustainable Energy Transitions. Environment and Planning C: Government and Policy, 30(3), 381–400. https://doi.org/10.1068/c10222

Seyfang, G., & Smith, A. (2007). Grassroots innovations for sustainable development: Towards a new research and policy agenda. Environmental Politics, 16(4), 584–603. https://doi.org/10.1080/09644010701419121

Shannon, D., Nocella, A. J., & Asimakopoulos, J. (Eds.). (2012). The accumulation of freedom: writings on anarchist economics. Oakland: AK Press.

Sheppard, E., & Barnes, T. J. (2017). Economic Geography. In D. Richardson, N. Castree, M. F. Goodchild, A. Kobayashi, W. Liu, & R. A. Marston (Eds.), International Encyclopedia of Geography: People, the Earth, Environment and Technology (pp. 1–19). https://doi.org/10.1002/9781118786352.wbieg0844

Shove, E. (2017). Matters of Practice. In A. Hui, T. R. Schatzki, & E. Shove (Eds.), The nexus of practices: connections, constellations and practitioners (1 Edition, pp. 155–168). London; New York: Routledge

Shove, E., Pantzar, M., & Watson, M. (2012). The Dynamics of Social Practice. Everyday Life and how it Changes. https://doi.org/10.4135/9781446250655.n1

Shove, E., & Walker, G. (2007). Caution! Transitions Ahead: Politics, Practice, and Sustainable Transition Management. Environment and Planning A, 39(4), 763–770. https://doi.org/10.1068/a39310

Shove, E., & Walker, G. (2010). Governing transitions in the sustainability of everyday life. Research Policy, 39(4), 471–476. https://doi.org/10.1016/j.respol.2010.01.019

Shove, E., Watson, M., & Spurling, N. (2015). Conceptualizing connections: Energy demand, infrastructures and social practices. European Journal of Social Theory, 18(3), 274–287. https://doi.org/10.1177/1368431015579964

Simons, A., Petschow, U., & Peuckert, J. (2016). Offene Werkstätten - nachhaltig innovativ? Potenziale gemeinsamen Arbeitens und Produzierens in der gesellschaftlichen Transformation. Schriftenreihe des IÖW, 212(16).

Simpson, P. (2017). Nonrepresentational Theory. In D. Richardson, N. Castree, M. F. Goodchild, A. Kobayashi, W. Liu, & R. A. Marston (Eds.), International Encyclopedia of Geography: People, the Earth, Environment and Technology (pp. 1–4). https://doi.org/10.1002/9781118786352.wbieg0273

Smith, A., Voß, J.-P., & Grin, J. (2010). Innovation studies and sustainability transitions: The allure of the multi-level perspective and its challenges. Research Policy, 39(4), 435–448. https://doi.org/10.1016/j.respol.2010.01.023

Smith, T. S. J. (2017). Of Makerspaces and Hacklabs: Emergence, Experiment and Ontological Theatre at the Edinburgh Hacklab, Scotland. Scottish Geographical Journal, 133(2), 130–154. https://doi.org/10.1080/14702541.2017.1321137

Smith, T. S. J. (2019a). Sustainability, wellbeing and the posthuman turn. Cham: Palgrave Macmillan.

Smith, T. S. J. (2019b). 'Stand back and watch us': Post-capitalist practices in the maker movement. Environment and Planning A: Economy and Space, 0308518X1988273. https://doi.org/10.1177/0308518X19882731

Soja, E. W. (2010). Seeking spatial justice. Minneapolis: Univ. of Minnesota Press.

Spaargaren, G. (2011). Theories of practices: Agency, technology, and culture. Exploring the relevance of practice theories for the governance of sustainable consumption practices in the new world-order. Global Environmental Change, 21(3), 813–822. https://doi.org/10.1016/j.gloenvcha.2011.03.010

Späth, P., & Rohracher, H. (2012). Local Demonstrations for Global Transitions—Dynamics across Governance Levels Fostering Socio-Technical Regime

Change Towards Sustainability. European Planning Studies, 20(3), 461–479. https://doi.org/10.1080/09654313.2012.651800

Spivak, G. C. (2011). Can the subaltern speak? Postkolonialität und subalterne Artikulation. Wien: Turia + Kant.

Springer, S. (2014a). Human geography without hierarchy. Progress in Human Geography, 38(3), 402–419. https://doi.org/10.1177/0309132513508208

Springer, S. (2014b). Why a radical geography must be anarchist. Dialogues in Human Geography, 4(3), 249–270. https://doi.org/10.1177/2043820614540851

Springer, S. (2017). The limits to Marx: David Harvey and the condition of postfraternity. Dialogues in Human Geography, 7(3), 280–294. https://doi.org/10.1177/2043820617732918

Spurling, N., & McMeekin, A. (2015). Interventions in practices. Sustainable mobility policies in England. In Y. Strengers & C. Maller (Eds.), Social practices, intervention and sustainability: beyond behaviour change (pp. 78–94). New York; London: Routledge.

Srnicek, N., & Williams, A. (2016). Inventing the future: postcapitalism and a world without work. London: Verso.

Steffen, W., Richardson, K., Rockstrom, J., Cornell, S. E., Fetzer, I., Bennett, E. M., ... Sorlin, S. (2015). Planetary boundaries: Guiding human development on a changing planet. Science, 347(6223). https://doi.org/10.1126/science.1259855

Strengers, Y., & Maller, C. (Eds.). (2015). Social practices, intervention and sustainability: beyond behaviour change. New York; London: Routledge.

Swyngedouw, E. (2012). The Marxian Alternative: Historical-Geographical Materialism and the Political Economy of Capitalism. In E. Sheppard & T. J. Barnes (Eds.), A Companion to Economic Geography (pp. 41–57). Malden; Oxford: Blackwell Publishers.

Tarrow, S. G. (2011). Power in movement: social movements and contentious politics. Cambridge; New York: Cambridge University Press.

Taylor Aiken, G. (2015a). Community Number Capture. Soundings, (58), 81–90.

Taylor Aiken, G. (2015b). (Local-) community for global challenges: carbon conversations, transition towns and governmental elisions. Local Environment, 20(7), 764–781. https://doi.org/10.1080/13549839.2013.870142

Taylor Aiken, G. (2017). The politics of community: Togetherness, transition and post-politics. Environment and Planning A, 1–19. https://doi.org/10.1177/0308518X17724443

Thornton, P. H., Ocasio, W., & Lounsbury, M. (2012). The Institutional Logics Perspective: A New Approach to Culture, Structure and Process. Oxford: Oxford University Press.

Thrift, N. (1996). Spatial Formations. https://doi.org/10.4135/9781446222362

Thrift, N. (2004). Intensities of feeling: towards a spatial politics of affect. Geografiska Annaler: Series B, Human Geography, 86(1), 57–78. https://doi.org/10.1111/j.0435-3684.2004.00154.x

Till, K. E. (2009). Ethnography. In International Encyclopedia of Human Geography (pp. 626–631). https://doi.org/10.1016/B978-008044910-4.00430-2

Tormey, S. (2012). Anti-Capitalism. In G. Ritzer (Ed.), The Wiley-Blackwell Encyclopedia of Globalization. https://doi.org/10.1002/9780470670590.wbeog025

Trefzer, Jackson, McKee, & Dellinger. (2014). Introduction: The Global South and/in the Global North: Interdisciplinary Investigations. The Global South, 8(2), 1. https://doi.org/10.2979/globalsouth.8.2.1

Tsing, A. L. (2015). The mushroom at the end of the world: on the possibility of life in capitalist ruins. Princeton: Princeton University Press.

van den Bergh, J. C. J. M. (2011). Environment versus growth. A criticism of "degrowth" and a plea for "a-growth." Ecological Economics, 70(5), 881–890. https://doi.org/10.1016/j.ecolecon.2010.09.035

van der Laak, W. W. M., Raven, R. P. J. M., & Verbong, G. P. J. (2007). Strategic niche management for biofuels: Analysing past experiments for developing new biofuel policies. Energy Policy, 35(6), 3213–3225. https://doi.org/10.1016/j.enpol.2006.11.009

van Griethuysen, P. (2010). Why are we growth-addicted? The hard way towards degrowth in the involutionary western development path. Journal of Cleaner Production, 18(6), 590–595. https://doi.org/10.1016/j.jclepro.2009.07.006

van Parijs, P., & Vanderborght, Y. (2017). Basic income: a radical proposal for a free society and a sane economy. Cambridge, Massachusetts: Harvard University Press.

van Parijs, P., & Vanderborght, Y. (2018). Basic Income and the freedom to lead a good life. In H. Rosa & C. Henning (Eds.), The good life beyond growth: new perspectives (pp. 153–161). London; New York: Routledge.

van Treeck, T. & Urban, J. (Eds.). (2017). Wirtschaft neu denken: blinde Flecken der Lehrbuchökonomie. Berlin: iRights Media.

Vandeventer, J. S., Cattaneo, C., & Zografos, C. (2019). A Degrowth Transition: Pathways for the Degrowth Niche to Replace the Capitalist-Growth Regime. Ecological Economics, 156, 272–286. https://doi.org/10.1016/j.ecolecon.2018.10.002

Vetter, A. (2018). The Matrix of Convivial Technology – Assessing technologies for degrowth. Journal of Cleaner Production, 197, 1778–1786. https://doi.org/10.1016/j.jclepro.2017.02.195

Victor, P. A. (2008). *Managing without growth: Slower by design, not disaster*. Elgar.

Wackernagel, M., & Rees, W. (1997). Unser ökologischer Fußabdruck: Wie der Mensch Einfluß auf die Umwelt nimmt. Birkhäuser.

Walsh, K. (2009). Participant Observation. In International Encyclopedia of Human Geography (pp. 77–81). https://doi.org/10.1016/B978-008044910-4.00489-2

Walter-Herrmann, J., & Büching, C. (Eds.). (2013). FabLab: of machines, makers and inventors. Bielefeld: transcript.

Warde, A. (2005). Consumption and Theories of Practice. Journal of Consumer Culture, 5(2), 131–153. https://doi.org/10.1177/1469540505053090

Wartenberg, T. E. (1990). The forms of power: from domination to transformation. Philadelphia: Temple University Press.

Watson, M. (2017). Placing Power in Practice Theory. In A. Hui, T. R. Schatzki, & E. Shove (Eds.), The Nexus of Practices. Connections, constellations, practitioners (pp. 169–182). New York; London: Routledge.

WBGU. (2011). Welt im Wandel: Gesellschaftsvertrag für eine Große Transformation. Berlin: Wiss. Beirat der Bundesregierung Globale Umweltveränderungen.

Welzer, H. (2011). Mental infrastructures how growth entered the world and our souls. Berlin: Heinrich Böll Foundation.

Welzer, H. (2014). Der Abschied vom Wachstum als zivilisatorisches Projekt. In H. Welzer & K. Wiegandt (Eds.), Wege aus der Wachstumsgesellschaft (pp. 35–59). Frankfurt am Main: Fischer Verlag.

Werner, K. (2015). Performing Economies of Care in a New England Time Bank and Buddhist Community. In G. Roelvink, K. St. Martin, & J. K. Gibson-Graham (Eds.), Making other worlds possible: performing diverse economies (pp. 72–97). Minneapolis: Univ. of Minnesota Press.

Werner, R. A. (2014). Can banks individually create money out of nothing? — The theories and the empirical evidence. International Review of Financial Analysis, 36, 1–19. https://doi.org/10.1016/j.irfa.2014.07.015

Westley, F. R., Tjornbo, O., Schultz, L., Olsson, P., Folke, C., Crona, B., & Bodin, Ö. (2013). A Theory of Transformative Agency in Linked Social-Ecological Systems. Ecology and Society, 18(3). https://doi.org/10.5751/ES-05072-180327

White, R. J., & Williams, C. C. (2012). The Pervasive Nature of Heterodox Economic Spaces at a Time of Neoliberal Crisis: Towards a "Postneoliberal" Anarchist Future. Antipode, 44(5), 1625–1644. https://doi.org/10.1111/j.1467-8330.2012.01033.x

White, R. J., & Williams, C. C. (2016). Beyond capitalocentricism: are non-capitalist work practices 'alternatives'? Area. https://doi.org/10.1111/area.12264

Wiegand, F. (2016). David Harveys urbane politische Ökonomie: Ausgrabungen der Zukunft marxistischer Stadtforschung. Münster: Westfälisches Dampfboot.

Wilkinson, R. G., and Pickett, K. (2010). The spirit level: why equality is better for everyone. London: Penguin Books.

Wood, E. M. (2017). The origin of capitalism: a longer view. London: Verso.

Woodward, K. (2017). Poststructuralism/Poststructural Geographies. In D. Richardson, N. Castree, M. F. Goodchild, A. Kobayashi, W. Liu, & R. A. Marston (Eds.), International Encyclopedia of Geography: People, the Earth,

Environment and Technology (pp. 1–10). https://doi.org/10.1002/9781118786352.wbieg1101

Wright, E. O. (2019). How to be an anticapitalist in the twenty-first century. London: Verso.

Wright, E. O. (2010). Envisioning real utopias. London: Verso.

Zademach, H.-M., & Hillebrand, S. (Eds.). (2013). Alternative Economies and Spaces. New Perspectives for a Sustainable Economy. Bielefeld: transcript.

Zanoni, P., Contu, A., Healy, S., & Mir, R. (2017). Post-capitalistic politics in the making: The imaginary and praxis of alternative economies. Organization, 24(5), 575–588. https://doi.org/10.1177/1350508417713219

Žižek, S. (2018). Der Mut der Hoffnungslosigkeit. Frankfurt am Main: Fischer Verlag.

Social and Cultural Studies

Ashley J. Bohrer
Marxism and Intersectionality
Race, Gender, Class and Sexuality under Contemporary Capitalism

2019, 280 p., pb.
29,99 € (DE), 978-3-8376-4160-8
E-Book: 26,99 € (DE), ISBN 978-3-8394-4160-2

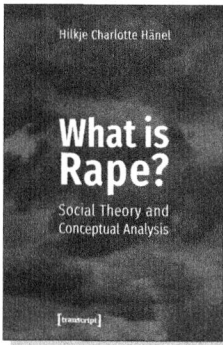

Hilkje Charlotte Hänel
What is Rape?
Social Theory and Conceptual Analysis

2018, 282 p., hardcover
99,99 € (DE), 978-3-8376-4434-0
E-Book: 99,99 € (DE), ISBN 978-3-8394-4434-4

Jasper van Buuren
Body and Reality
An Examination of the Relationships between the Body Proper, Physical Reality, and the Phenomenal World Starting from Plessner and Merleau-Ponty

2018, 312 p., pb., ill.
39,99 € (DE), 978-3-8376-4163-9
E-Book: 39,99 € (DE), ISBN 978-3-8394-4163-3

All print, e-book and open access versions of the titles in our list are available in our online shop www.transcript-verlag.de/en!

Social and Cultural Studies

Sabine Klotz, Heiner Bielefeldt,
Martina Schmidhuber, Andreas Frewer (eds.)
Healthcare as a Human Rights Issue
Normative Profile, Conflicts and Implementation

2017, 426 p., pb., ill.
39,99 € (DE), 978-3-8376-4054-0
E-Book: available as free open access publication
E-Book: ISBN 978-3-8394-4054-4

Michael Bray
Powers of the Mind
Mental and Manual Labor
in the Contemporary Political Crisis

2019, 208 p., hardcover
99,99 € (DE), 978-3-8376-4147-9
E-Book: 99,99 € (DE), ISBN 978-3-8394-4147-3

Iain MacKenzie
Resistance and the Politics of Truth
Foucault, Deleuze, Badiou

2018, 148 p., pb.
29,99 € (DE), 978-3-8376-3907-0
E-Book: 26,99 € (DE), ISBN 978-3-8394-3907-4
EPUB: 26,99 € (DE), ISBN 978-3-7328-3907-0

All print, e-book and open access versions of the titles in our list
are available in our online shop www.transcript-verlag.de/en!